MARK

NCCS | New Covenant Commentary Series

The New Covenant Commentary Series (NCCS) is designed for ministers and students who require a commentary that interacts with the text and context of each New Testament book and pays specific attention to the impact of the text upon the faith and praxis of contemporary faith communities.

The NCCS has a number of distinguishing features. First, the contributors come from a diverse array of backgrounds in regards to their Christian denominations and countries of origin. Unlike many commentary series that tout themselves as international the NCCS can truly boast of a genuinely international cast of contributors with authors drawn from every continent of the world (except Antarctica) including countries such as the United States, Puerto Rico, Australia, the United Kingdom, Kenya, India, Singapore, and Korea. We intend the NCCS to engage in the task of biblical interpretation and theological reflection from the perspective of the global church. Second, the volumes in this series are not verse-by-verse commentaries, but they focus on larger units of text in order to explicate and interpret the story in the text as opposed to some often atomistic approaches. Third, a further aim of these volumes is to provide an occasion for authors to reflect on how the New Testament impacts the life, faith, ministry, and witness of the New Covenant Community today. This occurs periodically under the heading of "Fusing the Horizons and Forming the Community." Here authors provide windows into community formation (how the text shapes the mission and character of the believing community) and ministerial formation (how the text shapes the ministry of Christian leaders).

It is our hope that these volumes will represent serious engagements with the New Testament writings, done in the context of faith, in service of the church, and for the glorification of God.

Series Editors:
Michael F. Bird (Crossway College, Queensland, Australia)
Craig Keener (Asbury Theological Seminary, Wilmore, KY, USA)

Titles in this series:
Romans Craig Keener
Ephesians Lynn Cohick
Colossians and Philemon Michael F. Bird
Revelation Gordon Fee
John Jey J. Kanagaraj
1 Timothy Aída Besançon Spencer
2 Timothy and Titus Aída Besançon Spencer

Forthcoming titles:
James Pablo Jimenez
1–3 John Sam Ngewa
Pastoral Epistles Aída Besançon-Spencer
Mark Kim Huat Tan
Acts Youngmo Cho and Hyung Dae Park
Luke Diane Chen
2 Peter and Jude Andrew Mbuvi

Matthew Scot McKnight
1 Peter Eric Greaux
1–2 Thessalonians David Garland
Philippians Linda Belleville
Hebrews Tom Thatcher
Galatians Brian Vickers
1 Corinthians Bruce Winter
2 Corinthians David deSilva

MARK

A New Covenant Commentary

Kim Huat Tan

CASCADE *Books* • Eugene, Oregon

MARK
A New Covenant Commentary

New Covenant Commentary Series

Copyright © 2015 Kim Huat Tan. All rights reserved. Except for brief quotations in critical publications or reviews, no part of this book may be reproduced in any manner without prior written permission from the publisher. Write: Permissions, Wipf and Stock Publishers, 199 W. 8th Ave., Suite 3, Eugene, OR 97401.

Cascade Books
An Imprint of Wipf and Stock Publishers
199 W. 8th Ave., Suite 3
Eugene, OR 97401

www.wipfandstock.com

ISBN 13: 978-1-60899-512-7

Cataloging-in-Publication data:

Tan, Kim Huat

Mark : a new covenant commentary / Kim Huat Tan.

xviii + 268 p. ; 23 cm. —Includes bibliographical references and index(es).

New Covenant Commentary Series

ISBN 13: 978-1-60899-512-7

1. Bible. N.T. Mark—Commentaries. I. Title. II. Series.

BS2585.53 T17 2015

Manufactured in the U.S.A.

MOCH

הנך יפה רעיתי

Contents

Acknowledgments | ix
Preface | xi
Abbreviations | xiii

Introduction | 1
The Beginning of the Gospel (1:1–13) | 12
   Fusing the Horizons | 15
The Gospel in Galilee: The Mighty Acts of the Messiah (1:14—8:21) | 22
   Excursus: Was Jesus Incensed or Compassionate? | 29
   Excursus: The Pharisees | 38
   Fusing the Horizons: Blasphemy against the Holy Spirit | 50
   Excursus: The Location of the Story | 65
   Excursus: Discrepancies Over What is Allowed | 76
   Excursus: Mark and Josephus on John the Baptist | 78
   Fusing the Horizons: Paltry Resources and a Needy World | 86
   Excursus: Food and the Tradition of the Elders | 91
   Excursus on "Corban" | 93
   Fusing the Horizons: Divine Integrity and the Abrogation of the Purity Code | 95
On the Road to Jerusalem: The Gospel and the Suffering Messiah (8:22—10:52) | 109
   Excursus: The Place of Jesus' Transfiguration | 118
   Excursus: Elijah must first come | 123
   Fusing the Horizons: Prayer and the Disciples' Failure | 125
   Excursus: Jewish Attitudes Towards Divorce | 132
   Fusing the Horizons: Marriage, Social Inequality, and Wealth | 140
   Excursus: The Suffering Servant of Isaiah 53 and Mark 10:45 | 144
   Excursus: The Son of David | 147
The Climax of the Gospel: The Messiah and Jerusalem (11:1—16:8) | 149
   Excursus: Problems of the Parable | 162
   Excursus: The Appropriation of Psalm 118:22–23 | 163
   Excursus: The Chronology of the Last Supper in the Four Gospels | 191
   Excursus: The Passover Meal | 195

Excursus: Caiaphas the High Priest | 204
Excursus: Sanhedrin | 206
Excursus: Pontius Pilate | 208
Excursus: Mark and John on the Hour of Crucifixion | 212
Fusing the Horizons: Mark's Achievement | 219
A Sketch of Mark's Theology | 226

Bibliography | 235
Scripture Index | 249
Ancient Sources Index | 257
Modern Authors Index | 264

Acknowledgments

The sense of being an indebted member to a large and nurturing community grows with the writing of a commentary. It is not an exaggeration to say that a tome is certainly needed for me genuinely to thank everyone. Perhaps this is why I find the Christian concept of eternal life so enthralling. But this also means I find writing just a page of acknowledgments so difficult.

Nevertheless, opportunities must be seized, even if they are not ideal. I would like therefore to thank the editors, Mike Bird and Craig Keener, for their patience, encouragement, and trust. I mention trust because they have committed to me the task of writing a commentary on one of the most significant books of the Christian church and, dare I also say, of this world. Great is your faith, my friends! If there are faults in this enterprise, it has nothing to do with vision but everything to do with execution.

The Principal of Trinity Theological College, Singapore, deserves special mention for his support and understanding, as I stole what little time I had left over from administrative duties to pen some rather "bitty" thoughts. My colleagues have been stimulating, and I find myself inexorably applying some of their wisdom and insights into my work. Thanks also should be given to the librarian, Michael Mukunthan, for helping me trace some obscure sources.

A busy husband also means a harried wife, especially when there are three children in tow. That my home remains one that is orderly and nurturing bears testimony to her patience, love, and competence. Perhaps I may one day write a book on Proverbs 31 as penance! But I do hope her sacrifice has not been in vain.

Preface

When there are so many major commentaries on the Gospel of Mark available in the market, what place is there for another? This question has been uppermost in my mind as I write this volume which the reader now have in his/her hands.

Without competing with these major commentaries, I have nonetheless utilized their research findings, and summarized them for an audience which may not have the time or expertise to pore through them. Moreover, I have kept in view the notion of a New Covenant Commentary Series. A new covenant presupposes a previous one, I have therefore sought assiduously to show how Mark is connected to the OT. Furthermore, the word covenant reminds me of a community, and hence, I have written this with a view to making Mark's message applicable to the challenges of being a Christian community in this complicated world. I have introduced as best as I can some Asian insights—I hope this has not been too obtrusive—believing that my social location may bring some benefits to a worldwide audience, for after all this may very well be the reason why the editors of the series approached me to contribute this volume.

I have kept in mind that my primary task is to explain Mark's message, not to show the prehistory of his sources, or attempt to justify his point of view (although I must add that at times resistance was futile). No attempt is made to treat completely or eruditely every issue connected with the interpretation of the Markan text. There are commentaries that have taken on this task, and there is no need to match their feat. Focusing on Mark's text also means I've given scant attention to historical issues or problems raised by parallel accounts in the other Gospels. My task is to explain Mark's tale, and not to assess whether it stands up to historical or synoptic scrutiny. Otherwise this commentary would have been twice as long.

As this is not a commentary on commentaries of Mark, certain issues that have taken much space in them are sometimes given scant notice, if I have judged that their resolution does not illuminate Mark's text. On the rare occasion I have struck out on my own, generating new issues and offering interpretations hitherto not found in other commentaries.

Abbreviations

1. OLD TESTAMENT APOCRYPHA AND PSEUDEPIGRAPHA

Bar	*Baruch*
2 Bar	*2 Baruch*
3 Bar	*3 Baruch*
1 En	*1 Enoch*
2 Esd	*2 Esdras*
4 Esd	*4 Esdras*
Jub	*Jubilees*
1 Macc	*1 Maccabees*
2 Macc	*2 Maccabees*
3 Macc	*3 Maccabees*
4 Macc	*4 Maccabees*
Pss Sol	*Psalms of Solomon*
SibOr	*Sibylline Oracles*
Sir	*The Wisdom of Ben Sira, or Ecclesiasticus*
TJos	*Testament of Joseph*
TMos	*Testament of Moses*
Tob	*Tobit*
Wisd	*Wisdom of Solomon*

2. DEAD SEA SCROLLS

CD	*Cairo Damascus Document*
1QH	*Hodayot Hymns* from Cave 1

1QM	*War Scroll* from Cave 1
1QpHab	*Pesher on Habakkuk* from Cave 1
1QS	*Community Scroll* from Cave 1
4QFlor	*Florilegium* from Cave 4
11Q13	*Melchizedek Scroll* from Cave 11
11QT	*Temple Scroll* from Cave 11

3. RABBINIC AND TARGUMIC LITERATURE

'Abod.Zar.	*'Abodah Zarah*
b.	Babylonian Talmud
B.Bat.	*Baba Batra*
Ber.	*Berakhot*
'Ed.	*'Eduyyot*
'Erub.	*'Erubin*
Git.	*Gittin*
Hag.	*Hagigah*
Hul.	*Hullin*
Ker.	*Keritot*
Ketub.	*Ketubbot*
m.	Mishnah
Naz.	*Nazir*
Ned.	*Nedarim*
Nid.	*Niddah*
Mak.	*Makkot*
Meg.	*Megillah*
Mid.	*Middot*
Ohol.	*Oholot*
Para.	*Parah*
Pes.	*Pesahim*
Pesiq. R.	*Pesiqta Rabbati*

Pirque R. El.	*Pirque Rabbi Eliezer*
Sab.	*Sabbat*
Sanh.	*Sanhedrin*
Seq.	*Sheqalim*
Sipre Lev.	*Sipre on Leviticus*
Suk.	*Sukkah*
t.	*Tosephta*
Ta'an.	*Ta'anit*
Tg.Ps.	*Targum on the Psalms*
Tg.Zech.	*Targum on Zechariah*
Toh.	*Toharot*
Yad.	*Yadaim*

4. EARLY CHRISTIAN WRITINGS

Did.	*Didache*
Epiphanius	Epiphanius
Haer	*Adversus Haereses*
Eusebius	Eusebius
H.E.	*Historia Ecclesiastica*
Irenaeus	Irenaeus
A.H.	*Adversus Haereses*

5. OTHER JEWISH, CLASSICAL AND HELLENISTIC LITERATURE

Josephus	Josephus
Antiquities	*Jewish Antiquities*
Apion	*Against Apion*
Life	*Life of Josephus*
War	*The Jewish War*
Philo	Philo
Decal.	*On the Decalogue*
Leg. Gai.	*Embassy to Gaius*

Virgil
   Georg.

Virgil
   Georgicon

6. MODERN WORKS

AASF	Annales Academiae scientiarum fennicae
AB	Anchor Bible
ABD	*The Anchor Bible Dictionary*, ed. D. N. Freedman (6 vols.; Doubleday, New York: 1992).
ABRL	Anchor Bible Reference Library
BAR	Biblical Archaeology Review
BDAG	*A Greek-English Lexicon of the New Testament and Other Early Christian Literature*, W. Bauer, trans. and rev. by W. F. Arndt and F. W. Gingrich; 2nd edn rev. by F. W. Gingrich and F. W. Danker; 3rd edn rev, by F. W. Danker (Chicago: University of Chicago Press, 2000).
BDF	*A Greek Grammar of the New Testament and Other Early Christian Literature*, F. Blass and A. Debrunner, trans. and rev. by R. W. Funk (Chicago: University of Chicago Press, 1961).
BECNT	Baker Exegetical Commentary on the New Testament
BETL	Bibliotheca Ephemeridum Theologicarum Lovaniensium
Bib	*Biblica*
BNTC	Black New Testament Commentary
BTS	Biblical Tools and Studies
BZNW	Beiheft zur Zeitschrift für die neuetestamentliche Wissenschaft
CBQ	*Catholic Biblical Quarterly*
CBQMS	Catholic Biblical Quarterly Monograph Series
ExpT	*Expository Times*
HNT	Handbuch zum Neuen Testament
HTR	*Harvard Theological Review*

HTS	Harvard Theological Studies
JANES	Journal of the Ancient Near Eastern Society of Columbia University
JBL	Journal of Biblical Literature
JBT	Jahrbuch für biblische Theologie
JETS	Journal of the Evangelical Theological Society
JSJSup	Supplements to the Journal for the Study of Judaism
JSNT	Journal for the Study of the New Testament
JSNTSup	Journal for the Study of the New Testament Supplement Series
JSOT	Journal for the Study of the Old Testament
JSOTSup	Journal for the Study of the Old Testament Supplement Series
JSS	Journal of Semitic Studies
JTS	Journal of Theological Studies
LNTS	Library of New Testament Studies
LSJ	*A Greek-English Lexicon*. By H. G. Liddell and R. Scott, new edn by H. S. Jones and R. McKenzie. Oxford: Oxford University Press, 1940 (supplement, ed. E. A. Barber, 1968)
NA28	*Novum Testamentum Graece*, 28th edn, ed. E. Nestle, K. Aland et al, Stuttgart: Deutsche Biblestiftung, 2012.
NICNT	New International Commentary on the New Testament
NIGTC	New International Greek Testament Commentary
NovT	Novum Testamentum
NovTSup	Novum Testamentum Supplement Series
NTOA	Novum Testamentum et Orbis Antiquus
NTS	New Testament Studies
NumenSup	Numen Supplements

PNTC	Pillar New Testament Commentary
RB	*Revue biblique*
SBEC	Studies in the Bible and Early Christianity
SBLDS	Society of Biblical Literature Dissertation Series
SBLSP	*Society of Biblical Literature Seminar Papers*
SBLSS	Society of Biblical Literature Semeia Studies
SBT	Studies in Biblical Theology
SHBC	Smyth & Helwys Bible Commentary
SNTSMS	Society for New Testament Studies Monograph Series
SOTBT	Studies in Old Testament Biblical Theology
TDNT	*Theological Dictionary of the New Testament.* 9 vols. Ed. G. Kittel and G. Friedrich. ET. Grand Rapids: Eerdmans, 1964-74.
TGST	Tesi greogariana, Serie theologia
TZ	*Theologische Zeitschrift*
WBC	Word Biblical Commentary
WUNT	Wissenschaftliche Untersuchungen zum Neuen Testament
ZNW	*Zeitschrift für die neuetestamentliche Wissenschaft*

Introduction

Larger works have detailed discussions on what is usually known as "Introduction." Consequently, we will provide only a sketch of where this commentary stands in relation to such matters.

AUTHORSHIP

There is no explicit mention of who the author is in the text of the Second Gospel[1] but we believe him to be Mark. The case for this is based mainly on two considerations: the superscription and the external testimony.

Superscription

In ancient times the author's name is found usually in the superscription—something that precedes the actual work, and may be treated as the equivalent to the title page in modern books. The text proper seldom identifies the author.[2] All the available Greek manuscripts of this Gospel featuring a superscription unanimously name Mark as the author.[3] The earliest manuscripts that have this feature come from the fourth century.[4] Later manuscripts contain superscriptions in different forms, usually expanded from the simple *kata Markon*.[5] Some scholars use this to infer that all superscriptions are artificial, leading to the thesis that this Gospel circulated anonymously at the first until a couple of centuries later.[6] What remains significant, however, is that despite the varied forms, all of them consistently state that Mark is the author. Such consistency cannot be ignored.

    1. "Second" here refers to the canonical order. We use this label in order not to pre-judge the issue of authorship.

    2. Collins 2007: 2–3. She points out that in antiquity the giving and use of titles belonged more to the reception of a work than its production.

    3. It is unfortunate that the earliest manuscript (P^{45}, third century) is missing the superscription, as it is fragmentary.

    4. Codex Sinaiticus (א) and Codex Vaticanus (B).

    5. Translated into English it means "according to Mark."

    6. Marcus 2000: 17; Pesch 1980: 4.

Moreover, Mark is not the name of an apostle, or an important figure in the history of earliest Christianity. Why should a rather obscure name be passed off as the author of this important work, when there were better candidates? Indeed, the two-document hypothesis[7] adds strength to this argument, as it means our Gospel was significant enough to be utilized by both Matthew and Luke. If a name has to be fabricated to identify a significant anonymous work, we would not have expected "Mark." The name "Mark" therefore carries with it a ring of authenticity.

Furthermore, written Gospels started circulating as early as the first century. We may use John's Gospel as an illuminating example. This work was already being copied in Egypt by AD 125,[8] a mere thirty years or so after its composition, which is usually believed to be in Ephesus. Although we do not have similar evidence in the case of the Second Gospel, we may posit that it must have started circulating in the first century, since it was used by Matthew and Luke. Early circulation of Gospels necessitated some sort of labelling, so as to distinguish the one from the other.[9]

All the above observations mean that even if the Second Gospel was published anonymously, this anonymity would have disappeared almost from the very start, when it started circulating. In other words, even if we deem the superscriptions as secondary, we will still have to accept that they may very well have enshrined a truth. Significantly, there is only one name offered by them as the author: Mark.

Early Patristic Testimonies

The earliest and most-discussed testimony comes from Papias, the bishop of Hierapolis in the early second century. His work, *Exegesis of the Lord's Oracles*, was written around AD 110,[10] but it is now lost except for excerpts that are cited in Eusebius's book, *Ecclesiastical History*, written in the fourth century. Papias testifies that Mark wrote the "oracles of the Lord," dependent on Peter's memories.[11] Of course, this does not necessarily mean that our current Gospel is being referred to. That said, it is clear that as early as the

---

7. The hypothesis that Mark and a source known as Q are the key sources used by Matthew and Luke.

8. The evidence of P^{52}.

9. See Hengel 1985: 64–84, for a magisterial treatment of such issues.

10. Bauckham 2008: 13–14; Gundry 1993: 1027–29, thinks it is even earlier: AD 101–108.

11. Eusebius, *H.E.* 3:9:15.

beginning of the second century, Mark was connected with the writing of a compilation of Jesus' teachings.

Irenaeus supports Papias's testimony. Since Irenaeus is defending the authenticity of the four canonical Gospels as we now have them, it is important that he had a strong case, as otherwise his opponents could have easily destroyed it. He indicates clearly that Mark is the author of the Second Gospel, and that Peter is his source.[12] We do not have room to cite all the relevant testimonies from other early Church Fathers. Suffice it to say that their testimonies are consistent with what has been presented.

Some scholars have dismissed the significance of the consistency of these testimonies by arguing that they were all dependent on Papias. So the many and varied witnesses are reduced to only one. The onus of proof is really on them, and they have not clinched their case. Moreover, it is more reasonable to believe this united testimony as reliable than to think it has been fabricated or confusingly mentioned by someone prominent, and from henceforth became the stuff of influential tradition.

To draw the threads of our argument together: Papias testifies that Mark wrote the "oracles of the Lord." Patristic testimonies and the superscriptions in their varied forms speak with one voice: Mark wrote the Second Gospel. This Gospel was significant enough to be linked to Peter, and used by Matthew and Luke. That an important work is connected with an insignificant name indicates authenticity.

The Evangelist Mark

Who exactly is this Mark? The early patristic testimony identifies him as someone closely associated with Peter. As no other descriptors of his identity is given, we may surmise that the brief datum was enough for early Christians to decipher his identity. If this consideration is correct, we are led to look for a Mark in the earliest accounts of the rise of the church. The NT books are key here.

The Acts of the Apostles mentions a certain John Mark was once a travelling companion of the apostle Paul, and left him later (Acts 12:12, 25; 13:5, 13; 15:37). This is probably the same person mentioned in the Pauline tradition (Col 4:10; 2 Tim 4:11; Phlm 24). All this testimony, if it refers to one person, puts Mark as someone associated with Paul. In 1 Peter 5:13, however, a certain Mark is expressly referred to as "son" by the writer of the letter. Early tradition does not cast any doubt that behind 1 Peter stands Peter the apostle. If all this evidence speaks of two or three well-known Marks,

---

12. Irenaeus, *A.H.* 3:2:2, c. AD 175.

we should have expected some sort of differentiation: either by assigning a title, or a toponym. Since there is no such attempt, it is reasonable to think that only one person is referred to: John Mark who was once the travelling companion of Paul but who became closely associated with Peter later on.

Can we know more about John Mark? Additional information may be found in the Anti-Marcionite Prologues (c. AD 180), that is if these enshrined an authentic traditions. In the relevant Prologue, Mark is described as stumpy-fingered. This datum might interest some readers but it adds nothing significant to our interpretation of his book.

What if our identification is wrong? Nothing substantial is affected in terms of exegesis if we are only concerned with unpacking the message of the book. Of course, if it is true that the book is written by John Mark, and that Peter was his source, the implication for historical reconstruction of earliest Christianity would certainly be significant.

DATE

Many scholars date the composition of Mark's Gospel to a time before the destruction of Jerusalem in AD 70.[13] One reason for this is that in chapter 13 Jesus is recorded as predicting the destruction of the Temple. Since Mark is fond of adding editorial comments (e.g., 7:3–4), we should expect a mention that this prophecy had been fulfilled if the book was written post-70. Furthermore, Josephus tells us that there was a great fire that destroyed the Temple. The fact that none of these is mentioned speaks for a pre-70 composition.

Is it possible to be more precise? The text offers little help here, except for 13:14, that is, if we can decipher its referent. In this verse Mark signals to the reader to take special note of what is said ("let the reader understand"). This suggests either the abomination of desolation has already been set up or the event is imminent. If we are right in identifying this as the occupation of the Temple by the Zealots and the forced appointment of Phanias as the High Priest (see the treatment of chapter 13), this brings us to the shadow of AD 67–68. However, the identification of the abomination of desolation is a highly contentious issue, and so we must look to other evidence.

We turn, once again, to early patristic testimony. When we compare the relevant statements of Papias and Irenaeus, an apparent discrepancy surfaces. Was Mark's Gospel written before or after Peter's death? Much hinges on how we interpret the term *exodos* in Irenaeus's testimony (i.e.,

---

13. E.g., Collins 2007: 14; and Guelich 1989: xxxi–xxxii. The prominent scholars who opt for a post-70 date are Pesch 1980: 14; and Evans 2001: lxiii.

whether it means a literal departure from a certain locality or a euphemism for death). That said, a case has been made that Irenaeus may, after all, be consistent with Papias.¹⁴ Whatever the case may be, it does not contradict the proposed pre-70 date. Taking all this into consideration, the range AD 64–68 appears cogent.

What is of significance here is that these were turbulent years, occasioned by Nero's persecution of Christians in Rome (AD 64) and the Jewish conflict with Rome (AD 66–70), concluding in the destruction of Jerusalem in AD 70. As Gaston observes, it is in this particular time span that all the motifs of Mark 13 would be operative to the fullest extent.¹⁵

PROVENANCE AND AUDIENCE

The questions of provenance (i.e., where the document originated) and audience may be answered by looking at the evidence provided by early patristic testimony, and by the text itself.

To start with the former, the two best candidates are Rome and Egypt (probably Alexandria). Early and wide testimony supports Rome as the place of composition (the evidence is provided by Irenaeus, Clement of Alexandria, and the Anti-Marcionite Prologues among many others). This is further supported by the presence of Latinisms in the Gospel (see especially Mark 7:26; 12:42; 15:16).¹⁶ These are either Latin terms that have been transliterated into Greek, or terms that have a uniquely Roman flavor. Furthermore, Mark's text assumes a Gentile audience (cf. 7:3–4), especially one that was well-versed in the OT because he cites from it and alludes to it in many places. The Christian community at Rome fits this bill: Paul's letter to the Romans paints a picture of a Gentile community that knows its LXX well.

The other candidate attested in patristic writings is Egypt. The testimony is provided by one lonely voice: John Chrysostom (c. 347–407). Measured against the early and widely-attested Roman provenance,¹⁷ the Egyptian provenance appears improbable. That said, there is a rich tradition that locates Mark in Alexandria, but this does not necessarily contradict the testimony that the Gospel was written in Rome. Eusebius mentions that

---

14. France 2002: 37.
15. Gaston 1970: 468.
16. For a complete listing, see Gundry 1993: 1043–45.
17. See Incigneri 2003. The whole monograph is devoted to demonstrating a Roman provenance.

Mark was sent to Alexandria after he had written his Gospel in Rome.[18] Epiphanius's testimony supports this, with the additional detail that it was Peter who sent him there.[19]

Interestingly, a handful of scholars have argued that Mark was composed in Syria-Palestine.[20] However, no external testimony supports it. The case is derived from internal evidence, inferring from passages such as 7:31 and 15:21.

If the Gospel of Mark has a Roman provenance, we may presume Mark is writing for a Roman audience, particularly the church at Rome. Much of Markan scholarship then utilizes this assumption to reconstruct the profile of the community to which Mark is writing. He mentions some details such as the young man who fled naked (14:52), and Simon of Cyrene (15:51–52) who is also described as the father of Alexander and Rufus. These details would interest only a particular community.

There are, however, other considerations to bear in mind. Recently, Bauckham has argued that unlike the letters, the Gospels are meant for a wider circulation, and not just for one community.[21] The ably-argued case need not be rehearsed here. Consider the itineraries of the apostles, the frequent communication between churches, and the fact that we could not expect an elaborate work such as Mark's Gospel to be written only for a community of about fifty to one hundred Christians. That said, Bauckham's case must be balanced against the quaint details found in Mark. The resultant picture is that of a writing that has been shaped by a specific audience, but without limiting itself to that audience.[22] Mark certainly wrote for his immediate community but he also had in mind Christians all over the Empire who might find his writing beneficial and edifying.

OCCASION AND PURPOSE

To answer the questions of occasion and purpose we must depend substantially on our reconstruction of the origin of the writing, especially the dating, the provenance, and the audience. But the text itself may also play a part.

It has frequently been observed that Mark's Gospel shows a heightened interest in discipleship, focusing especially on the suffering awaiting them,

18. *H.E.* 2: 16:1.
19. *Haer.* 6: 10.
20. Kee 1977: 100–105; Theissen 1991: 259; cf. Boring 2006: 17–19; and Marcus 2000: 33–37.
21. Bauckham 1998: 9–48.
22. Cf. Mitchell 2005: 36–79.

either in the form of repudiation or persecution. From this observation, it is often thought that Mark was written to an audience experiencing persecution from society or state. Thus Mark's Gospel would have the purpose of reaffirming the importance of the gospel to a beleaguered community, and helping them fall in line with the way of the Lord, especially during times of persecution. The way of the cross is the way of Jesus, and this is the way that would lead ultimately to glory. History tells us Nero began an intense persecution of Christians in Rome in AD 64. This might have been the impetus for Mark's Gospel to be written.[23]

The other possibility is that Mark intended to set in writing the oral apostolic tradition, especially Peter's, as the band of apostles was passing away. This serves the purpose of preserving the tradition for future generations. The evidence from Papias lends support to such a theory, for he implies that Mark wrote before Peter's death.

There is no need to choose between the two, as Mark could conceivably have had a few purposes in mind (including those not discussed earlier). Here it may be instructive to note the subtle difference, and yet inter-dependability, between occasion and purpose. The occasion which led to the writing may arguably have been the onset of persecution or the aging of the apostles. This might have triggered an intention to write a document to achieve not just one but a set of objectives.[24] Such objectives may have been pastoral in nature, didactic or polemical (i.e., Mark might be countering some false teaching),[25] or all of the above. So we need not come down firmly on a particular purpose.

Literary Characteristics

What sort of writing is the Gospel of Mark? Comparing it with the whole range of ancient literature, what comes closest to it is known as the *bios* or "Life."[26] This is an ancient form of biography, often written to encourage the audience to follow the example of the featured life. To be sure, Mark's writing would appear rather different from such *bioi* in that the focus is on the passion and death of his "hero." But what makes it different is the character not the genre. Mark wants his audience to know that his central character, Jesus of Nazareth, is unlike any other in the ancient world, indeed in the whole of

---

23. Guelich 1989: xl–xliii. Cf. Winn 2008: countering imperial propaganda post-70.
24. Cf. Collins 2007: 102; France 2002: 23.
25. E.g., Weeden 1968: 145–58 and Gundry 1993: countering errant Christology and staurology respectively.
26. Stanton 1974; Burridge 1992.

human history. This character's significance is intimately connected to his passion and death, and hence the nature of the focus. In this regard Mark is not inventing a new genre. Later on, others emulated his writing, and such writings became known as "Gospels" or churchly writings. It is only after this that one can speak of a new genre, or better, a sub-genre.

It may be claimed that Mark intended his writing to be read in the setting of worship (cf. Acts 2:42; 5:42; Col 4:15). Moreover, literacy rates were rather low in the ancient world.[27] Hence Mark would have designed his work not for self-study but to be read aloud to Christian communities gathered at worship. Certain features of Mark's text demonstrate this. His style is vivid (e.g., Mark 14:32–52; compare this with the parallel accounts in Matthew and Luke), and is often replete with dual expressions—a feature of oral communication and not formal writing. An example of this dual expression is found in Mark 1:32, where the time of the event is described as "evening, when the sun has set." This may appear tautologous to the trained eye of a good writer. But for oral communication, such dual expressions make the message memorable. Furthermore, repetitiveness is a feature (e.g., the threefold passion prediction: 8:31; 9:31; 10:33), which helps especially a listening audience, who would not have the document to refer to. All these stylistic devices are in keeping with a text written for oral presentation.[28]

Certain corollaries follow. First of all, it calls into question the many complicated and convoluted chiastic structures proposed by scholars.[29] How could a listener perceive such grand schemes and structures which are transparent only after sustained analysis? That said, this criticism must not be taken as rendering void all rhetorical studies of Mark's text. Rather, it is to say, secondly, that we should expect Mark to employ small-scale techniques, utilizing small chunks of text so that the listener might not be lost in a wealth of details. Indeed, Mark makes use of flashbacks, small-scale chiastic structures, the sandwich technique for relating one story to the other, suspense, paradox, and topical arrangements. Such techniques hold the listeners' interest, and help them to connect episodes or passages so that a profounder message may be perceived. Finally, it suggests that the structure of the book is straightforwardly simple and predominantly linear. Our proposed structure will take this into account. But before this is offered,

---

27. The best authorities estimate literacy of the Roman Empire at around 10 percent and that of Roman Palestine, around 3 percent. See Harris 1991: 22; and Hezser 2001: 25, 445–50, 496–500. Given the importance of learning Torah in Jewish culture, the estimates might possibly be higher for Jewish Palestine. See Millard 2000.

28. Bryan 1993: 72–81; cf. Hartvigsen 2012.

29. Cf. Van Iersel 1989: 19–26, 75–86, who proposes elaborate concentric structures.

we must consider an important datum often missed by scholars emphasizing that Mark's Gospel is written for oral presentation.

In Mark 13:14, Mark inserts his editorial remark "let the reader understand." This directive to the reader is important for our consideration of the kind of text Mark's Gospel is. If Mark were written merely for oral presentation, we should expect the remark to be "let the listener understand." The fact that the reader is alerted, without giving him explicit clues as to the meaning of the abomination of desolation, implies that this reader is no ordinary reader but someone who has been trained. He could then be expected to explain to the audience the meaning of v. 14. This certainly means he is also expected to explain or clarify Mark's teaching to the audience.

Moreover, Mark's text is too long for a one-sitting reading. A reader must know the appropriate points to stop his reading. He must be guided by the contents, rather than by length. Thus we should expect a clear structure to be found and clear indications of breaks in the text.

If the above conjectures are correct, an important rider must be added to the valid concept of the Gospel of Mark being written for oral presentation. It is a *bios*, written for oral presentation *by an informed or trained reader*, who has the duty to study his text so he knows where to stop the reading for the day, and so he can prepare himself to explain certain aspects of it to his audience. Therefore, we must allow for some sophistication to Mark's Gospel, even if the structure is straightforwardly simple.

We can now present a proposed structure for it. We argued earlier for a structure that is clear and simple. Two cues are provided at the beginning and at the end respectively. First, Mark has announced his primary subject matter right at the start—the gospel of Messiah Jesus—and this must guide us in our construal of the structure. The second is obtained by considering the sort of denouement Mark has adopted for his narrative. Scanning through the text, one observes that the Passion narrative takes on a prominent role. Moreover, Mark narrates only one trip of Jesus to Jerusalem, which is a climactic and fateful one. Of course, Jesus would have made many trips to that city, historically speaking. So Mark's narration of only one trip indicates to us where his narrative emphasis is, and what sort of structure he is adopting. It describes the progression of Jesus' gospel ministry, using a geographical approach that is easily remembered: beginning with Galilee and ending with Jerusalem.

The Structure of Mark

I. The Beginning of the Gospel (1:1–13)

II. The Gospel in Galilee: The Mighty Acts of the Messiah (1:14—8:21)

1:14–15	Jesus' Inaugural Gospel Message
1:16–45	Typical Activities of Jesus' Ministry
2:1—3:6	Conflict with Religious Authorities
3:7–12	Summary of Jesus' Deeds
3:13–35	New People of God and Jesus' True Family
4:1–34	Kingdom in Parables
4:35–41	Stilling of the Storm and Unveiling of Jesus' Identity
5:1–20	Healing of the Demoniac of Gerasenes
5:21–43	Jairus's Daughter and the Woman with Chronic Bleeding
6:1–6a	Rejection at Nazareth
6:6b–30	Mission Extended and Martyrdom Foreshadowed
6:31–56	Miracles Around the Lake
7:1–23	Redefining the Unclean
7:24–36	Extension of Jesus' Ministry to the Gentiles
8:1–10	Feeding of the 4,000
8:11–21	Demand for a Sign and the Yeast of the Pharisees and Herod

III. On the Road to Jerusalem: The Gospel and the Suffering Messiah (8:22—10:52)

8:22–30	Stuttering Beginnings of a True Perception
8:31—9:1	Messiah Must Suffer
9:2–13	Transfiguration and Transformation of Expectations
9:14–29	Boy with an Unclean Spirit
9:30–50	"The Messiah Must Suffer" and Sundry Lessons on Discipleship

10:1–31	More Revolutionary Values for Disciples
10:32–45	Following the Messiah in Service
10:46–52	Restoring Bartimaeus's Sight

IV. The Climax of the Gospel: The Messiah and Jerusalem (11:1—16:8)

11:1–25	Challenge in Jerusalem: Symbols of Fulfillment and Judgment
11:27–33	Jesus' Authority Questioned
12:1–44	Further Controversies
13:1–37	Eschatological Discourse on the Mount of Olives
14:1–11	Anointing at Bethany
14:12–31	Last Supper
14:32–52	Gethsemane and the arrest of Jesus
14:53–72	Hearing by the Sanhedrin
15:1–20	Roman Trial
15:21–41	Crucifixion and Death of Jesus
15:42–47	Burial of Jesus
16:1–8	Resurrection

Within each phase two entities stand out: the Messiah and his people/disciples. What connects the Messiah and his people is the gospel that is preached, enacted through mighty acts, and embodied through suffering obedience.

The Beginning of the Gospel (1:1–13)

THE HEADING (1:1)

In a world where many things compete for the interest of a potential reader, the beginning of a book must be written in such a way as to be attention-grabbing. Its role is therefore critical because not only has it to perform the aforesaid function, it has also to inform the reader, at least in an implicit way, of what is to come.

What we now have shows that Mark has opened his narrative admirably. Not only are highly potent terms in his culture used ("beginning," "gospel," "Christ" and possibly "Son of God"), they are also expressed with an unexpected twist, signaling that what follows may be both explosive and subversive. We will explain how this takes place, but first, a question concerning the exact limits of the opening section of Mark has to be discussed.

Verse 1 serves certainly as a heading. What is disputed among scholars is whether it is the heading of the entire work or just a section, such as 1:1–13 or 1:1–15. By virtue of its compressed style and the presence of numerous significant words, we incline to the view that it serves as the heading of the entire work.[1] A parallel that illuminates this is Hosea 1:2. We may also mention the fact that Mark does not write sectional headings, not even for his important Passion Narrative.

That said, we note that the Greek *kathōs* ("just as") introduces vv. 2–3. Without the usual complement of a *houtōs* ("so") clause, it implies that *kathōs* introduces a statement (i.e., vv. 2–3) to complete an earlier one (i.e., v. 1). This means v. 1 does not stand alone as a sentence, as we might expect the heading of the work to be. Verse 1 may then be understood as both the heading of the work and forming part of the opening section.[2] This may appear confusing but it may have come about because Mark is not concerned with formal style. It is also possible that Mark is creatively ambivalent.[3]

---

1. Collins 2007: 130; France 2002: 50.
2. Cf. Boring 2006: 29.
3. Cf. Becker 2006: 112.

With regard to the extent of the opening section, we think it ends in v. 13,[4] as there appears to be a clear break in content and plot with 1:14–15. These verses speak of John's imprisonment—implying the end of one phase—and introduces Jesus' message to the readers.

We return to v. 1, especially the meaning of the significant terms in their context. The "beginning of the gospel" was certainly a loaded phrase. A calendar inscription from Priene (9 BC) illuminates this.[5] We provide the English translation of Danker:[6]

> In her display of concern and generosity on our behalf, Providence, who orders all our lives, has adorned our lives with the highest good, namely Augustus ... And Caesar, [when he was manifest], transcended the expectations of [all who had anticipated the good news], not only by surpassing the benefits conferred by his predecessors but by leaving no expectation of surpassing him to those who would come after him, with the result that *the birthday of our god signaled the beginning of good news for the world because of him.*[7]

We can detect some subversion by Mark. The Greek word he uses for "gospel" is *euangelion*, which was important for the early Church, just as it is for Christian faith today. It was also important for the Roman Empire, although it is usually found in the plural form (*euangelia*). The Christian usage was *always* singular. What must not be missed is that the calendar inscription speaks of the *beginning* of the *euangelia*, stating its connection with Augustus Caesar's birth, calling him a god and proclaiming a universal impact. Mark connects the beginning of the one gospel with Jesus Christ instead. If the phrase "Son of God" was original to Mark's text, there is another point of contact that may be discerned. We know from other sources that Augustus Caesar was known as the son of god, after his adoptive father Julius Caesar was divinized by the Roman senate. In Mark's text, Jesus Christ is the Son of God. Markan subversion is clearly at work.

---

4. France 2002: 59.

5. This was previously known as the Priene Inscription. However, copies of this inscription were found in at least five cities in Asia Minor, showing how widespread this piece of propaganda was. Augustus' reign was widely hailed in Asia Minor because of his shrewd policies. The economy of the region boomed, and in response the leaders of these cities proposed to start a new calendar to coincide with Augustus's birthday. The beginning of good news in this light meant a new world order. See further Stanton 2004: 9–62, esp. 30–33.

6. Danker 1982: 216–17.

7. Our italics and they translate the Greek *ērxen de tōi kosmōi tōn di' auton euangeli[ōn ē genethlios hēme]ra tou theou*.

We now take a closer look at the meaning of Mark's *euangelion*. That the word means good news is accepted by all scholars. But the framework within which we are to understand it has been disputed. Taking all the scholarly discussions into consideration but without going into detail, it seems best to understand this term against the OT and Jewish background,[8] without negating the possibility that Mark would have been familiar with the Roman propaganda that uses the term. In other words, Rome may be the dialogue partner, but she does not define the meaning for Mark. That meaning comes from the OT, which the verses that follow make clear.

Of importance are the Hebrew words *bāśar* (verb) and *mĕbaśśer* (participle). These words are found in passages with potent theological nuances, such as Isa 40:9; 52:7 and 61:1. These passages speak of the announcement of the good news of God's return to Zion, ending Israel's exile and rooting out evil from the world. Mark's use of *euangelion* may then be regarded as pointing to the fulfillment of these promises.

Two more words need to be explicated in the heading: "Christ" and "Son of God". With regard to "Christ", it is best to treat it as a title: Messiah. "Christ" is the anglicized version of the Greek *Christos*, which is in turn a translation of the Hebrew *māšiah* (anglicized into "Messiah"), which basically means "the anointed one." In Jewish thought of the Second Temple period, the reference is often—though not always—to a royal figure from the line of David, who is expected to come to deliver Israel from her enemies (cf. 4QFlor 1:10–13, 18–19; *Pss Sol* 17:21–32).[9] What is more important, however, is Mark's use of the term, which means a firm decision can only be made when the whole work has been analyzed.

The connection between the term "Son of God" and Roman propaganda has been explained earlier but we note here two further things. First, it is not clear whether this phrase was part of Mark's original text. Much has been discussed and there is no consensus.[10] Assuming it is original, it will be instructive to explore its Jewish background. In its Jewish context, the "Son of God" is often used in relation to the concept of election, principally the choice of Israel as God's special people, and the choice of the Davidic king as God's vicegerent. This fits into the ancient concept of divine adoption, where someone or a nation is singled out as a god's special love. For many Jews of Jesus' day, the term when used on human beings did not

---

8. See the magisterial treatment of Stuhlmacher 1968; and ably summarized in Guelich 1989: 13–14.

9. For a judicious treatment see Horbury 1998; and Horbury 2003. See also the essays in Charlesworth 1992; and the succinct treatment in Wright 1992: 307–20.

10. Head 1991: 621–29 vs. France 2002: 49 (cf. recently Wasserman 2011: 20–50, who supports the longer reading).

mean he/she was divine, but the chosen ruler or king of Israel. The Qumran scrolls (4QFlor and 4Q246) offer clear evidence that this is so. Of course, the Christian Church could have poured new content into the title, based on their understanding of who Jesus was. That is, as Son of God he was not simply king but more than king. However, Mark has intentionally left the meaning unexplained in the prologue. He will clarify this as his narrative proceeds. Modern scholarship has often regarded this title as the key to Mark's Christology.[11]

It remains for us to summarize what Mark has achieved with his heading. Mark has certainly introduced the key character, identified him with title(s) and indicated his importance with the correlate phrase "beginning of the gospel". All this is indeed explosive because set in the first century Roman Empire, the terms such as "gospel" and "son of God" formed a significant part of the unifying propaganda of an Empire that comprised many subjugated kingdoms and peoples. These terms laud the ruling power, usually making reference to the one who was touted as the greatest among them all: Augustus Caesar. But Mark speaks of a different gospel and a different Son of God, who is none other than Jesus of Nazareth, hailing from what may be regarded as the backwater of the Empire, and belonging to a people often regarded as strange at best, or a pest at worst. In other words, right from the very start, the alert reader would perceive that a contrast—indeed, a contest—is being set up between Augustus Caesar and Jesus Christ, between Rome and the Christian Church.

Fusing the Horizons

Mark's prologue was a shrill challenge to his society. What is striking in this challenge is the use of significant terms to flesh out the meaning of the Christian gospel. In other words, the potent content is given relevant packaging so that its power can be perceived much more quickly. Indeed, the packaging also hints at the contrast between the Roman gospels and the Christian gospel. One was plural, needing frequent re-enactments and connected with the might of this world; the other is singular, being the one true gospel, and is connected with the might of heaven but displayed, as Mark will show, in the crucified form of the Messiah. Popular and significant terms are thus being subverted by the Christian message.

---

11. The seminal work here is Kingsbury 1983.

Evangelistic endeavors in our world may take a leaf from Mark's book. Too often the gospel is presented in a garb that comes from another time or culture. We must, instead, seek ways to use significant terms in our time and culture to present the gospel. The rich theological terms of yesteryears, or from a far country, would simply pass our generation by if we do not make the effort to connect. In this light, the gospel message is not a mantra to be repeated but a performance that needs creative re-enactments.

This does not mean we are merely repeating what is fashionable. Rather, we are to use it as contact points or for subversion. In this sense, while the gospel can indeed be quickly understood, it is still a challenging message, as it calls people to abandon old and entrenched patterns of thinking and living in order to embrace the new and liberating. Hence, gospel preaching cannot just be about packaging, important as this may be. The content is supremely important, for it is this that will ultimately subvert and transform. To reiterate what was adumbrated earlier: we need *creative* performances, but such performances are also to be *re-enactments*, following the plot but with different props.

Mark's prologue indicates that the content of gospel preaching is to be informed by the story of Jesus Christ. This is the reference point. As such it serves as a challenge to how the gospel is being presented today. We may mention here, as an example, the weekly sermons of some churches where the focus is on how their members may be healthy or wealthy. God is presented as the doting, generous Creator and we are therefore fools if we remain sickly or poor. Such a counterfeit message contradicts Mark's presentation of his central character and actually sounds more like the gospels of the Caesars.[12] Such gospels certainly brought material benefit, but often only for a select group: the rich and powerful, the decision makers and the investors. Never mind the cries of the powerless many. Sadly, Christians may be complicit in such matters. As long as business or governmental schemes can enrich us, we are tempted to take them as God's blessing, without considering whether they are moral or just. Any gospel preaching that takes our eyes away from Christ must therefore be treated with suspicion.

---

12. Cf. the contribution of Horsley 2002: 137–47, where he has the gumption to equate the United States of America with the rapacious Roman Empire, leading to angry reactions from some quarters. We think, however, authentic Gospel preaching should sometimes be disturbing, making us realize that the enemy is not out there, but within, and may very well be ourselves.

JOHN THE BAPTIST AND JESUS' MINISTRY (1:2–13)

If the gospel is fundamentally connected with Jesus Christ, its origins actually predate his ministry and reach back to the Old Testament. Mark cites a fused text from Exod 23:30; Isa 40:3; and Mal 3:1 but attributes it only to Isaiah (v. 2). Sensing that there is an apparent contradiction here, later scribes changed the reading to "the prophets." However, the early manuscripts should be followed and there is no need to think that Mark has blundered. Three reasons may be posited for this "limited" attribution. First, Mark is in good company, as many biblical writers understood prophecy as being related to the one ongoing story of God and Israel, or the world.[13] So it is often assumed there is a theological force driving forward and unifying history. Earlier Scripture may then be regarded as contributing to the development of the same divine plot as later scripture, giving rise to the Jewish exegetical practice of linking texts containing similar subject matter (known in its Jewish form as *gezerah shawah* or analogy). Secondly, Mark singles out Isaiah because he regards him as the best exponent of the evangelical message of the Old Testament (i.e., Isaiah is the prophet of the gospel par excellence). What this implies is that we are given a hint as to how we may understand Mark's concept of the gospel, and from this, the ministry of Jesus may therefore be better understood.[14] Indeed, Isaiah is the only writing prophet mentioned by name in Mark's Gospel. Thirdly, Mark wants to introduce John the Baptist as the predicted forerunner of Jesus Christ. John's role dovetails best with the Isaianic prophecy of the voice in the wilderness. The citation of Isa 40:3 therefore prepares the reader for the next narrative development: a description of John's ministry.

The use of Isa 40:3 is highly significant here. The Qumran community which produced the Dead Sea Scrolls, appropriated it to explain its establishment in the wilderness (1QS 8:14; 9:19–21). It was there to prepare the way of God, signifying the imminent fulfillment of the great divine promise of restoration. The focus on this is not surprising, as Isaiah contains the powerful theme of a second exodus and a return of God to Zion to reign. When this is realized, there will be profound transformation in both flora and fauna, to the extent that the term "new creation" may be used (cf. Isa 65:17). In Mark's hand, the same prophecy is used for signaling the imminence of divine restoration, but astonishingly he explicates it as the coming of Jesus Christ. The significance of this will be made clear as Mark's narrative progresses.

---

13. See the treatments of this fascinating topic in Beale 1999; and Fishbane 1985.
14. Cf. Boring 2006: 36: "Mark writes an 'Isaian story.'"

The herald of the Isaianic prophecy is identified as John the Baptizer (v. 4). John's characteristic practice is introduced together with a brief description of the way he is dressed (vv. 4-6). The reference to his attire is meant to evoke memories of the prophets (2 Kings 1:8; Zech 13:4), and also to confirm that John was indeed a desert dweller, dovetailing with the prophecy of the voice in the wilderness.

John is called "Baptizer," implying that this was his characteristic activity and for which people remembered him, which Josephus the Jewish historian confirms (*Antiquities* 18:117-19). Mark explains the theological rationale for John's baptism as being connected with repentance and the forgiveness of sins. Such forgiveness is ratified through the outward act of baptism for the repentant. This fits in with the conceptual background of the fused text used in 1:2-3: a people truly prepared for the advent of God must have genuinely turned away (i.e., repented) from their disobedience, and embraced the gracious overtures of God (i.e., forgiveness). Moreover, against the first century Jewish background and the evidence provided by Josephus, John's baptism may also be understood as a call to join a new community. His use of the wilderness as the place of ministry could therefore have arisen from both practical and theological concerns, as the wilderness was the place that could fit crowds and was also evocative of Israel's exodus traditions.

Based on the data above, scholars have speculated whether John was ever connected with the Qumran community, since there is a convergence of text, location, and practice. However, given the paucity of the evidence and some crucial differences in relation to how baptism was administered (mainly frequency and agency), it is best to leave the question open.[15]

Verses 7-8 summarize John's message. The forerunner theme is further developed, but with the focus now on the coming one. He may also be known as "the stronger one," perhaps harking back to the Isaianic idea of God as "the mighty one" (28:2; 49:26), or possibly his messenger (Isa 11:2). Whatever the case, this person is so mighty that John is unworthy even to do one of the lowliest tasks in society: to stoop down and untie the thong of his sandals.

Significantly, this person will also baptize, but with the Spirit. The Holy Spirit is connected with the OT end-time expectation of a great moment of cleansing, resulting in the renewal of Israel. This promise is often described with liquid metaphors (Isa 32:15; 44:3; Ezek 11:19; 36:26-27; cf. Ezek 37:14; Joel 2:28-29; and 1QS 4:20-22). Such metaphors show spiritual cleansing is an important concern of God. The upshot of all this is that the Spirit's work

---

15. For discussion, see Webb 1991: 140-52; updated in Taylor 1997: 20-43.

may be regarded as "baptism." The similar saying in Matt 3:11||Luke 3:16 adds the word "fire." This may gel with what Mark is portraying, as fire is also an image for cleansing, albeit with the added notion of judgment.

Mark skillfully follows his description of John's message with the public appearance of Jesus. Astonishingly, Jesus comes to be baptized by John! This may reduce Jesus' status to being ordinary, but Mark prevents this by describing the divine portent that takes place at Jesus' baptism: the heavens are rent open, the Spirit descends in the form of a dove, and the divine voice speaks, affirming Jesus to be his beloved son. The significance of all this may be unpacked as follows.

First, Mark uses the Greek *schizō* to describe what took place in the heavens. This is a graphic word, which speaks of "tearing asunder." Mark uses this word only once more, in the account of the tearing of the Temple veil (15:38). The other Gospel writers use *anoigō*, which means "open," so as to avoid suggesting violence was done to heaven (Matt 3:16; Luke 3:21). Mark knows the meaning of *anoigō* and uses it in 7:35. All this implies *schizō* is being used intentionally and not because Mark lacks the vocabulary. The reason for this may be that Mark is thinking of Isaiah. This suggestion is supported by the fact that the book of Isaiah is important to the composition of Mark's Gospel. In Isa 64:1 the prophet pleads before God to rend[16] the heavens and come down, so as to restore the nation of Israel. For Mark, Jesus' baptism signifies God has answered this prayer.[17] The long-awaited intimate involvement and restorative action of God has come to pass.

Secondly, the descent of the Spirit takes on the bodily form of a dove. The Greek syntax[18] can mean either "the Spirit, appearing as a dove, descends" (i.e., understanding it adjectivally)[19] or "the Spirit descends as a dove does" (i.e., understanding it adverbially).[20] Since Mark describes Jesus as seeing something tangible, many commentators take the simile as adjectival.[21] The image of the Spirit as a dove is remarkable in two ways. First, the description is a stable datum across all four Gospels, when they contain many variations in the accounts of Jesus' baptism. The second is that this is a unique description of the Spirit, not even paralleled in the account of Pentecost (Acts 2:1–4). Against all comers, this image of the Spirit has stuck in Christian art, but what does it mean?

---

16. The LXX uses *anoigō*, but the MT uses *qāra'*, which means "tear open."
17. Cf. Boring 2006: 45.
18. The phrase is *to pneuma ōs peristeran katabainon*.
19. Guelich 1989: 32–33.
20. Keck 1970–71: 41–67.
21. France 2002: 78.

Avian images have been used of the Spirit's work of creation in the OT and Jewish literature (Gen 1:2; *b. Hag.* 15a; cf. 4Q521 1:6, where eschatological re-creation is in view). This theme does relate to the theological nuances of Mark's description of the beginning of the gospel. However, why does Mark specify a dove? In the alleged parallels, a dove is never mentioned. Recently, it has been proposed that Mark is countering the Roman symbol of an eagle with the dove.[22] There is much mileage in this but in our opinion it is still deficient, as it neglects the Jewish background. The dove often stands for Israel in Jewish literature (Hos 7.11; *b. Ber* 53b; *b. Sab* 49a), but never once is it used of the Spirit, with the possible exception of *Targum to Canticles* 2:12, where the voice of the turtledove is interpreted as the voice of the Spirit. Even so, it is clear that this parallel is not exact.

One possible solution is to regard the simile as a complex reference to the Spirit's work of remaking Israel as having been devolved upon Jesus through his spiritual anointing and empowerment. After all, the Spirit is understood in the prophetic literature as the end-time gift that remakes Israel (see especially Ezek 36–37). All this will explain why Jesus in Mark represents Israel, and at the same time calls upon the nation to follow him in order to gain the kingdom. Admittedly this is speculative, but its consonance with many Markan themes makes it somewhat appealing. However, if a safe but bland answer is required, it is that the dove is a clean animal for sacrifice (Gen 15:9; Lev 1:14; 12:6; 15:14, 29).

Thirdly, the visual symbol is accompanied by the divine voice, which affirms Jesus as his beloved Son. If we discount the occurrence of this nomenclature in v. 1 because of textual uncertainty, this will then be the first time Jesus is called God's Son. Scholars have debated the precise nature of the background to this verse: whether it is based on Ps 2:7; Isa 42:1 (for this to work, it must be conjectured that an original *pais* has been transmuted to *huios*); or Gen 22:2. If we are right to propose that sonship language should first and foremost be understood as election language when used of human beings, Ps 2:7 appears to be the more suitable background, being a verse from an enthronement psalm. But there is no need to think of a precise passage. What is more important is the *story and role* underlying such a title. Jesus as God's beloved Son takes Israel's role upon himself and rule as God's vicegerent. This divine pronouncement gives the true perspective on Jesus' identity for the reader.

As the Son of God, Jesus is then led by the Spirit to be tempted by Satan in the wilderness, which Mark describes rather briefly (vv. 12–13). Jesus may be regarded here as recapitulating the experience of Israel in the

---

22. Peppard 2010: 431–51.

first exodus. Instead of forty years, he is tempted for forty days by Satan. The mention of Satan also serves to foreshadow the conflict to come in Jesus' ministry. Interestingly, Jesus is described as being with the wild beasts (v. 13). The significance of this remark is unclear. It may refer either to the intensity of his temptation (i.e., threat of wild beasts), or the restoration of paradisiac conditions (i.e., wild beasts are tamed).

The Gospel in Galilee: The Mighty Acts of the Messiah (1:14—8:21)

Jesus' Inaugural Message (1:14–15)

The programmatic significance of these verses must be highlighted. This is the first time that Jesus speaks in Mark's Gospel, and with this Mark sums up Jesus' message. If the preceding section formed the beginning of the gospel, this passage may be understood as the hinge moment in the gospel story.

Mark prefaces Jesus' proclamation with the arrest of John. The point is that the forerunner has done his part, and Mark will explain later why he was arrested (see 6:17–18). The stronger one who baptizes with the Spirit (1:7–8) now proclaims. The locality of this proclamation is not in the wilderness but in Galilee, a cosmopolitan region belonging to Herod Antipas. The message concerns the gospel of God. For the alert listener, a connection between this and 1:1 is at once detected.

The statement of Jesus in v. 15 may be broken into two parts. First he announces what is happening, and Mark uses the Greek perfect tense here (*peplērōtai* and *ēngiken*) to signify that what Jesus proclaimed continues to have currency for his readers. Secondly, Jesus counsels a response, and Mark depicts this with the present tense, signifying that the actions of repentance and faith are to be ongoing. The key themes of Jesus' ministry and Mark's Gospel are therefore given in a nutshell: fulfillment, kingdom, repentance, faith, and gospel.

Fulfillment speaks of plot, with currents reaching back to the past. What is described as taking place is therefore to be construed as being once foretold. In this regard, there is meaning to history, and more precisely, it implies God has been faithful to his promises. It is this quality that gives his people hope.

The word kingdom (the Greek is *basileia*) should be understood primarily in the abstract sense of "reign," rather than in the concrete sense of "realm," as the Hebrew *malkût* or the Aramaic *malkûta'* makes clear. But the two ideas are associated, as reign often entails realm. Israel believes her

God is the only true ruler and creator, and so his reign cannot be abstractly divorced from history. Indeed, Israel was chosen to be God's true subjects to demonstrate concretely to the world what his reign meant. But her disobedience sent her into exile. Consequently an eschatological expectation of God's return to Zion shows in a climactic way that he is the sole king of the universe and that Israel is his special people (Ps 145:10–13; Isa 52:7). While the meaning of the kingdom may indeed be polyvalent, it should not therefore be conceived as referring to anything. Instead, it is to be anchored in the ongoing story of the one God and his people, and understood in relation to the yearning for eschatological closure.[1]

Is there an OT passage that may help us situate Jesus' announcement? Isaiah 52:7 is a good candidate. This is supported by Mark's having named Isaiah as the key inspiration behind his idea of the beginning of the gospel in 1:2–3. Furthermore, the notions of God's reign and the proclamation of good news are explicitly joined together in Isa 52:7. In this passage, God returns to Zion to reign as king. Consequently, the herald announces to Zion and the cities around her the good news. This divine advent signifies for the Israelites the end of exile and the onset of eschatological blessings. Jesus' message of the kingdom may be said to relate to such a hope.

The puzzling thing is that the kingdom is described as "having come near," which contradicts on the surface the fact of fulfillment. Not surprisingly, scholars have debated the precise meaning of the original Greek, whether *ēngiken* means imminence[2] or arrival.[3] The consensus is that it means imminence, but this does not bring us any closer to a resolution of the apparent contradiction. That said, this phenomenon of the "now-and-not-yet" actually forms the substructure of much of Markan theology, indicating that Mark sees in it a potent theological theme. Indeed, as his narrative progresses, the reader will see that the resolution of this oxymoron lies in answering correctly the question of who Jesus is, and how the kingdom is intimately bound up with him. In this regard, "paradox" is a better word than "contradiction" (i.e., the kingdom is in a sense still future but in an important sense it may be claimed to have arrived).[4] We will return to this topic in our treatment of chapter 4.

The response counselled by Jesus is repentance and faith. While such qualities have an important role in general piety, their special connection

---

1. Cf. Wright 1996: 220–26; and the perceptive re-examination of the data in Allison 2010: 164–204.
2. Boring 2006: 50–51; France 2002: 91–92; Marcus, 2000: 172–73.
3. Classically, Dodd 1941: 36–37.
4. Cf. the judicious treatment of Kümmel 1957.

with the kingdom of God should not be missed. In the prophetic literature, repentance (often described with the Hebrew *šûb*) is often the precondition of forgiveness and restoration (Isa 44:22; Jer 3:10–14; Hos 14:1–9). All this is often couched in corporate terms.[5] In this regard, the pattern of sin-exile-restoration, found frequently in the story of Israel and God, may plausibly be latent here.[6] More significantly, there can be no repentance if we do not agree with God's statement of our condition or his promise of forgiveness. Hence, repentance and faith are two sides of the same coin: we repent believingly, and we believe repentantly. Note the link back to John's ministry, as his baptism is a baptism of repentance for the forgiveness of sins (1:4).

Leading from the above point is the idea that this faith, while directed ultimately to God, must also take the form of believing the message of Jesus. As Mark will demonstrate later, faith is not so much about trusting generally in God's faithfulness as confessing that *through the ministry of Jesus* God's faithfulness is seen. In this regard, the promises that Israel longed for are now encapsulated in the ministry of Jesus.

The Gospel in Action and Typical Activities of Jesus' Ministry (1:16–45)

In this section the typical activities of Jesus' ministry are presented in cameo form. Mark narrates Jesus' call of his first disciples (1:16–20), his teaching activity which is connected with the performance of miracles (1:21–39), and the foreshadowing of conflict through the story of the healing of the leper (1:40–45). Discipleship, teaching, miracles, and conflict will be motifs occupying much of Mark's Gospel. Through all these cameo-like stories, Mark gives his listeners an idea of what it means for the gospel to be in action.

The Call of the First Disciples (1:16–20)

If according to the prophetic literature, God's return to Zion takes place in tandem with the reconstituting of a covenantal community (Isa 59:20–21; 61:1–8; Jer 31:31–34; Ezek 37:21–28; Hos 2:18–23), and if, through the Spirit's anointing, the task of this reconstitution has been devolved upon Jesus, then it is not surprising that together with the gospel proclamation, Jesus would call disciples as the first step in building this reconstituted community. This is precisely what is presented in vv. 16–20.

---

5. Sanders 1985: 106–8.
6. See the stimulating discussion of this pattern in Stanton 1985: 377–92.

The Sea of Galilee provides the setting of the call story. Strabo (*Geography* 16:2) and Pliny the Elder (*Natural History* 5:15)—both naturalists of the first centuries that straddle the Common Era—and Josephus (*War* 3:506–508) testify to its being full of fish. Many settlements arose close to its shores and gave the whole region a rather cosmopolitan character.

When understood against the first century Jewish background, Jesus' call of disciples becomes striking. As Martin Hengel has noted, the call of Jesus to follow after him goes beyond the practice of Jewish teachers or rabbis. There are no stories of a Jewish teacher calling disciples to follow him. On the contrary, people chose to follow famous teachers on their own accord (cf. *b. 'Erub.* 30a; *b. Ketub.* 66b). Hengel therefore proposes that Jesus' call resembles that of a charismatic or revolutionary leader, summoning people to a revolutionary war.[7] However, this notion has to be read into the narrative, as there is no explicit mention of it. Indeed, what differentiates Jesus' call from that issued by Jewish revolutionaries is that he included a promise of transformation (v. 17). With reference to the call story of Elisha (1 Kings 19:19–21), it may be argued that the persona adopted by Jesus is that of a prophet and not a teacher. But Mark will soon describe Jesus as a teacher (1:21)! What is more important is to observe that Mark portrays Jesus' call as absolutely authoritative, as those summoned dropped their vocational tasks "immediately." Hence, we may conclude that while parallel call-stories offer insights into the meaning of the present story, it should not be used to limit the possibilities.

What does being made fishers of men mean (v. 17)? Jesus is possibly using a memorable word-play. Surprisingly, all the uses of this image in the OT are ominous, for they speak of divine judgment (Jer 16:16; Ezek 29:4–6; Amos 4:2; Hab 1:14–17). This does not seem to fit with the general drift of Mark's presentation of Jesus' ministry, especially his announcing the good news of God. Could the gospel message also entail judgment? And would the disciples help in the realization of that? Whatever the precise meaning, the summoned disciples would certainly be embarking on a new vocation that would touch the destiny of human beings.

We offer, finally, some interesting observations about the first disciples. The first named, Simon, will be given the nickname Peter later (3:16), indicating the key role he will play. His name is always mentioned first in groupings (3:16; 5:37; 9:2; 13:3; 14:33). Accordingly, he often functions as the spokesman for the disciples. We may also expect him to be the older brother of Andrew, since he is named first in that pair (v. 16). Simon, James,

---

7. Hengel 1981: 18, 21, 52.

and John together form the inner circle, and become the privileged audience of Jesus' special miracles and revelation (5:37; 9:2; 14:33).

Jesus' Teaching and Miracles (1:21–34)

Mark introduces his readers to yet another important locality in Jesus' Galilean ministry: Capernaum (v. 21). The name in Hebrew means "village of Nahum." According to Josephus, it was prosperous and had a thriving fishing industry (*War* 3:516–21). This explains why a toll-booth was set up in its vicinity (2:1; 14). A detachment of Roman troops was also stationed there (cf. Matt 8:5–13), further indicating its importance. It was also Peter and Andrew's village (1:29), and probably the center of Jesus' Galilean ministry (see 2:1; 9:33; Matt 8:5–17 || Luke 7:1–10).

The first miracle story of Mark takes place on a Sabbath and it concerns both word and deed: these are described as being performed with unrivalled authority (vv. 22, 27). The comparison with the scribes to the latter's detriment prepares Mark's readers for more stories about the conflict between Jesus and the scribes later on (2:6, 16; 11:27).

The appearance of a demon-possessed man in the synagogue (v. 23) sets the stage for the introduction of one hallmark of Jesus' ministry: his exorcistic work. Three other accounts of exorcism are given in 5:1–20; 7:24–30; and 9:14–29. Mention of such an activity is also found in summaries or general reports such as 1:32–34; 1:39; 3:11–12, and in the Beelzeboul controversy of 3:22–30. All this indicates how important the motif is. Although there was much interest in exorcism in the Mediterranean world around the time of Jesus, there were actually very few exorcistic narratives available and very few exorcists named.[8] This scarcity throws into bold relief the frequent depiction of Jesus as an exorcist.

Exorcistic practices of Jesus' day are often referred to by scholars for understanding better his exorcism. Accordingly, the mention of Jesus' identity (v. 24) is construed as the demon's attempt to gain power over him, and Jesus' silencing word (v. 25) becomes his countermove to regain the initiative.[9] As interesting as such parallels may be, they fail to explain what Mark is doing. In all his exorcism stories there is no power struggle but the simple giving of a command, uncluttered by techniques or incantations. The

---

8. Apollonius (Philostratus *Life of Apollonius* 1:3–5, 19); Eleazar (Josephus *Antiquities* 8:45–48) and possibly Hanina ben Dosa (*b. Pesah.* 112b). Solomon was also regarded by some as an exorcist. See discussion in Witmer 2012: 22–60.

9. Hull 1974: 67–69.

exclamation of the crowds that his teaching (i.e., shown by exorcism) is new and authoritative (v. 27), says just as much.

Jesus is addressed as "the Holy One of God" (v. 24). A similar title is used in the OT for Aaron (Ps 106:16), Elisha (2 Kings 4:9), and possibly Samson (a variant reading of Judg 16:17 in the LXX). Judging from these occurrences, the title's meaning may simply be that a certain person has been set apart for some special ministry. But Mark's portrayal of Jesus, while certainly containing this notion, also goes beyond it. He shows how Jesus, as the bearer of the Holy Spirit, drives out uncleanness. In this respect, it may be instructive to note the passages in the Dead Sea Scrolls that speak of the eschatological elimination of ritual impurity by "the holy Messiah" (1Q30) and by God's holy Spirit (1QS 4:18–23). This testifies to the Jewish belief that only at the eschaton can all forms of uncleanness be rooted out of Israel by an agent of God who bears the Spirit.

There are some other significant points that bear mentioning so as to complete this Markan motif. The first is that Mark usually describes the demons as unclean (*pneumata akatharta*), indicating what sort of framework we are to use to understand these stories. The issue of ritual uncleanness looms large in Mark's Gospel (1:40–45; 6:25–34; 7:1–23). Ritual uncleanness separates the affected from the corporate life of the nation of Israel. In the case of demon possession, not only is the person unclean, he is also controlled by what is antagonistic to God. Hence, being exorcised meant that he was liberated to belong to God and to participate in the corporate life of his people.

Secondly, the exorcism leads the crowd to exclaim that Jesus has taught with authority (v. 27). This signifies that Jesus' activities of teaching and exorcism cannot be divorced from each other, as his word and deed are intimately related. His exorcism is in a profound sense also his teaching.

Thirdly, it is the exorcism that leads the crowd to introduce the adjective "new" to describe Jesus' teaching with authority. The word "new" is significant, as it points to eschatological newness. The demons' fear of being destroyed supports this proposal, as it shows they do not regard Jesus as any ordinary exorcist. Early Jewish and Rabbinic thought locates the destruction of demons at the eschaton (see *Pesiq. R.* 36:1 where the agent is the Messiah; *Num. Rab.* 19.8; cf. Zech 13.2). This fits in with the eschatological horizon of Jesus' gospel proclamation (1:15), with the added implication that the kingdom of God has invaded the territories long held by demonic forces. There is therefore a Markan escalation in the two confessions of the crowds (1:22; 1:27) which incidentally forms an *inclusio* (bracket).

Fourthly, the authority by which Jesus performs exorcisms is absolute. This was mentioned earlier but it bears repeating. Jesus does not use formulas or incantations, or make appeal to God's word. A simple command is issued and there is no tussle. Perhaps this is the significance of the crowd's confession that ends the story: "He commands even the unclean spirits and they obey him" (1:27).

Fifthly, the demon reveals the true identity of Jesus. Thus far, the true identity of Jesus has not been fully revealed to or discerned by people. The voice that spoke in 1:11 was probably meant only for Jesus to hear. Indeed, Mark's narrative has this characteristic: demonic forces know Jesus' identity but people continue to puzzle over it.

Finally, Jesus commands silence. Why? It may be that unclean entities are not allowed to confess the identity of clean entities. More probably, it is part and parcel of an important theme in Mark: the theme of secrecy. Mark will narrate many stories hereafter exhibiting a similar phenomenon. Why this is so will be clarified only when the whole Gospel has been read.

Once the tone is set, Mark goes on to show another aspect of Jesus' ministry: healing (vv. 29–31). Interestingly, the healing is performed on Peter's mother-in-law, to rid her of fever. By a simple grasping of her hand, Jesus raises her from bed (v. 31). Upon being healed, she serves Jesus and his company. Some scholars detect here a paradigm for discipleship.[10] The raising of Peter's mother-in-law is analogous to resurrection from spiritual death, and her immediate service to Jesus sets the example for later believers: they are raised so as to serve.

Widening of Jesus' Ministry (1:35–39)

The story hints at Jesus' prayer-life (the Greek imperfect *prosēucheto* suggests habitual praying). Mark mentions three times that Jesus prays, and these reports are made at important moments of his ministry: here at the beginning of his ministry; in 6:46 after the feeding of the 5,000 (John 6:15 tells us the crowds want to make Jesus king because of this miracle); and in 14:32–42, where the Father's will is affirmed and unswervingly followed in the Garden of Gethsemane.

The description of Jesus' praying, the comment of Peter and Jesus' response may be seen as a whole. Through prayer the temptation of reveling in a celebrity status is preempted, and one's calling from God is affirmed and strengthened. Hence, instead of meeting those who were so desirous of seeing him, Jesus declares the one reason for his having come is to preach the gospel. This must mean leaving Capernaum—even if he was treated as a celebrity there—in order to go to other villages which have yet to hear his message. Through this cameo, Mark achieves elegantly his purpose of

---

10. Boring 2006: 66.

portraying the spread of Jesus ministry. At the same time he explains what this ministry is all about: not self-aggrandizement (we will see later how important such a theme is to Mark), but the propagating of the gospel of God.

Healing of the Leper (1:40–45)

With this story Mark hints at the religious ramifications of Jesus' ministry, especially his healings, and how these may lead to conflict with the religious authorities.

What is known as leprosy in the Bible is not Hansen's disease. Instead the term is used to refer to a variety of skin diseases. Leviticus 13:45–46 shows the lengths to which someone afflicted with it has to go to avoid contaminating others: he had to wear torn clothes, leave his hair unkempt, wear a mask to cover the lower part of his face, and cry out, "Unclean! Unclean!" in order to ward people off. He also had to live in colonies, separated from society. More burdensome was the religious meaning of such a dreaded disease. It was regarded as incurable, being a result of God's judgment (see Num 12:9–15; 2 Chron 26:16–21; cf. also the telling remark in 2 Kings 5:7). Such a person could not appear before God in the Temple. With this background, we can understand the desperation that drove the leper to meet Jesus and thus violate some social customs. Instead of standing afar and calling to Jesus, this leper goes to him, falls poignantly on his knees and beseeches Jesus to heal him (v. 40).

Jesus shows his compassion (see excursus) and does the surprising thing by touching him, thus breaking a taboo. Moreover, Jesus declares him clean. To show the efficacy of Jesus' declaration, Mark uses his favorite word "immediately." If Jesus can declare someone clean, what becomes the role of the priest, since in the OT he is the only one who can pronounce a leper clean (Lev 13:2–6)? With this, we come to the ominous note in vv. 43–44.

Excursus: Was Jesus Incensed or Compassionate?

The attitude of Jesus towards this breaking of an important social custom is occluded by a textual uncertainty: whether Jesus was incensed or compassionate (v. 41). Many commentators choose to follow the reading *orgistheis*,[11] found in manuscript D (*Codex Bezae*) and supported by some

---

11. This means "being incensed." See France 2002: 115; Guelich 1989: 72; Marcus 2000: 206; for a contrary view, see Collins 2007: 177, 179; Gundry 1993: 95; Metzger 1994: 76.

old Latin manuscripts. Their decision is based mainly on the consideration that it is the harder reading and *splanchnistheis*[12] is therefore to be construed as introduced by later scribes to ameliorate a difficult reading. The reading adopted by NA28 (*splanchnistheis*) and followed by the NRSV is not without its strengths. First of all, an overwhelming majority of manuscripts support this reading. This weight of external attestation, which is early and wide, should not be easily dismissed. Secondly, D is a rather eccentric manuscript.[13] When D is the only Greek manuscript that offers support, we should be wary of the reading. Thirdly, elsewhere in Mark 3:5 and 10:14, the potentially embarrassing description of Jesus' anger has not been tampered with in the manuscript tradition. If scribes purportedly introduced an "easier" reading at 1:41 because of the potentially embarrassing reference to Jesus' anger, one would have expected them to do the same in the later two passages. But this did not happen. Finally, *orgistheis* could be the "easier" reading after all, in that it chimes in better with *embrim samenos*[14] just two verses down. We will adopt the reading *splanchnistheis* in our commentary.

The word *embrimaomai* in v. 43 is often used to describe the uncontrollable rage or fury of animals. Why is this word used of Jesus? Was it the failure of the leper to follow an express order that Jesus in his prescience saw? Was it the ravages of disease? Was it the temple authorities? Mark does not tell us, but what may be instructive here is to think of the narrative function of such a tantalizing description of Jesus' emotion. Mark is probably foreshadowing unpleasant conflict to come in his narrative. The phrase "testimony to them" (v. 44) may be discussed in this connection. The word "them" may possibly bring together Moses and the priest to form one group. More probably, it refers to the entire group of priests, without implicating Moses.[15] What is more crucial is the determination of the force of the Greek dative *autois*. Is it to be construed as a dative of advantage (i.e., "to them") or disadvantage (i.e., "against them")? If it is the former, the testimony is meant to show that all the regulations of the priests have been complied with (see Lev 13–14).[16]

12. This means "being compassionate."
13. Metzger and Ehrman 2005: 71–73.
14. This means "warning sternly."
15. Hooker 1983: 82.
16. Gnilka 1978: 91; Marcus 2000: 207.

If the latter, the testimony is meant to indict them.[17] The two other occurrences of such a phrase in Mark are found in 6:11 and 13:9, and they are all used in contexts of opposition. This prompts us to treat the dative here as a dative of disadvantage. So the healing of the leper becomes damning evidence either for the priests' unbelief in Jesus' ministry (but Mark has not said anything about this yet) or the failure (whoever these people are) to effect true purity in Israel.

Why is there a need for silence in v. 44? The next verse gives the effect of the leper's failure to keep Jesus' injunction, and this may be regarded as a partial explanation of Jesus' charge: the resultant publicity prevented Jesus from entering villages openly. However, it has also been suggested that Jesus does not want to be misconstrued as challenging the Temple authorities, since it is their function to make ritual purity possible.[18] But such a proposal is problematic, because the priest does not play the role of a miracle worker but a certifier. Accordingly, Jesus' healing would not have been perceived as challenging the priest's authority. It may be better to look at the immediate Markan context, and at the larger interest Mark has in Jesus' commands to silence (i.e., the secrecy motif).[19] As the Markan narrative unfolds, it will be seen that this motif has an important theological function. The meaning of Jesus' identity and ministry (incorporating here the spectacular healings and miracles) can only be grasped fully in the light of the cross.

Conflict with Religious Authorities (2:1—3:6)

Up to this stage, Mark has shown the reader the critical significance of Jesus' ministry. He has also narrated the increasing popularity of Jesus. However, Jesus does not have the requisite social credentials. This sets the stage for conflict. Mark 2:1—3:6 brings together five controversy stories to paint with a broad brush the key issues between Jesus and the religious leaders. These stories also foreshadow the final conflict in Jerusalem.

Mark uses structural devices, so as to help his audience better to appreciate and remember the critical points. An influential proposal suggests that a concentric (chiastic) structure may be found. In this scheme, the first story corresponds with the last, or fifth in this case, the second with the fourth, and the third stands as the center piece (see Diagram 1).[20] The center piece reveals the real cause for the disagreements between Jesus and the

17. France 2002: 120; Guelich 1989: 77.
18. Crossan 1991: 322.
19. Collins 2007: 179.
20. Dewey 1980: 109–30.

religious leaders (i.e., the coming of the new demands and the abandoning of the old).

Diagram 1
Chiastic Structure of Mark 2:1 – 3:6

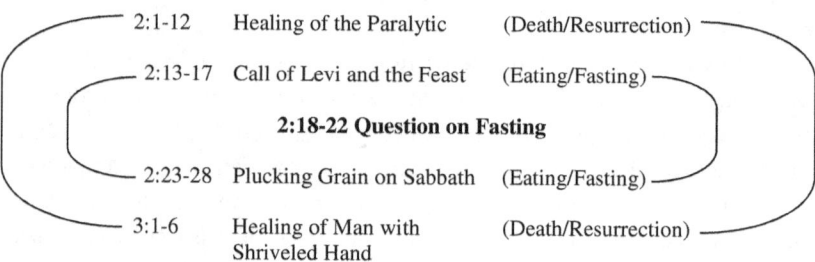

2:1-12	Healing of the Paralytic	(Death/Resurrection)
2:13-17	Call of Levi and the Feast	(Eating/Fasting)
2:18-22 Question on Fasting		
2:23-28	Plucking Grain on Sabbath	(Eating/Fasting)
3:1-6	Healing of Man with Shriveled Hand	(Death/Resurrection)

The correspondence between the first and the fifth, the second and the fourth, appears to be forced, as the main points of the stories lie elsewhere. A linear structure is more cogent. The first will then be linked with the second by the theme of sin and forgiveness, the third stands alone as the center and explanatory piece.[21] The fourth and the fifth correspond through the Sabbath theme (see Diagram 2).

Diagram 2
Linear Structure of Mark 2:1 – 3:6

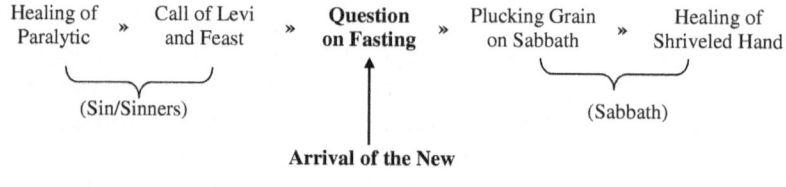

Healing of Paralytic » Call of Levi and Feast » **Question on Fasting** » Plucking Grain on Sabbath » Healing of Shriveled Hand

(Sin/Sinners)   (Sabbath)

Arrival of the New

Intensification of Opposition to Jesus

Unspoken question (2:6) → query put to disciples (2:16) → query put to Jesus (2:18) → accusatory question put to Jesus (2:24) → no question, but plot to indict and kill (3:2, 6)

---

21. Kiilunen 1985: 68–80; but cf. also Dewey 1980: 109–10, where the point is intimated.

There also appears to be an intensification of hostility as the stories progress, climaxing in the plot to put Jesus to death by widely-divergent groups.

Healing of the Paralytic 2:1–12

This first conflict story may be regarded as setting the tone for the other conflict stories. The main issue between Jesus and the religious authorities revolves around his claims, which they think threatened their inherited traditions. In some ways, the story also foreshadows the final conflict with the religious authorities in Jerusalem. In the passage about the Jewish hearing of Jesus (14:55–65), the twin themes of blasphemy and the Son of Man are found (14:62, 64), just as they are in this episode. Notably, Jesus refers to himself as the "Son of Man" for the first time. This is Jesus' preferred way of referring to himself, and carries important christological freight.

Capernaum is the setting. Depending on how the Greek phrase *en oikō* (v. 1) is construed, it may refer either to Jesus' home[22] (so NRSV) or Peter's house (cf. 1:29).[23] As usual, a crowd gathers. Roofs of houses in first-century Galilee might be reached easily by the wooden ladder outside.[24] Since they were thatched and made of mud, they could be dug through easily. Such an inconsiderate act would usually have led to angry reprisals, but Mark does not tell us the reaction of the crowd or the owner of the house because his focus is elsewhere. We may assume that the paralytic was participatory in the initiative to seek Jesus. Hence, Mark tells us that Jesus sees their (i.e., the whole group) faith, but speaks to the paralytic (v. 5).

Jesus' response in v. 5 appears somewhat inappropriate, but it becomes comprehensible when we bear in mind the biblical assumptions that (i) the greater problem bedeviling humanity is their estrangement from God (i.e., sin); and (ii) sin and sickness may be related. The latter is amply attested in the literature of the ancient world and the OT (e.g., Deut 28:27; Ps 107:17–18). A rabbinic saying runs: "A sick person does not arise from his sickness until all his sins are forgiven him" (*b. Ned.* 41a). Hence, healing and forgiveness often intersect (e.g., Ps 41:3–4; 103:3; Isa 38:17; 53:4–6).[25] However, this is not always the case (cf. John 9:2–3), as there may be other factors at work.

Jesus' speech caught the attention of the scribes. These were people of letters, as the Greek *grammateus* makes clear. However, in the Jewish

---

22. Collins 2007: 184 (tentatively).
23. France 2002: 122; Marcus 2000: 215.
24. Roubos 1986: 350–92.
25. Brown 1995.

context, the primary body of learning was the Torah, and hence, scribes in Mark's Gospel were people who knew and taught the Torah.[26] From their point of view, only God can forgive sins.[27] So they criticize Jesus inwardly: "He's blaspheming" (v. 7). To be sure, the priest has been given the role to pronounce God's forgiveness through the rituals of the Temple. But it is unlikely Jesus is challenging the Temple here.[28] In fact, as the drift of the narrative indicates, Jesus' pronouncement is deemed to have arrogated to himself the sole prerogative of God.[29]

Blasphemy in the OT is a capital offense (Lev 24:10–16). Although there was no technical definition of what constituted blasphemy in Jesus' day, the extant Jewish evidence connects it to speaking against God, pronouncing his unique name or claiming the unique prerogatives of God (*m. Sanh.* 7:5).[30] Forgiveness of sins is one such prerogative (Exod 34:6–7; Isa 43:25; 44:22). This is reinforced continually through the annual Yom Kippur festival. However, there may be one instance where forgiveness of sins is attributed to a human being. In a fragment from the Qumran caves (4Q242), it is said that a Jewish diviner (or exorcist?) forgave Nabonidus's sin. Because of its fragmentary nature, its meaning remains highly debated.[31] Alternatively, this fragment may be regarded as the exception that proves the rule. All this means the religious leaders' response in Mark is historically credible.

Mark's phrase *ei mē heis ho theos* (v. 7) should be translated "except 'God is one.'" This clumsy construction serves to make reference to the Shema (Deut 6:4–5), which functions somewhat like a Jewish creed. The Shema confesses that for Israel there is only one God, and she is to love this one God with her entire being.[32] From the way the Markan narrative is set up, Jesus' claim is interpreted by the scribes to have transgressed the sacred boundaries of their confession of one God. Jesus is therefore regarded as having put himself in an equal position with that one God. The Shema, therefore, should be the frame of reference for understanding this controversy.

Jesus' reply to the scribe's unspoken accusation (v. 9) has puzzled many readers. It is often assumed Jesus wants to demonstrate that it is easier to talk

---

26. Saldarini 1988: 152.

27. This implies we are not taking the verb of v. 5 as a "divine passive." Jesus then becomes the one who offers forgiveness. See France 2002: 125–26; cf. the fine study of Hofius 1994: 125–43.

28. Klostermann 1950: 23; Witherington 2001: 115.

29. Collins 2007: 185; Gundry 1993: 112.

30. On Jewish attitudes, see Bock 1998.

31. See discussion in Hägerland 2011: 154–58; and Hogan 1992: 149–57.

32. See Tan 2008: 181–206.

(i.e., to pronounce forgiveness of sins) than to act (i.e., perform a healing),[33] but is there more than meets the eye? Furthermore, it is puzzling that Jesus would seek to demonstrate his authority to forgive by healing, since the ability to work miracles was not understood as proving that one possessed the special prerogative of God. As the narrative plays itself out, *Jesus does not answer which is easier*, but proceeds to demonstrate his authority by healing. Perhaps the way forward is to think of Jesus as conveying the notion that the healing and the offer of forgiveness are regarded as closely integrated, and not dichotomized. Both are beyond human ability, and come only as a gracious gift from God. This falls in line with much prophetic expectation, where the concept of eschatological shalom involves both reconciliation and renewal (Jer 33:6–9; Hos 2:16–23). But for those who have eyes only for the tangible, the healing will speak to them.

There is also an implicit challenge to the scribes' theological understanding. If Jesus has indeed blasphemed by usurping God's authority, how could he have healed, since God is presumably the one behind the healing?

The phrase "Son of Man" is used in Mark's Gospel for the first time in v. 10. Much has been discussed about this title;[34] we offer here just a summary of the key proposals, and indicate the stance taken.[35] This phrase has been understood as a circumlocution for "I," as referring to generic man or to an indefinite man, or even to a special class of men. It has also been understood as a messianic title. The view adopted here is that in its Aramaic form it can refer to man in general. In Dan 7:13, however, the phrase (without the article) is used poetically to contrast the beasts representing the earthly empires with the human figure that stands for God's purpose and kingdom. Because of the importance of the book of Daniel in Jewish speculation on the end time, this literary figure is often utilized to speak of the climax of the kingdom story and the deliverance of God's beleaguered people. In fact in the Similitudes of Enoch (*1 En* 37–71, dating unsure)[36] and *4 Ezra* (post AD 70), this figure is regarded as the Messiah. What all this means is that Dan 7:13 becomes the seedbed for the understanding of the role of the Son of Man in some circles, and may thus add new possibilities to an ordinary phrase.

With this serving as background, we can then argue: (1) that Jesus uses this designation to refer to himself (always with the definite article);[37]

---

33. Marcus 2000: 217–18; Stein 2008: 120.
34. See discussion in Burkett 1999; and recently, Hurtado and Owen 2011.
35. This is similar to Dunn 2003: 759–61.
36. See discussion in Boccaccini 2007: 415–98.
37. See Hurtado's conclusion in Hurtado and Owen 2011: 166: "the expression's

(2) that he may have in mind the figure of Dan 7:13 as the exposition of the meaning of his ministry; (3) that such a term does not automatically convey the above idea, as the ordinary usage may refer to man in general; (4) that Jesus sees fit to remain ambiguous for important reasons; (5) that he sometimes also pours in new content to the meaning of the phrase such that even the usage of Dan 7:13–14 cannot fully explain it; and (6) that there is a profound convergence between his kingdom message and his self-understanding, because in both instances, hiddenness/ambiguity is a characteristic which could only be penetrated by faith. This is precisely how Mark presents Jesus, and it will be demonstrated as his narrative progresses.

To be sure, Dan 7:13–14 does not mention the authority to forgive sins. However, since the Son of Man is the figure who brings an end to the dominions of the world and unleashes the eschatological age, it is not difficult to extend this further to suppose he may be connected with the reconciliation between God and his people, a concept within which forgiveness is to be understood.

Without allowing the details to cloud the main point, we may say this controversy story highlights a major aspect of Jesus' work: the forgiveness of sins. What has troubled Israel throughout her checkered history, namely the problem of sin, may potentially be resolved by Jesus. That said, we must not miss how the story is presented. Some scribes perceive Jesus' actions as arrogating to himself the unique prerogative of God. There is no attempt on the part of Jesus either to clarify this or to avoid being misunderstood. Every dutiful Jew would have the obligation to do so when it concerns so important a tenet of the community as the Shema. Instead, Jesus provokes the scribes further by claiming to have the authority, as the Son of Man, to forgive sins, and backs it up with healing. The exclamation of the crowd serves, then, to highlight Jesus' uniqueness (v. 12). So an implicit question is raised. It is not about Jesus' status vis-à-vis the Temple. Instead, it is about his claims and the one God confessed in Israel's Shema.

---

primary linguistic function is to refer [to Jesus], not to characterize . . . it is the *sentence/ saying* that conveys the intended claim or statement, *not the son of man's expression itself.*" This is brilliantly put but we would like to add that the expression was not plucked out of thin air, meaning it was used because it could potentially carry a profound freight that was bequeathed by tradition. In other words, saying "The Son of Man is so-and-so" conveys more significance to the community than saying "Jesus is (or I am) so-and-so." This being the case, the referential directions run in both ways: Daniel 7 and Jesus of Nazareth. The phenomenon shows creativity at work, a creativity that is consistent with the type that surrounds also Jesus' kingdom message. All this means the tradition is mined for creative speech and act, which in turn breathes new life into the tradition.

Improper Table Fellowship (2:13-17)

From the theme of the Son of Man's authority to forgive sins, Mark moves on to show how Jesus receives sinners, especially the tax collectors. This controversy story contains no miracles, and it is often known as a pronouncement story because the main point of the story is found in the pronouncement given at the end.

Since Galilee was ruled by a client king supported by Rome, the toll envisaged here must have been collected for Herod Antipas's government. This toll is not to be equated with the poll tax (cf. 12:13-17) or land tax which was paid directly to Rome and collected by royal officials in the case of Galilee. Rather, the toll was levied on goods or for the right of passage.[38] As the Sea of Galilee was teeming with fish, Levi's toll collection probably came mainly from the fishing trade. The collection of these indirect taxes was farmed out to the highest bidder, and such privatization often resulted in overcharging: to cover possible future losses, to receive remuneration for enterprise, or simply because of greed. In the Talmud, toll-collectors are lumped together with murderers and robbers (*m. Ned.* 3:4). Moreover, their frequent contacts with the Gentiles exposed them to ritual defilement (so *m. Tohar.* 7:6), and their work, which helped support the conqueror, earned them the label of quislings. Hence, Jesus' calling a toll collector to follow him is highly significant.

Levi's prompt response (v. 14) recalls that of Jesus' first disciples in 1:16-20. Based on the parallel in Matt 9:9, it is often concluded that Levi is Matthew, who is also mentioned in the list of apostles in Mark 3:18 (cf. Matt 10:3, where Matthew is called a toll collector in the list).[39]

A meal ensues and two things may be said about it. First, the venue is ambiguous (v. 15). The Greek *en tē oikia* could refer either to Jesus' house or to Levi's house. Since Luke 5:29 tells us it is Levi who prepares the feast, the latter is to be preferred. Secondly, this is not an ordinary meal because of the posture adopted. The Greek word *katakeimai* means to recline. This posture is adopted among Jews only for feasts or formal celebrations, such as the Passover.[40] Otherwise they sit for meals.

The scribes belonging to the Pharisaic party (see excursus) have questions over Jesus' dining with toll collectors and sinners (v. 16), presumably because such people were not scrupulous about ritual purity, or many other regulations of the Torah. Moreover, to eat with someone in ancient times

---

38. Donahue 1992: 6:337-38.
39. Lane 1974: 100-101.
40. Jeremias 1966a: 48-49.

often meant to be identified and reconciled with him. Hence, Jesus' eating with the wrong company suggests he has no reservation about being identified with such people, and may convey the scandalous message that God accepts them.

Excursus: The Pharisees

The general consensus is that Pharisees were certainly not people who were simply "keeping up appearances." The term probably comes from the Hebrew *pārûš*, which means "separated one," and was probably first coined by their opponents. According to Josephus, the Pharisees were one of four major sects (the others being the Sadducees, the Essenes, and what Josephus calls "the Fourth Philosophy," who were probably the Zealots; see Josephus *War* 2:162–66 and *Antiquities* 13:171–73; 18:11–25). They were accorded the high honor of being accurate interpreters of Torah. Their origins remain shrouded in mystery but they were active in the two centuries straddling the beginning of the Common Era. Comprising mainly lay members, they nevertheless exercised powerful pressure on Jewish religion and policy. Their aim was to purify Israel through an intensified observance of Torah, inspired by the tradition of the elders, so the nation would be prepared for God's promised return. So they set up what might be termed as "eating fellowships" so as to eat food in a state of purity, befitting that of the Temple. This concern for purity was not regarded simply as an inward form of piety, since the Pharisees were also linked with revolts (notably Saddok in the revolt of AD 6; see Josephus *Antiquities* 18:4). Purity could also be a political issue.[41]

Jesus identifies his mission in a proverb-like statement[42]: to restore sinners. It also implies that offering help to those who do not need it is futile. Understood this way, the term "righteous" is in the statement primarily as a kind

---

41. Baumgarten 1997; Deines 1997; Neusner 1973; Saldarini 1988.

42. There were statements in the ancient world that were similar in effect (e.g., "it is not the custom of doctors to spend their time with the healthy, but where people are ill," Plutarch *Apophthegm Laconica* 230F). See other examples in Collins 2007: 195–96.

of rhetorical counterpart to the "sinners." It does not suggest Jesus thinks the Pharisees are really righteous.[43]

Incompatibility between the Old and the New (2:18–22)

Being the centerpiece of the collection of five controversy stories, the story contains the explanation of the key issue between Jesus and the religious authorities. The feasting theme is still maintained (as it is in the second story) through the implicit reference to a wedding banquet (v. 19). Jesus disciples' lack of fasting sets them in contrast with the Pharisees and the disciples of John the Baptist, and this engendered a controversy.

The only fast prescribed in the Torah is connected with Yom Kippur or the Day of Atonement (Lev 16:29–31; 23:26–29). By the post-exilic period, a few other fasts were added to the national calendar (cf. Esth 9:31; Zech 8:19). Individuals might choose to fast whenever they deemed it necessary, such as to show piety and penitence. But such fasts were not placed in the same category as the prescribed national fasts. According to Luke 18:12, the Pharisees fasted twice in a week, and from other evidence we know this to be on Mondays and Thursdays (cf. *Did.* 81; *m. Ta'an.* 14:5; *b. Ta'an.* 10a). There is also evidence to show that the Pharisees and other Jews might have connected their fasting with the hastening of the eschaton (*b. Sanh.* 97b–98a; *Life of Josephus* 290; cf. Zech 8:19; 1 Sam 7:6; 1 Macc. 3:47, where fasts are performed to bring about victory in a holy war). Against this background we can understand the concern of the Pharisees, and why Jesus defends his disciples' lack of fasting with the sort of illustrations he uses. The issue is not about the prescribed national fasts, but those undertaken personally to show penitence and hasten the coming of the eschaton.[44]

On the surface, Jesus seems to be using a common-sense analogy (i.e., fasting should not take place at weddings [v. 19]). However, there is a deeper meaning to this analogy. The climax of God's restoration of the nation is expressed in Isaiah as a wedding (Isa 62:5). God, the bridegroom, will marry the land, or Zion, which means restoration for the nation. There are also other passages in the Prophets that describe God's relationship with Israel, using the marital metaphor (Hos 2; Ezek 16; Jer 2:2; Isa 54:5). These passages presuppose a rupture in this relationship, brought about by Israel's disobedience. Consequently, the repair of this rupture may be pictured as (another) wedding. Such a picture is also found at the climax of the book of Revelation (Rev 19:7–8; 21:1–3, 9–10).

---

43. Stein 2008: 131. He also discusses other options.
44. Lane 1974: 109; Marcus 2000: 236.

The background clarifies why Jesus chooses the wedding metaphor. The point is that, through his ministry, the long-anticipated climax of God's relationship with Israel has now come to pass. It is possible that the bridegroom refers to Jesus.[45] What is notable is that there is no evidence of the Messiah's being described as the bridegroom in Jewish literature before the sixth century AD (the first attestation is found in *Pesiq. R.* 37:2).[46] Hence, the metaphor is not messianic. Instead, it implies that Jesus puts himself on par with the one God of Israel.[47]

What would the departure of the bridegroom mean (v. 20)? Clearly, it signals the end of festivity. What event is envisaged as corresponding to it? Usually this is believed to be Jesus' departure, which would reintroduce the practice of fasting for his followers. It is equally possible, however, that it refers to divine abandonment, if we bear in mind the rich meaning of the nuptial metaphor in the OT. Being Jews, the disciples will share in the pain of the nation of Israel. The one possible event that is being referred to would be the destruction of Jerusalem in AD 70. Perhaps the originator of this saying intentionally kept it ambiguous.

The nuptial metaphor is followed by two pictures that speak of incompatibility (vv. 21–22). New cloth in ancient times was unshrunk, unlike old cloth which had been shrunk through repeated washings. Patching an old garment with new cloth only adds to the problem. This notion of incompatibility extends to wineskins. New wine is still fermenting and produces carbon dioxide. This causes the wineskins to swell. New wineskins can take this pressure but not old wineskins because they have become brittle with age. So this centerpiece in the collection of five controversy stories points out the incompatibility of old practices with the arrival of the new. As such, it hints at what the real issue is between the religious authorities and Jesus: whether they would accept that the new or eschatological has come in Jesus' ministry.

Plucking Grain on a Sabbath (2:23–28)

With the fourth controversy story, a new issue is presented, which is about the Sabbath. The occasion is the plucking of grain by Jesus' disciples to satisfy their hunger (v. 23). The Pharisees regard the disciples' action as work (v. 24), and this sparks a controversy between them and Jesus. Jesus defends

---

45. Boring 2006: 85; Collins 2007: 199.
46. Marcus 2000: 237.
47. Collins 2007: 199; but interestingly not Marcus 2000: 237.

his disciples by appealing to an OT precedent (vv. 25-26), concluding with a pronouncement on the real meaning of the Sabbath (vv. 27-28).

The Sabbath commandment was first given in Exodus 20:10 and it serves as a pointer both to creation (Gen 2:2-3) and to the Exodus. In this respect it may also be regarded as a sign of the covenant, reminding the Jews of their covenantal status. Crassly understood, it forbids work on that day, but when it is set within the framework of creation and Exodus, it should also be viewed positively, such as rest and worship. What sort of activity is regarded as forbidden work, and by what criterion should such a decision be made, have naturally led to some debates among Jews. The Qumran community applied it strictly and forbade even the humanitarian action of helping an animal or a man out of a pit on Sabbath day (CD 11:13-17).

The disciples' plucking grain to eat reflects the Jewish institution of *pe'ah*, which has its basis in the Torah (Lev 19:9-10; 23:22; Deut 23:24-25). This was promulgated for the sustenance of the poor and the destitute. At issue in the text is whether the disciples are breaking a Sabbath regulation, as Exod 34:21 expressly forbids reaping on that day. Philo of Alexandria confirms this when he writes (in the first century) that Jews are not allowed to pluck fruit or cut any tree or plant on the Sabbath (*Life of Moses* 2.22; cf. the rabbinic pronouncement in *m. Sab.* 7:2). So the controversy is not over whether Jesus' disciples could feed themselves on a Sabbath day, but over *what they were doing* to feed themselves.

Jesus defends his disciples' actions by appealing to David's example in 1 Sam 21:1-9. This incident probably took place on a Sabbath day, since the bread was presented before God each Sabbath (Lev 24:8).[48] It is clear from 1 Sam 21:1-9 that Ahimelech was the high priest, and not his son Abiathar. Has Mark made a mistake in v. 26?[49]

Much depends on how the Greek phrase *epi Abiathar archiereōs* is to be understood, principally the construction *epi* + genitive. In Mark 12:26 the same *epi* + genitive construction is found (in this case *epi tou batou*), which does not mean "upon the burning bush," but "in the account of the burning bush" (i.e., construing the *epi* + genitive as having locative force). So Mark may then be regarded as meaning "in the section of scripture having to do with Abiathar"[50] in the present passage. Even so, it is hard to understand how 1 Sam 21 may be regarded as a passage featuring Abiathar the high priest. He is not even mentioned.

---

48. According to a Jewish tradition, the bread was removed and eaten by priests at the next Sabbath (*Midrash Rabbah Lev.* 32: 3).

49. France 2002: 146; Marcus 2000: 241.

50. Proposed long ago by Wenham 1950: 156.

A second possibility is to translate the *epi* + genitive construction as "at the time of" (i.e., construing the *epi* + genitive as having temporal force), but to think of the title as being given prospectively.[51] This will result in the translation "in the days of Abiathar, who later became the high priest," just as we might say the Queen was born in such and such a time, when she was not actually queen at her birth. If the objection is raised that Abiathar's name is not mentioned in the account, it may then be answered that Jews remembered him better because of his connection with David and with the first Temple. All this may smack of special pleading, because if there were no historical problem in the first place, every reader would have construed Mark as saying that David met Abiathar the high priest. Perhaps the best that we can do now is to say the jury is still out on this question.

What is more important is the point of comparison that Jesus hopes to make. The regulations governing the consecrated bread are found in Exod 25:30 and Lev 24:5–9. The point of comparison can either be that of (a) human needs justify the infringement of Torah regulations;[52] or that (b) an anointed royal figure has the authority to override them.[53] What is common to both cases is that there is precedence in Scripture for the overriding of a Torah regulation. As the latter point carries an important christological freight, we will explicate it further. Just as David was not condemned for performing something illegal, neither should Jesus be, provided the Pharisees were willing to consider Jesus in the same category. In this light, we may regard Jesus as speaking of his own special status.[54] He, like David, is the yet-to-be-fully recognized (i.e., enthroned) king, and can dispense with a sacred regulation in order to sustain life: the life of his disciples.

Jesus' pronouncement in v. 27 makes the lesson clear. It explains what has priority. Some Jewish writings state a similar viewpoint (*Jub.* 2:17; 2 *Bar.* 14:18; *b. Yoma* 85b). Perhaps the most relevant is that from the *Melkita on Exodus* 31:14: "The Sabbath is handed over to you, not you to it," which means God's gift of the Sabbath was given not to destroy but to bring about true humanity. However, this principle, while putting things in their proper place, is not meant to teach that any human being can decide when sacred regulations may be dispensed with. So the next pronouncement is needed to complete the thought (v. 28).

"Man" (v. 27) and the "son of man" (v. 28) may be construed as synonyms. But no Jew will accept that human beings in general may be the

---

51. Derrett 1975: 2–15.
52. Collins 2007: 203.
53. Note the emphasis on David in the text.
54. Dewey 1980: 98; France 2002: 145–46.

lords of the Sabbath.⁵⁵ So this wordplay should be regarded as pointing to something more significant. If the Sabbath is made for men, then the divinely appointed ruler of true humanity, who is described as "one who is like a son of man" in Daniel 7, must have the authority to decide when this Sabbath regulation may be dispensed with in the wider interest of humanity. Much has been discussed on the meaning of the Greek connective *ōste*. It is possible to regard it as a loose transition.⁵⁶ Alternatively, we may posit Mark's editorial hand is at work here⁵⁷ (i.e., he is drawing the conclusion from the story for his audience).

This second usage of the "Son of Man" phrase gels very well with the first (2:10). Twice the phrase is used in connection with prerogatives belonging solely to God: the forgiving of sins, which also mean the transgression of divine regulations, and the Lord of such regulations, especially the Sabbath. The "Son of Man" phrase therefore carries very significant christological freight for Mark.

Healing on a Sabbath (3:1-6)

The final controversy story in the cycle is again over the Sabbath, but the locality is now the synagogue (v. 1). As this is the final story, Mark makes it clear that deep animosity has taken root. The religious leaders are no longer interested in explanations, but are simply looking for a cause to condemn Jesus (v. 2).

The question of v. 4 is full of irony and, not surprisingly, unanswered. If one may synthesize from the Mishnah and the Talmud, it may be inferred that some Jews believed saving lives overrode the Sabbath (*m. Yoma* 8:6; *b. Yoma* 85b). For illnesses which were not life-threatening, however, they might not be treated (*m. Sab.* 14:3-4; cf. CD 11:9-10).⁵⁸

The Greek behind "stubborn hearts" (v. 5) is *pōrōsis tēs kardias*, which is derived from the Hebrew *šĕrirût lēb* and means literally "hardness of heart." This description is typically used of Pharaoh (Exod 4:21; 7:3; 8:32; 14:4), and is often found in prophetic denunciations of the nation of Judah just before the exile (Jer 3:17; 7:24; 9:14; 11:8; 13:10; 16:12; cf. Deut 29:18; Ps 81:15). This description is now applied to Jesus' opponents. There is irony here. The charge of being stubborn and hard-hearted is a typical prophetic charge against the Israel of old. Now it is applied to those who claimed to

---

55. Stein 2008: 149; Casey 1988: 160.
56. BDF 391.2.
57. Lane 1974: 119-20.
58. Marcus 2000: 248.

know better, and should know better, being religious leaders (3:5). The prophets' audience were Torah breakers but Jesus' audience are supposedly Torah upholders. All the poignant lessons of the exile appeared to have an opposite effect on those who lead.

It is astonishing that the Pharisees and the Herodians can collude together (v. 6), but nothing brings enemies together like having a common archenemy. The term "Herodians" denotes probably not a religious sect but the supporters of the ruling dynasty of Herod[59] (cf. *War* 1:319, where a similar term is used), which was not Jewish but Idumean, and was in place only because of Rome. This was a dynasty which was resisted by the Pharisees (cf. Josephus *Antiquities* 17:41–47; *War* 1:571).

Mark's Achievement with this Cycle of Stories

Within a short span of narrative, Mark succeeds in showing what the key issues between Jesus and the religious authorities are, and what the central reason behind them all is. This will prepare Mark's readers for the rest of his Gospel, where resistance will be evident and culminates with the crucifixion of Jesus. So a pale shadow has fallen over Jesus' ministry. All is not well, even when stupendous deeds of healing and restoration are performed. Why? Mark reminds his listeners that it is due to a hardness of heart, the same condition which led to Pharaoh's destruction and Israel's exile, a theme that will be picked up again in chapter 4.

We must not forget, however, that all this actually serves as a foil to a more important theme at work—Jesus' identity. He performs deeds that put him on the side of the one God of Israel. The use of the Son of Man designation exhibits this phenomenon. Introduced for the first time in the first controversy story, and repeated again in the fourth, it resonates with prerogatives that are uniquely God's. In this light, all the controversies boil down to the question of who Jesus is, and what he claims to be doing in relation to Israel's covenantal story.

SUMMARY OF JESUS' DEEDS (3:7–12)

This Markan summary presents Jesus' typical activities (teaching and miraculous deeds), the typical venue (by the lake, often on a boat), and the typical responses (of crowds and demons). While performing a transitional function,[60] it also carries the plot forward. Verse 7 speaks of a withdrawal

---

59. Meier 2000: 740–46.
60. Marcus 2000: 255.

of Jesus and his disciples to the lake, and this is appropriate as a response to the controversial atmosphere of the previous cycle of stories (2:1—3:6). Not only this, a large crowd follows Jesus, indicating his rising popularity, and perhaps serving as a contrasting picture to the response of the religious authorities. Some in the crowd come from faraway places such as Tyre and Sidon, perhaps preparing the reader for the story of 7:24–30. So great is this crowd that Jesus has to use a boat to prevent the people from crowding him. With this description, Mark introduces a new vehicle of Jesus' ministry (v. 9). He would frequently be in a boat, teaching large crowds gathered at the shore of the Sea of Galilee, and moving across that lake with the same boat. Indeed, Mark will later narrate interesting incidents involving this boat (4:35–39; 6:45–52).

Jesus' encounters with unclean spirits continue, with a recurrent pattern: these spirits know the true identity of Jesus but they are commanded to be silent. But this time round, the confession made by the unclean spirits is that Jesus is the Son of God (v. 11). Up to this stage, we see that apart from God's declaration of Jesus' divine sonship, no other being on earth has acclaimed Jesus to be such, except those possessed by unclean spirits.

THE NEW PEOPLE OF GOD AND JESUS' TRUE FAMILY (3:13–45)

The material here covers three stories. The first is the appointment of the twelve apostles (3:13–19). The second and third stories strike a different note, as they feature opposition to Jesus. These two stories are integral to each other because one is sandwiched by the other—a story is told partially (3:20–21) before moving on to the next (3:22–30), and then back again to complete it (3:31–35). The opposition depicted comes from Jesus' family and the scribes. Both groups regard Jesus as "beyond the pale" (mad or demon-possessed). Together the three stories clarify the true members of Jesus' family.

Making of the Twelve (3:13–19)

The Greek phrase *apēlthon pros auton* (v. 13) means literally "they departed to him" (i.e., the disciples left a larger parent group to join Jesus). Henceforth, they form a group of specially chosen people, differentiated from the crowds.

To say that Jesus appointed the Twelve does not quite capture the Markan idea (vv. 14–15). The Greek verb used is *epoiēsen*, and it is best translated as "made,"[61] with a possible allusion to the story of creation. Jesus' action in calling the Twelve is like a new creational act.[62] Furthermore, the number Twelve alludes to the twelve tribes of Israel: their formation and promised reconstitution (Isa 49:6; Ezek 45:8; cf. Matt 19:28; Luke 22:30), made urgent by the two deportations from the land in 721 BC (Northern Kingdom) and 586 BC (Southern Kingdom). In this light, the use of such a term to designate his disciples speaks volumes about Jesus' intention.

The term "apostles" should most probably be understood in the light of the rabbinic concept of *the šālîaḥ*. This refers to a legal agent who is sent out with the full authority of the sender, to act on his behalf. A memorable sentence captures this concept: "The one sent by a man is as the man himself" (*m. Ber.* 5:5). The main functions of the apostles are also described (vv. 13–15). First of all, they are to be with him. This defines succinctly what discipleship means. By being with Jesus they can know him intimately and understand his teaching. It also implies that they will be taught things not available to the crowds. From this point onwards, Mark will recount stories where Jesus' disciples ask questions of Jesus privately, or relate teaching situations involving only the Twelve. Only by being with Jesus can they perform the next two functions: preaching and casting out demons. These are principal features of Jesus' ministry (1:21–27, 35–39), but they are now inherited by his apostles.

The names of the Twelve are given, with the occasional nicknaming by Jesus. Mark does not explain why this is done. One theory suggests that it has to do with either their character (cf. 9:38; Luke 9:54)[63] or the role they would henceforth play (Matt 16:18).[64] Simon is nicknamed Peter (v. 16), indicating his foundational role in the early Church. James and John are given the name Boanerges (v. 17). This word is usually explained as a Greek transliteration of the Hebrew *benê regeš* or *benê rōgez*. They mean respectively "sons of commotion" or "sons of agitation." However, "sons of thunder" is not an impossible rendering.[65]

Three other names deserve some discussion. The passage mentions a certain James, who is the son of Alphaeus (v. 18), but no Levi, who was also called the son of Alphaeus in 2:14. Even if Levi is Matthew, as the parallel in Matt 9:9 tells us, it is still puzzling why this is not clarified. Furthermore,

---

61. This is the case with classical Greek, although the LXX contains instances where the meaning is "appointed" (1 Sam 12:6; 1 Kings 12:31; 13:33).
62. Boring 2006: 100; Marcus 2000: 267.
63. France 2002: 161.
64. Marcus 2000: 268.
65. France 2002: 161–62.

how is Levi related to James the son of Alphaeus? Were they brothers, or did they happen to have fathers with an identical name? Mark does not answer these questions. Perhaps his focus was on the concept and role of the Twelve, rather than their identity, apart from the prominent ones.

Another Simon is mentioned, who is nicknamed *kananaios* (v. 18). This is certainly not a Greek word, and most scholars think it is a transliteration of the Aramaic *qan'ānā'*, which means an enthusiast or a patriot.[66] If this suggested derivation is correct (cf. Luke 6:15; Acts 1:13), Simon was remembered either as someone who was patriotic to his nation, or perhaps someone who had affinity with the Zealots, a Jewish party that came into prominence during the Jewish war with Rome (AD 66–70). If we are right about the identity of Matthew and this Simon, we then have an interesting coming together of two people who once subscribed to diametrically opposed agendas. One once worked for the Empire, and the other once worked against the Empire. The significant thing is that Jesus brings together people with opposing agendas, and remakes them into the restored people of God.

Completing the list is Judas Iscariot (v. 19). The term "Iscariot" has been explained differently in the scholarly literature. By far the most popular is to split it up into *'îš + qĕriyyôt*, which means in Hebrew "the man from Kerioth," thus indicating Judas's place of origin.[67] We do not know where Kerioth is exactly because there are many places with such a name (cf. Josh 15:25; Jer 41:24). Perhaps this geographical reference is added to differentiate him from another Judas (cf. John 14:22). The other serious possibility is to construe the Greek as being derived from a semitized form of the Latin *sicarius*, which means a bandit or a freedom fighter.[68] If this is correct, Judas may then be regarded as joining the movement of Jesus because he thought he would be overthrowing the Romans to give Israel political freedom. When this idea was finally disabused, he betrayed him. This is a clever hypothesis but the derivation appears too complicated to carry conviction.

Jesus' True Family (3:20–35)

Two stories are combined here—the visit of Jesus' family (vv. 20–21, 31–35) and the *Beelzeboul* accusation by the scribes (vv. 23–30)—the latter being intercalated by the former. This ancient rhetorical technique is designed to bring episodes of similar meaning together, so that they may be mutually

---

66. Collins 2007: 222; Stein 2008: 173.

67. Collins 2007: 223.

68. Boring 2006: 103, combines both meanings. A good survey of possibilities is given by Brown 1994: 1410–16.

illuminating.[69] That which intercalates completes the meaning of that which is intercalated by explicating the deeper issue. In this case it is about the true members of Jesus' family, or God's family (v. 35). The intercalation is not artificial because in both incidents, Jesus was labelled. The family labels him mad while the scribes from Jerusalem label him demon-possessed. Demon-possessed people were also regarded as mad in antiquity (John 10:20).

The setting is in a house, a place where much of Jesus' teaching is given. Jesus' family[70] comes to restrain him. In good ancient Semitic tradition, the family assumes responsibility for the disciplining of a wayward or deviant son, even if he is already grown up. Moreover, this is done to protect the family's honor. All this means Jesus' teaching, deeds, and claims must have been quite shocking to his peers.

The scene changes with v. 22, and some scribes from Jerusalem accuse Jesus of being possessed by Beelzeboul. The meaning of this term is uncertain although "lord of the house" or "lord of the heavenly abode" seems most cogent. In any case, in so charging Jesus the scribes tacitly agree that Jesus' ministry has been characterized by extraordinarily authoritative exorcisms, since the alleged power behind his work is attributed to no less a figure than the prince of demons.

Jesus responds in "parables" (v. 23). This is the first time the Greek *parabolē* is used in Mark's Gospel. The concept takes after the Hebrew *māšāl*, which means basically "dark saying," in contrast to the Greek which speaks of a comparison. Nevertheless, their semantic domains do overlap. Given that the story is set in Palestine, it is best to understanding it according to the Semitic way. Being inherently loose in semantic boundaries, the term may refer to pithy sayings or even extended narratives in which some comparison is made and an encrypted message given. So we must avoid prejudging the meaning of Jesus' message based merely on some definition of what a parable should be. How Jesus uses it to convey his message in a particular text should be the main guide to interpretation.

The parables make two comparisons, using the images of kingdom[71] and house (vv. 24–27). Their purpose is to show the logic of the accusation to be absurd. If there is civil war or internecine division, a kingdom or a household cannot stand. What Jesus hopes to convey is that his exorcisms indicate an *invasion* of Satan's kingdom and not an internal revolt.

---

69. Geert van Oyen 1992: 949–74

70. On the plausibility of construing the Greek *hoi par' autou* to mean "family," see Collins 2007: 226; and France 2002: 166.

71. After the ground-breaking announcement of Jesus in 1:15 regarding the imminence of the kingdom, the word "kingdom" is not used again until 3:24, where it occurs twice.

The formula "Amen I say to you" (v. 28) appears to be unique to Jesus. The word "amen" is Hebraic in origin and has as its root meaning "truth" or "trustworthiness." It is also used in Jewish liturgy as an affirmative response, or at the end of a doxology (Deut 27:15–26; 1 Chron 16:36). The LXX translates the Hebrew *āmēn* as *genoito*, which means "let it be," and thus many understand the Hebrew term to mean "so be it."[72] In the context of Jesus' sayings, it means a solemn truth is being given, somewhat akin to "Thus says the Lord."[73] Jesus' usage is unique in that the term is used to preface a saying and not to conclude it. Some scholars have also regarded it as carrying important christological freight.[74]

The scribal charge of blasphemy in 2:7 now rebounds to them (3:29–30). In the Markan context the blasphemy against the Holy Spirit means an outright rejection of Jesus' ministry. This may be derived from the fact that his ministry derives its power from the Holy Spirit, and its feature is the exorcism of unclean spirits. Furthermore, the forgiveness of sins is often linked to the work of the Spirit in the eschaton (see excursus on "Blasphemy against the Holy Spirit").

The words "will never," standing as a counterpart to "eternal sin" (v. 29), are a translation of the Greek *eis ton aiōna*, which is in turn derived from the Hebrew *lĕ'ōlām*. This Hebrew phrase refers to the age to come, which may be associated with the consummation of history (i.e., the eschaton). Through the work of the Spirit in Jesus, the eschaton has proleptically invaded the present age, without ending it. Hence, by rejecting Jesus' ministry by assigning his exorcistic work to Satan, the scribes stand in danger of committing an eschatological or eternal sin.

The scene reverts back to the first story in v. 31, with the depiction of the arrival of Jesus' family. There is something interesting about the composition of this family contingent, because the responsibility for reining in or bringing home a wayward adult male member of the family usually rests with males: either the father or the elder brother. In Jesus' case, the mother comes along with his brothers, suggesting that Joseph is probably dead or ill. This also suggests that Jesus is the eldest son.[75] If Jesus had an older brother, the mother need not be present. But if Jesus is the eldest brother, the mother has to be responsible if Joseph is not around, since younger brothers do not have the authority to rein him in. Their coming along must be for the reason that if the situation becomes ugly, they can then help their mother.

---

72. Hawthorne 1992: 7–8
73. Jeremias 1966b: 149; Donahue and Harrington 2002: 131.
74. Jeremias 1971: 35–36; France 2002: 175 (basing on Isa 65:16).
75. Cf. Marcus 2000: 275–76.

Mark locates the family contingent "outside." This may be coded language to refer not just to a physical position but also to a theological position (i.e., although they might be Jesus' physical kin, they were not truly his family).

Jesus asks about kinship (v. 33) and his reply to his own question is astonishing (vv. 34–35). The family bond was regarded as almost sacred in the first century Palestinian context, because of the fifth commandment (Exod 20:12). Thus for Jesus to speak of his real family as comprising those who obey God, and not those who are related to him by blood, serves to relativize the importance of such blood ties. Of course, Jews would accept that God's claims supersede those of family. However, to claim that those who obey God are Jesus' mother, brother, and sister goes beyond this in some ways in that a new type of kinship is envisaged. Such a concept dovetails with the story of 3:13–19, which connotes the idea of Jesus' creating the new people of God, through the calling of the Twelve.

Interestingly, the answer of Jesus does not contain the all-important word "father." There may be two possible explanations for this. It may be that Jesus is adapting his answer to the situation. Joseph is not there and so there is no need to mention who his father is. Alternatively, Jesus may be thinking of his special relationship with God who is known to him as Abba.[76] This may also allude to the virgin birth of Jesus. Of course, both explanations need not be regarded as being mutually exclusive.

Fusing the Horizons: Blasphemy against the Holy Spirit

The blasphemy against the Holy Spirit has intrigued many people. Modern readers, anxious to know whether they or their close relatives have committed it, often ask what Jesus is referring to exactly. Not surprisingly, many theories have been propounded throughout the history of the Church to explain it.

We present here the biblical perspective, assuming that the OT forms a continuum with the NT. It may surprise many that what is being referred to is actually clear but *what is unclear is the logic* that is at work. The blasphemy against the Holy Spirit is committed when opponents of Jesus ascribe his exorcisms to the work of *Beelzeboul*. This is so because the Holy Spirit is the power behind Jesus' distinctive exorcisms. But why should this blasphemy be regarded as an eternal sin without the possibility of forgive-

---

76. Boring 2006: 110.

ness? Using the OT as a resource, we see that in the prophetic promises, God's end-time restoration of Israel involves also the forgiveness of her sins (Isa 40:2; 43:25; 44:22; Jer 31:34; 33:8; Ezek 36:33), as it was sin that brought about her exile in the first place. The end-time restoration is to be achieved by the powerful work of the eschatological Spirit, who is also the agent of cleansing, revelation and regeneration (Isa 32:14–20; 59:15–21; Ezek 36:24–36; 37:1–14; 39:21–29). Without his work, restoration could not occur and Israel would be regarded as being still in her sins. Although the Spirit is not said expressly to bring about forgiveness of sins, we can infer this from his work of cleansing, restoring and regenerating: these aspects sum up God's definitive return to his people to repair the broken covenantal relationship once and for all.

This restoration, Jesus claims, is taking place in his ministry as the eschatological Spirit moves mightily through him to bring about the collapse of Satan's kingdom. Once this logic is appreciated, it can be seen that when the work of the Spirit is rejected, there can be no way of entering this eschatological kingdom of God. In brief, the rejection of the Spirit's work is a rejection of God's program of restoration and redemption. Eschatological overtures when maliciously slandered — and so resisted — can only result in an eschatological (eternal) destiny. The opponents of Jesus have thus painted themselves into a corner. If the only cure is rejected, how else can they be cured?[77]

From the Markan perspective, it also appears that the work of the Spirit in relation to the irruption of the kingdom is expressed significantly in exorcism. Mark has already indicated this by narrating Jesus' first spectacular deed as an exorcism (1:21–28), shortly after the Spirit descended upon him. The implication is that maligning Jesus' exorcisms takes on greater gravity than maligning Jesus' other miracles.

Finally, we need to emphasize that this sin is not committed whenever any accusation of demonic inspiration is made against any Christian exorcist. Instead, Jesus' warning is valid only in so far as the accusation is made against *his* ministry of exorcism. Hence, Christians should not jump to the conclusion that whoever speaks against Christianity today, even if it is done in vitriolic terms, has committed this very particular sin. So the present story speaks as much of Jesus' unique status as the reverence that is to be given to the Spirit.

---

77. Lövestam 1968: 62.

THE KINGDOM IN PARABLES (4:1-34)

Preamble

Mark has recorded some parabolic teaching of Jesus while depicting him in debate with his opponents (3:23-27; cf. 2:19-22). But now in chapter 4, Mark includes an extended parable of Jesus, together with the hermeneutical key for decoding all parables (v. 13). This major teaching block—one of two, the other is found in chapter 13—will help Mark's audience gain a proper perspective on what has preceded and prepare them for what is to follow.

In the previous chapters Mark has narrated the reactions of different people (the crowds, the tax-collectors and sinners, the religious authorities, Jesus' family) to Jesus' teaching and deeds. If Jesus' ministry signifies the dawning of the long-awaited hope of Israel, namely the coming of God's kingship, why does it engender different responses? The parables in this chapter go to the heart of the issue by illustrating the nature of the kingdom that has come through Jesus' ministry. It is full of paradoxes, and not what his contemporaries thought it would be.

In this section, we are also informed for the first time that Jesus teaches lessons that are exclusively for his disciples. The explanation of the Parable of the Sower is laden with talk about "insiders" versus "outsiders." This may be regarded as a further development of the theme in chapter 3. Not the outsiders, but the members of God's family may grasp the essence of Jesus' teaching because they will be given special insights (v. 10).

Since this section treats very significant themes, we should expect some coherent structure. The key lies in understanding the function of vv. 21-25. If this passage is regarded not as parables but as containing pithy sayings that provide a counterpoint to the sayings of vv. 10-12, then all the parables in this chapter feature only seed. The parable placed first in this collection (i.e., the Parable of the Sower) may then be regarded as the archetype, since the understanding of it opens doors to the other parables (v. 13). So Mark includes the interpretation of Jesus (vv. 14-20), something which he does not do for the other parables.[78]

But can we say vv. 21-25 are not parables? We should first notice that they are not explicitly named as such, unlike the three seed parables. It is better to regard them as disparate sayings that have been strung together. Secondly, their content differs from that of the other three parables in that they speak of light and concealment, and not seed and growth. This fits in

---

78. In vv. 33-34 the fact that Jesus did explain his parables is stated, but not the content.

better with the theme of vv. 10–12. Thirdly, they develop the theme of vv. 10–12 further by stating that there will be illumination and revelation eventually (i.e., all "hiddenness" will ultimately end because the lamp comes for the purpose of illumination). This gives the christological resolution to the paradoxical kingdom, and promises that all things will finally be made clear.

In short, we have an ABA'B' structure for vv. 3–25 (see Diagram 3). The archetypal parable is taught in vv. 3–9 (A), followed by comments on the concealing function of parables in vv. 10–12 (B). Next, the explanation of the archetype parable is given in vv. 13–20 (A'), and this is then followed by sayings on concealment and revelation in vv. 21–25 (B'). Mark then includes two further seed parables to illustrate the hidden nature of the kingdom (vv. 26–32). No interpretation from Jesus is provided for them, probably because Mark regards this as unnecessary once the meaning of the Parable of the Sower has been explained, and Jesus' role in all this is understood. Of course, in the summary Mark reiterates that Jesus typically explains the parables to his disciples (vv. 33–34).

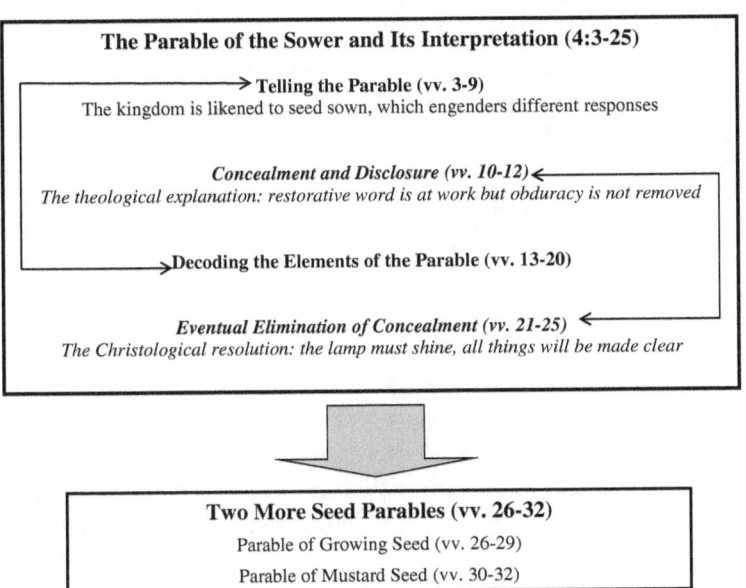

Diagram 3
The Structure of 4:3-32

All the above then raises a pressing question: why does Mark choose only seed parables to explain what the kingdom is? We may think of three reasons. The first is that Jesus ministered in what is largely an agrarian society. Farming images would be most suitable for his listeners. Secondly, the image of planting and harvesting is frequently used in the OT to convey God's creative work in the nation, especially his restorative work (Hos 2:21-23; Amos 9:13-15; Zech 8:12). Jewish eschatological discourses make use of such an image too (cf. 2 *Bar.* 70:2). Moreover, the seed is most congenial for representing the restorative word of God which works to bring about his eschatological will (cf. Isa 55:10-11; 4 *Ezra* 8:41; 9:31). Indeed, in Jer 31:27-28, the image of sowing seed is used in relation to the prophecy of the repopulation of Israel and Judah. Finally, the image of seed conveys aptly the nature of the kingdom. Just as a seed is hidden in the soil but will germinate to bring forth life and fruit, so also will the kingdom be hidden, but its effect will be tangible and unstoppable.

Parable of the Sower (4:1-9)

The setting (v. 1) serves to raise the expectation that something spectacular is about to happen because it contains a hyperbole. Usually crowds are just described as "great" (3:7-8; cf. 5:21; 6:34; 8:1; 9:14; 12:37), but in 4:1, Mark uses the Greek phrase *ochlos pleistos*, which means literally "the greatest crowd." This "mammoth" crowd has gathered at the shore of the lake to listen to Jesus and subsequently he has to use the boat as a vehicle for teaching. Verse 2 tells us that Jesus teaches in parables, but the focus will just be on one.

Two verbs are joined in the opening statement of Jesus: "listen" and "look."[79] The implication is that mere listening is not enough. The listeners must also perceive. In other words, their hearing should lead to a new outlook. To be sure, the importance of "hearing" is not to be belittled, as it occurs again in vv. 9, 12, 15-16, 18, 20, 23-24, 33, and especially so when it is the first word of the Shema[80] (see Deut 6:4-5). The upshot of all this is that something important is being conveyed by Jesus, and it will take one's total concentration and keen perception to grasp his meaning.

The parable speaks of a sower (the Greek is *ho speirōn*). There may be an allusion to Jer 31:27-28, which pictures God as a sower who works to

---

79. English translations sometimes use only one verb (e.g., NRSV), denuding the statement of an important nuance.

80. Cf. Gerhardsson 1967-68: 165-93, who argues that the whole parable may be interpreted with reference to the Shema.

bring Israel back from her exile.[81] It has also been suggested by some commentators that the sower in the parable could also be Jesus.[82]

A familiar scene taken from the agrarian context of his listeners is used: a small landholder casts seed in all types of soil in the hope of getting optimal yield.[83] He would also sow seeds before ploughing (cf. *Jub.* 11:11; *t. Sab.* 7:2; *b. Sab.* 73b).[84] The parable is constructed artfully and uses ideas which are easy to follow. Seeds are sown on four different types of terrain: the ground beside the path, the rocky places, the thorny patches, and good soil. The seeds face different conditions and give different results. These are arranged in the form of a gradation: no germination → quick germination but also quick termination → no fruit → abundant fruit.

The first terrain is properly "the ground beside the path,"[85] in keeping with the Greek *para tēn hodon*, and not "along the path," as it is in many English versions. This is the unplowed part of the field. The seeds on it are easily accessible to birds. More importantly, such a description may be theologically loaded, because the word *hodos* (way) is used positively in Mark to represent the "way" of three intimately related entities: the way of the gospel (1:2), the way of Jesus (8:27; 10:32), and the way of discipleship (9:33; 10:52).[86] So the people who are represented by the ground that is "beside the path" are those who do not belong to the way. As a result, the seed or word is taken immediately from them. Feeding birds are often an ominous image (Gen 40:17, 19; Deut 28:26; 1 Kings 14:11; 16:4; Ps 79:2; Isa 18:6; Jer 7:33; 34:20; Ezek 29:5; 32:4; cf. *Jub.* 11:11).

The second are the rocky places. Terrain of this nature has only a thin layer of soil, which does not allow the germinating plant to take root deeply. Exposed to the scorching sun, it will wither quickly. The description that the plant sprang up quickly in such a terrain has puzzled many readers, as there is no scientific basis for it. Perhaps the solution lies in construing the parable as adopting an observer's perspective. Seeds sown on rocky terrain are nearer the surface as compared to seeds sown on ploughed soil. As it takes a shorter time for the shoot to break out from this thin soil, it gives the impression that it germinates more rapidly. The point of the description lies in the contrast: quick growth but shallow roots. "Rootlessness" is a

---

81. Wright 1996: 232.
82. Hooker 1991: 122–23.
83. Boring 2006: 116.
84. Cf. Payne 1978: 123–29.
85. Cf. the grammatical observations of Marcus 2000: 292.
86. Stanton 2002: 44–49.

stock image for describing the infidels or the wicked in Jewish literature (Sir 23:25; 40:15; Wis 4:3).

The third type of terrain contains thorns. Due to competition from the thorns, the sown seed cannot reach its full potential of bearing fruit. Jer 4:3 warns against sowing among thorns in his sermon encouraging repentance and return.

The final terrain is good soil, which yields great results. The enumeration of the yields is interesting. If taken as crop yields they are indeed phenomenal, since usual yields were less than tenfold. Even so, this pales in comparison with the exaggerated expectations of the fruitfulness of the eschaton by the rabbis, where yields can be as much as 150,000 times (*b. Ketub.*11b-12a)! The point is that great fruitfulness, a symbol of the eschaton (Jer 31:12; Hos 2:21-22; Joel 2:22; Amos 9:13; Zech 8:12), has come.[87] But if it is taken as the yield of the individual seed, the description is realistic.[88]

Verse 9 harks back to the "Listen" of v. 3, and together they form a frame for the parable. The saying also serves two functions. First, it makes the parable applicable to all, with the words "those who have ears." But secondly, "those who have ears *to hear*" suggests that not everyone uses his/her auditory organs properly, and in this respect the exhortation is narrowed to a special group. The two ideas are not mutually exclusive. All are summoned to hear but it is implied that not all will do so.

The Meaning of the Parable (4:10-25)

This section may be broken up into three units. The first (vv. 10-12) tells us why Jesus explains the parables only to his disciples and not to the crowds or "outsiders." This sets the stage for the second unit (vv. 13-20), which reiterates the importance of the parable of the sower, and also decodes for the disciples the meaning of the different images in the parable. The third (vv. 21-25) comprises four different sayings: two each on the theme of revelation/concealment, and the need to respond appropriately. All this enriches the meaning of Jesus' parable teaching by promising ultimate clarity, albeit with a warning thrown in.

The Purpose of the Parables (4:10-12)

Mark probably envisages a group larger than the Twelve in v. 10 (cf. 2:15). The plural "parables" is intentional, and not a result of poor composition.

---

87. Cf. Jeremias 1954: 150.
88. White 1964: 301-3; Payne 1980: 181-86.

The point is that the key to understanding Jesus' many parables lies with one particular parable. Conversely, to ask about the meaning of the Parable of the Sower is to ask about the parables.

In v. 11 Jesus speaks of the "secret" of the kingdom of God. The Greek word used here is *mystērion*, and it occurs only once in Mark's Gospel. It refers to God's secret purpose which is known only through revelation. Indeed, it harks back to the Aramaic *rāz*, used in Dan 2:18-19, 27-30, 40, where Daniel interprets Nebuchadnezzar's dream of the compositely-made statute by referring to God's secret. In this sense, what Jesus is about to teach his disciples cannot be obtained through human ability, but comes as a gift, a revelation. This means the images generated by the parables will remain in the minds of Jesus' hearers, teasing them into active thought but never providing them with the requisite meaning until the light from Jesus' teaching shines into them. It is also to be noted that with this verse, the connection between Jesus' parables and the reign of God coming through his ministry is made explicit.

Who are those who are described as "on the outside" (v. 11)? In chapter 3, those who were described or implied to be "outside" (3:31) were Jesus' family and the scribes respectively. It may then be inferred that the "outsiders" here are those who are quick to dismiss Jesus' claims and teaching. To the "outsiders" everything about Jesus' ministry remains as a parable or a *māšāl* (i.e., a dark saying), but the "insiders" are given the secret for decoding it. Two contrasts are thus set up: revelation versus concealment, and insiders versus outsiders.

Verse 12 presents intractable interpretation problems. There is debate on how the Greek *hina*, and the corresponding *mēpote*, may be construed. The question concerns chiefly whether the Greek words convey intention or result. Because of space constraint, only the main lines of interpretation are discussed here.[89] (1) If the Greek *hina* is telic (i.e., stating purpose), then Jesus is saying that the parables are told with the express purpose to make outsiders remain ignorant, so that their sins remain unforgiven. The counterpart *mēpote* (lest) confirms the statement's telic force. The problem facing this interpretation is that it appears to contradict Jesus' proclamation of good news to all and sundry. (2) One variant of this approach is to treat the Greek *hina* as being a short hand for *hina plērōthē* (i.e., in order that it may be fulfilled), a formula for citing scripture. This redirects the intention from Jesus to Scripture. But the troublesome intentionality is still there. (3) If it is ecbatic in force (i.e., stating result), the statement of Jesus may be interpreted thus: the result—not the intention—of teaching in parables is

---

89. For a good discussion, see Evans 1989b: 91-106.

that some would remain ignorant, and their sins would therefore not be forgiven. The fault then lies not with the parable speaker but the hearers, whose stubborn hearts prevent them from understanding the parables. The Greek *hina* is usually telic in force, although at this stage of its development in the first century, it could be used to indicate result.[90] However, *mēpote* proves a challenge and has to be arbitrarily construed as being tentative or conditional. There are unambiguous words to serve this function, such as the Greek *ei mē*. Hence, while this interpretation makes good theological sense, it is weak grammatically. (4) Some scholars prefer to dig back to the Aramaic substratum, and argue that in the process of translating it into Greek, a misunderstanding has arisen. They contend that *hina* probably translates the Aramaic *dĕ*, which although telic in force, can also be used as a relative pronoun, (such as "who"). *Mēpote* is then construed as reflecting the Aramaic *dîlĕmā'*, which may be translated as "unless."[91] This produces the sense: "Everything is in parables to those who are outside *who* may look and yet not perceive ... *unless* they repent ..." Consequently the verse describes those who are the "outsiders," but with a hope held out to them that if they repent they will no longer be outsiders. However, this approach does not quite solve the problem, since it is clear that Mark depicts Jesus as typically explaining parables only to his disciples (see vv. 11, 34). Privileged information is given only to the insiders, implying that it is Jesus' intention not to make the meaning of his parables transparent to all. This is confirmed in vv. 33-34.

Notwithstanding the interpretational problems, it should be pointed out that, if we bracket off theological concerns, the grammar is actually clear (especially the pairing of *hina* with *mēpote*). It speaks explicitly of intentionality. The fact that Jesus explains parables only to the insiders supports this further. Moreover, the original context of the Isaianic quotation in v. 12 speaks clearly of intentionality too (see below). Resorting to a putative Aramaic substratum will not do, as we do not have it and any retroversion is precarious. All we have is the Greek text of Mark, and the contextual indicators he provides us. The difficulty lies not with the grammar but with the presupposed theology. It is jarring to human ears.

One way to solve the problem is to limit the saying to a small group, (i.e., the religious leaders who opposed Jesus).[92] But the fact that the insiders are differentiated from "the largest crowd" (v. 1) suggests that a much bigger group is envisaged. Indeed in chapter 3, those who were described

---

90. Moule 1959: 142-46.
91. Cf. Manson 1937: 75-80; but countered by Black 1967: 212-14.
92. Watts 1997: 194-210.

as being "on the outside" are the relatives of Jesus. That said, Mark would surely know that James, the Lord's brother, did come to trust in Jesus after his resurrection! This means the "outsiders" can become "insiders."

Perhaps the way forward is to start from Isa 6:9–10 and acknowledge that the harshness in Mark 4:10–12 comes mainly from the quoted words. Our preferred interpretation is therefore option 2. It retains the telic idea, which is suggested not simply by the Greek *hina* but also by the way the story is told. This intention is the divine intention, connected with the words used by Isaiah on the obdurate nation just before her exile. The full force of this obduracy has yet to be unleashed, and Jesus' ministry does precisely that, fulfilling Scripture (i.e., making it full).[93] It will attract rank stubbornness to itself. All this is part of God's plan and may be construed as the secret of the kingdom. Of course, the Isaianic quotation need not be regarded as totalizing. Other aspects must be brought in to ensure a full-orbed view of Jesus' ministry. The fact that Jesus appealed to people to hear does not indicate that fatalism is at work.

That said, we must not miss an important implication here, which actually undergirds the whole of 4:1–34: the kingdom works in the midst of great rebellion without cancelling it, at least not yet. Hence, there is a division among the people, making them into insiders and outsiders. Furthermore, Jesus' ministry is seen as eschatological, drawing together the different narrative threads of the biblical story, both positive and negative. Hence salvation is announced together with judgment (and Mark will have more to say about this later).

The Interpretation of the Parable (4:13–20)

Jesus' questions in v. 13 make explicit the hermeneutical significance of the Parable of the Sower. It provides the key to unlocking the meaning of all Jesus' parables.

Jesus' explanation of the parable begins with the all-important sentence that guides us to its meaning: it is about the sowing of the *word*.[94] The soils are only part of the message. If this is missed, then this parable has been domesticated of all its revolutionary effect. The importance of the word is also suggested by its frequent occurrence in the explanation.[95] The absolute form "the word" is never found in the OT; it is always qualified by another noun or in a genitive relationship with something else. How-

---

93. Cf. Schneck 1994: 114–23.
94. Cf. the keen observations in Marcus 2000: 308, 311.
95. Eight times out of twenty-four, a third of the total usage of the Gospel of Mark.

ever, the absolute use of it is often found in the NT. This gives it a technical sense—the word of the gospel, which is also the eschatological word.[96] We may compare this with the OT depiction of God's word: that which creates, reveals, judges, restores, and recreates (Ps 19; 33:6; 119:105; Isa 55:10–11). The gospel has similar functions.

Only through recognizing the momentous importance of the "word" could the different responses symbolized by different soils become significant and not just run-of-the-mill comments about life. The eschatological "word" is sown in different kinds of soils, indicating different conditions of the heart. The different points along the spectrum of responses are highlighted: those who lost it straightaway, through to those who gave up because of persecution, and those who were hampered by the cares of this age, and finally to those who respond positively. As interesting as these responses may be for a psychological enquiry or homiletical application, the main point lies elsewhere. It is that the promised restorative word is given while obduracy still works. This is because the full measure of obduracy has yet to come, although it is now in process in Jesus' ministry. This being the case, the word given through Jesus' ministry could be easily rejected by the unbelieving as an impotent word and thus not God's restorative word. But the point of Jesus is that the word is now sown, and what is regarded as impotent is actually potent, albeit hidden! The time that the Jews longed for ardently has indeed come, although it is not accompanied by an open blaze of glory. So faith is needed and the hearers are exhorted to listen carefully. The parable then speaks of the paradoxical timing of the kingdom and the paradoxical nature of its revelation. This manner of reading it ties up vv. 10–12 neatly with the parable interpretation, and dovetails with the thrust of the next paragraph.[97]

Hidden in Order to Reveal (4:21–25)

The paragraph comprising vv. 21–25 picks up the theme of revelation versus concealment, sounded in vv. 10–12. It speaks of the lamp's coming to illuminate (see below) by being set on a lampstand, and not by being hidden under a bowl or a bed. This is then concluded with a clear statement that all things will ultimately be made clear, and the hidden open (v. 22). After that, the exhortation to hear, first sounded in v. 9 when the parable was told, is given (v. 23), indicating the utter importance of that statement. All this is further reinforced by the exhortation of v. 24: "to see what they are hearing."

---

96. Jeremias 1954: 77.
97. For other interpretative options, which are many, see Snodgrass 2008: 155–56.

The two sayings that follow speak of accountability and judgment. In other words, what is being heard is not a run-of-the-mill thing, because there will be a great day of reckoning.

The Greek *mēti erchetai ho lychnos* is often translated as "do you bring in a lamp," which is also supported by many commentaries, but it actually obscures a powerful Markan theme at work. The Greek *erchomai* is almost always deponent, and should be translated with an English verb in its active voice,[98] unless otherwise indicated.[99] This being the case, Mark's statement actually speaks of the lamp's coming. In the OT the lamp is an image for God's word (Ps 119:105), and it is used to signify the illuminative or revelatory aspect of his word. Since Jesus provides the world with new revelation, Mark may very well have Jesus in mind too.[100]

The implication of the lamp's coming is spelled out in v. 22, and it provides the counterpoint to the parable theory of 4:10–12: it is always God's intention for full clarity to come. The hiding is only a phase, and is subservient to the larger interest of revelation.[101] This means the kingdom will finally be tangibly experienced. So important is this truth that the exhortation to hear, sounded at the end of the Parable of the Sower (v. 9) is repeated here (v. 23). Although it is not stated when clarity will come, in Mark's Gospel this is either Jesus' crucifixion and resurrection, or his coming again.[102] One may then speak of a christological resolution of the kingdom's enigma.

A different image is conjured up with v. 24. The Greek *blepete ti akouete* aptly juxtaposes the senses of seeing and hearing. In the Markan context, seeing is an important activity especially when it is related to the things that are happening in Jesus' ministry (8:15, 18, 22–26; 12:14). Why it is important to "watch what you hear" is explained with the use of the metaphor of a measure. An escalation of the *lex talionis* principle may be detected here. What it means is that the negative judgments people pass on Jesus' ministry will result in negative judgments being passed on them. But because of the eschatological and salvific significance of Jesus' ministry, these future judgments will be infinitely more severe than what they themselves are passing on Jesus.

On the surface the saying of v. 25 appears rather capricious, but when it is understood in its particular context, it makes good sense. Those who

---

98. This means "does the lamp come?"

99. The parallels in Matthew and Luke (Matt 5:15; Luke 8:16; 11:33) use different verbs (Matthew uses *kaiō* and *tithēmi*, and Luke *haptō* and *tithēmi*).

100. Hurtado 1983: 79.

101. Cf. Boring 2006: 132–33; Hurtado 1983: 76.

102. Donahue and Harrington 2002: 154; Marcus 2000: 319.

are the "insiders" (i.e., people who are open to what God is doing in Jesus' ministry), are promised more revelation and insight. For those who do not have this attitude, even the little insight they once had will soon be gone. Rejection does not mean the status quo is preserved; instead, it leads to a downward spiral. The verse does not identify who takes this away. It could be Satan (cf. 4:15) or God.

Two Seed Parables (4:26–32)

Two seed parables are found here. Through them, the parable connection with the kingdom of God is made explicit.

For the first time, the phrase "this is what the kingdom of God is like" is used to preface a parable (v. 26). This parable is about the germinating seed, growing without any human input (vv. 26–29). What is emphasized is the inscrutability of the growth of the kingdom, but the results are assured and will be clear to all. The Greek of the final two clauses in v. 29 echoes the Greek translation of Joel 3:13 (LXX 4:13). The latter speaks of eschatological judgment against God's enemies. If the echo is intentional, Jesus appears to be using it with a different nuance: to speak positively of the final results of the kingdom.

The second parable is about the mustard seed (vv. 30–32), which develops further the idea of the previous one. The kingdom's goal will not only be reached inexorably, it will be more glorious than its inauspicious beginnings. Consequently, a more arresting image is used: not just any seed but the mustard seed. The Greek phrase *mikroteron hon pantōn tōn spermatōn epi tēs gēs* is literally "the smallest of all seeds on the earth," which may cause difficulty for some readers. This seed is probably the black mustard (*brassica nigra*), which is extremely small but can grow to a height of about ten feet. Although it is not the smallest seed on Earth, it is proverbial for its smallness (*m. Nid.* 5:2; *m. Naz.* 1:5). This proverbially small seed will become a plant that is the greatest of garden plants. On its branches birds of the air will make their homes. The image of birds nesting in this plant recalls the OT promises of the entry of Gentiles to the kingdom (Ezek 17:23; 31:6 [LXX]; Dan 4:20–22; cf. *1 En.* 90:30). So glorious will the kingdom be that Israel will not be the only beneficiary; the nations of the world will also be drawn into it, for God is the king of all creation. This prepares the Markan audience for the story he will narrate in the next chapter.

The two seed parables then convey the notion that the kingdom comes not as a giant tree transplanted from heaven, an image which may accurately describe much of Jewish eschatological speculation (cf. the "cosmic tree" of Dan 4:20–22; cf. Ezek 17:1–10; 31:6).[103] Nor does it come to make everything clear, and at a stroke deliver Israel from her enemies and consign them to everlasting punishment. No, the kingdom begins in a hidden way, like seed that is planted. But this seed will inexorably develop into that giant tree that Jews expect. So the kingdom does come but not in the way that is expected.

Summary (4:33–34)

Mark summarizes this section by reiterating the main themes (vv. 33–34). He starts by stating that many *similar* parables were spoken by Jesus. This dovetails with the hermeneutical emphasis of this section: the Parable of the Sower is the parable that unlocks others. It also states that Jesus' characteristic teaching method uses parables. Furthermore, the insider-outsider antithesis is reiterated: explanations are given only to those who are Jesus' disciples.

STILLING THE STORM (4:35–41)

The statement that the lamp comes for the purpose of revelation and not concealment (4:21) is developed further with this story. Jesus' true identity is revealed, as the winds and waves obey him, just as they obey God. The story also initiates a series of miracle stories (four altogether), which culminates with the rejection of Jesus by his own townspeople, who are described as people without faith (6:1–6). Indeed, the theme of faith—especially that of the disciples—also receives significant treatment from this story onwards.

The instruction to the disciples to cross the lake while Jesus himself remained to dismiss the crowd sets the stage for the miracle story (vv. 35–36). The reason for this is not given, unless we think of the next story in chapter 5 (i.e., the encounter with the Gerasene demoniac) as implicitly providing it.

It is peculiar that someone should be sound asleep in a small boat tossed by a tempest and yet this is precisely what Jesus does (v. 38). Perhaps Mark wants his audience to recall the OT concept of sleeping peacefully as a sign of trusting in God (Ps 3:5; 4:8; Prov 3:24).[104] However, from the perspective

---

103. Concepts of the cosmic tree abound in ancient culture. Indeed, as Wyatt observes, "the tree is both an *axis mundi* . . . that is, the central pillar of the universe . . . and an allomorph of the Primal Man," (Wyatt 2001: 166). See also Collins 1993a: 223; James 1966; and Widengren 1951.

104. Cope argues that a parallel to the story of Jonah is intended, but the case is unconvincing (e.g., Jesus is not fleeing from God's call); see Cope 1976: 96–97 followed by Collins 2007: 259–60; cf. Aus 2000. Highly suggestive is the idea that the depiction

of the disciples, nothing can be more disheartening than to see their master soundly asleep in a crisis (v. 38), and hence the rebuke: "Teacher, don't you care that we perish?" Jesus addresses the storm as though it were a person (v. 39). Although his words recall the exorcism of 1:25, there is no compelling reason to think an exorcism is also taking place.[105]

The questions of Jesus reveal what the main problem with the disciples is they lack faith (v. 40). The Greek adverb *oupō*, which means "not yet" or "still," indicates that by now the disciples should have developed a robust faith. This is especially so if they have been given privileged insights not available to others (cf. 4:10–12). At this point an alert audience should have perceived that two aspects of the theme of faith have been presented: trust *like* Jesus and trust *in* Jesus.[106]

The final statement of the disciples (v. 41) reveals another important aspect of the story. In the OT, the sea often represents primeval chaos, which only God can tame (Job 26:11–12; Ps 104:7; Isa 51:9–10). Up to this stage Mark has presented Jesus as an authoritative teacher, a healer and also an exorcist. However, a new datum is given now: Jesus can also control the forces of nature. He can calm storms like God. Indeed, the thrice occurrence of the word "great" in a short compass of six verses ("great storm" (v. 37), "great calm" (v. 39) and "great fear" (v. 41)) further supports this insight. Jesus' authority evokes awe and any description of it must befit the adjective "great."

However, the juxtaposition of the theme of "faith" with "Jesus' greatness" gives rise to an irony: great power should engender great faith, but this is not the case here. This irony looms large in the chapters that follow.

HEALING THE GERASENE DEMONIAC (5:1–20)

This story is strange by many standards, ancient and modern, and often leaves students of Mark baffled. Although having links with earlier exorcism narratives (1:21–28; 1:32–34; 3:11–12), it goes beyond them in terms of intensity (a legion of demons), setting (a thoroughly unclean place), and dialogue (an extended one). It also has links with the next two miracle stories via the theme of ritual impurity. In this sense they show Jesus' cleansing power at work. Furthermore, it shows for the first time Jesus ministering in

---

of a sleeping Jesus is meant to show his likeness to God (see Marcus 2000:338; cf. Batto: 1987: 153–77).

105. Cf. Collins 2007: 261.
106. Marcus 2000: 334.

overtly Gentile territory, developing the idea already suggested in the Parable of the Mustard Seed (4:30–32).

Excursus: The Location of the Story

The Greek manuscript tradition is quite confused here, mirroring the ancient confusion over where this town is located. Based on the most ancient manuscript testimony (א and B, fourth century), the reading Gerasenes should be preferred over against competitors such as Gadarenes (attested by the majority of manuscripts but they are unfortunately late), Gergesenes (few and late) or even the strange Gergystenes (unique to W, fifth century). There is, however, a problem with the earliest reading Gerasenes. If this is the ancient name of the modern town of Jerash in Jordan, it means it is located about thirty-seven miles from the banks (SE) of the Sea of Galilee! It appears incredible that the pigs would have run this distance before drowning in the lake (v. 13). Furthermore, no steep banks may be found. Gadarenes fares slightly better, since it is five miles from the lake in a south-easterly direction. Moreover, this city has limits reaching all the way to the shore. This reading seems to prevail in Matt 8:28. However, it suffers from the same problem as the earlier one, as steep banks cannot be found on the south-eastern bank of the lake. In terms of topography, Gergesenes is the best candidate, that is, if we identify it with the modern day Kursi. This is situated on a plateau, on the east bank of the lake. But the reading is attested by a few manuscripts only, and they are all late witnesses (eighth century onwards). One possible way of harmonizing textual testimony with geographical reality is to regard the name Gerasenes as being derived from the Hebrew root *grš*, which means "to banish." This is a term commonly used to describe exorcism.[107] Accordingly, the event may be regarded as historical but the name of the place as given symbolically. If this is the case, we will not be able to locate where the exorcism took place.

In ancient Palestine the deceased were buried in caves, which explains why tombs could be a dwelling place for social outcasts. What led the demoniac to meet Jesus, Mark does not say (v. 2). One may surmise it was the magnetic authority of Jesus (cf. 1:23–24).

107. Marcus 2000: 342.

The state of the demoniac is poignantly described. His superhuman strength renders him uncontrollable. But behind such strength lies a wrecked human being, alone and naked—a pain to others and a pain to himself (vv. 3–5, 15). Regarded as posing a danger to the community, he is therefore restrained by chains. Such actions do not, however, solve the root problem.

In pleading with Jesus not to torture him, the demoniac also confesses his status (v. 7). Jesus is called the Son of the Most High God, the longest title to be accorded him in Mark's Gospel. Interestingly, the same title is also found in Luke 1:32 and 4Q246. In the latter passage, it functions most probably as a messianic title.[108] There is also a certain aptness to the title, in that the term "Most High God" is often used in a polytheistic context to refer to the supreme god (cf. Gen 14:18–20; Pindar *Nemean Odes* 1:60; 11:20, where Zeus is referred to as the "Most High."). In Jewish literature, Gentiles are sometimes described as calling Yahweh the Most High God (Num 24:16; Dan 3:26; 4:2; 2 Macc 3:31; 3 *Macc.* 7:9; cf. Acts 16:17). Thus the title serves the function of a monotheistic polemic, and hints at the ethnicity of the demoniac.

The fascinating conversation that ensues should not be regarded as a tussle for power between the demons and Jesus, since Mark's narrative consistently portrays Jesus as having unrivalled and unchallenged authority when it comes to evil or chaotic forces.[109] In fact, the conversation serves a pedagogical purpose. The name "Legion" is certainly a Roman military term. A Roman legion comprised about five thousand troops when in full strength, but most legions were normally not at full strength. This will then bring the number closer to the 2,000 pigs which they will later inhabit (v. 13). The presence of this term, among some other indicators,[110] suggests to some commentators that the story may be a sort of political commentary.

---

108. Fitzmyer, 1993: 153–74; Collins 1993b: 65–82.

109. Cf. France 2002: 228–29. The demoniac's petition "Swear to God that you won't torture me" has elicited an interesting proposal. The Greek behind the word "swear" is *orkizō*. This is often used in exorcistic contexts, by the exorcist and not the exorcised (cf. Acts 19:13). Consequently, some commentators have taken this as implying the demoniac's intention to preempt or counter any exorcistic action by Jesus, (i.e., using the exorcist's term on the exorcist himself). This, however, is making too much out of just one term.

110. E.g., "a large herd of pigs" (v. 11). The word for "herd" here is *agelē*, which is rather unusual for pigs because it is typically used to describe troops. This is further indication that Mark intends his listeners to treat this story as alluding to the Roman military annexation of Palestinian territory. Pigs are regarded as unclean animals in the OT (Lev 11:7–8; Deut 14:8), and have also become a symbol of paganism (cf. Matt 7:6; 2 Pet 2:22).

It alludes to the Roman Empire's legions, by which the Empire has annexed many territories to itself (i.e., possessing them), jealously guarding what has been unjustly arrogated, and causing terror in its wake.[111] This proposal has mileage but it would be wrong to think of the episode as simply an allegory of Roman occupation and oppression. Ancient people had no trouble believing in the power of evil spirits. What the legion of demons did to the man was similar to what the Empire did to the territory. Mark sees the parallels and relates the story in a context where such parallels will be easily perceived. It should also be noted that the passage does not issue a call to Christians to take arms and rebel against the Roman Empire. Instead, the way out of the terror of Roman occupation is to go on "exorcising" (i.e., speaking the authoritative word of Jesus). This will overcome evil powers and re-humanize the oppressed.

We can also understand the pedagogical point behind the recounting of the reference to pigs as containers (vv. 11–13): unclean spirits should dwell in unclean vessels, and not humans. That said, the demons' request does appear to be somewhat illogical, since the pigs proceeded to destroy themselves after being demonized. Perhaps Mark is suggesting that evil entities ultimately destroy themselves.[112]

Most herds of pigs are small. A size of three hundred is already considerable.[113] Not surprisingly, the villagers reacted negatively to their destruction (vv. 14–17). To those who have eyes only for economics, two thousand pigs are worth more than one formerly insane man. Accordingly, the people of that town beg Jesus to depart from them. It is much cheaper to consign a person to an ancient mental institution (the tombs) or to buy chains. All this means Jesus is not welcomed—not because they do not believe in his power, but because they do not accept his program.

Jesus' response to the man's request to follow him is fascinating (vv. 18–19). This is the first time the Markan audience hears of Jesus' not allowing someone to follow him, but there may be strategic reasons for this. Jesus may be refused entry to this community to minister, but he can plant his witness. The former demoniac would be a strategic witness, having himself personally experienced the healing ministry of Jesus. Interestingly, it is also the first time in Mark's Gospel that Jesus expressly commands a person to publish abroad what has happened to him! This is probably to be explained by the need for a witness in Gentile territory, and also that Gentiles are not

---

111. Marcus 2000: 351; Myers 1988: 190–94.
112. See Collins 2007: 271 for other suggestions.
113. Boring 2006: 152.

affected by the bellicose ideas of much of Jewish messianism.[114] Jesus bids him to return to his family to testify to them but the man does this and more, for he proclaims (cf. 1:14–15) to all and sundry in the Decapolis,[115] causing amazement to many. Perhaps it is not too inaccurate to call this unnamed person the first apostle to the Gentiles.

Jairus's Daughter and the Woman with Chronic Bleeding (5:21–43)

We have here another fine example of intercalation in Mark's Gospel (the others are found in 3:20–35; 6:7–32; 11:12–26; 14:1–11; 14:54–72). The story of the healing of the woman with a menstrual disorder is sandwiched by the story of the raising of Jairus's daughter.

Menstrual blood and death are regarded as rendering people ritually impure, but Jesus overcomes this without being made impure, even though he comes into contact with them. Hence, there is a thematic connection with the healing of the Gerasene demoniac where there was extreme ritual impurity. It must also be stressed that the theme of faith remains dominant.[116] In this regard, we may claim there is also a connection with the miracle story in 4:35–41, where the theme of faith is prominent. We shall explain how this theme is further developed in this passage.

The Humility of Faith: the Request of Jairus (5:21–24)

The story takes place on the Jewish side of the Sea of Galilee (i.e., after Jesus has returned from Gerasenes). Although a great crowd comes to Jesus (v. 21), the spotlight falls on Jairus (v. 22). Jairus is "one of the synagogue rulers," meaning that he is not the presider who has overall responsibility for the synagogue, but a member of the body of elders that elects the presider.[117] He is certainly a man of high standing and means: his house has rooms (v. 40), the family can afford professional mourners (v. 38), and he probably has servants too (v. 35).

---

114. France 2002: 232–33.

115. The Decapolis (literally: ten cities) was part of the kingdom bequeathed to Philip the Tetrarch, the brother of Herod Antipas. This is located to the east of the Jordan River, beyond the Sea of Galilee, and is known for its Hellenistic culture. The extant evidence seems to indicate the number is only nominal, and exactly what cities belonged to this region are not clearly defined (Pliny *Natural History* 6:18, 74; cf. Josephus *Life* 341, 410).

116. See the helpful treatment of Marshall 1989: 90–110.

117. Cf. Schürer 1979: 432–36.

Being Jesus' social superior, and given the fact that Jesus has been rejected by the religious authorities, it would have been very humbling for Jairus to approach him for help. However, Jairus does precisely this because of his daughter's plight (vv. 22–23). Perhaps we may discern here the humility of faith. Without humility, faith cannot germinate.

One interesting Greek word used to describe Jairus's request in v. 23 is *sōthē*, which means "be saved." While being appropriate for the situation of Jairus's daughter, it also serves as a link-word with the story of the woman with a menstrual problem (see vv. 28, 34). Moreover, the *sōzō* word creates special resonances for the Markan audience, as salvation comes through faith in Jesus.

Mark tells us that Jesus accepts his plea for help and goes with him. The seemingly innocuous detail about a larger crowd following them (v. 24) prepares the audience for the sandwiched story.

The Power of Faith: the Healing of the Woman with Chronic Bleeding (5:25–34)

Mark informs his audience that in the crowd there is a woman who has suffered from a menstrual disorder for twelve years. According to the Torah, menstruation rendered a woman ritually impure (Lev 15:19–33). So concerned were the Jews to avoid being ritually contaminated by menstruants that a whole tractate was devoted to it in the Mishnah (tractate *Niddah*). There is also evidence, albeit in the third to fourth centuries, for the Jewish notion that a menstruant could also neutralize a healer's power (*Hekhalot Rabbati* 18). If this notion has roots reaching back many centuries earlier, Jewish listeners to Mark's tale would have certainly caught a deeper significance: Jesus should not have been able to heal the woman. The datum "twelve years" emphasizes how longstanding the problem has been. All avenues of healing known to her have been tried, and all resources exhausted, only to receive the dividend of a worse condition (vv. 25–26). Such a poignant description prepares the way for Mark's audience to appreciate how astonishing her eventual healing was.

The woman's action indicates she wants to touch Jesus' robe surreptitiously, not wishing for attention (vv. 27–28). This is because in the Jewish context, this woman is regarded as chronically impure, and whatever she touches will be impure too. For her then to be present in a crowd is already scandalous, not to mention touching a holy healer. Her action, while scandalous, actually sets the stage for a powerful theological theme to be disclosed.

The healing is immediate, in contrast to all the futile remedies she has tried (v. 29). It is also palpable, because she can feel it in her body. What is however much more significant is the effect on Jesus. He senses that power has gone out of him, and asks who has touched his clothes (v. 30). Since the crowd is pressing upon him, this appears to be a rather silly question, and Jesus' disciples think exactly that (v. 31). However, the point of the Markan story is that it is only one particular touch that draws forth power from Jesus: the touch of the impure. The usual Jewish notion is that the impure corrupts the pure whenever the two come into contact. This is why measures must be taken to protect the pure from ritual contamination. This story expresses the reverse: the pure cleanses the impure when the two meet. A further implication is that the boundaries that are enacted for the protection of purity are no longer needed. We have here a fistful of revolutionary ideas!

The fear of the woman is understandable (v. 33). She has done what is socially unacceptable. An impure person must not mingle with the crowd, as this will spread ritual impurity. She has contravened social and ritual codes in her desire to be healed.

However, faith must not be kept hidden. Hence, Jesus' insistent search for the person who has touched him (v. 32) is also designed to draw the woman out from the camouflaging crowd. Mark ends the story with the important words: "Your faith has healed (or 'saved') you" (v. 34). These words are also relevant for Jairus, as they can instruct him on the power of faith. This being the case, this sandwiched story is more than just an interlude. It contributes to the thickening plot of the story of Jairus.

The Test of Faith: the News of Death (5:35-40)

The interrupted story is resumed, with dire news coming from Jairus's household. His daughter has died, and hence, there is no need for the visit to be made (v. 35). All human experience teaches that the onset of death should be the cessation of all effort.

Significantly, Jesus ignores such logic. Instead, he exhorts Jairus to believe in the face of finality and the impossible (v. 36). These words express the main theme of the story. In the shadow of death, and going against the grain of typical human responses, Jesus challenges Jairus to believe. This is highly significant because Mark is recounting a resurrection miracle for the first time. The words also recall those that were spoken at the stilling of the storm (4:35–41), and the healing of the woman with a menstrual disorder. But can death, which is something far worse, be overcome? Together Jesus and Jairus make the journey, the conclusion of which offers either grief or joy.

Upon reaching the house, the sight of professional mourners[118] wailing for Jairus's daughter (v. 38) may have served to reinforce his sense of hopelessness. To moderns the employing of professional mourners may seem hypocritical, or at least strange. But such an arrangement could actually help the bereaved to vent their grief without fear of embarrassment.

Jesus' statement that the girl is asleep has a double meaning (v. 39). The language of sleep is often used in the Bible as a euphemism for death (Dan 12:2), and this should be the interpretation here. Mark's narrative is certainly about a miracle being performed and not a misunderstanding being cleared. Behind this euphemism lay a powerful theological idea: death is not final, since Jesus has the power to raise dead people. However, the statement is understood in the literal sense by the characters in the story and hence, it engenders scorn (vv. 39–40). All this may have raised further doubt for Jairus. His faith is challenged. Has he done the right thing by trusting Jesus?

The Vindication of Faith: the Raising of Jairus's Daughter (5:41–43)

In the girl's room with a small group,[119] Jesus takes her by the hand and utters the Aramaic words, "*Talitha koum!*" which Mark translates for his audience as "Little girl, I say to you, get up." This is the first time that Mark inserts Aramaic words into his narrative. There are three other instances where Aramaic words are retained: *ephphatha* in 7:34, *abba* in 14:36, and of course the *eloi eloi lama sabachthani* of 15:34. What may be the significance of recording this Aramaic utterance here? Scholars are puzzled, as no theological theme may be found.[120] Probably this is a detail that has remained

---

118. We may call them thus for the following reasons. First of all, Jesus throws them out (v. 40). It is hard to envisage Jesus' doing this if they were members of the family. Secondly, the really bereaved would not have derided a statement offering hope (v. 40). The same would not be true for professional mourners. Thirdly, it was common practice for those who could afford it to hire professional mourners. See Culpepper 2007: 177–78.

119. Mark does not explain why only three among Jesus' twelve apostles are allowed into the room. Presumably these have a special relationship with Jesus (the inner circle), and constitute his most important witnesses.

120. Marcus thinks the use of a foreign language is part of the repertoire of ancient faith healing techniques, and also that its presence heightens mystery (Marcus 2000:

ingrained vividly in an eyewitness's mind. The dead girl responds, rises, and walks about. Jairus's faith in Jesus is vindicated.

We are also informed by Mark that Jesus does not want this miracle to be published abroad (v. 43). This means that those who derided him will be left guessing whether a miracle has occurred or a misunderstanding cleared. This fits in well with the theme of secrecy in Mark's Gospel.

Mark's Achievement with the Cycle of Four Miracle Stories

With the cycle of four miracle stories (4:35—5:43), Mark has gone beyond simply depicting Jesus as a miracle worker. He has succeeded in showing Jesus in more dramatic and spectacular terms. All this makes the question of his identity more urgent. Who is this person who can control forces associated with the primeval chaos, tame a legion of evil forces, cleanse the chronically impure, and raise the dead?

Alongside this urgent question chimes the theme of faith. Will faith be put in Jesus when circumstances seem to indicate otherwise: when boisterous waves break upon the bow; when the majority reject him; when all human ability fails in solving a medical problem; and when all hopes are gone because death has come about? The words "Do not be afraid, only believe" (5:36) are absolutely apt, and serve also as an exhortation to faith.

This cycle then brings together in creative fashion the themes of Jesus' identity and faith in him. This fits hand in glove with the earlier emphasis in the collection of parables (4:1–34) about the hidden nature of the kingdom. If the kingdom is hidden, faith is certainly the needed response.

THE REJECTION AT NAZARETH (6:1–6A)

Mark has not forgotten the staggering message he has conveyed in 4:10–12, regarding the purpose of parables. He follows his collection of four miracles (4:35—5:43) with an episode of rejection (6:1–6a), highlighting yet again the obduracy theme. What makes this more poignant is that the rejection comes from the people who are from the same hometown as Jesus. Of course, the alert listener would know this was not a new twist to the plot. Already in chapter 3 Jesus was portrayed as a stumbling block even to his own family members.

363; cf. also Collins 2007: 286). However, the fact that Mark provides a translation would mean that he is intent on removing the mysterious element, and the language used, though foreign to Greek speakers, is native to the characters of the story.

Mark does not name the town, but given the toponym in 1:9 and 1:24, we may with justification conclude that it is Nazareth. Interestingly, this is the only story in Mark that is located in Nazareth.

The story is set on a Sabbath day, with Jesus teaching in a synagogue (v. 2). This may be construed as the community's wishing to honor him. Or it is for them to hear for themselves his message that has brought him acclaim in other towns and villages. As it is also true in previous episodes, Jesus' teaching amazes his own townspeople. But what appears to be a positive note actually contains latent misgivings. Words of wisdom and works of wonder certainly have astonishing qualities (these are associated with the ideal Davidic ruler or Messiah; cf. Isa 11:2; *Pss Sol* 17:23), but what Jesus' townsfolk cannot accept is that these are coming from someone they know. Astonishing claims and familiar neighbors are not allowed to coexist in the minds of many people, especially for an ancient Semitic village where everyone supposedly knew everybody.[121] Jesus is known to them simply as the son of Mary, and a carpenter at that. The listing of the names of Jesus' siblings serves to emphasize this familiarity (v. 3). Incidentally, all this means Jesus could not have performed many miracles before his public ministry, otherwise the amazement of the people would not have made much sense. This contradicts many childhood stories of Jesus in the apocryphal gospels.[122]

The above reconstruction of what could have led to Jesus' rejection by his own townspeople is given confirmation by Jesus' own assessment of the problem bedeviling all this skepticism (v. 4). The third person pronoun is emphasized: "A prophet is not without honor except in *his* hometown, among *his* relatives and in *his* household." Similar sayings are found in the cultures surrounding Palestine. Apollonious of Tyana (first century AD) remarks that "Until now my own country alone ignores me" (*Epistle* 44). The sentiment resonates also with much of the experience of OT prophets. Stories abound of their rejection by their own people. This allows us an inroad into another aspect of Jesus' self-understanding. He aligns himself with the prophets.[123]

As the result of unbelief, few miracles are performed (v. 5). Such a statement should not be taken as an indication that Jesus is powerless to perform miracles when faith is not present because this makes nonsense of the miracle of the stilling of the storm in 4:35–41. Mark's language may

---

121. Similar sayings are found in the cultures surrounding Palestine. Bultmann mentions an Arabic proverb that laments, "The piper has no friends in his own town." See Bultmann 1963: 31.

122. E.g., the stories in the *Protevangelium of James*.

123. On the theme of Jesus as a prophet, see the treatment of Allison 1998; and Keener 2009: 238–55.

be strong, but he should not be expected to contradict his own paramount interest of showing that Jesus' miracles stem from his own authority. The explanation of Glöckner should be considered seriously: unbelief makes a miracle not so much impossible as meaningless, and therefore in most cases futile.[124]

It bears mentioning that there is something significant in the way that Jesus was described (v. 3). Jesus is called Mary's son, which is somewhat peculiar. Indeed, nowhere else in the canonical Gospels is Jesus called as such (cf. Luke 4:22; John 1:45; 6:42 where he is known as "son of Joseph"). It may be that some sort of derision is implied (i.e., Jesus was regarded as an illegitimate child, and Mark is alluding to the virgin birth of Jesus, which is perniciously reinterpreted by those who do not believe in this claim).[125] Alternatively, it may indicate that Joseph is dead and so it becomes possible to call a son by his mother's name (cf. 3:31). However, the usual practice is still to identify the son by the name of his deceased father (see b.Yoma 38b).[126]

The episode ends with a description of Jesus' amazement (v. 6), answering the amazement of the townspeople (v. 2). The datum of Jesus' amazement is found only here in Mark's Gospel, which may be construed ironically. Lack of faith in Jesus is the really amazing thing, especially by people who should know him better. Once again, Mark ends his cycle of stories on a downbeat. But all this becomes a foil to the importance of faith.

Mission Furthered and Martyrdom Foreshadowed (6.6b–30)

The sending out of the Twelve for mission, and their return to give a report to Jesus, frame the story of the death of John the Baptist. Through the intercalation of stories, Mark also ties up some loose ends. In the earlier chapters, Mark's audience was informed there were two aspects to the call of disciples: to be Jesus' envoys to extend his ministry (1:16–20; 3:14–15), and also to be with him (3:14) in order that they may receive instruction and training. The latter aspect has been well developed (see especially 4:10, 34), but not the former. This is precisely what Mark makes good at this juncture. Furthermore, although Mark has mentioned the arrest of John the Baptist earlier (1:14), he did not describe the circumstances leading to it. This lack

---

124. Glöckner 1979: 81.

125. Wilson 1995: 188. See the judicious discussion in Marcus, especially the refutation that the matronym is used because Jesus' siblings had a different mother (Marcus 2000: 374–75).

126. Cf. McArthur 1973: 38–58 in which he proposes that no slur was intended. But this is untenable. See the apt comments of Marcus 2000: 375.

is remedied now, but in a way that gives it an ominous ring: Jesus' fate is expected to be quite similar to John's.

The Twelve Sent (6:6b–13)

The Twelve are sent out in pairs (v. 7), probably in line with the tradition that two witnesses are needed to validate a testimony (cf. Deut 17:6). There may also be a practical reason: a companion provides encouragement and support (cf. Eccl 4:9–12). Not surprisingly, it was a Jewish custom to send official representatives in pairs (*b. Sanh.* 26a, 43a). The Twelve may therefore be construed as the envoys of Jesus, bearing testimony to his word and deed. In relation to this, the task of exorcism is emphasized (v. 7). We have seen how this activity characterizes Jesus' ministry as that which inducts the kingdom. Verses 12–13 show that this activity has correlates: exorcism takes place alongside kingdom preaching and healing.

The instructions given to the Twelve are ascetically stringent, and the emphasis appears to be on mobility (i.e., theirs is a task that demands quick travelling and not lengthy tarrying [vv. 8–11]). What is allowed—staff, sandals and tunic (but not an extra one)—serves mainly this function, although self-preservation is also in view. So urgent is the task that the basic necessity of food and shelter must be sought from those who would be hospitable to them. Seen this way, the rationale for such stringent instructions becomes transparent. They are given in anticipation of a swift and hazardous mission.

For the unwelcoming or intransigent, the Twelve are to shake the dust off their feet when they leave, as a symbolic gesture and testimony against such people (v. 11). The rabbis were known to have shaken dust off their feet upon leaving Gentile territory, to avoid carrying defilement back to Israel or their homes (*m. 'Ohol.* 2:3; *m. Toh.* 4:5). Probably a similar intention may be posited of the action commanded by Jesus. Their action effectively means that those who reject the message are regarded as defiling outsiders to the kingdom of God.[127] In this regard, the action serves also as a testimony against them (cf. Acts 13:51; 18:6).

Much of what the Twelve do in their mission (v. 13) has a parallel in Jesus' ministry. There is proclamation of repentance (cf. 1:15), exorcism, and healing (cf. 1:32). The anointing of the sick is new. Anointing is often performed with olive oil, which is believed to have medicinal qualities. It probably symbolizes God's presence—and in this instance, healing presence—and special care.[128]

---

127. SB 1.571.

128. There is no evidence that Jesus performed anointing to heal but it is a practice

Excursus: Discrepancies Over What is Allowed

The items (staff and sandals) that are allowed the Twelve in Mark's account are expressly denied them in the parallel account in Matthew (10:10). The parallel in Luke mentions only the forbidding of a staff, and is silent over whether sandals are allowed (Luke 9:3; but sandals are forbidden in Luke 10:4). There appears to be no fully satisfactory solution to this discrepancy. The popular ones appeal to contextual or grammatical explanations. One theory posits that Mark has altered the originally stringent forms of Jesus, which are attested in Matthew and Luke, to suit the changed circumstances of his time.[129] (Even if this were the case, it would not help those seeking harmonization). Another argues that what Matthew and Luke actually mean is that the disciples are not allowed to carry a second staff, or a second pair of sandals.[130] (If so, why don't Matthew and Luke make this clear?) As important as harmonizing the parallel accounts may be, our concern here is with Mark's message.

The Reaction of Herod Antipas (6:14–16)

These verses speak of Jesus' increasing popularity, leading to speculations about his identity. Herod Antipas's reaction is highlighted and this prepares the way for the narration to follow. Although he is given the title of "king" here, Augustus Caesar actually refused to grant him the said title, but had him conferred instead as tetrarch (derived from a Greek word which means "ruler of a quarter;" cf. Matt 14:1).[131] Such a technical nicety, important to politicians, is of no great interest to Mark or many members of his audience. In his territory, Antipas calls the shots.

What is reported amounts to nothing less than John the Baptist's being raised from the dead in Antipas's opinion (v. 16). There is more than meets the eye in this simple datum. First of all, Jesus' growing fame is due, in part, to the work of the Twelve. In other words, the success of the Twelve is implied, even though it is not narrated.

---

prevalent in the early Church (Jas 5.14).

129. Boring 2006: 175.
130. Carson 1984: 245; but refuted by France 2002: 249.
131. On the material evidence, see Braund 1992: 3:160.

Secondly, there must have been some sort of "family resemblance" between the ministry of Jesus and his disciples and that of John the Baptist to warrant the remark that the latter has been raised from the dead. Verse 14 suggests the two may be associated via powerful deeds. Unfortunately there is no record of John ever performing a miracle (cf. John 10:41). That said, the verse may simply mean John has become more powerful after he has been, presumably, raised from the dead. All this dovetails with the opening verses of Mark, where John's ministry is described as the beginning of the gospel of Jesus Christ.

Thirdly, this particular detail is given to pave the way for a flashback that explains how John the Baptist came to be imprisoned and executed. This is one loose thread that was left hanging after 1:14, which Mark now ties up.

Some other popular responses are given in v. 15: Elijah or one of the prophets. This is the first time Elijah is mentioned in Mark's Gospel; Jesus will be associated with Elijah again in 8:28. This name also appears in the account of the Transfiguration (9:4–5), and the dialogue between Jesus and his disciples that follows. In that dialogue, John the Baptist is regarded as Elijah (9:11–13). There was great expectation among the Jews for the return of Elijah (cf. Mal 4:5–6) to herald the eschaton.[132]

The statement about Jesus' being "a prophet or one of the prophets" shows that in popular thought there are at least two kinds of prophets: a general one and a classical one. The NIV attempts to make this distinction even clearer with the phrase "of long ago," but it is not found in the Greek text. The classical ones were deemed pre-eminent, as they were OT personages who were reformers and doers of mighty deeds. The line of classical prophets was thought to have ceased until the great day of restoration (cf. 1 Macc 4:46; 14:41).

Flashback: John's Death (6:17–29)

This flashback provides the circumstances leading to John's arrest and his subsequent death. John was arrested for criticizing Herod's marriage to Herodias, the wife of his half-brother, Herod Philip (not Philip the tetrarch). There is a parallel account in Josephus (*Antiquities* 118:116–19) and much has been discussed about the supposed discrepancies between the accounts. They revolve around three issues: (i) the reason for John's arrest; (ii) the location of his prison; and (iii) the name of Herodias's previous husband. As interesting as this discussion may be, our interest is in Mark, and the issue

---

132. Cf. Collins 2007: 304.

will therefore be treated in an excursus. Suffice it here to say that Mark's account is historically credible and is crafted adroitly to hold the audience's interest. The story makes a moral point in the setting of wantonness, lust and a macabre execution.

Excursus: Mark and Josephus on John the Baptist

Josephus records that the main reason for John's arrest was Antipas's fear of a possible uprising (*Antiquities* 18:118). This may be construed as a political reason. Mark seems to suggest a moral reason instead. But the two may be harmonized without great difficulty, since in Jewish culture there is no dichotomy between public office and private life, and morality is seen to be an inseparable component of politics. This is even more so if the ruler is deemed an outsider. So it is eminently possible that John's criticism of Antipas's marriage, illegitimate from the standpoint of Jewish morality, might provide the tinder for an already tense situation to become explosive, especially when the Herods's rule was unwelcome by most Jews. Indeed, Antipas's marriage to Herodias did lead to tension between him and Aretas IV, the king of the Nabateans and the father of the wife whom Antipas divorced. Antipas would not want internal problems to surface, as he was already facing an external foe. John's criticism of the marriage by using a moral principle strongly held by the Jews could do just that. Hence, Antipas believed some sort of preemptive action would be in order.

Josephus also mentions that John's incarceration was at Machaerus in Peraea, where he would also be executed (*Antiquities* 18:119). This datum is quite peculiar, as Josephus informs us just a few lines before that this was under the control of Aretas IV (*Antiquities* 18:112). Why would a purportedly seditious element be placed by Antipas, and a birthday banquet held, at a stronghold that belonged to someone (Aretas IV) who was having a quarrel with him? Mark's location appears to be more logical, as v. 21 suggests that the banquet was held in Galilee. However, this is an inference that is drawn from the presence of Galilean noblemen (v. 21), as Mark does not state explicitly where the banquet was held. Given such uncertainties over the data, it would be premature to speak of Mark's unreliability.

Finally, there appears to be confusion over the name of Herodias's husband. Mark calls him Philip, while Josephus calls him Herod, and never Philip (*Antiquities* 18:109). Interestingly, Mark never mentions Philip the

Tetrarch (although Luke does in Luke 3:1, but he does not name the first husband of Herodias!) and whenever Josephus refers to Philip, it is always Philip the Tetrarch. To make matters worse, Josephus informs us that Philip the Tetrarch was married to Salome, the daughter of Herodias and Herod (*Antiquities* 18:136)! In the light of all this evidence, some scholars who give pre-eminence to Josephus's account, think that Mark was confused in naming Herodias's first husband as Philip. But this is unwarranted, as first of all, Herod the Great's family tree is actually quite complicated. Moreover, "Herod" can be a personal name or a family name in Josephus's account. There is no reason why the first husband of Herodias could not have more than one name. A simplified family tree of Herod the Great, derived from J. Marcus, may make all this clear:[133]

Diagram 4
Simplified Family Tree of Herod the Great

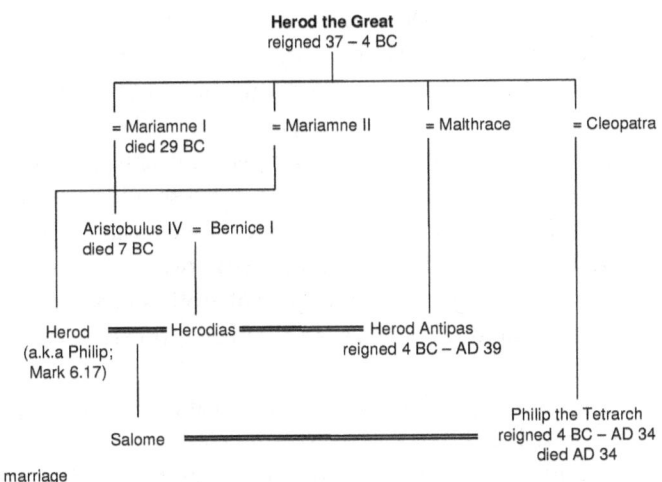

What was exactly the reason for John the Baptist's opposition to Antipas's marriage to Herodias (v. 18)? It was not because it entailed Herod's divorcing his first wife. Divorces were allowed under Jewish law (Deut 24:1-4). Nor was it because Herodias, a woman, had initiated divorce proceedings. She did not have that right under Jewish law, but it was permissible under

133. Marcus 2000: 394.

Roman law. Rather, it was because the levitical rules governing marriage (Lev 18:16; 20:21) did not allow a man to marry the divorced wife of a brother who was still alive.[134] This explains why John's criticism was powerful: it came from a man respected for his religious views. Furthermore, it had great political liability for Herod Antipas because he was regarded as not properly Jewish, and therefore not properly the ruler of the Jews (cf. Josephus *War* 1:123; Josephus *Antiquities* 14:9). Any flouting of Jewish sensibilities would make his position even more untenable.

In Mark's account, the prime movers are two women (something which Josephus does not mention): a mother and a daughter. There is a textual problem here. Some early manuscripts (ℵ B D) read "his daughter Herodias,"[135] instead of "the daughter of Herodias."[136] The latter reading is attested later (A C Θ). If we follow the reading which has the earlier attestation—and the harder reading—Mark is saying it was Antipas's daughter, by the name of Herodias, who performed. But the account seems to suggest it was Herodias's daughter who performed. The possibility that Herodias's daughter was also known as Herodias seems rather remote. Moreover, if Josephus is reliable at this point, Herodias's daughter should be called Salome (*Antiquities* 18:136), who was also (later?) married to Philip the Tetrarch. Hence, the NIV's choice is probably correct.

Semitic decorum would not usually permit a daughter, let alone a royal one, to dance to please banqueting men. What should be remembered, however, is that Herod's household was highly Romanized.[137] This being the case, it would follow Roman customs much more readily than Jewish ones. Roman customs allowed for flagrant display of eroticism. The dance could not be an ordinary kind, as it would not explain Antipas's over-generous offer in v. 23.

Antipas's offer of up to half of his kingdom appears at first sight to be an incredible reward for a dance. However, three mitigating factors must be borne in mind. First, the expression may be a hyperbole and is not therefore meant to be taken literally. In this case, it connotes a good offer rather than denoting a mathematically precise fifty percent of the kingdom (cf. Esth 5:3, 6; 7:2). Secondly, it is well-known that drunken men often made promises that were exaggerated, with no intention of fulfillment. Finally, it was not uncommon in those days even for sober royalty to make extremely

---

134. Josephus levelled a similar criticism, but targeting mainly Herodias, in *Antiquities* 18: 136.

135. The Greek is *tēs thygatros autou Hērōdiados*,

136. The Greek is *tēs thygartros autēs tēs Hērōdiados*.

137. See Hoehner 1972: 156–57. Cf. Bauckham's study with respect in the names adopted in the Herodians circles in Bauckham 2002: 202–20.

generous promises in order to boast of their wealth or generosity (Herodotus, *Histories* 9:109).

Modern readers may also be puzzled by Mark's recounting that she finally asks for John the Baptist's head on a platter, as advised by her mother. Why did she settle for this when she could have so much more? A moment's reflection will show that she was actually acting prudently. As mentioned earlier, oriental monarchs were known for making generous offers at rash moments (perhaps to demonstrate their great generosity in front of honored guests) or in a state of drunkenness, which they actually had no intention of fulfilling. If Herodias's daughter had greedily asked for half of Herod's kingdom, the request might be granted in word, but in actual fact she would not receive it. There were ways to ensure this. Stories of mysterious deaths often emanated from royal courts. So she was wise to consult her mother, since the latter, being intimate with Antipas, must have known what might safely be asked. Asking for the execution of John the Baptist was a request that could be fulfilled straightaway, without much loss to Antipas, and would rid the family of a pesky foe. The macabre detail of having John's head on a platter is not mentioned in the suggestion of Herodias in 6:24b, and may perhaps be construed as the dancing girl's own contribution. Putting John's head on a platter suggests it was part of the banqueting menu. Such black humor indicates the sort of depravity that was at work.

Antipas's predicament is also historically credible. He had a fascination for John, but this did not translate to loyalty (vv. 19–20). Moreover, any postponing of the girl's request would bring about a great loss of face for him, as important and powerful guests were present. The execution was thus carried out, and John's corpse was later collected by his disciples for burial.

The Return of the Twelve (6:30)

The return of the Twelve provides the end-framing component to the story of John's death. Their work has been effective, which has also led Antipas to wonder whether John the Baptist was raised from the dead. The narration of this return prepares the way for the next episode: the story of the feeding of the 5,000.

MIRACLES AROUND THE LAKE (6:31–56)

Two miracle stories taking place around the lake are narrated here. The first is the feeding of the 5,000, a miracle Jesus performs using just five loaves and two fish (6:31-44). The second describes Jesus walking on water in the midst of a storm. This results in great fear among his disciples, which Jesus also allays (6:45-52). These two miracles may be known as nature miracles. They prompt the question about Jesus' identity. In this regard they may be seen as a further development of the theme first introduced in 4:35-41, which is held in abeyance until now. The collection of miracle stories is concluded by a brief description of Jesus' healing ministry in Gennesaret and other towns (6:53-56).

The Feeding of the 5,000 (6:31-44)

The abortive attempt at ensuring the disciples have a time of quiet and rest sets the stage for this miracle story (vv. 31-33). So great is the enthusiasm for Jesus that the crowd succeed in reaching Jesus' intended destination on foot, before he and his party arrive by boat. How they managed to outrun the boat—and taking a much longer distance at that—we will never know. Not surprisingly, many commentators think Mark is exaggerating here.[138] Be that as it may, Mark certainly intends to depict the great enthusiasm of the crowds.

The sight of a great crowd eagerly awaiting him leads Jesus to have compassion on them (v. 34), as they appeared to him as sheep without a shepherd. This simple description is latent with great meaning. First, the verb *splanchnizomai* (which means "having compassion") is not common in Mark (here and in 8:2, and possibly 1:41). Whenever it is found, it is used of Jesus. He is thus presented as the compassionate one. Instead of regarding the crowd as a nuisance, he cares for them. This datum must be kept in mind as we attempt to decipher the meaning of the miracle. Secondly, the image of sheep without shepherd provides the hermeneutical key for what is to follow. It is also a common biblical description of Israel when she is bereft of capable and godly leadership (Num 27:17; 1 Kings 22:17; Isa 13:14; Ezek 34:5; Zech 10:2). Indeed, the restoration of Israel may be described as the raising up of the one shepherd, who is God's vicegerent, to lead his flock (Ezek 34:23; 37:24; Mic 5:4). The miracle of the feeding of the 5,000 answers such a hope. Many details of the story also convey that this miracle is profoundly significant, which will be examined in the course of the commentary.

Ever watchful of time, the disciples suggest to Jesus that the crowd should be dismissed in order that they may get food for themselves (vv. 35-36). The reply of Jesus that they should be feeding the crowd is astonishing,

---

138. France 2002: 264-65; Marcus 2000: 417.

because it will take 200 denarii (i.e., eight months' wages), to do so (vv. 37–38). This rather unreasonable challenge should not be understood as being spoken tongue-in-cheek, or as a foil to revealing how stupendous the miracle will be. Instead, it should be regarded as indicating what is to be part and parcel of the disciples' work. As envoys of Jesus, they are to minister to those in need. But how can their paltry resources be enough to feed so many? What happens next is familiar to many Bible readers—five loaves and two fish are used to feed 5,000—but there are layers of deeper meaning found in the details, which will be explicated below.

The Greek text of v. 39 presents interesting possibilities. The word used for the people's posture is *anaklinō*. To a Gentile audience this is certainly the posture for a banquet.[139] For a Jewish audience, it has the added possibility of recalling the posture for the Passover.[140] Furthermore, the Greek word used for the groupings is *symposia*, a word occurring only once in the whole of the NT. The word means literally "drinking together," and it was used originally to designate a drinking party. By extension, it later carried the meaning of a banquet. A counter-banquet to that which was held by Herod Antipas in 6:21 is being presented.[141]

The datum that the grass is green is also significant, and it is found only in Mark's account of this feeding story. In Galilee grass grows in the wilderness only during springtime, as this is the time of rainfall.[142] Spring is also the season in which the Passover is celebrated.[143] Mark may be presenting Jesus as the shepherd who leads his flock to green pastures, recalling the Shepherd Psalm (Ps 23).[144]

The word used to describe the groupings in v. 40 is *prasiai*. This is yet again a word which occurs only once in the entire NT, and its usage here is puzzling. In secular Greek it actually means flowerbeds, and is never used to describe a grouping of people.[145] Perhaps Mark uses it for vividness: the people are grouped together in an orderly way like flowerbeds. Some scholars have also argued that the division into fifties and hundreds recalls the action of Moses in Exod 18:21, where he divides Israel into such groupings

---

139. BDAG s.v.

140. Jeremias 1996a: 48–49.

141. Cf. Fowler 1981: 85–86.

142. See Marcus 2000: 408.

143. John's account explicitly mentions that the miracle takes place near the Passover (John 6:4).

144. Guelich 1989: 341.

145. BDAG s.v.

for military purposes.¹⁴⁶ If this is the case, an Exodus typology may also be said to be at work.

Although some commentators have regarded the actions described in v. 41 as alluding to the Eucharist, it must equally be said that this was the typical action of the head of a Jewish household during meals.¹⁴⁷

The munificence of the miracle¹⁴⁸ is being emphasized in v. 42. Not only are the people fed, they are also "filled to the brim," as the Greek word *chortazomai* indicates. Furthermore, the disciples picked up twelve basketfuls of broken pieces. The word for "basket" here is the Greek *kophinos*, and it refers to a distinctively Jewish receptacle.¹⁴⁹

It has been suggested that the numbers in the story are also symbolical. It is highly plausible that the number five alludes to the Torah. Moreover, Jews sometimes compare the Torah with bread.¹⁵⁰ The number twelve may be symbolic of the twelve tribes of Israel, and the underlying theological message is that these twelve tribes are reconstituted through the work of the eschatological shepherd.

It may be instructive to mention here that some scholars have detected echoes of the exploits of the prophets Elijah and Elisha in this episode (1 Kings 17:8–16; 2 Kings 4:42–44).¹⁵¹ While this cannot be totally ruled out, it is important to emphasize the dissimilarities. A large crowd is fed in this episode and not just one widow. Furthermore, the description of the crowd as sheep without shepherd suggests a different connection. Indeed, the next episode of Jesus' walking on the water, which is connected with this feeding miracle, shows that the prophetic connection, if it is present at all, is at best secondary.

We may now sum up the significance of the miracle as a whole.¹⁵² The datum provided by 6:4 is critical. As explained above, this is an image recalling Israel bereft of godly leadership, with the hope that God would one day

---

146. Collins 2007: 324–26; Marcus 2000: 419.

147. Jeremias 1966a: 108–9.

148. Feeding miracles are known in Judaism, but not on such a scale. In *b. Ta'an.* 24b-25a some bread is said to have appeared miraculously in Hanina ben Dosa's empty oven.

149. *Juvenal* 3:14; 6:54; see BDAG for description. We are not sure of its actual size.

150. Cf. Borgen 1965: 104; Marcus 2000: 407.

151. Collins 2007: 319–20.

152. It has been suggested that no miracle actually took place (Myers). Instead, what happened was that the miserly hearts of the crowd were stricken by a boy's contribution (cf. John 6:9), and everyone took out food he had surreptitiously hidden to share with those seating next to him. This is unscholarly in the extreme, as this theory aims not to exegete what Mark's narrative means, but to defend a naturalistic worldview. Clearly, Mark intends his audience to understand a miracle has taken place.

raise up his shepherd (Num 27:7; 1 Kings 22:17; Ezek 34:5-16; Zech 13:7). We should also note Mark's emphasis that the event takes place in the wilderness (*erēmos*). This is mentioned thrice (vv. 31, 32, and 35). Indeed, this detail is found only in Mark's Gospel and not in the parallel accounts of the other three Gospels. When all this is combined with the Jewish speculation of a re-enactment of the manna miracle (2 *Bar* 29:8; *Mekilta on Exod* 16:5; cf. Rev 2:7), we have the components that make up the significance of this episode in Mark. Jesus is here presented as the messianic shepherd who would lead the people on a greater Exodus, during which their needs would be met in miraculous ways.[153] The messianic aspect of this miracle, while implicit in Mark, is clearly expressed in the Johannine account where the crowd is described as seeking forcibly to make Jesus *king* (6:4-15). In Mark's hands, however, the story is told to emphasize the *compassion* of the messianic shepherd.

The question is often asked whether this episode also looks forward to the Last Supper in which Jesus again takes bread, blesses and breaks it, and distributes it to those partaking of the meal. In that later account, the Last Supper is also presented as that which foreshadows the messianic banquet to be served when the kingdom is consummated. All this means that while Jesus now makes use of what has been offered to feed the crowd, he will later offer himself to feed the world. The similar words used for Jesus' action with respect to the bread may support such a thesis. In both accounts (see 6:41 and 14:22), there is a taking (*lambanō*), a blessing (*eulogeō*), a fragmenting (*kataklaō* in 6:41, but *klaō* in 14:22) and a distributing (*didōmi*). Moreover, the datum of the green grass points to spring, the season in which the Jewish Passover is celebrated. Such an attractive hypothesis is not without its problems. First, the Passover connection of the feeding of the 5,000 is not explicit (only John's account in John 6:4 makes this plain). More importantly, Mark says nothing of the multiplication of wine or drink, and the datum that fish are also present does not quite square with a eucharistic symbolism. Finally, the action of blessing and breaking of bread is commonplace: the head of a household often does this during mealtimes. As fascinating as the suggestion may be, it is unclear whether Mark intends it to be understood in this way.

---

153. It should be noted that *Pss Sol* 16.23-46 presents the Messiah as a shepherd.

Fusing the Horizons: Paltry Resources and a Needy World

Over the centuries, many readers have found in this episode the comforting thought of the multiplying power of God. More than that, it has also become an inspiration for many a Christian enterprise to be set up and kept running against all odds.

The Church is often confronted with the sheer scale of human need. When she looks at the physical resources that are available, the hiatus is so wide that none without faith will dare take up the call to answer this need. However, this episode instructs us that our paltry resources may be offered up to God to be blessed and multiplied for the benefit of the world. Mother Teresa's ministry is a fine example of this dynamic. A lone nun, without much, answered the need to minister to the poor and dying in Calcutta, which resulted in much attention and effort being given to such lost causes.

Lest it be missed, Mark also teaches through this episode that God does not "feed" his people out of a sheer miracle. Instead, he uses resources already present, paltry as they may be, and meets their needs through his servants, sometimes in spectacular ways and other times more mundane.

There is much that the Church can and must do. With God's multiplying power available, she should then be daring and venturing, not daunted by seemingly impossibilities. The entire world is our scope, but we can start with our immediate neighbors and neighborhoods.

Jesus Walks on Water (6:45-52)

This miracle story shares similar details with the earlier miracle of calming the storm in 4:35-41. In both accounts a late crossing of the lake takes place, strong winds blow, the disciples are terrified and bewildered at the end of the experience, and Jesus calms storms. However, the differences are telling: Jesus now walks on water and utters words suggestive of divine disclosure. In this respect, the identity of Jesus receives further development.

There is an interesting problem with respect to the locality. Luke tells us the feeding of the 5,000 takes place at Bethsaida (Luke 9:10). This has been identified as Bethsaida Julius on the northeastern shore of the lake. But in v. 45 Mark informs us the disciples are ordered to get to Bethsaida, after the 5,000 have been fed. They end up instead in Gennesaret, which is on the western shore (v. 53). A possible solution is to think of two Bethsaidas (i.e., Bethsaida Julius and the hypothetical "Bethsaida in Galilee"), but unfortunately there is no material evidence to support this.[154] Of course, if Mark's account is read on its own there will be no difficulty. We are not informed about where the journey started from; only that it ended up in Gennesaret, because their intention to go to Bethsaida was foiled by the high winds.

Focusing on the Markan story then, we notice first of all the puzzling actions of Jesus at the beginning of the episode (vv. 45–46). The disciples are bundled[155] into a boat and ordered to cross the lake by themselves to Bethsaida, while Jesus remains on land, to pray on a mountain. Mark later tells us expressly that Jesus is aware the disciples are struggling against a headwind all through the night, and yet nothing is done until the fourth watch (i.e., the hours just before dawn [6:47–48]). This implies Jesus is intentionally leaving his disciples to struggle for quite a while, which is rather peculiar.

The Romans divided the night—from dusk to dawn—into four watches (cf. Diodorus Siculus 19:26:1; Josephus *Antiquities* 18:356). The fourth watch (v. 48) would then be the hours just before dawn. Such a time note may carry a deeper significance, as in the OT and Jewish tradition dawn is the time connected with the coming of God's help (see especially Exod 14:24 and Ps 46:5; cf. *Joseph and Aseneth* 14:1–2).

In the history of interpretation, some rather curious explanations have been given to this episode which avoid reading supernatural elements in the narrative. Some suggest that Jesus was either wading through the surf near the hidden shore or walking on a sandbank. The disciples in their terror thought that he was walking on water.[156] Such a misunderstanding gave rise to the circulation of a miraculous account of Jesus' walking on water, which later reached Mark, the fallacy of which modern scholarship has managed to spot. All this ignores one thing: some of Jesus' disciples were experienced fishermen; they should be given credit for knowing whether or not they were just inches above the lakebed or a few yards from the shore. Indeed, no amount of naturalistic explanation or exegetical procedures can change the fact that Mark intends his audience to understand that a miracle is taking place.

---

154. It may possibly be identified as el-Araj, on the North-eastern shore of the lake, but convincing evidence for this is yet to be found. See Strange 1992: 1:692–93.

155. The Greek *anankazō* is strong, meaning "compel."

156. Taylor 1952: 327; cf. also Derrett 1981: 330–48.

The really puzzling thing, then, is not that Mark is narrating a spectacular miracle, but that he depicts Jesus as intending to pass the disciples by (v. 48). The NIV reading ("he was *about* to pass by them")[157] represents an amelioration of a difficult idea. However, by so doing it has obscured the significance of the event. The Greek phrase (*ēthelen parelthein autous*) actually means "he *intended* to pass them by," as *thelō* certainly denotes volition. The question then comes, "Why would Jesus intend to pass the disciples by, if his going to them by walking on the water was meant to help them?" Not surprisingly, it has been proposed that the easiest way out of this conundrum (without resorting to improbable theories such as Jesus' desiring to overtake his disciples in getting to the other shore in order to surprise them) is to think of the verb as representing the disciples' perspective on Jesus' action.[158] They thought he was trying to pass them by when actually he was not. If this were correct, Mark expressed it rather clumsily. But there is no reason to think Mark has been clumsy here. Once again, the OT background provides a plausible solution to the problem. The verb *parerchomai* (to pass by) is used almost like a technical term in the LXX for a divine epiphany. The seedbed for such a usage is Exod 33:17—34:8. In this account, the verb in question is used thrice—33:22 (twice) and 34:6—to depict God's passing by Moses (i.e., revealing his glory in a manner Moses has not seen before). Such a description of the divine epiphany is later utilized in the account of Elijah's coming before God at Mt Horeb (1 Kings 19:11-13). Moreover, the express mention of Jesus' walking on the water is meant to be a parallel to God's walking on the sea (Job 9:8; Ps 77:19; Hab 3:15; cf. Sir 24:5-6), which signifies his sovereignty over chaotic forces. All this provides the answer to Jesus' strange intention. This is to provide a theophany so as to encourage the disciples.[159]

Jesus' words "I am" in v. 50 further supports this interpretation. The Greek expression *egō eimi* in the LXX translates the Hebrew *'anî hû'*, which is used as the divine self-declaration of Israel's God, in contexts where his unique sovereignty as the one and only God is emphasized (Exod 3:14; Deut 32:39; Isa 41:4; 43:10-11). Not surprisingly, this divine self-declaration is also used in connection with commissioning or comforting because God's unique sovereignty is critical for assurance. Indeed, in Isaiah the words "I am" or the claim of God's sole supremacy are given to awaken faith in his people, and comfort them in their difficult undertaking. So they are often coupled with the encouraging "Fear not" or "Take heart" (e.g., Isa 41:10, 13;

---

157. My emphasis.
158. France 2002: 272.
159. Marcus 2000: 426.

43:1, 5 etc.). We should also note that the expression *'anî hû'* occurs in the Isaianic passages that speak of God's promise of deliverance through the waters of a second Exodus (Isa 43:1-25; 51:10-12). This motif is certainly relevant to Mark's Gospel, which utilizes significantly the second Exodus concept. To be noted finally is that the expression is also related to the covenantal name of Yahweh. All this means that Jesus' use of these words, especially in the context of his walking on water, is theologically charged.[160]

Mark's message to his readers is now clear. He wants them to understand that as they struggle in "tumultuous waters" in obedience to Jesus' commands, they are to remember that he who commands is also he who, like God, walks on water and is present with them.

The security that comes with Jesus' presence is emphasized in vv. 51-52. The calming effect is immediate, and the disciples were greatly amazed (indicated by the Greek *en heautois*). Mark attributes their fear—or lack of faith—to the disciples' failure to understand the meaning of the feeding of the 5,000. This, in turn, is brought about by their hardness of heart, a condition dangerously close to that of the Pharisees (3:5). The reason given is rather mystifying, as Mark has not explicitly said what it is about the feeding story that should have strengthened the disciples' faith. Perhaps we may surmise that the disciples have forgotten Jesus is the compassionate eschatological shepherd, upon whom the disciples can rely for timely help.

Further Healings (6:53-56)

Apparently frustrated by the high wind, they end up in Gennesaret instead of Bethsaida. The name Gennesaret refers not to a town, but to a strip of land between Tiberias and Capernaum,[161] on the western shore of the Sea of Galilee. Once Jesus steps on to shore, the crowds recognize him and start to flock to him, bringing with them the sick. Connecting with the idea from the story of the healing of the woman with chronic bleeding (5:27-30), Mark tells his audience that many beg Jesus to allow them to touch the edge of his cloak. So the stories of nature miracles end with the note that Jesus' popularity continues to grow.

REDEFINING THE UNCLEAN (7:1-23)

In the course of narrating some miracles, Mark has presented Jesus as relativizing Jewish purity regulations (e.g., 1:40-45; 5:1-20). In fact, in the

---

160. For a fine study on the use of this phrase, see Williams 2000.
161. Edwards 1992: 2:963.

case of the healing of a woman with a menstrual problem (5:25–34), the theological message given was that purity should not recoil in the face of impurity, but should reach out to restore and heal. Such a revolutionary view of holiness would certainly have led to great controversies in first century Palestine. In recent memory, famous Jewish martyrs of the Maccabean period lost their lives precisely because of their unflinching loyalty to the purity code, especially the regulation banning consumption of pork. It was believed that such loyalty would induce God to come alongside the nation. Small Israel could then triumph over any big kingdom. Hence, purity issues were not simply about hygiene. Bound up with them were the triad of Torah, tradition, and politics, and as such they were loyalty indicators. What served as loyalty indicators could easily become *boundary markers*. Indeed, food was especially effective as a boundary marker, because eating together in ancient societies served also the function of social integration.

The Controversy Presented (7:1–13)

To indicate how high the stakes are, Mark informs his audience that a delegation of scribes from Jerusalem is sent to hear Jesus on this matter, together with local Pharisees (v. 1). The other instance where a delegation of religious leaders came from Jerusalem to observe Jesus is found in 3:22, where the important issue of the power behind Jesus' exorcism was discussed. The present controversy is sparked when Jesus' disciples were seen to be eating food with unwashed hands. This is not because of negligent hygiene. Rather, it ignores the provisions of the purity code, as interpreted by the Pharisees and their sympathetic scribes.[162]

Mark's parenthetical remarks in vv. 3–4 indicate that he expects most members of his audience to be Gentiles. The phrase "all the Jews" have caused some difficulty. From the extant evidence, we may gather that while the Pharisees did have a special concern for ritual purity,[163] it is not strictly accurate to attribute such a concern to all Jews. However, the Pharisees did have a great influence over ordinary Jews.[164] Their influence might be regarded as significant enough for Mark to present this practice as a broadly Jewish phenomenon to his Gentile audience.

Mark uses an unusual word to describe the washing of hands in v. 3: the Greek *pygmē*. It literally means "fist," and this is where the trouble starts.

---

162. Baumgarten 1987: 5–17.

163. Neusner 1973: 80; but objections were raised by Sanders 1992: 428–43. The overall case of Neusner remains cogent.

164. Marcus 2000: 440.

What would washing hands with a fist mean? Not surprisingly, some Greek manuscripts either omit the word, or substitute it with the similar sounding *pykna*, which means "often" or "thoroughly." The latter is rightly regarded by many scholars as a secondary reading, introduced into the manuscript tradition to solve a difficulty. So if *pygmē* is the original reading, what does it mean? One proposal is that it refers to a washing that was done up to the wrist (i.e., the fist may be taken to extend up to the wrist), and *m. Yad.* 2.3 pronounces that the hands are rendered clean by the pouring of water over them up to the wrist. Another possibility is to interpret the word as referring to a fistful of water that was used in ceremonial washing (see *m. Yad.* 1.1). And finally, it has been suggested that what is meant is attested in modern Jewish practice: washing the hands while they are in a cupped shape. Whatever its meaning, what is clear is that it is performed for ceremonial reason, and with this we must be content.

The charge made is that the disciples did not follow the tradition of the elders (v. 5). This tradition is a result of interpretation of texts that has developed, discussed and tested over the many years of study and practice of Torah (cf. Josephus *Antiquities* 13:297). One of its goals may be described as "fencing" the Torah (i.e., creating a buffer zone between the explicit requirements of Torah and day-to-day practice), such that if the elements of the tradition were observed, transgression of Torah would definitely be prevented (*m. Abot* 1.1). In this particular instance, the Torah regulation which is most directly relevant is that which commands the priests ceremonially to wash their hands before offering sacrifices (Exod 30:18–21; 40:30–32). The extension of this principle to the laity—to cover all foods consumed, and not just sacrifices made to God—was a later scribal development in the interest of making all Israelites as pure as the priests.[165] Purity formed a key component of the agenda of the Pharisees, which was connected with their expectation that God would mercifully come to the plight of the nation and deliver her from her enemies.

Excursus: Food and the Tradition of the Elders

Eating common food with unwashed hands does not contradict the Torah. Mark does not negate this principle but states instead that it contradicts the tradition of the elders. What causes difficulty for biblical scholars is that there is no evidence for such a tradition in the Mishnah. Indeed what is made clear in is that common hands could not communicate defilement to

---

165. Neusner 1973: 80.

ordinary food, but only to consecrated food that priests eat (*m. Para.* 11:5). That said, it would be premature to think that Mark has been unreliable in this matter. First, a good case may be made for there being a relaxation of strict regulations after the two tragic wars fought with Rome in AD 66–70 and 132–35. So what is written in the Mishnah does not fully reflect what took place in the years before these two great wars. Secondly, it is a well-nigh consensus among scholars that the Pharisees may be typified as a movement which sought to extend the purity of the temple to the home (see excursus on Pharisees). So for Pharisees to be particularly interested in this issue should not be surprising. Finally, the practice of praying with washed hands was widespread in the Diaspora (*Epistle of Aristeas* 305). Since prayers often preceded the partaking of food, eating with washed hands was the usual practice. This could itself become a boundary marker, separating the Jews from the Gentiles. All this means Mark can justifiably paint with a broad brush by including other Jews in this Pharisaic interest.

Jesus replies by quoting Isaiah (Isa 29:13) to show that what once obtained in the nation remains, albeit in a different form (vv. 6–8). In its original context, God was rebuking the Israelites for their superficial religious observances. In using this text, Jesus implies that this condition is present among his interlocutors, the religious leaders, who are also denounced as "hypocrites." The Greek word *hypocritēs* is used only once in Mark. Its rarity belies its importance, for the use of this word heightens the poignancy. It meant play-acting originally. Hence, tragically, what the Pharisees and some religious leaders are striving to achieve is illusory, possible only as a play on stage. According to the evidence available, Pharisees were often pejoratively described as such through the use of similar terms (Josephus *Antiquities* 17:41; 1QH 4:7–15).

Jesus' charge then is that although their practice conforms to the external requirements, their hearts are actually far from their original intent. The purity code was given by the God of Israel not for its own sake but to serve as a reminder of his holiness. A holy God can only be approached by a holy people and not by one who tries to circumvent the force of certain commandments.

As an instance of such play-acting, Jesus cites the provision which, after being developed by many years of traditioning, relates to the fifth commandment. The financial support of impoverished parents could be set aside by invoking the practice of "Corban" (see excursus). Jews understand that the fifth commandment entails the concrete practise of providing for parents. However, the "Corban" principle may be invoked to redirect God-given resources from their proper and compassionate use for selfish ends, in the name of devoting such resources to God! This makes a mockery of God since it was he who gave the fifth commandment in the first place. The will of God is thus put in a secondary place.

Excursus on "Corban"

The Hebrew or Aramaic word means literally "gift," but in the context of the Jewish sacrificial system, it refers to an offering made to God. So the term may, by definition, refer to anything that has been devoted exclusively to God, which means no one else may lay claim to it. In actual practice, however, there was some latitude on how the principle was applied.

A piece of inscription taken from an ossuary discovered near Jerusalem has the words, "Everything that a person will find to his profit in this ossuary is an offering (qōrban) to God from the one within it."[166] What is so interesting is that Jewish ossuaries are boxes constructed for the storage of an ancestor's bones. But the dedication of bones to God as an offering or gift is unthinkable, given that they are considered ritually unclean. This implies that the word qōrban is not really used to indicate an offering to God, but to prevent any use of it. The word may then refer to a ban, rather than an offering.

Furthermore, there is evidence from the rabbinic discussions on vows that what is rendered qōrban may still be used by the owner in some ways (m. Ned. 5.6). So the provisions of Torah (precisely that which speaks of not breaking vows and dedicating things to God) are twisted, and loopholes are searched and exploited for the sake of one's benefit. In this light, it is perfectly understandable why Jesus' teaching puts emphasis on the heart.

The Conclusions Promulgated (7:14-23)

This sequel tackles an unexpressed question. Wouldn't God be pleased with the zeal to make all Israel follow the regulations prescribed for their priests?

---

166. Baumgarten 1984: 5–17; Fitzmyer 1959: 60–65.

In tackling this unspoken question, the basic principle with which Jesus contradicts the tradition held dearly by the Pharisees is disclosed.

Jesus turns to address the crowd (v. 14), signifying that what is to be pronounced has great relevance for all. It defines what being unclean means. Once this is understood, the crowd would know where defiling sources might be found. Jesus begins with the polar opposites of inside and outside. He then defines uncleanness as not coming from the outside, but arising from inside a person (v. 15). In essence, this relativizes ceremonial washing, as the contagion is now regarded as coming from the inside and not the outside.

To clarify this notion further, Mark moves the scene to inside the house (v. 17). Whose house it is does not really matter. It is more important to recognize that in Mark's Gospel, the house is the locality for special teaching to be given to a privileged group, namely Jesus' disciples. So in the house Jesus' disciples ask him about the dark saying or riddle (the Greek is *parabolē*). This is similar to the situation envisaged in 4:10-12. Perhaps the unspoken question they have is: "If defilement is from the inside, won't this make nonsense of the whole purity code?" What justification does Jesus have for defining defiling sources as internal and not external?

Jesus' answer to that implied question has sometimes been interpreted as being humorous, referring to what takes place naturally in the toilet:[167] undigested food, pure or impure, is passed out of the system and into the latrine (vv. 18-19). But there may be something more profound going on. Verse 19 tells us that food does not affect the heart, which is the seat of personality in ancient thought.[168] In this regard, we can see that the heart of the matter is the heart. It is this that gives rise to impure thoughts and actions, making people really impure (vv. 20-23). Ethics have precedence over rituals, and rituals are set in place not as an end to themselves but to remind the community of a greater reality.

What is the implication of such a teaching? Mark draws out one, and this is announced in a parenthesis at the end of v. 19: Jesus declares all foods clean. This is a momentous remark, as what has been regarded as differentiating the elect people of God from the Gentiles was partly the food they ate. If no food can make a person unclean, then laws governing pure and impure food were no longer necessary. The boundary marker of food laws is then taken down. For Mark's audience this is of great consequence, for it means Jews and Gentiles can come together to eat at the same table.

---

167. On the humor of Jesus, see Buckner 1993 and Iverson 2013: 2-19.
168. Donahue and Harrington 2002: 224.

Fusing the Horizons: Divine Integrity and the Abrogation of the Purity Code

One nagging question arising from the episode is whether God contradicted himself, since he was the one behind the food laws or purity code. In this regard, it is important to remember the biblical emphasis that the heart is the heart of the matter. The purity code is given not out of divine caprice, but to serve as a concrete reminder of the holiness of God. That code must never be understood as a talisman or as something to mask the evil of the heart. This is one criticism the prophets made repeatedly (Amos 5:21–27; Hos 6:6). However, the one who is greater than the prophets has come, and brings with him the good news of the kingdom. This addresses the heart to which the purity code served as a vivid signpost. When the destination is reached the signpost is no longer needed. Or as Paul would put it, things pertaining to childhood are put away when one reaches adulthood (1 Cor 13:11), not because they are bad or shameful but because maturity for which childhood is an important preparatory phase is reached. So when the evil of the heart is addressed and cured, the ceremonies that point to such a reality are no longer required. The will of God is therefore upheld. Hence, Jesus is not teaching that frivolity is the answer to rigid ceremonies, but the heart of the matter of these ceremonies must always be kept in mind. We can see why Mark's Jesus is truly he who proclaims good news.

"ALL FOODS MADE CLEAN" AND THE EXTENSION OF THE MINISTRY TO GENTILES (7:24–36)

Following the narration of a controversy that led Jesus to pronounce sayings implying the obsolescence of the purity code, Mark now depicts Jesus going to Gentile territories. While in these territories, Jesus performs an exorcism (vv. 24–30) and a healing (vv. 31–36). Note that these are hallmarks of the kingdom's presence (1:21–28, 32–39; 3:22–30). Mark has already prepared his audience for this by depicting in chapter 5 Jesus' going to Gerasenes to deliver a man from a legion of unclean spirits.

However, this does not mean Mark is merely repeating himself. The key difference is the ethnic explicitness. Mark did not tell his audience that the demoniac of Gerasenes was Gentile. They were left to infer this from the indicators Mark strategically placed. But in 7:24–30, Mark states explicitly that the woman who comes to Jesus is Gentile. More importantly, Mark uses this story to set the theological parameters for understanding what it means for Jesus to go to Gentile territories. The "going to" is not to be equated as a "going over to," that is, the Jews are not neglected in favor of the Gentiles. The primary emphasis remains the house of Israel. Such priority must be respected, as it stems from God's promise to the patriarchs: to the Jews first and also to the Gentiles would be one Pauline formula that sums this up well (Rom 1:16).

The Syro-Phoenician Woman (7:24–30)

Mark makes it clear that it is Jesus' intention to go to the vicinity of Tyre, a Gentile area (v. 24). In ancient times Tyre was an important trading city (cf. Isa 14) and it developed close economic ties with the kingdom of Herod the Great.[169] Its coins were the only ones that the Temple authorities would accept for the Temple tax, because the quality of their silver was highly trusted.[170] Interestingly, Josephus describes the Tyrians as "notoriously our bitterest enemies" (*Apion* 1:70; cf. *Antiquities* 14:313–321; *War* 2:478). Politics, economics and popular sentiment did not always coincide. Indeed, there is also evidence that the economic ties Tyre had with Galilee resulted in benefit only to the Tyrians, and many Galileans resented this as a result.[171] This implies Jesus' visit to that vicinity might have been offensive to his own people, indicating yet again that the visit was deliberate. The same pattern found in earlier passages (e.g., 1:35; 3:13; 6:31–32) is seen here in Gentile territory: Jesus intends to get away from public attention but does not succeed. This also indicates that his fame has spread far and wide, and beyond Jewish Palestine.

The imploring woman is described as being of Syro-Phoenician origin (the modifier "Syrian" is needed in order to make the designation precise, as there were also Phoenicians in North Africa) and also a Greek (vv. 25–26). Although the word "Greek" (*Hellēnis*) as used in biblical literature usually refers to people who could speak Greek, and not strictly ethnic Greeks, it is also often a synonymous term for *ethnē* or Gentiles (cf. Rom 1:16; 1 Cor

---

169. Donahue and Harrington 2002: 232.
170. Abrahams 1917: 83–84.
171. Theissen 1991: 72–80.

1:22-24). Mark could not have chosen a better story to speak of the implication of rendering all foods clean, as what may be regarded as utterly disadvantageous comes to the fore: it is a woman who implores Jesus; the request is about driving out an unclean spirit; the one who comes to Jesus is a Gentile.

The verbal exchange between Jesus and the woman is highly fascinating (vv. 27-30). In an apparent refusal to answer the woman's request, Jesus states the children must be fed first, as it is not right for their food to be given to dogs. The use of this image would certainly have caused offense for first-century Mediterranean people, just as modern readers may regard it as harsh. Dogs were regarded by Jews as unclean, and their status in the eyes of many Gentiles did not fare better, even if they were household dogs. OT references to dogs are usually pejorative (e.g., 1 Sam 17:43; 2 Sam 16:9; Ps 22:16; Isa 56:10-11). Indeed, Jews often call Gentiles dogs (*1 En* 89:42, 46-47, 49; cf. *Pirque R. El.* 29). Interestingly, Mark does not clarify what kind of dogs Jesus is referring to, although the woman thinks of them as domestic ones, waiting anxiously under the table.[172] The question arising from all this is whether Mark has portrayed Jesus as being callous and offensive.

The word "first" of v. 27 shows there is more to the plain meaning of Jesus' statement. If there is a "first," one may logically expect a "second." This has implication for our understanding of Jesus' statement, which we will elaborate below. Moreover, the woman actually perceives a more powerful insight suggested by the image constructed by Jesus. Addressing him as "Lord," she reasons that there is no need for the children to be fully fed first, as the crumbs that drop from the table may be given to the dogs. Jesus' response is that it is precisely such a reply that brings about the exorcism (v. 29). This is the only instance in Mark's Gospel that anyone has won (apparently) an argument with Jesus! But what is the underlying message here? There are four things that warrant a closer look. The first concerns Jesus' apparently indifferent attitude. The second is the word "first" used by Jesus. The third has to do with the image Jesus employs. And the fourth is the reply made, for Mark tells us this is precisely the reason that her child is delivered (v. 29). We will elaborate on these points below.

First, Jesus' rather laconic reply smacks of an unwillingness to help. To be fair, this conclusion is gathered primarily from the words used. We do not have access to the tone or manner in which these words were given. A twinkle in the eye while speaking these words or an affirming gesture can mitigate the harshness of words and transform them into something

---

172. France 2002: 298.

playful.[173] In narrating a story, the apparently contradictory may be left in suspense by which the plot thickens. The resolution at the end will shed light on the apparently contradictory.

Secondly, the phrase "permit first" with which Jesus begins his reply is pregnant with meaning. What is significant is that there is no mention of a sequel. The gaping semantic ditch must be leapt across by the woman herself. We may assume the woman picked up the implication and did the semantic leap. So Jesus' answer would have come across as "not yet," rather than a flat "no." We shall see later that the woman actually went further than this implication.

Thirdly, the image is highly suggestive. Dogs may still eat of the crumbs that fall from the children's table, without arrogating to themselves what rightfully belongs to the children. Theologically speaking, the meal may allude to the banquet of the last days that God will throw for his children (cf. Isa 25:6). This concerns the restoration of Israel in which the nation will finally dine in perfect fellowship with God. It is thus connected with the actualizing of the eschatological kingship of God. Once this is grasped, the sequence inherent in the image may be seen as speaking of salvation history. Restoration and redemption must first come to Jews, because of God's promises to the patriarchs. The eschatological pilgrimage of the Gentiles takes place after Mt Zion is raised to the highest heights (Isa 2:2-4; 49:6). This divine sequence must be respected. Indeed, this should be something the Gentile audience of Mark could also celebrate. If God reneged on his promises to Israel, it would offer no comfort to the Gentiles, as he could easily renege on those he made to the Church. Furthermore, the word "bread" connects us immediately with the feeding miracle in the previous chapter and the feeding miracle in the next. As we shall see later, the later feeding miracle is performed for Gentiles. These stories fill out the meaning of the words "first."

Finally, the woman's reply demonstrates she understands Jesus' hints about the theology undergirding the image. In fact, her understanding went further than the boundaries dictated by the redemptive sequence, and grasps the character of the One behind it all. Rightly so, Mark's emphasis is on her reply (v. 29) because it accepts the validity of Jesus' image. However, it also furthers the image boldly and legitimately for her daughter's benefit: the dogs may eat of the crumbs *now*. The woman is not using extraneous arguments or appealing to extrinsic considerations. Everything in her reply comes from the image Jesus has used. This certainly evidences submission to the lordship of Jesus. However, it also evinces a clear grasp of the presence

---

173. E.g., Camery-Hoggart 1992: 150–51; and Filson 1960: 180.

of grace, a grace that can benefit even those who are outside God's current program, so to speak. Priority therefore does not necessarily mean watertight exclusivity. What leads her to do this must surely be attributed to faith, which Matthew the evangelist duly informs us that it is so (Matt 15:28).

We can therefore posit that Jesus intentionally drops clues for further thought, and invites engagement.[174] Being a wise teacher, Jesus is encouraging her to argue, with the hope that in the process certain powerful insights will open up. Indeed, he has provided enough ammunition for her to destroy his own case.

To summarize: this episode ties together masterfully the Jewishness of Jesus and the worldwide efficacy of his ministry that is still future. In this regard, Mark's audience will understand why Jesus spent most of his time reaching out to the Jews, even if he is to be the ruler of this world. They will further understand why this does not mean Gentiles are neglected. Crumbs from the table may still be eaten by dogs. But the day will come when these dogs will be children, and sit together with other children at the great banquet of reconciliation and renewal.[175]

The Deaf and Speech-impaired Man (7:31–36)

The story of the healing of the man who is deaf and speech-impaired is unique to Mark's Gospel. It reinforces the theme of the previous episode by showing that Jesus' kingdom ministry is also available to Gentiles.

The travel itinerary given by Mark seems odd. Sidon was to the north of Tyre, while the Sea of Galilee lay in the southeast (v. 31). Furthermore, the Decapolis was on the eastern shore of the Sea of Galilee. The itinerary envisaged by Mark involves going first to the north and then turning around to head in a south-easterly direction for the Decapolis. Why this is so, Mark does not explain. If Jesus wanted to give himself as wide a berth as possible from Antipas's kingdom, there was no need to head north first. From this rather strange itinerary, some scholars have concluded Mark does not know his geography.[176] Not surprisingly, there arose a textual variant, which speaks of Jesus not as departing Tyre for Sidon but as departing the Tyre-Sidon region and heading for Galilee. This has early support (P45, from the third century), but most scholars deem this reading as secondary, based mainly on the consideration of transcriptional probability (i.e.,

---

174. Pokorný 1995: 321–37, suggesting it is a test of faith.

175. The recent thesis of Alonso argues along a similar line, positing that with this episode, Mark invites his readers to cross boundaries; see Alonso 2011.

176. Lührmann 1987: 132; but cf. the refutation in Hengel 1985: 148.

if this easier reading were correct, it would be difficult to account for the rise of the harder reading, especially when the harder reading has early and wide manuscript support). Some scholars think that Markan theological interest may be at work here, as he wants to show that the communities in that region are touched by Jesus, because either Mark comes from that region or is writing for the communities of that region.[177] It may be assumed that it was at Decapolis that a person who is deaf and speech-impaired is brought to him. Mark's audience, if alert, would have been familiar with this topographical reference, as the healed Gerasene demoniac went throughout the Decapolis, proclaiming the work of Jesus (5:20). The proclamation has borne fruit.

The actions of Jesus appear mystifying (vv. 32–35). In antiquity, saliva was often believed to be a healing agent associated with both magical incantations, and also physicians' prescriptions (Galen *Natural Faculties* 3:7; cf. the rabbinic evidence in *t. Sanh.* 12:10 and *b. B. Bat.* 126b). With regard to the Aramaic word *ephphatha*, there is no evidence that it was ever used in magical incantation. The word is recorded here probably as a result of a vivid remembrance of some eyewitness. Some scholars think the actions and the word have exorcistic associations.[178] But we cannot be sure about this. The "deep sigh" should more properly be translated as a "deep groan,"[179] indicating the difficulty of the miracle. Of course, Jesus might have accommodated himself to the cultural mores of the people around him, but such an explanation does not clarify the main message of this story. The vividness of the account suggests that Mark has something important to say.

Many allusions to the OT may be detected in the exclamation of the people (v. 37), which also serves to reveal to us the true significance of the miracle. The words "he has done everything well" may echo Gen 1:31 (cf. Eccl 3:11). A superlative is used in the response of the people ("overwhelmed"[180] with amazement), indicating how significant this miracle is. Furthermore, the phrase "he even makes the deaf hear and the mute speak" most probably alludes to the promise of Isa 35:5–6, where the transformation of the people of God at the restoration of Zion is envisaged. This proposal is supported by the use of the word *mogilalos* in v. 32. This extremely rare word occurs only once in the NT, and also only once in the LXX at precisely the passage which we believe the episode alludes to: Isa 35:6! Since this OT passage is also used in Matt 11:4–6 || Luke 7:22–23 as a summary of the gospel

---

177. Theissen 1991: 234–45.
178. E.g., Marcus 2000: 478.
179. The Greek is *stenazō*.
180. The Greek is *hyperperissōs*.

ministry of Jesus, we can conclude it is of great importance to the nascent Christian movement. All this lends strength to our speculation that Isa 35:6 is lurking in the background. Mark is therefore saying that the fulfillment of this Isaianic passage has come, and that the Gentiles are the unexpected beneficiaries of these blessings.

If the earlier episode (7:24–30) speaks of crumbs benefiting dogs, this story speaks of dogs having more than just crumbs, as Gentiles now participate in the benefits brought about by the second Exodus and the eschatological restoration of God's people. So Jesus' deep sigh (v. 34) may symbolize the great exertion connected with drawing the Gentiles into the kingdom. Not surprisingly, the people's reaction to the healing is to acclaim with words never spoken before in Mark's Gospel: Jesus has done all things well (*kalōs panta pepoiēken*)—and this must be the inclusion of Gentiles in the blessings of the kingdom.

The feature found in v. 36 is familiar, as it is found in earlier stories (e.g., 1:44–45). The Greek tenses used (imperfect) suggest Jesus repeatedly commanded the people who were privy to the miracle to remain silent about it, but they repeatedly did not heed his command and therefore spread the news. While this may point to a pragmatic concern, there may also be a deeper theological motif at work. Jesus' miraculous deeds cannot be fully understood or authentically appreciated apart from the cross.

THE FEEDING OF THE 4,000 (8:1–9)

If this feeding miracle is regarded as taking place in Gentile territory, we have three miracle stories associated with the Gentiles (starting from 7:24). But can a Gentile provenance be demonstrated?

It has to be noticed first of all that Mark does not provide a topographical note. What we have is a general time note: "in those days." Since the locality of the previous story was the Decapolis, a case may be made that this feeding miracle also takes place there, which is a Gentile region. Secondly, the term used for the baskets is different (*spyrides* instead of *kophinoi*, v. 8). As we mentioned earlier in 6:43, *kophinos* is a distinctively Jewish receptacle, but the same cannot be said for *spyrides*, which is a more general term. Thirdly, some scholars have argued that the description of the crowd as "having come from a long distance" (*apo makrothen*) may imply that these were Gentiles, since they have sometimes been described with that phrase (Deut 28:49; 1 Kings 8:41; Isa 60:4; Jer 46:27; cf. Eph 2:13 for similar terminology).[181] This hypothesis is strengthened when we realize that if the people are with Jesus in a remote place, it is superfluous to mention that some of them have come from far away. The individual arguments may not be compelling on their own, but together they do form a cogent case. Indeed, the parallel in Matthew makes this clear, when it provides the datum that the crowd glorifies the "God of Israel" (Matt 15:31), a term more congenial for non-Jews. One other consideration that supports the case is that Mark loves grouping stories in threes. If this feeding miracle is interpreted as having been performed for the Gentiles, what we then have are three stories of Jesus performing the signs of the kingdom for Gentiles. If the foregoing is on target, we are then in a position to consider the deeper significance of this story.

The word "another" in v. 1 signals that a story similar to what has been narrated before will be told. True enough, Mark tells us a large crowd gathers in a remote place (v. 4; see the parallel in 6:34–35), and has followed Jesus for three days (v. 2). Their lack of food draws Jesus' compassion, prompting a discussion with his disciples (vv. 2–4). Jesus' concern for the crowd bewilders the disciples: where could such a large amount of food be found in the wilderness? Some commentators find it impossible that the disciples should make such a response since they have witnessed a feeding miracle before. They therefore argue that there was only one story but Mark has repeated it for a theological purpose.[182] We do not deny that Mark has a theological purpose in narrating this. Whether Mark composed this story as a doublet or derived it from tradition is a more complicated question, which this commentary cannot delve into.[183] We will therefore focus on Mark's message. If we are right about the Gentile setting, the point must be that very similar blessings of the Jews are also given to them.

The significant differences are chiefly the use of different words for thanksgiving over the bread, and the numbers involved: 4,000 people (gender not specified) instead of 5,000 men; seven loaves instead of five; seven basketfuls of leftovers instead of twelve (do note that the words used for the receptacles are different). We do not think the difference in the words used for thanksgiving is important (*eucharisteō* in 8:6 versus *eulogeō* in 6:41). First of all, they are synonymous. Secondly, *eulogeō* is also used in 8:7, for the thanksgiving of the fish. What remains to be discussed is the difference in numbers. Are there symbolic meanings to the different numbers?

---

181. Guelich 1989: 404.
182. A sort of doublet but see Gundry 1993: 398–401.
183. See the discussion in France 2002: 305–7; and Gundry 1993: 398–401.

One popular hypothesis is that in the former miracle, the numbers 5 and 12 represent Jewish theological concepts. Five thousand is an intensification of the number "five," and it stands for the five books of Torah, while "twelve" is the number of the tribes of Israel. In the present story, the number "four" stands for the world as it was regarded in ancient times as having four corners and "seven" is the number of completeness. Together these numbers stand for the complete worldwide mission of the Messiah. Theories of this nature are difficult to prove or refute, and one wonders whether Mark intends this, and if he did, would his audience have picked it up?

What is clear, though, is that Mark wants his audience to understand there are two miracle stories of feeding large crowds. He does this for good reasons. If we were right to conclude that the feeding miracle in Mark 6 served to demonstrate Jesus as the compassionate eschatological shepherd who would inaugurate the second exodus for the Jews, then what Mark is saying by the feeding of the 4,000 is that such an exodus also draws in the Gentiles. There is no better place to relate this story, since Mark in chapter 7 has depicted Jesus as declaring the purity code obsolete.

Mark, therefore, has led his audience on a narrative journey that features increasing participation of Gentiles in the benefit of the second Exodus Jesus is inaugurating. This is first adumbrated when the purity code is made obsolete. So there should be no barriers between Jews and Gentiles, at least in the area of food. What is theory has to be shown in practice. Hence following this, Mark goes on to narrate a story which shows that even while bread is being served to Jews—the children of promise—scraps from the table may be still be consumed by Gentile dogs there and then. Priority still belongs to the Jews, but priority does not mean exclusivity. After this, Mark indicates that Gentiles also participate in the blessings of the second Exodus (i.e., the deaf hear and the mute speak). And finally, the third story in the sequence provides the climax. These Gentiles do not just have scraps; they are also invited to participate at the table of the eschatological shepherd just as Jews were. They are fed with the same food and are all satisfied. Clearly, the kingdom is also for the Gentiles.

THE SIGN AND THE YEAST (8:10–21)

It is best to read the demand for a sign together with the discourse on the yeast of the Pharisees and of Herod, as a follow-on from the feeding of the 4,000. Once this is done, the placement of these stories will not appear whimsical or muddled. There is a parallel tradition preserved by Q (Matt 12:38–41 || Luke 11:29–32), where it is said that a sign will nevertheless be given and this is the sign of Jonah. This raises many interesting historical and literary questions but our concern is with Mark.

The Pharisees Demand a Sign (8:10–13)

The name Dalmanutha does not appear in any other ancient source, and we are left with absolutely no knowledge of where it was. This is why in the manuscript tradition some other names are suggested: Mageda, Magdala, Magada, and even Melegada. But the earliest and the most-widely attested reading is Dalmanutha. Based on the data provided by this episode, and especially v. 11 (a crossing of the lake and the appearance of Pharisees; or, a crossing from Decapolis to a place where Jews may be found predominantly), scholars conjecture that this unknown place should be located on the western shore of the Sea of Galilee.[184]

Much may be seen as lurking below the surface of this brief story, comprising mainly a question and answer session. Mark shows what sort of motive the Pharisees have by the use of *peirazō* (v. 11). In Mark's Gospel this word is reserved only for Satan (1:13) and the Pharisees (together with the Herodians in 12:15). The upshot of this is that the Pharisees are grouped together with Satan in their testing of Jesus.

But how exactly are the Pharisees testing Jesus? The sign they ask for is "from heaven" (v. 11). This can mean something performed by God (i.e., heaven being a circumlocution for God)[185] or something done to the heavens (i.e., a celestial sign).[186] However, it clearly refers to something that will confirm Jesus' claims once and for all.[187] It bears mentioning in this connection that Mark has been careful with his vocabulary. He has referred to Jesus' miracles mainly as *dynamis* but never as *sēmeion*, which is now the word used for denoting what the Pharisees are requesting to be done. According to the background of the Second Temple period, many Jews were frequently looking out for harbingers of God's decisive intervention in history.[188] In this regard, Jews speculated that when the Messiah finally came he would perform such a sign. This had a precedent in Moses' ministry,

---

184. France 2002: 309; Marcus 2000: 498.
185. Guelich 1989: 413–14; Pesch 1980: 1:407.
186. Gibson 1986: 42–53.
187. Culpepper 2007: 258.
188. See discussions in Allison 1993: 85–90; and Gray 1993: 123–30.

where he performed signs to show that God was on the side of the Jews, and would be acting powerfully to rescue them from Egypt.

Jesus' description of the Pharisees as "this generation" is significant (v. 12). The phrase *hē hautē genea* is used four times in Mark. Two of its occurrences are found in this verse (the other occurrences being 8:38 and 13:30). Verse 9:19 has a phrase which resembles it closely (*ō apistos genea*, which means "O unbelieving generation"). Furthermore, it is found only on the lips of Jesus in the gospel traditions and is almost always used negatively. It is plausible that behind such a phrase stands the story of the testing (cf. *peirazō*) of God by Israel at Massa and Meriba (Exod 17:1–7).[189] So significant is this story that, just before entering the Promised Land, Moses refers to it again in his summary of their wilderness experience (Deut 6:16; 9:22 and 33:8). The re-telling of this episode is also done in Ps 95:7–11, where those people are expressly called a generation in v. 10. The upshot of all this is that the Pharisees are reprising the role of the wilderness generation, a generation which tempted God repeatedly with demands for signs because of their chronic obduracy.

Jesus' reply is curt and is prefaced with the words, "Amen, I say to you," a clause indicating that what is to follow is of great significance. This appears in Greek as a conditional sentence that provides only the protasis (i.e., the "if" clause) without giving the apodosis (i.e., the "then" clause). This is indicative of an underlying Semitic syntax, which uses only the protasis of a conditional clause to make a solemn declaration. The imprecation that is to be provided by the apodosis is left unspoken. Fully translated it runs: "Amen I say to you, if a sign were to be given to this generation, *may God then do such-and-such to me*" (the words in italics are left unsaid). So it is certainly correct to regard the sentence as indicating a strong negative: no such sign will ever be given. See 2 Kings 6:31 for a similar but fuller expression.

Jesus' curt reply can now be unraveled. What the Pharisees are asking for is to some extent already being performed. The signs that God is now establishing his eschatological rule are found in Jesus' ministry, precisely through his teaching, his reconciling activity and chiefly that of his healing and exorcism. Those with eyes to see will know that the eschatological age has dawned, even while mundane history continues to run its course. But these activities are not regarded by the religious authorities, especially the Pharisees, as constituting the signs of the kingdom. What they want is something "open." They want a sign that is both apocalyptic and triumphalist (i.e., demonstrating God's powerful rescue of the Jews by the destruction of their enemies and the bequeathing of glory to them). If this is what authenticates

---

189. Marcus 2000: 500–501.

the presence of the kingdom, Jesus will have to reply that such a sign will not be given, because it is antithetical to all that he has taught about the kingdom. As we shall see later, it is not about triumphalism but humble service. Not surprisingly, Jesus' reply is in the form of an asseveration.

At its deepest core, the demand for a sign by the Pharisees stems from a different vision of the kingdom. So the point is not that it is wrong to ask for signs, for Scripture allows this and sometimes endorses it (see especially Judg 6:36-40; 1 Kings 18:24, 36-38; and especially Isa 7:13-14). Instead, the dispute is over kingdom-visions and kingdom-realities. If the signs performed by Jesus do not convince, it must mean these people are imbibing a different kingdom-vision. So it is not surprising that Mark tells us Jesus took leave of the Pharisees after their short dialogue, and crossed the lake to the other side (i.e., away from Galilee and into Gentile territory yet again). And it becomes clear why, on the way to the other side, Jesus warns his disciples of the yeast of the Pharisees and of Herod.

The Warning to the Disciples (8:14-21)

Once the basic issue in the demand for the sign is uncovered, we are in a position to understand the meaning of this episode — one which has baffled many commentators and led to many scathing remarks about Mark's compositional technique.[190] The feeding of the 4,000 prompts the demand for a sign from the Pharisees. The Pharisees offer an alternative vision of the kingdom, a vision described by Jesus as yeast (i.e., the element that corrupts the unleavened bread of the true kingdom vision). It is against this that the disciples are warned. Herod is mentioned here because his vision of the kingdom is also antithetical to that of Jesus. With this serving as introduction, the story will now be discussed in detail.

The story begins with the mention that the disciples have forgotten to bring bread with them, except for one loaf (v. 14). Just the mention of the "one loaf" has prompted scholars to consider whether there is a deeper meaning to it. Moreover, the Markan syntax is peculiar in that it appears to be in two minds. Translated literally, v. 14 says: "And they forgot to take breads (the Greek is plural) — and they had no bread except for one — with them in the boat." Hence, it has been suggested that the one loaf refers either to Jesus (the bread of life)[191] or the Eucharistic bread (the one loaf of the church).[192] Approached this way, Mark is then commenting either on the

---

190. Cf. Beavis 1989: 105-14.
191. Hooker 1991: 192.
192. Marcus 2000: 509-10. Cf. Quesnell 1969: 231-32, 242-43.

situation of the disciples or that of the church, or perhaps both. Respectively it means either that Jesus' presence is sufficient to meet the physical needs of the disciples even though they do not have sufficient provisions, or that the Eucharist Jesus instituted is sufficient for whatever needs the Church may have. It is hard to be certain whether such symbolic undertones are to be detected, when the narrative as it stands makes perfect sense without any recourse to symbolism. The Markan syntax, clumsy as it may be to some refined writer, makes its point quite clearly: the disciples have forgotten to bring ample provisions, but they do have one physical loaf with them in the boat.

In line with the above suggestion, Gibson has recently proposed that the Markan syntax is entirely appropriate if we posit the following. The disciples deliberately carried only one loaf with them in order to prevent Jesus from performing another bread-multiplying miracle on Gentile soil. Jesus' warning then is that they should watch out for the yeast of the Pharisees and of Herod, because both these groups do not accept Jesus' kingdom vision. The upshot of this is that the disciples' deliberate neglect is for keeping the messianic blessings within Israel.[193] As attractive as this hypothesis is, there are some insuperable problems,[194] the chief of which concerns the meaning of the verb *epilanthanomai* (v. 14). For the hypothesis to stand, it must be translated as "(deliberately) neglecting" which is not what it usually means. It means simply "to forget." In other words, it is unintentional.

Perhaps, it is wise not to read too much symbolism into the bare statement of v. 14. Instead, we should construe Jesus as using the occasion as a stepping stone to an important teaching, namely that of avoiding the yeast of the Pharisees and of Herod. This prompts the disciples to wonder whether the remark is given because they have forgotten to bring ample provisions. And this raises another problem. How could the disciples think that Jesus was concerned over their paltry resource, when he had already performed two multiplying miracles? Doesn't this make them incredibly obtuse?

Truth may sometimes be stranger than fiction, or perhaps the clumsiness in the construction of the episode arises from Mark's desire to relate the theological with the historical in one breath. Whether or not Mark has been fair to the disciples, his intention must not be missed: the feeding miracles have deeper meanings that are not easily grasped by all (enemies and disciples included). We may tentatively unpack the significance as follows. First, these feeding miracles are not simply performed to feed but, more importantly, to demonstrate that the compassionate eschatological

---

193. Cf. Gibson 1986: 42–53.
194. Collins 2007: 385–86; France 2002: 315.

shepherd has enacted in a definitive way the second Exodus. This second Exodus is a closely allied concept with the kingdom. Secondly, the feeding stories show that both Jews and Gentiles may be beneficiaries of the kingdom. The eschatological shepherd feeds them both. Thirdly, the focus on the leftovers in Jesus' questioning emphasizes the abundance of such provisions. There is a generosity to the kingdom that the disciples have yet to fully appreciate. They, like many of Jesus' interlocutors, are still thinking of the earthly, not grasping the spiritual truths of his ministry. The issue is not so much whether they believe Jesus can provide bread; more profoundly, it has to do with the transformation of a deeply entrenched kingdom vision—something that will require a lot of time, effort and teaching.

How does Herod fit into all this? His vision may be seen as representing the non-Jewish viewpoint, where to rule means to exercise power. Here religion serves only to bolster one's political position, and may be conveniently sidelined or violently removed when that religion calls into question the ruler's ethics (6:14–29). The kingdom is not about intrigue or eliminating opponents to seize power (something Mark will return to in chapter 10). The irony is that both the Pharisees and Herod, bitter enemies as they may be, actually have similar kingdom-visions. They want something that is openly glorious, with the vindication of their own group, and the elimination of enemies. It becomes clear why it is imperative that the pure bread of the true kingdom must not be corrupted by the yeast of triumphalism and narrow-mindedness.

So Jesus' one refrain is, "Do you still not understand?" The disciples are the "insiders" but display attributes of the "outsiders"—they have eyes but do not see; they are taught repeatedly but do not yet understand (vv. 17–18; cf. 4:12). The least Mark's audience can gather from all this is that to be a true disciple of Jesus is never easy, for it involves a revolution of values and outlook. This is achievable not by human strength but divine grace.

On the Road to Jerusalem: The Gospel and the Suffering Messiah (8:22—10:52)

THE STUTTERING BEGINNINGS OF TRUE PERCEPTION (8:22-30)

The episodes of the two-stage healing of the blind man (8:22–26) and Peter's confession (8:27–30) both take place away from Galilean soil. Coming as they are, after the poignant questions asked by Jesus about the disciples' spiritual sight and understanding (8:14–21), these episodes may be regarded as a kind of narrative commentary on what treatments of this malady may look like.

It should also be noted that from the story of the healing of the blind man onwards, Jesus seldom sets foot again on Galilee. Instead, he charts a course for Jerusalem, after wandering for a while in Gentile territory (Bethsaida and Caesarea Philippi). As it is well known, Mark narrates only one trip of Jesus to Jerusalem. Hence, many commentators regard this story as beginning the second half of Mark's Gospel, where Jesus is depicted as being inexorably drawn to Jerusalem for the climax of his ministry.[1] Many lessons on discipleship are taught and the phrase "on the way"[2] (8:27; 9:34; 10:17; 10:32) occurs frequently, indicating that the journey to Jerusalem is also a foil to clarifying what discipleship means.

The Healing of the Blind Man at Bethsaida (8:22-26)

This is the first time Mark relates a story of the healing of a blind person. What is so striking about it, however, is that it is the only miracle that shows a two-stage healing process, giving the impression that the initial action of Jesus is not fully efficacious. Perhaps this is one episode that early Christian preachers would quite happily forget, as the other three Gospels do not contain such a story. However, Mark sees in this a deeper significance, and

---

1. Marcus 2009: 589–92. He calls it "the royal way of Jesus" (591).
2. The Greek is *en tē hodō*.

uses the story to hammer home the point that getting true spiritual insight is indeed difficult.

The story is set most probably in Bethsaida Julius (vv. 22–23), located on the northeastern shore of the Sea of Galilee, in a region governed by Herod Philip. Surprisingly, Bethsaida is called a village,[3] when it was actually a fortified city in Jesus' day (Josephus *Antiquities* 18:28; cf. Matt 11:20). It has been suggested that Mark may be referring to an outlying settlement that was joined to the city.[4] However, it is more plausible to posit that since it was only in recent memory that Bethsaida became a fortified city, it might still be known by many as a village.

Why Jesus takes the blind man outside the village, Mark does not explain, and we are left to make our own inferences. Since the man will be commanded later not to enter the village, one may surmise it has something to do with Bethsaida itself.[5] As it was a large fortified city, Jesus may have wished to avoid publicity yet again. Similar to an earlier story (7:33), Jesus uses saliva to effect the healing: he spits on the man's eyes and puts his hand on him (where exactly, Mark does not tell us).

What the man says may contain a touch of humor (vv. 24–26). There is probably no symbolic content in the description; it is given only to illustrate the indistinct vision the man has. Jesus' second attempt results in full and clear vision, as the Greek *diablepō* indicates.

Scholars suggest this strange episode is a sort of parable, explaining the spiritual condition of the disciples.[6] Their sight has been restored through Jesus' gracious call and teaching. They do indeed see, but only partially. To see fully, more work needs to be done. This is precisely what the major section of 8:22—10:52 seeks to narrate.

The Confession of Peter (8:27–30)

The scene is set in the villages around Caesarea Philippi. It was formerly named Paneas or Panion in honor of the god Pan. After enlarging it, Herod Philip gave it a new name—Caesarea Philippi—so as to honor Augustus Caesar. Not surprisingly, the imperial cult (i.e., the worship of Augustus) was staunchly observed there (Josephus *War* 1:404–406; *Antiquities* 15:363–64).

---

3. The Greek term Mark is *kōmē*.

4. France 2002: 324; cf. the comment of Hecateus of Abdera that the Jews have only one fortified city, namely Jerusalem, but many villages (Josephus *Against Apion* 1:197).

5. Marcus 2009: 598 thinks it is meant to allude to God's taking Israel by the hand to lead them out of Egypt (Jer 31:32).

6. Marcus 2009: 601–2; cf. Johnson 1979: 370–83.

The distance from Bethsaida to Caesarea Philippi was about twenty-five miles. As the distance is quite considerable for one on foot, it implies that the place was chosen by Jesus because of its significance. Perhaps this was done to ensure some confidentiality for what he would be revealing to his disciples because messiahship is often linked to bellicose ideas in the Jewish context. Another possibility is that it was chosen to subvert the Empire's propaganda. To confess Jesus as Messiah at such a place was to challenge the propaganda that deliverance came from the Caesars of the Empire.

Interestingly, Mark describes Jesus' questions as being posed "on the way." The Greek phrase *en tē hodō* is used frequently in chapters 8–10 and may be thus regarded as a sort of technical term. The way Jesus is taking leads towards Jerusalem, where he would be crucified. Hence, it may also be regarded as the way of the cross. Along this way many lessons of discipleship are given, signifying that the way of the cross is also the way of discipleship. This further implies that rejecting the cross (i.e., its meaning for Jesus, the Christian movement and the divine redemptive program), means also rejecting discipleship. Do also note that Jesus' identity is asked "on the way," implying that Jesus' identity, the cross, and discipleship are all bound up together. Much, therefore, is at stake here.

The popular answers that the disciples volunteer (vv. 28–29) all belong to one category: the prophetic. They were previously mentioned in 6:14–16. It seems Jesus was better known in his day as a prophet than as the Messiah. However, Jesus' question in v. 29 indicates the popular answers are not adequate. At the same time, he wants personal answers. In the Greek text the word "you" comes first in the sentence for emphasis. What the disciples think of Jesus should not be dependent on the crowds.

Peter calls Jesus the Christ (v. 29). The word "Christ" is the Greek form of the Hebrew "Messiah." On the meaning of this word, see our earlier discussion of 1:1. Many Jewish writings give evidence that Jews awaited a kingly Messiah, from the line of David, to fight wars for Israel and eliminate her enemies. This would usher in an age of glory for Israel, and certainly for the pious and righteous within her (see *Pss Sol* 17; CD 19:10–11; 4Q252 and 1QM 4:13; 14:4–8).

Peter's confession is therefore momentous. It shows that for the first time one of Jesus' disciples grasps his true identity. However, Mark uses a strong word to describe Jesus' response. The Greek *epitimaō* means literally rebuking or scolding (v. 30). This prompts an important question: is Peter's response rejected by Jesus?

If we look back at the instances where Jesus silences confessions, we will discover such confessions are usually on target even if the timing is wrong. The case here is similar. Peter's confession is not wrong. It demonstrates that he is not blind like the crowds but "perceives" Jesus' true identity. A look at the word-statistics will confirm this. The title "Messiah" is used of Jesus only once in the heading of the work before this passage. No other character has confessed Jesus with this title up to this stage. After this, the word will be used a few times in Mark's Gospel, for discussing and disputing over Jesus' identity (12:35; 14:61; cf. 9:41; 13:21–22).

However, Peter's confession is only partially right, as what messiahship truly entails has to be hammered out on the anvil of following the suffering Jesus. In other words, although Peter perceives the true identity of Jesus, he has yet to perceive the true *significance* of that identity. This may be part of the reason why this confession, which appears to be something like a breakthrough in the plot of Mark's Gospel, is to be kept under wraps, at least for the time being.

THE MESSIAH MUST SUFFER: THE FIRST PASSION PREDICTION (8:31—9:1)

This passage is closely connected with the previous one, and serves an important theological purpose in Mark's Gospel. It explicates what messiahship means, and also what confessing Jesus as Messiah entails for the true confessor. It is not the triumphalism (cf. the "yeast" of 8:15) of the Pharisees or Herod. Instead it is about taking up the cross and denying oneself. So a new twist is given to the traditional notion of messiahship, a twist that even the hitherto perceiving Peter has not fully grasped.

The Rebuke of Peter (8:31–33)

Mark informs us that after Peter's confession, Jesus begins to teach that the Son of Man must suffer, be killed, and be raised again after three days (vv. 31–32). A few things must be noted here in order the full impact of what Mark intends is felt.

The first is that Jesus responds to Peter's confession with his own favorite self-designation of Son of Man. It is as though Jesus is qualifying the notion of Messiah with the Son of Man. This designation has been held in abeyance since 2:28, but it appears now at a critical juncture of the narrative. We have earlier argued that the background that best explains Jesus' use of this designation is Daniel 7. We find a new twist to the concept here, as it is stated that the Son of Man must suffer. There is no clear indication of this in Daniel, only that this figure is identified with God's beleaguered people (Dan 7:18, 21–22, 25). Even so, his introduction results in their vindication, and the triumph of God's kingship. This is really the image that takes the spotlight and therefore endures. Perhaps all this explains why there is no extant Jewish exegesis that describes the Danielic figure as a suffering one.[7] What we have here is therefore a revolutionary idea; or if not, at least a revolutionary emphasis. As Mark will show later, the shocking idea of the suffering Son of Man is not due to political circumstances, but is traceable to the inscrutable divine will.

Secondly, this response is actually a piece of teaching. The implication is that it is not given as a knee-jerk reaction or made off the cuff. Being a piece of teaching means there will be new elements for the disciples to grasp. All this adds to the significance of the saying.

Thirdly, the domain of enemies has enlarged. It does not comprise just the Pharisees of Galilee or the Herodians in that same region. The focus now falls on a formidable group: elders, chief priests, and teachers of the law. These are leaders in different aspects of the life of the Jewish community. Tradition (elders), cult (priests), and Torah (teachers of the law) will come together to condemn Jesus.

The fourth is that this constitutes the first passion prediction of Jesus in Mark's Gospel. There are three such predictions (8:31; 9:31; 10:33-34) altogether. These sayings always end with a prediction of resurrection "after three days." In Jewish usage, this is understood to mean "the day after tomorrow" (i.e., on the third day [cf. Josephus *Antiquities* 7:280-81]). To be noted too is Hosea 6:2, where such a formula is not meant to be chronologically precise, but signifies "a short while." Verse 31 provides therefore the first reference to Jesus' resurrection in Mark's Gospel.

The final thing to note is that Mark informs us such a prediction is spoken plainly (v. 32). This is an important datum as the Greek word *parrēsia* is found only once in Mark. Thus far, Mark has told his audience that Jesus' ministry in its relation to the kingdom is often in riddles. But now Jesus speaks plainly. So the word signals how important this piece of teaching is, and also that it is not esoteric but graspable by the disciples, if they are willing to accept it.

---

7. Some scholars argue that in Daniel 7, the Son of Man is identified with the beleaguered and vindicated people of God, and in this sense, one may speak of a suffering Son of Man (e.g., Hooker, *Son of Man*, 189-98; Marcus, 613). The fact remains that speculations on the Son of Man figure in other Second Temple Jewish writings do not make it explicit or develop the idea. Instead, the figure is always portrayed as glorious and triumphant, coming to the rescue of beleaguered Israel. Of course, it may be argued that behind this description lies the notion of identification. But this is a very imprecise way of stating things and circumvents the clear intent and theme of such Jewish presentations: the Son of Man comes to deliver in great power and pomp, and not to be suffer. See Collins 1992: 448-66.

Plain as it may be, it is still shocking and challenges received notions of messiahship. Consequently, Peter responds negatively and a dialogue with Jesus ensues (vv. 32b-33). Peter rebukes Jesus and is, in turn, rebuked by him with stinging words. In Peter's mind, the Messiah does not suffer. Indeed, the predominant assumption is that a Messiah who suffers and dies shows himself only to be a false claimant. Hence, Peter seeks to set his teacher straight, basing himself on solid tradition. We have here a fistful of ironies! The disciple rebukes the master. The disciple seeks to instruct the master. He gets the plain message of Jesus right (i.e., Jesus will die), but he also gets it all wrong. In so doing, the chief disciple plays out the role of Jesus' chief enemy (Satan)!

Peter is typed as a "satan" in Jesus' rebuke, not because he was demon-possessed but because in opposing Jesus' intention to go to Jerusalem to be repudiated and executed, he has played out the role of Satan, the one who opposes God's purposes. The final sentence of v. 33 makes this clear: Peter minds the things of men and not the things of God. The fact that "Jesus turned and looked at his disciples" (v. 33) suggests that Jesus' harsh words to Peter may be intended to prevent the other disciples from imbibing Peter's viewpoint.

The Greek phrase *hypage opisō mou* is highly interesting, as it may be understood as a Semitic idiom for commanding someone to get out of sight, or get back in line (i.e., get back to discipleship principles). A similar phrase, *deute opisō mou*, is used in 1:17, where Jesus summoned his disciples, especially Peter, to follow him. Hence, Jesus is not saying "get lost" to Peter but "get back in line."

Following the Suffering Messiah (8:34—9:1)

The scene now changes, although the theme continues. Jesus calls the crowd. He explains to them what being his disciple means. It does indeed entail recognizing Jesus to be the Messiah and the Son of Man. But such recognition must be followed by the kind of praxis described in this passage. We will attempt to expound this in greater detail.

The Greek phrases that speak about following Jesus at the beginning and the end of the saying in v. 34 form an *inclusio* or brackets (*opisō mou akolouthein* and *akoloutheitē moi*). What is framed is explained by these brackets, the content of which are painful but practicable actions. Being thus framed means such actions are taken not to show heroism but principally to follow Jesus.

The passage mentions two actions: to deny oneself and take up one's cross. The meaning of the first may be grasped quickly. It is about the giving up of one's rights in order to be at the disposal of a higher call. The second item needs some explanation. The word "cross" occurs for the first time here in Mark. As an instrument of execution, it was viewed with horror because it not only tortured but also shamed. What is worse is that in Jewish theology, being crucified also means being cursed (Deut 21:23; cf. Gal 3:13). The Romans reserved it mainly for violent revolutionaries or slaves. The image suggested by the phrase "take up the cross" is that of a person carrying the horizontal beam (the *patibulum*) to his place of crucifixion.[8] There cannot be a more vivid way of stating the cost of following the Messiah. In the first-century context, the implication of this saying is that the followers of the Messiah are not those who carry swords to depose pretenders to the throne, but crosses to die with him. No greater statement of self-renunciation and opposition to violence can be stated.

This proverb-like saying to support the injunction of v. 34 is notable for its irony (v. 35). Saving life equals losing it and vice versa. But it is true only if the qualifications to the equation are considered: saving one's life by denying Jesus or the gospel results in the loss of one's true life, now and at the eschaton. Losing one's life for Jesus and the gospel results in saving one's true life, now and at the eschaton. Life, then, is not defined by one's ability to hold on to it, but by its relation to Jesus and the gospel.

The word "gospel"—first introduced in 1:1, and mentioned at the strategic 1:14–15—has been kept in abeyance until now. It will appear again at 10:29; 13:10; and 14:9 (not counting 16:15). When one takes a closer look at how it has been used thus far, some insight into what Mark may be trying to do surfaces. In 1:1 and 1:14–15, the word is used to speak of Jesus' message. Especially in 1:14–15, this message is that which signals to the world God's fulfillment of his promises to redeem his people. This is indeed the good news that subverts the counterfeit of the Empire's. But with the use in 8:35, a different key is played. That which marks the fulfillment of God's promises and ushers in a new age is also that for which one may lose one's life, because this generation is sinful and adulterous. In this regard, the gospel is not just about salvation but also about discipleship. And this latter theme will be the focus of the use of the word in 10:29 and 14:9.

The verses in vv. 36–37 clarify the meaning of the ironical saying in v. 35, and serve also to encourage Jesus' audience to make the right choice. They also give hermeneutical balance to the earlier verse. The way of the cross is not about destroying life—not even one's own—but it is fundamentally

---

8. Hengel 1977: 62.

about attaining life: new and true. So the comparison in vv. 36-37 warns the disciples that the world and its glory cannot measure up to the great value of life itself. Some English translations unfortunately obscures this by translating the Greek *psychē* as "life" in v. 35 but "soul" in vv. 36-37.[9] In Hebraic thought the "soul" is the "life."[10] Hence, what is referred to is not the immaterial portion of one's being; rather it includes all that is human. All that the world can offer is not worth life itself. So if a person gains the whole world and loses his true life, he has not made a profit but a loss. And if he discovers he has made a big mistake by engaging in that transaction, there is no way back for him, as what he has gained is of a lower value than what he has lost. He has irretrievably lost himself.[11]

The words of v. 38 are important for they promise the certainty of Jesus' vindication. They also serve the function of reinforcing the message of vv. 35-37. Losing one's true life is now defined by the Son of Man's being ashamed of that person. A sort of *lex talionis* is at work here. When one is ashamed of Jesus, Jesus will be ashamed of him. What increases the stake to immeasurable proportions is that this shaming is done when Jesus comes in glory with his angels (i.e., at the irreversible eschaton). Being ashamed in the ancient Semitic context means rejection. It usually has domestic connotations, leading to the idea that being ashamed means treating that person as not belonging to the family. This means the person is cut off from the Messiah's family, and because the setting is the eschaton, there is a dreaded finality to it.

As such, v. 38 provides a counterpoint to the concept of the suffering Son of Man. He will not always be suffering, as though suffering is the supreme thing. No, he will claim his rightful status in God's time, and be glorified. The suffering precedes the glory.

We come now to 9:1, which bristles with many difficulties. "Will not taste death" is a Semitic expression for death. In the Markan context the statement refers to some of Jesus' contemporaries, and not to the OT heroes who were taken up to heaven, without having tasted death (e.g., Enoch, Moses, and Elijah).[12] Jesus' statement in 9:1 is also prefaced by the formula "Amen I say to you," reflecting its sobriety and veracity. But what does he mean by "the coming of the kingdom of God in power?"

---

9. E.g., the NIV.
10. Hartman 2010: 329-33.
11. Cf. Marcus 2009: 627-28, where he appeals to the notion of "eschatological life."
12. Chilton 1987: 267-74.

Some scholars think it must mean the Parousia (i.e., the conclusion of human history).[13] They will then take it that Jesus has made a mistake. Since that prediction, two thousand years of history has transpired, and those who heard these words have all tasted death. A popular notion among some conservative Christians runs in a similar vein, but regards Jesus as referring to the Jewish race instead. Jesus is then saying the Jewish race will not be obliterated at all; it will, instead, experience the Second Coming of Christ. If this were correct, Jesus would have a strange way of putting things. This makes us wonder whether we also got it right with his other sayings.

We must pay close attention to the Markan hints. In Mark, the kingdom of God has indeed come through Jesus' ministry. So Jesus is not speaking about the coming of the kingdom per se but its coming *in power*: a visible and clear display of the hidden kingdom that has come. This means any event that shows clearly God reigns and has vindicated Jesus.[14] The Parousia of Jesus qualifies but it is not the only candidate. Secondly, the saying in the Markan context is given as a supplement to v. 38. The implication then is that the vindication of the Messiah will, indeed, be given at the eschaton, but before that comes a foretaste of this may be given too. So Jesus expects something that will fortify his disciples in their belief that they have not followed a lunatic. Consequently, it must be an event that takes place in their lifetime. So much is clear, but the difficulty comes in trying to pin down the exact event. Some scholars take the sequel to be the case—the transfiguration of Jesus demonstrates to the disciples that the one who is going to suffer is indeed God's Son, divinely chosen to rule as God's vicegerent.[15] Others will take this to be the resurrection of Jesus—a clear-cut divine vindication of Jesus in the eyes of the apostles and the early Church (cf. Rom 1:4)[16]—or perhaps even the crucifixion.[17] Still others think that it is the destruction of Jerusalem, as that event vindicates Jesus' prediction and hence his status and his ministry.[18]

The problem here is that Mark, while he does give clues, does not give enough of them to help us adjudicate amongst these competing views. Perhaps there is no need for this, since the main message is not affected. Jesus

---

13. Kümmel 1957: 27; Hooker 1991: 212.

14. Cf. the OT dynamic concept of the day of the Lord. See Von Rad 1957: 97–108; and Moore 1987: 193–205.

15. Cranfield 1959: 287–88; Marcus 2009: 630.

16. Edwards 2002: 260

17. Bird 2003: 23–36.

18. McKnight 1999: 128–30.

Transfiguration and Transformation of Expectations (9:2–13)

When the first Passion prediction was made (8:31), it was so controversial that even Jesus' chief disciple rebuked him (8:32). The Transfiguration may then be understood as an event designed for the disciples, to vindicate Jesus, especially his view of his vocation as the suffering Messiah. Not only is he vindicated by God, his hidden glory is also allowed to emanate for just a moment, indicating that suffering and glory need not be regarded as incompatible.

The conversation that takes place after the event (vv. 9–13) focuses on the suffering aspect of the kingdom. Not only must the Son of Man suffer and be rejected, but the eschatological Elijah has also been maltreated by humans. So the whole section (vv. 2–13) shows that the opposite poles of suffering and glory may be reconciled in Jesus. This is the lesson the disciples must learn as they grapple with the mystery of the kingdom and the mystery of Jesus' messiahship.

The Transfiguration (9:2–8)

Mark informs his audience that this event takes place after six days, presumably from the time Jesus made his discipleship demands in the previous story. Jesus takes his three closest disciples up to a high mountain (v. 2). Where this place is, we do not know and probably the adjective "high" is meant to speak more of theology than topography (see excursus). Mark describes what happens to Jesus with the word *metamorphoō*, which means basically a change in form.

Excursus: The Place of Jesus' Transfiguration

The place is not specified but a time note is given, which is rare in Mark. Using the time note as a cue and the description that the mountain is high, some scholars have conjectured this place must be within a six-day reach from Caesarea Philippi. The one high mountain that is reachable in six days is Mt Hermon, which is 9230 feet in height and about twenty miles northeast of Caesarea Philippi. This would be a spectacular candidate and would brook no rivals if it were not for the sequel which speaks of Jesus' descending the mountain and meeting the scribes (9:14). Believing it is quite inconceivable for scribes to be found so far from Jewish territory, other scholars prefer to place the Transfiguration within Galilee. The chief candidate, and what is traditionally recognized as the site, is Mt Tabor, 1929 feet in height and about fifty miles southwest of Caesarea Philippi.[19] The drawback of this suggestion is that Mt Tabor is not actually high, although its solitariness gives the impression it has a commanding height. Furthermore, it requires quite a lot of walking from Caesarea Philippi (about fifty miles as the crow flies). The one other possible candidate is Mt Meron, which is 3962 feet in height and about twenty-five miles southwest of Caesarea Philippi.[20] It is close enough to Caesarea Philippi but because it is situated near other mountains of roughly the same height, it does not have a commanding presence.

Another factor complicating the site's identification is that height of mountains is sometimes construed theologically, in good biblical tradition (i.e., a high mountain is so only because of theological significance [cf. Isa 2:2]).

Verse 3 focuses on Jesus' clothes, which become more dazzlingly white than any process on earth could hope to match. The description of dazzlingly white clothes does carry important theological implications. Heavenly beings and saints at the eschaton shine resplendently (1 En 62:15; cf. Rev 4:4; 7:9). Jewish descriptions of God often use light and whiteness to describe his garments (cf. Dan 7:9). So the question for many theologians is: does the Transfiguration point to what the saints will finally have, of which Jesus is the forerunner? Or does it set Jesus apart from the rest of creation because only he shares his Father's glory?[21] The answer is probably the latter, in that Mark's story is structured to show the uniqueness of Jesus. He does not describe Elijah and Moses as shining in resplendent glory, although Luke did in Luke 9:31.

As was said earlier, two visitors were present: Elijah and Moses. Much has been discussed on why it is precisely these two who show up. It could be

---

19. Stein 2008: 416.
20. Leifeld 1974: 162–79.
21. For early theological interpretations, see Lee 2009.

that they belong to the class of the "deathless ones."[22] The traditional view that they represent the Law and the Prophets has no basis in Mark or in biblical literature, and is rightly rejected by many scholars today.[23] The best answer, in our opinion, is that they both have unique mountaintop experiences, and both are connected to the covenantal story of God and Israel in which the Exodus concept looms large.[24] Moses led Israel out of Egypt and was instrumental in forging a covenant between God and Israel. Elijah was the covenantal reformer and is expected to return at the end time to prepare the way for the second Exodus (Mal 4:4–5), through which the definitive and eschatological people of God will be constituted. Whatever the case, the focus is on Jesus. Moses and Elijah are key points in the covenantal story, but Jesus is the climactic point. They prepare, but he fulfills.

Such a magnificent vision certainly stupefies ordinary human beings, and not surprisingly, Peter blurts out comments he has not quite thought through. Peter's comment may then be understood as his answer or response[25] to the vision (v. 5). What was Peter's intention when he proposed to build three booths for these three majestic figures? The making of such booths is often connected with the Feast of Tabernacles, through which Israel recalls the great liberating event of the Exodus (Lev 23:33–43; Num 29:12–38; Neh 8:14–17). Consequently, eschatological significance is also given to it, as it reminds the nation of a greater Exodus.[26] But if Peter was thinking of the Feast of Tabernacles, would he not have suggested building shelters for all six of them and not just three? Recently Heil has suggested the shelters allude to the Tent of Meeting in which divine revelation was received, and over which the divine presence as a cloud descended (Exod 33:9).[27] Such a suggestion has its merits, but if he is right, why would Peter propose to build three and not just one? Furthermore, Elijah is never associated with the Tent of Meeting in Jewish thought. So it seems best to regard Peter as trying to be hospitable even though he is not thinking clearly when such words are uttered (9:6).

Verse 7 is crucial for the story. God speaks in response to Peter's suggestion, and this gives us the hermeneutical key to the whole vision. An overshadowing cloud is often used as a symbol of the divine presence, or a

---

22. Stein 2008: 417.

23. The classic statement is in Origen, *Commentary on Matthew* 12:38.

24. Similarly Marcus 2009: 632, who suggests that it is Mt. Horeb that connects the two figures.

25. The Greek *apokritheis* clearly conveys the idea of "responding."

26. The case is first made in detail by Riesenfeld 1947. Cf. Rubenstein 1994: 371–87.

27. Heil 2000: 161

precursor to the giving of divine oracles (Exod 19:19; 40:35; Num 9:18-23; Job 38:1; Ezek 1:4). For the second but final time in Mark (cf. 1:10-11), the divine voice affirms Jesus' status as the Son of God. Significantly, this time around, the words are directed not at Jesus but at the disciples. They hear for the first time the unmediated voice of God, affirming the status of Jesus as the unique Son and the one to whom they must listen. The word "listen" plays a critical role in Mark's Gospel (cf. 4:3, 9, 24; 7:14; 8:18).

We note too that this command is placed at a strategic point. Jesus has been teaching the reality of the kingdom in unprecedented and shocking ways. Not only that, but his perspective on what the Messiah is to do, and what the glorious Son of Man is to experience at the hands of mortal men, is scandalous. But the divine voice commands that only Jesus be heard, vindicating thus his perspective.

Some scholars have been impressed with the many allusions the Transfiguration story has with the receiving of Torah by Moses on Mt. Sinai.[28] The following are possible parallels: (1) the time note of "after 6 days" (Exod 24:16; Mark 9:2); (2) the presence of companions (Exod 24:1, 9; Mark 9:2); (3) the cloud that covers (Exod 24:16; Mark 9:7); (4) the divine voice (Exod 24:16; Mark 9:7); (5) a transformed appearance (Exod 34:30; Mark 9:3); and (6) the reaction of fear (Exod 34:30; Mark 9:6). How much should be made of this, Mark does not tell us. But if this is latent in Mark's story, we may safely say that just as Moses spoke God's will to his people, so also does Jesus, but in a way that is climactic. And just as Moses received a theophany (a visible manifestation of the presence of God), so also do the disciples receive a Christophany (a visible manifestation of Jesus' glory). All this serves to bolster the importance of Jesus.

The Son of Man and Elijah (9:9-13)

As Jesus descends the mountain with his disciples, he charges (the Greek is *diastellomai*, which means "sternly warns") his disciples to keep what they have experienced quiet. This pattern of great revelation to be followed by secrecy has been encountered many times previously. But what is significantly different here is the time limit to this secrecy: until the Son of Man has risen from the dead. This implies that Jesus' resurrection, which of course entails his prior crucifixion, serves as an important hermeneutical lens. It is through this event that the glorious deeds of Jesus' ministry may be understood correctly. Of course, this will also ensure that fanatical messianic enthusiasm is forestalled until all things are made clear. Why is the

---

28. Marcus 2009: 1114-18.

time limit given at this juncture of the narrative and not earlier? Jesus has spoken plainly about the Son of Man's passion in 8:31–32, and hence other profound things may be stated plainly.

Mark tells us the disciples wonder what resurrection means (v. 10). This is peculiar, as Jews should know what resurrection means, unless what mystifies the disciples is not so much the general concept of bodily resurrection as the resurrection of the Son of Man. Jewish ideas of resurrection do not include the rising again of the Son of Man of Daniel 7. Furthermore, resurrection, as opposed to mere corpse resuscitation, is expected to take place en masse at the end of time, when God winds up his redemptive program for the Jewish nation. So referring to the resurrection of just one person called the Son of Man may have puzzled the disciples.

We can now see how the question of v. 11 follows naturally. Talk of a resurrection inexorably leads a first century Jew to think of the eschaton. Coupled with this, the disciples have also seen Elijah, who is regarded by many Jews as being the herald of eschatological times. This being the case, the question about Elijah may be asked, specifically the scribal view that Elijah must first come (see excursus). The nagging doubt implicit in the question is that if the scribes are right, and if Elijah is not actively at work in Jesus' day, what ground is there for any talk of the arrival of the eschaton or for believing Jesus is the Messiah or Son of Man?

Jesus' answer affirms the scribal view, and for clarity connects Elijah's coming with the restoration (v. 12). The term "restoration" may be understood as speaking of the time when God finally returns to reign in Zion. Connected with this is the notion that people will be restored to him and be reconciled with one another, and that all flora and fauna will return to their ideal state. But the Son of Man is more important than Elijah, just as the fulfiller is more important than the forerunner. So Jesus moves on to speak of the Son of Man, principally about his suffering. As the suffering of the Son of Man is absent in Jewish eschatological expectations, Jesus' question serves the purpose of goading the disciples to reshape their perspective on the coming of God's kingdom.

A major challenge for commentators and biblical scholars is the deciphering of what OT texts Jesus is referring to. Did the OT really prophesy that the Son of Man must suffer? Perhaps the way forward is to think of Jesus as creatively combining the passages of Daniel 7 and Isaiah 53. This will then give rise to the notion that the one who plays the role in the eschatological vindication of God's people is also the one who suffers for them. There is a basis to this conjecture. We have argued that Mark 1:15 has Isaiah 52:7 as its background. If this is the case, there is no preventing someone from combining this with Isaiah 53, a passage that is close to it. This will relate the realizing of God's kingship to the role of the Suffering Servant. If we are right about the primary background to Jesus' use of the Son of Man title (i.e., Dan 7 and the kingdom connection), it is not impossible to imagine someone who is steeped in Scriptures combining all these aspects.

The next statement about Elijah's being maltreated by men (v. 13) is unexpected but a moment's reflection will show that it is nevertheless relevant to the trend of thought started, in that it serves two purposes. The first is that it aligns Elijah's work with the Son of Man's. One has been ill-treated, so would the other. It is all of a piece, perhaps indicating that God is behind such a revolutionary idea. Secondly, the statement serves to point in a cryptic way to the identity of this Elijah. If Elijah has come and suffered, the natural question that follows is who is he and where may he be found? Although Mark does not give us his identity explicitly (cf. however, 6:14–15 and Matt 11:14), his Christian audience would easily think of John the Baptist, as he was the forerunner of Christ.

Perhaps surprising for readers today, Jesus states that it is written that Elijah must first suffer. Did the OT really prophesy that Elijah must suffer? One possible answer is to think of the trials of the first Elijah. By invoking the Jewish exegetical concept of typology, the second Elijah may be said to undergo a similar experience.

With all the above said, what must not be missed is the narrative function of the story of the Transfiguration and the present story. Both combine to teach Jesus' followers that glory and suffering need not be prised apart. Jesus is truly that glorious Son of Man, but it is written that he must suffer. This is true also for Elijah. He has indeed come, signaling that all things are being restored. What they must not forget is that he too has been ill-treated by his contemporaries. All this serves as a further response to Peter's rebuke of Jesus in 8:32, and a further explication of 9:1.

Excursus: Elijah must first come

It should be emphasized that Mark 9:11 is ambiguous about who or what exactly Elijah is to precede. However, since the question of Jesus' identity is hovering in the background, readers may justifiably think of Mark as implicitly saying that Elijah comes as a forerunner of the Messiah.

This is where the problem begins, as nowhere in Scripture is Elijah said to come as a forerunner of the Messiah, although in Mal 4:5–6 he is said to herald the day of the Lord. This day refers not to a 24-hour period but an event. The event that is envisaged is God's great coming to his people. In this sense, the day of the Lord may also be a related concept to God's returning to Zion to reign (i.e., the kingdom of God). But since the ushering in of the great day of the Lord is often related to the coming of the Messiah, it is not surprising that scribes are depicted in Mark as believing Elijah to be his herald.

The passage in Malachi also speaks of the restorative work of Elijah in that he is expected to reconcile family members to each other. The LXX makes this clear by translating the Hiphil of *šûb* with the Greek *apokatastēsei*. This notion is enlarged upon in later Jewish thought to refer to all the tribes of Israel. A fine example is found in Ben Sira 48:10:

> It is written that you are to come at the appointed time with warnings, to allay the divine wrath before its final fury, to reconcile father and son, and to restore the tribes of Jacob.

Elijah's coming at the eschaton is also attested in many other Jewish sources (4Q558; *m. 'Ed* 8:7), including its connection with the resurrection (*SibOr* 2:187–88; *m. Sota* 9:15).

The Boy with the Unclean Spirit (9:14–29)

The group of disciples that were not involved in the Transfiguration event failed to exorcise a demon-possessed boy, and a dispute arose between them and the teachers of the law. The fact that the disciples have successfully cast out demons before (6:13) makes their failure reprehensible. Indeed, exorcism is to be part and parcel of their kingdom work (3:15; 6:7).

It is puzzling why when the crowd see Jesus coming to them, they are overwhelmed with wonder and run to greet him (v. 14). Usually in Mark's Gospel the crowd is astonished only after witnessing a miracle (e.g., 1:22), and not before. This has led some scholars to suggest that the glory of the Transfiguration continues to linger on Jesus' face,[29] or that Mark is continuing his echoes of Exodus 34:29–35, which narrates also the people's awe over Moses' shining face.[30] An alternative is to think of it as an extravagant use of the term by Mark to denote Jesus' commanding presence.[31]

---

29. Evans 2001: 50; Gundry 1993: 487–88.
30. Hooker 1991: 223.
31. France 2002: 364.

Whatever the reason, Jesus is soon informed of the boy's condition and the disciples' failure in vv. 17–18. His response in v. 19 indicates that a deep malaise is at work. The label of "unbelieving generation" is applied to his disciples because they stand foursquare with their contemporaries as people who have little or no faith (cf. 8:12). Brought before Jesus, the unclean evil spirit immediately throws the boy to the ground, making him convulse and foam at the mouth (v. 20).

The ensuing dialogue between Jesus and the boy's father (vv. 21–24) offers a fascinating insight into how faith germinates and grows. The father's desperation surfaces upon the description of the woes of the boy. His plea is passionate and evokes sympathy. His words "if you can" probably indicate he thinks Jesus may not be up to the task, rather than that Jesus may not be willing to do so. At this stage, faith is still not present. Jesus' challenge in v. 23 throws the responsibility back at him. The question is not whether Jesus can but whether he has faith, for everything is possible for him who believes. As it is the case in 6:5–6, Jesus does not perform miracles when there is unbelief. Realizing that the responsibility is his, the father cries out for help: "I believe; help my unbelief!" This oxymoron indicates the turmoil the father is going through. Faith has germinated but it is weak, and so there is a cry for help. But faith, however weak, is still faith and the exorcism is duly performed (vv. 25–27).

The disciples want an explanation of their failure when they are alone with Jesus in the house (v. 28). Mark does not say whose house it is, but he consistently sets the private teaching of Jesus for his disciples in a house. Jesus' reply emphasizes the importance of prayer. The meaning of this is examined in "Fusing the Horizons" below. Most Greek manuscripts add the phrase "and fasting," which is missing in the early manuscripts (fourth century). Almost all scholars regard this phrase as having been added by scribes in the interest of bolstering ascetic practices, or explaining more clearly why the exorcism failed.

Fusing the Horizons: Prayer and the Disciples' Failure

In Jesus' explanation of the failure of the disciples to cast out the demon, the blame is not placed on the lack of faith on the part of the boy's father. To be sure, lack of faith is a grave problem, as Mark's Gospel frequently castigates it. That said, what remains fascinating is that the blame is assigned solely to the disciples' failure in prayer. As it is quite incredible that the disciples did not engage in prayer, does Jesus mean they did not *pray hard enough*? Would this also suggest there are different levels of prayer and also different degrees of difficulty connected with exorcisms, since the disciples did manage to perform some earlier? If this were so, it would be natural for a special class of spiritual elites to arise. Such a pernicious phenomenon is found in many religions, including institutionalized Christianity, but it does not square with the tenor of the gospel of Jesus Christ.

All this invites us to think of what prayer is in essence. If prayer denotes total reliance on the Almighty to perform the deed, the failure of the disciples may be explained as their relying on something else other than God. This is also a form of unbelief, a theme which is prominent in the story. Being able to cast out demons in the past is no guarantee the disciples can do so in the present. Faith must not be put on past accomplishments, however glowing that may be, but on the one true object of faith. Thus, exorcism comes by prayer (i.e., by trusting in the Almighty and not on anything else).[32] Interpreted this way, Jesus' reply need not be construed as trying to speak of different grades of difficulty in performing exorcisms, or different levels of praying; it simply points his disciples back to certain fundamentals connected with discipleship which are frequently forgotten. The emphasis on prayer serves then to inoculate us from a reliance on formulas or past achievements. Instead, it directs Christians to place their trust wholly in God.

THE SECOND PASSION PREDICTION AND SUNDRY DISCIPLESHIP LESSONS (9:30–50)

There may be a thematic thread linking together the Second Passion Prediction with the following three clusters of teaching, viz. true greatness (vv. 33–37), generosity of attitude (vv. 38–41), and the severity of stumbling the little ones (vv. 42–50). Discipleship remains the concern here, but the three clusters center on the concept of greatness, with the attendant need to deflate one's sense of self-importance. This then dovetails neatly with the anti-triumphalistic nature of following the Son of Man, first announced in the sayings on discipleship after Peter's recognition of Jesus as the Messiah. This has not been forgotten by Mark, and it hardly needs to be said that in

---

32. Cf. Schweizer 1971: 189–90.

a society shaped significantly by the honor-shame dynamic, this key lesson must be learned repeatedly if the disciples are to walk in the way of Jesus.

The Second Passion Prediction (9:30–32)

Mark tells us expressly that the second Passion Prediction is given in the interest of discipleship (vv. 30–31). One item of information not found in the first Passion Prediction is the prediction of betrayal. The Greek verb *paradidōmi*, which is used by Mark, does not in itself mean that. The technical term for this is *prodidōmi* or, if the noun is used, *prodotēs*. That said, its root meaning of "being handed over" may be used to depict adequately such an idea, especially when the word was used in 3:19 to characterize the infamous disciple of Jesus. The present tense in Greek tells us that the process of betrayal has started. For the characters of the story, this is the first time Jesus mentions he will be betrayed. This may explain why the disciples are baffled by Jesus' prediction (v. 32).

True Greatness (9:33–37)

The story is situated in a house in Capernaum. We have noted how significant Capernaum is to Mark's Gospel (1:21–27; 2:1–12). Furthermore, the house is the place where special instruction, primarily for Jesus' disciples, is given. The conversation between Jesus and his disciples is occasioned by an argument among his disciples (v. 33). The phrase "on the road" is linked with discipleship—discipleship being following in the way of Jesus (cf. 8:27; 10:32–45).

What follows is a piece of teaching that speaks of a total reversal of conventional attitudes. Being great is not having the ability to command others to serve, but to be the one who serves all. True greatness must always be tied up with a servant's heart. Once this is grasped, it means that the argument on the road should not have arisen at all. Mark will return to this topic at 10:35–45.

Jesus uses a child to illustrate his teaching. In first century Palestine, the child was not usually regarded as a precious little thing who exemplified what trusting means, as is commonly understood in many Christian circles today. Instead, the child was regarded as a minor: someone without status and easily ignored.[33] The one without status is thus linked with Jesus and the Father. To receive someone was also an important social convention (Acts 18:27–28; Gal 4:14; *Did.* 11:1–2; 12:1). This was usually extended to equals

---

33. Donahue and Harrington 2002: 285.

or to respectable people. The despised are not received; they are tolerated. The great are happily received. In this sense, it is the most natural thing to receive Jesus or the Father. But Jesus teaches that to receive him or the Father, a disciple must receive the little child (i.e., the one without status). This receiving is done in the name of Jesus. In its Semitic context, this phrase is often used in connection with agency and allegiance (i.e., acting on behalf, and for the honor, of the person named).[34] Hence, the phrase signifies here that such an action is performed because the person wants to be Jesus' authentic disciple. When the child is received in Jesus' name, it is tantamount to receiving also Jesus and the Father. Do note that the concept of Jesus' being sent by the Father is found only here in Mark's Gospel, although it is frequently mentioned in John.

Largeness of Heart and Vision (9:38-41)

The identity of this exorcist is not given, as the whole point of the story is to show that working for Jesus is not a franchise for a selected few. The discourse which follows is peppered with the phrase "in my name." This provides the hermeneutical key for understanding the meaning of this passage.

John's objection is quite understandable. He has abandoned many things to follow Jesus. He is one of the designated few who has been given the commission to perform the kingdom's acts and to proclaim the kingdom's presence. The unnamed man is not. In reply to John's objection Jesus makes three points (indicated by the three *gar*-clauses in Greek).

The first is that anyone performing a miracle in Jesus' name will not speak against him because he is using Jesus' authority. This indicates the person is open to Jesus' ministry. So he cannot at the next moment speak evil of Jesus. The word "next moment" is important, since Judas' later betrayal of Jesus may otherwise invalidate Jesus' statement.

Secondly, if someone is open to Jesus' ministry (i.e., not against it), he may be counted as being for Jesus and his disciples. Of course, one who is not against something is not, by definition, one who is for that thing. To understand how the logic of v. 40 works, we need to bear in mind the controversial nature of Jesus' ministry and the eschatological urgency connected with it. In other words, there can be no sitting on the fence by way of response. Jesus' ministry is such that if one is not for it, opposition will be shown. What needs to be observed too is that the logic of v. 40 is indicative of inclusiveness and not exclusiveness.

---

34. Hartman 2010: 390.

The final point is given in v. 41 and the thrust is similar. Those who really belong to Jesus need not be identified with a social or even action group. So Jesus says anyone giving water to his disciples (in Greek it is plural, *hymas*) in his name will not lose his reward. The qualifier "because you belong to Christ" is added for clarity.[35] Giving a cup of water to them in Jesus' name means recognizing that they belong to the Messiah. Such recognition in the time of Jesus' ministry and in the time of the first-century Church is explosively controversial, and might lead to ostracism. So that person who gives only a cup of water—an activity understood as the least one can do to help—will not lose his reward, even though he may not be directly involved or identified with apostolic work or the preaching of the gospel. In Mark's Gospel, rewards to be given by God because of a connection with Jesus' ministry are always understood as things which pertain to the new age (cf. 10:28–30). So an activity which is understood as showing basic courtesy when done in the name of Jesus redounds in great reward! This is a lesson for the disciples who are tempted to think that only they will be rewarded because of their special status as the chosen Twelve.

All the three reasons make this case: the disciples must abandon the conventional understanding of group boundaries. Serving Jesus is not about acquiring a franchise. Just as true greatness means being a servant of all in Jesus' name, it also involves having a largeness of heart that goes beyond focusing on one's in-group.

Not Causing the Little Ones to Stumble (9:42–50)

The sayings found in this passage appear abrupt. No indication of time and place is given. Since the paragraph begins with the injunction not to trip up the little ones who believe in Jesus, we must begin with deciphering their identity.

It can be argued that "the little ones who believe in me" are connected to those who cast out demons in Jesus' name without being known by the Twelve, or those who give a cup of water to them in Jesus name, in that their connection with the Jesus' movement appears slender to the human eye. So preventing them from doing service in the name of Jesus or erecting membership boundaries to protect the Twelve's status amounts to "stumbling" them. That person who causes the stumbling is better off having a large millstone tied round his neck and be thrown into the sea. The "large

---

35. This is the one clear instance that Jesus calls himself the Messiah in Mark's Gospel! Hence, it should put an end to any hypothesis that Peter's confession of Jesus as Messiah is rejected by Jesus.

millstone" here is actually that which is driven by a donkey (the Greek *mylos onikos* is literal, which means "donkey-millstone"). This is much larger than the common millstone. The picture is therefore exaggerated and grotesque, given in the interest of making the saying memorable. Such a grotesquely-pictured fate is better than the apparently innocuous tripping up of people with nascent faith.

Why should such a ghastly ending be described as a better option? The answer is given in the next three sayings, each featuring a part of the body as the instrument of stumbling (vv. 43, 45, 47). Together they speak of the basic activities of a human being: seeing, doing and walking. This is a poetically comprehensive way of referring to the major sources or instruments of sin and stumbling (cf. Prov 6:16-19; Job 31:1, 5, 7). The thrust of these three sayings is that it is better to lose many basic human functions than to be thrown into Gehenna. The word in Greek actually refers to the rubbish dump of the Valley of Hinnom, situated just outside Jerusalem, where fires burn continuously. In Jewish apocalyptic literature, this becomes a metaphor for the ultimate place of punishment (*1 En* 27:1-2; 54:1ff; 56:3-4; 90:26; *4 Ezra* 7:36; *2 Bar* 59:10; 85:13). Whether the metaphor speaks of annihilation[36] or of conscious punishment lasting all eternity,[37] the word itself does not say. However, this rubbish dump is described later in v. 48 as the place "where their worm does not die, and their fire is not quenched." The words are taken from Isa 66:24, and there it speaks of the dead bodies of God's enemies, left decomposing and smoldering in the battlefield. Such a combination of images is also found in later Jewish literature (Judith 16:17; Sir 7:17). So what is described as enduring are the agents of destruction and decay. The opposite of being cast into this eternal rubbish dump is entering the kingdom of God (v. 47).

The object of stumbling in v. 42 is the little one who believes, but in vv. 43-48 it is the person himself. Has the connection been lost? No, the catch-word *skandalizomai* is maintained, and Mark may then be construed as using it as a stepping stone to another idea: the disciples must watch themselves lest they also stumble. More important, the one who causes others to stumble also stumbles himself, or the one who makes discipleship to be almost an impossible option for others makes himself a non-disciple.

The mention of the fire that is not quenched in v. 48 leads to the enigmatic sayings of vv. 49-50. In deciphering them, the first thing to observe is that the final statement (v. 50) speaks about being at peace with one another. This dovetails with what we have been expounding. This collection of

---

36. Hooker 1991: 232.
37. Donahue and Harrington 2002: 294.

sayings is about what true greatness means, and how this involves service and a largeness of heart. Without these qualities it will be impossible for the disciples to have peace with each other or with those who show the slenderest connection with the Jesus movement.

Hence, a case may be made for construing the sayings on salt as being about discipleship.[38] If we invoke OT imagery, salt and fire are words connected with sacrifices offered to God (Exod 30:35; Lev 2:13; Ezra 6:9; 7:22; Ezek 43:24). If this is the primary horizon of meaning, the phrase "everyone will be salted with fire" has a limited reference to Jesus' disciples, and the total thrust of the saying is that every disciple must be dedicated like an offering to God. The verse that follows speaks of purification (i.e., if we now think of salt as a purifying agent).[39] This is eminently possible, since fire is also a purifying agent. Such purification is necessary before one may be offered to God. But purification implies testing. One test that may come to the disciples is the presence of those who appear to be connected to the Jesus movement by the slenderest of threads. Dedication to God therefore means the disciples have to learn to have the largeness of heart so as to be at peace with others, including those who appear to be "outsiders." This is, then, one possible way of linking these rather disparate sayings with the themes of the preceding passages.

MORE REVOLUTIONARY VALUES FOR DISCIPLES (10:1–31)

Mark 10:1–31 contains three stories that have as their central concern the revolutionary values of the kingdom of God. In this respect, these stories continue the basic thrust of the earlier ones (9:30–50): following Jesus involves re-envisioning societal mores and one's values. The values concern marriage, children, and possessions, three key preoccupations of human beings. Even today, statistics relating to the break-up of marriages, pictures of destitute and neglected children scavenging for food, and intrigues and betrayals brought about by a desire to gain a larger slice of the economic pie are news that still haunts.

Divorce and God's Original Intention for Marriage (10:1–12)

The itinerary given in v. 1 is peculiar, leading to interesting alternatives in the manuscript tradition. Supposing that the NIV has followed the original reading, what we have described is a journey from Capernaum (9:33) into

---

38. France 2002: 383–84.
39. Evans 2001: 73.

Judea, and crossing the river Jordan to arrive at Perea. While the itinerary is strange, it is not impossible. What is more pertinent is that this topographical note brings us back to the territory of Herod Antipas. The Markan audience does not need reminding that John the Baptist was beheaded precisely because of his criticism of Herod's divorce and subsequent remarriage to Herodias. In this light, the mention of the Pharisees as intending to test or trick Jesus by asking a question about divorce is apt (v. 2). Moreover, many Jews, and even the Pharisees themselves, are divided over such an issue (see excursus). Jesus is therefore put in a tricky situation. An unwise answer could land him in hot soup.

Excursus: Jewish Attitudes Towards Divorce

Although there were debates among Jews about what constituted legitimate grounds for divorce, all sides, except probably the Qumran community, took it as a given that divorce was allowed. The biblical text which was often referred to in such controversies was Deut 24:1–4. In the first-century Jewish world, the famous opponents in such debates were Hillel and Shammai, two prominent rabbis. The former may be regarded as holding a liberal view while the latter held the conservative view. In *m. Git.* 9:10, we have this interesting account:

> The School of Shammai say: A man may not divorce his wife unless he had found unchastity in her, for it is written, "Because he hath found in her *indecency* in anything [Deut 24.1]." And the School of Hillel say: [He may divorce her] even if she spoiled a dish for him, for it is written, "Because he hath found in her indecency in *anything*." R. Akiba says: Even if he found another fairer than she, for it is written, "And it shall be if she finds no favor in his eyes [Deut 24.1] ..."

The italicized words identify the concepts the different schools emphasized to build their ethics on. The School of Shammai allowed divorce only on the ground of unchastity, while the School of Hillel allowed it for many other reasons. The strictest view of all, which was almost identical with that of Jesus, came from the Qumran community. They prohibited divorce: certainly for leaders, but also probably for all its members (cf. CD 4:20—5:2; 11QT 57:17–19).

The first question asked by the Pharisees concerns the legality of divorce (v. 2). The reply of Jesus is shrewd and wise for three reasons. First, it will lead them back to Torah, the accepted norm for all Jews. Secondly, through a closer look at the relevant text (Deut 24:1–4) it will be seen that Moses did not command divorce. This will then set the ensuing discussion on the right premise: divorce was given as a concession and not a command. It is precarious to build ethics based on a concession. If the foregoing is accepted, the discussion will then, thirdly, move to consider the origin of marriage. Indeed, if there is a command pertaining to marriage and divorce in what Moses wrote, it is found in Gen 2:24. This assumes, of course, that Jesus and the Pharisees think of Genesis as being written by Moses.

The Pharisees reply that Moses permitted it (v. 4). In Jesus', day, a certificate of divorce would have been given which would allow the divorced woman—since only the husband could initiate divorce proceedings—to remarry. What needed to be ascertained, in order to prevent abuse, were the just grounds for divorce. Many of the rabbinic traditions touching on this topic are about such grounds.[40]

Jesus' reply acknowledges the existence of this provision (v. 5). However, in order to prevent concession from sliding to normalcy, he points out that the Mosaic regulation (Deut 24:1–4) was given because of the "hardness of hearts." This is a telling phrase, as it recalls the condition of Israel so often castigated by the prophets, which led ultimately to the rupture of the Sinaitic covenant and exile (Deut 10:16; Jer 4:4). The phenomenon is also referred to in Mark 4:12 and 8:17. In other words, the provision was given not to encourage divorce but to serve as a damage-control measure.

Jesus now appeals to first principles instead of casuistry (vv. 6–8) (i.e., the original intention behind the divine gift of marriage [Gen 1:27; 2:24]), before the deterioration of sin has set in which calls for legislation. That said, it must be noted the reference point is still Moses, as both Deuteronomy and Genesis are regarded as stemming from him. This is important, as it indicates that Jesus has not departed from the agreed frame of reference. Otherwise, the argument would have been weakened.

Citing from Gen 1:27 and 2:24, Jesus draws the implication that marriage amounts to becoming one flesh (v. 8). Although Jesus does not explain exactly what "one flesh" means, he nonetheless points out what it entails: what God has joined together, let none separate. The contrast between two acting agents, viz. God and human beings, makes the point clear: God wants marriages to last, and human beings must not use initiatives or institutions to break them. This sets the teaching of Jesus in stark contrast with the Hillel

---

40. See the tractate *Giṭṭin* in the Talmud.

school and the ruminations of Josephus (*Life of Josephus* 426; *Antiquities* 4:253). The upshot of this emphasis on the oneness lays the foundation for a permanent union, which is grounded in creation itself (i.e., God made humanity male and female). Since this is a union of two, and not the absorption of one into the other, both partners stand equal in the eyes of God in the marital relationship.

Looking back at the whole discussion, we can see how wise Jesus' answer is: it gives nothing incriminating away, and does not compromise the pure intention behind the institution of marriage. The point is that to start with casuistry (i.e., what cases may be deemed legal for divorce proceedings to take place), is to start at the wrong end. The right way to start is to ask what really is the divine intention behind marriage, what this intention is supposed to signify, and to reflect on how such an intention may be encouraged to flourish in all our laws and institutions. This is something that Antipas in all his power, and Herodias in all her cunning, would not dare contradict. Nor would the Pharisees dare to do so in front of the crowds.

Something more potent is also perhaps being hinted. If Moses gave the concession because of hard-heartedness, what would happen if this hard-heartedness is taken away? If the coming of the reign of God means restoration of people and creation, what ethics should be practiced once this restoration is at work? Jesus has proclaimed that the kingdom is dawning in and through his ministry. This means he is the one who can remove the hardness of hearts. If this is so, the attitude of his disciples towards marriage and divorce should be transformed. So the kingdom connection must be kept in mind. Not surprisingly, the parallel story in Matthew contains a discussion between Jesus and his disciples on how this original intention relates to the kingdom (Matt 19:10–12).

The suggestion made above may explain why the implications of his discussion with the Pharisees are made clear only to the disciples in a house (v. 11). They are "the insiders" in relation to kingdom realities. This motif has been encountered before in Mark's Gospel. Special teachings reserved for the disciples are taught in the house (cf. 7:17; 9:28, 33), without specifying whose house it is.

That Jesus' teaching in v. 12 is revolutionary may be seen in the following: both genders are covered, and that remarriage means committing adultery. The patriarchy of Jewish society, sponsored by texts such as Lev 20:10–12, easily led women to be regarded as chattels. Hence, they are never the offended party in any breakdown of marital relationships. This means men do not commit adultery against women, but only against other men (i.e., if a married man slept with the wife of his neighbor, he did not sin against his own wife but only against his male neighbor). Similarly, if a married woman has an extra-marital affair, she has not wronged the wife of the man she slept with, but only her own husband. In contrast to all this, Jesus teaches that the wife can also be sinned against. He is using the original principle of marriage that the two shall be one to derive the teaching that marriage is not only for the man but also for the woman. This is indeed radical and ground-breaking in his society. No Jewish rabbi or teacher in his time or before it has ever made such a pronouncement.[41]

Jesus goes even further. Remarrying someone after a divorce is construed as committing adultery against the divorced spouse. Why should this be the case? This is unthinkable in today's society and not surprisingly, a matter without consensus in NT scholarship.[42] Constraints of time and space do not afford us a detailed discussion of the matter. Suffice it here to point out that Jesus' pronouncement in vv. 11–12 is derived from the first principles he has expounded earlier. This means the one flesh union is still at work even after a divorce, which implies that all divorces, including those legitimated by human institutions, cannot break the marital bond in the eyes of God. So if a man were to marry again after a divorce, he would be committing adultery against his original spouse. The same applies also to a woman. An inference to be drawn from this is that Jesus commands monogamy. If polygamy is allowed, talk of committing adultery against one's wife makes no sense. Not surprisingly, such a radical pronouncement of Jesus is qualified by explanatory remarks by other early Christian writers in the interest of clarifying or softening,[43] which we are unable to discuss in this commentary.

Little Children and the Kingdom (10:13–16)

This short story fleshes out the essence of the kingdom by connecting it to little children, a motif encountered before (9:33–37). Mark describes Jesus' response to the disciples' hindrance of the children with the Greek *aganakteō*. This word speaks of irritation and repugnance, and it occurs once only in Mark's Gospel. It shows how gravely wrong the disciples' hindrance of children is. Why should an action performed in the interest of giving their Master some respite be greeted with such displeasure? The reason lies in vv. 14–15, and it is that children are somehow connected to the kingdom of God. First, the kingdom of God belongs to them. The second arises from

---

41. Marcus 2009: 711–13.
42. See the helpful discussion in Stein 1979: 115–21.
43. The exception clauses in Matthew and the directives of Paul. On the latter, see Wong 2002: 181–94.

the first: those who wish to receive the kingdom must do so as children. The phrase "as a little child" in Greek (*ōs paidion*) may be construed either as modifying the grammatical subject (whoever) or the grammatical object (the kingdom of God). Translated the alternatives are: (i) "Whoever, like a little child, receives the kingdom," or (ii) "Whoever receives the kingdom as one receives a little child." Both are possible and must not be regarded as mutually exclusive. The solemnity of this truth is reinforced by the prefatory words "Amen I say to you" (v. 15).

As explained earlier, children then were recognized as being without status. Being unable to fend for themselves they had to depend on others and would not be well received, since in ancient society, social reciprocity was the powerful dynamic that bound people together. So Jesus is saying that, contrary to what the majority in society is thinking, the kingdom belongs to such entities. Indeed, without this recognition of one's utterly dependent status on God, there is no way for one to receive the kingdom. The disciples fail because they regard the children as a nuisance to the Messiah, without remembering that all humans—because of their need for redemption and forgiveness—are also in some sense a nuisance. But it is to such people that God comes in his redemptive power. All this means that the least in society should be given the same welcome to the kingdom.

Wealth and the Kingdom (10:17–31)

The words of the young man who approached Jesus are interesting and significant. First, nowhere else in Mark's Gospel is Jesus called a good teacher. In fact, such an address is attested only once in all the extant Jewish literature. In a statement that contains a play on the word "good," Rabbi Eleazar of Hagronya is addressed thus: "Good greetings to the good teacher from the good Lord, who from his bounty dispenses good to his people" (*b. Ta'an* 24b). What is interesting in this parallel is the connection between the concept of goodness and God's bounty. We are not sure whether the young man is flattering Jesus, but clearly a similar connection of goodness and wealth is found in the story. Secondly, his question concerns "eternal life." This is probably a shorthand way of referring to the "life of the age to come" (the Hebrew would be *ḥayyê 'ōlām habbā,*' or, life in God's new order), which is, of course, everlasting.

The young man's opening words elicit from Jesus the radicalizing of the concept of goodness. In fact, he connects this to the Shema, the Jewish creed that confesses one God. The translation "except God alone," found in some

English versions,[44] does not quite capture the meaning of *ei mē heis ho theos*, which actually means, "except God is one." This strange phraseology is here because of the Shema. The point may be paraphrased thus: "No one is good except God, who is one; and this is what the Shema means." The upshot of this is that the teaching Jesus is about to give has its basis in the Shema and the Ten Commandments (which he would refer to again in 12:29–31). This heightens the status of the discussion, and suggests the following: if only God is good as the Shema requires, by calling Jesus good is the young man putting him on that level? Secondly, the commandments that are cited in v. 19 climax with the command to follow Jesus (v. 21). This suggests that Jesus puts himself on a high pedestal, as the one who sums up Torah. Thirdly, we may observe that the commandments cited may all be related to loving the neighbor. The requirement to follow Jesus, however, is not related. Is this requirement then to be understood as belonging to the Godward aspect of the Ten Commandments? If it is so, the implication is that following Jesus means loving God, bringing us back to the Shema. Admittedly, the foregoing is speculative but what gives us some confidence in thinking it possible is that a similar phenomenon may be found in 2:1–11, where Jesus claims subtly his identity may be understood via the Shema.[45]

Moving back to the concrete data, we observe that the commandments Jesus cites exhibit a peculiar order. He begins with the sixth to the ninth commandments. He then follows with "do not defraud," before moving back to the fifth commandment. What is interesting is the command of "do not defraud." This is not found in the Ten Commandments, unless we think of it as a loose application of the tenth commandment.[46] If it is not, we may wonder why the tenth commandment is left out, along with those which relate principally to God (commandments one to four). Before we offer an explanation for this phenomenon, the young man's response must be examined.

The man replies he has kept all those commandments since he was a boy. And now the climax comes and the penny drops. Jesus speaks about the *one thing* the man lacks, recalling the *one God* in the Shema, and enjoins him to sell all that he has and give to the poor, which will ensure heaven's rewards. And, then, he is to follow Jesus. The Markan text speaks of Jesus' looking lovingly at him (v. 21). This is an important datum, as it indicates that what follows is not given out of malice or to make things unusually difficult for the young man. Love must be the framework for understanding

---

44. E.g., the NIV and NASV.
45. Further on this see Tan 2008: 181–206; 2011: 2677–707.
46. Marcus 2009: 721.

the rationale for these demands, and love can be incisive. More importantly, the radical demands of Jesus show that the end of keeping the commandments is not philanthropy, as important as this may be, but following him (cf. 8:34–38). Perhaps all this is actually the working out of what the tenth commandment "You shall not covet" means. If this is the case, we can now appreciate why Jesus did not mention this commandment earlier. This is the commandment to emphasize, not by quoting but by discussing its implications. But all this the man cannot do. He has kept some commandments but his failure to give up his possessions to follow Jesus shows his loyalty is not really to the commandments but to his own opulent welfare. For him, obeying God's commandments may be done as long as one's preferred lifestyle is not compromised.

We are now in a position to understand why Jesus starts by radicalizing the concept of goodness. Far from being a non sequitur, it actually establishes the framework for understanding the apparently harsh requirement Jesus makes in v. 21. Jesus is not countering flattery here. Instead, he sees the need to emphasize the fundamental axiom for Jews in order that the discussion may move forward fruitfully. God is good such that goodness cannot be predicated of anyone except God himself! Remembering this will help the rich young man understand that the difficult tenth commandment is given not to make him miserable but to liberate him to be a good neighbor to those in need, and to follow the Messiah when he summons him. Conversely, the failure to give up all to follow the summons of God made through his Messiah will reveal that he has not authentically affirmed the goodness of God.

We can now appreciate certain curious aspects of the story, especially why the first four commandments were not cited. If they were, the man would certainly have replied that he had no other gods. But now that he is shown to be unable to give up all to obey the tenth commandment and follow the Messiah, he has been unmasked as one who cannot authentically confess the Shema (i.e., he does have other gods).

The sad pronouncement of Jesus in v. 23 is greeted with amazement on the part of the disciples. This is so because there is one powerful strand of Jewish thought that connects wealth with God's favor.[47] Along with some passages in the Bible (e.g., Deut 28:1–14; Job 1:10; Ps 128:1–2), which speak of God rewarding the wise and faithful with riches, there are other passages in Jewish literature of the Second Temple Period that speak of the rich as being the blessed of God. It is probably this latter concept that leads the disciples to remark: "Who then can be saved?" In other words, if those who are tangibly blessed by God cannot enter the kingdom, those who appear to

---

47. Dowd 1988: 76.

be ill-favored do not stand a chance. That said, it must also be pointed out that an opposite strand of Jewish thought also existed, where wealth was regarded as something that alienated a person from God.[48]

Jesus' pronouncement challenges the notion just described. Because of its importance, Jesus answers the disciples' amazement with a reiteration of what he said earlier: it is hard for the rich to enter the kingdom (vv. 23-24). This difficulty may be compared with a camel going through a needle's eye. There is a long-standing tradition that speaks of a small gate in Jerusalem by the name of "Needle" which camels must stoop to get through. This is then used to convey the concept of humility. As beautiful as this may be as an image, there is no such gate.[49] What Jesus uses here is a common proverb or an epigram to convey the message of impossibility. A parallel to this may be found in the Babylonian Talmud (*b. Ber.* 55b), where the image of an elephant going through the eye of a needle is used.

The perplexity of the disciples increases so that they remark, "Who then can be saved?" The answer given by Jesus brings his disciples back to the platform of hope: with men it may be impossible but with God all things are possible (v. 27). Those who are seemingly the ill-favored of God may be saved. Indeed, the saying probably also opens up the possibility to the rich: they may also be saved by the wonder-working power of God, certainly not by allowing them to cling on to their riches, but by opening their eyes to see their dependence on God.

At this juncture Peter reminds Jesus that the disciples actually have left everything to follow him (v. 28). This becomes the foil to the next piece of teaching, which gives closure to the whole concept of giving up everything to follow the Messiah. It is that following the Messiah is not about impoverishment. Instead, it means ordering one's values rightly. The items listed by Jesus (v. 29) may be considered as life's essentials in the first century Palestinian context: home, relations, and means of survival. Indeed, these were understood to be the blessings of the covenant (progeny and land as inheritance; cf. Gen 12:1-3). The giving up of all this for the kingdom results paradoxically in gaining them (v. 30), which echoes 8:35. Persecutions are mentioned, as not all will imbibe kingdom values. But the essential point is that giving up is not impoverishment but being free in order to share; such sharing enlarges one's home, family, and possessions. This thought connects us back to Jesus' radical demand in v. 21. We can now see the cohesiveness of the whole passage.

---

48. Schmidt 1987: 76-84.

49. Aquinas mentioned it is from Anselm that he learned it, in *Catena Aurea* on Matthew 19: 23-26.

The motif of reversal is mentioned again in an epigram (cf. 9:35). The function here is probably to prevent the disciples from adopting a triumphalistic attitude. Following Jesus has its rewards, but this must not be understood as going on a reward chase so as to be put on a pedestal above the rest of humanity. The first shall be last and the last first must be the slogan of the kingdom. It is all about honoring even the lowliest and serving them.

To sum up: the three stories of this section have as their central concern the values that relate to the kingdom of God. Such values cut across the grain of many an accepted institution, attitude or norm. But they do so not in the interest of being difficult and demanding, as though discipleship were a contest to see who might be the most ascetic or acerbic. No, they are what they are in the interest of returning to the divine intention behind the creation of this world. This intention is now revealed through the ministry of Jesus of Nazareth. The possibility of attaining this is graciously given also through it. All this is but another idiom for saying that God has begun his eschatological reign!

Fusing the Horizons: Marriage, Social Inequality, and Wealth

Marriage, inequality in society, and wealth are still explosive issues today. Divorce rates are on the rise in many societies, countering the belief that as societies further their economic development, families should be happier. Class distinctions, whatever the variety, continue to rear their ugly heads in ever subtle forms—and sometimes brazenly—in spite of laws that have been promulgated to prevent them. We happily sacrifice the future of the vulnerable for our own gain. The quest for wealth often becomes toxic, leading to greater economic polarization.

These areas come under the kingdom spotlight in the passage. It is by subjecting ourselves to the rule of God that we come to understand what being married means, how to treat our fellow human beings, and where true wealth may be found. We do not pretend to know everything about such explosive issues but the following may safely be claimed. Being married means faithfully cleaving to our spouse in spite of the slings and arrows of outrageous fortune. Furthermore, we are to accept all, especially the weak and vulnerable in society, because God accepts all. In God's kingdom, all are vulnerable children. Finally, wealth is to be shared. By sharing we bless and are blessed. We are not impoverished in the process but are actually enriched. He who gives up all to follow God's call will find in inscrutable ways that what he has given up is, in a profound sense, given back to him.

In Jesus' eyes, then, the health of a society is measured by how strong marriages are, how the lowly are welcome, and how wealth is shared. This calls into question what we find so often in our world. But before we wag our finger at it, we need to take a good look at what is happening in our churches. Faithful Christians continue to cringe at the news of embezzlement or sex scandals of prominent leaders. Moreover, big or wealthy churches are quite happy to pontificate where small or poor churches have gone wrong, without thinking whether perhaps they, for their size and wealth, may have imbibed the wrong values, or worse, belonged to the wrong kingdom. Furthermore, the conversion of a prominent person is jubilantly celebrated, and that of an illiterate unemployed person garners nary a notice. The Church should seek to live out what Jesus has taught about the explosive issues of family, acceptance and wealth in whatever society she finds herself and bear witness to the liberating and empowering nature of these values. Otherwise, we end up not as the salt of preservation but the bacteria of putrefaction.

Following the Messiah in Service: Third Passion Prediction (10:32–45)

The third Passion Prediction (10:32–34) is intended to be connected closely with the request of James and John (10:35–45). This is suggested by the fact there is no indication of any change of place or time. The latter story is simply introduced with the Greek connective *kai*, which means "and." In many ways the arrangement and composition of these two stories follow the similar narrative pattern of the second Passion Prediction, and share a similar concern. That said, it must still be emphasized that what is found here is not mere repetition, but a further development of a couple of central ideas. First of all, apart from its being the most detailed of the three, there is a significant new datum given in the third prediction: the Gentiles would be the ones to execute Jesus, even though the whole thing is contrived by the Jewish leaders. Secondly, the destination is explicitly named as Jerusalem, and it is in that city of peace that Jesus will be executed. Thirdly, the Son of Man, and not a child, is now used as the example in the teaching on true greatness. So this prepares the way for the reason, hitherto unexplained, why the glorious Son of Man must suffer. It has to do with service and providing a ransom.

The Third Passion Prediction (10:32-34)

The story begins with the description of the group being "on the way" (v. 32). We have pointed put earlier that this is a cipher for the way of Jesus, which is also the way of discipleship. In this passage the destination of this way is given: Jerusalem. It is in Jerusalem that the disciples will come to understand exactly the way of Jesus, and what following him means. And sadly, in Jerusalem their failure will be seen in all its lurid colors. Mark sows here the seed of his Gospel's denouement.

Something ominous is in the air, judging by the description of the astonishment and fear of the disciples and other followers. This is construed as being connected with Jesus' "leading the way." The reaction of the Twelve and other followers indicate it must be something about Jesus' manner that causes such consternation. Rightly, many commentators conclude it is Jesus' resolute march.[50] All this gives this third and final Passion Prediction a climactic quality.

The taking aside of the Twelve (v. 33) signifies yet again the privileged position these have in terms of revelation. Details of Jesus' forthcoming ill-treatment are given: being mocked, spat at, flogged, and finally killed. Such items are also connected with the Suffering Servant of Isaiah 53 (especially vv. 3, 5, 8-9, 12). Furthermore, the Gentiles are now mentioned as the executioners, although the Jewish leaders (the chief priests and the scribes) engineer this. The prediction of resurrection after three days ends the saying.

The Request of James and John (10:35-40)

James and John approach Jesus with a request that has, as its credit, boldness, but as its debit, rank self-centeredness (v. 35). It should also be noted that such a request is not incredible, as these two have seen Jesus transfigured. Perhaps they sense that Jerusalem will be the climax of Jesus' ministry, and hope that when this happens they will be seen as his faithful lieutenants, deserving to share his glory. That said, the request also reveals that the lesson on true greatness, first taught in 9:33-37, has not been imbibed.

---

50. France 2002: 41 Marcus 2009: 744 argues that the language speaks of pilgrimage, which has been fused with the idiom of holy war of Deutero-Isaiah. Cf. Watts 1997.

Not surprisingly, the reply of Jesus mentions that they do not know what they are asking for. The metaphors of cup and baptism are connected with Jesus' vocation. In the OT, the cup stands for the destiny to which one is appointed. In this sense it can convey the notion of blessing (Ps 11:6; 16:5; 116:13), judgment (Ps 75:8; Jer 25:15-29; Ezek 23:31-34; Hab 2:16), or simply suffering, without any judgment being implied (Isa 51:17-23; Lam 4:21). Since the next usage in Mark speaks of the suffering that has been destined for Jesus (14:36), the "cup" should mean suffering. Baptism is not a metaphor that is well developed in the OT, and so we will have to look at ideas contemporaneous with Jesus' time. Since baptisms are often water rites that involve the overwhelming of a person with a fluid, one may think of this as the dominant idea (cf. Luke 12:50). Combining this with the notions suggested by the metaphor of cup, the conclusion is that Jesus is speaking of being overwhelmed by suffering or judgment. That said, there may be a deeper level of meaning. The word "baptism" in Mark's Gospel may recall either the activity of John the Baptist, or more probably the baptism of Jesus through which his vocation was given. This then dovetails neatly with Jesus' challenge: what he will be going through belongs exclusively to his vocation.

Whatever the case, the two disciples answer that they are able. Jesus agrees. As disciples of Jesus, their vocation involves that too. But what is implicit is that the disciples think of suffering and judgment as only a phase or transition to glory. They have not grasped a more powerful connection between glory and suffering, especially when it is seen in the light of the Messiah's vocation. Jesus' next statement in v. 40 is, therefore, barbed. First of all, such positions are only for those for whom they are prepared. This theoretically may rule out these two disciples. But more significantly, Mark tells us in 15:27 with identical phraseology that the persons by Jesus' right and left are the two crucified malefactors! Mark may be suggesting the following: if ever there was an enthronement for the Messiah in Mark's Gospel, it would be the cross; if ever there were companions sharing Jesus' enthronement glory, it was the two crucified malefactors.

If our interpretation is on target, the conversation between Jesus and his two disciples is seen to be full of ironies. Mark already indicates this when he narrates Jesus as saying that James and John do not know what they are asking for. The suffering of the Messiah is something that is uniquely the vocation of Jesus. Suffering is not a means to glory, but is itself the display of the messianic glory. Although James and John claim they are able to drink Jesus' cup and be baptized with his baptism, when the crunch comes they fail.

The Lesson on True Greatness Once More (10:41-45)

The misguided and ambitious request of James and John understandably gives rise to unhappiness on the part of the other disciples. To defuse this tense situation, and to extend the lesson to the rest of the company, Jesus calls the Twelve together and teaches them what true greatness is. He begins with the Gentile concept of greatness: the great person is he who has the authority to lord it over many (v. 42). The disciples' perspective on greatness should be the opposite: the greatest is he who has the most to serve. This revolutionary value has its basis in the vocation of the Son of Man.

In order for its full significance to be grasped, the Danielic background of the Son of Man idea must be kept in mind. To reiterate, the Danielic Son of Man is he who will be given the kingdom, and through his work the saints of the Most High are to be vindicated (Dan 7:13-14). In this regard, the figure speaks of vindication, triumph, and glory. But in Jesus' interpretation, this figure is combined with the Suffering Servant in Isaiah 53, to which some key ideas of Mark 10:45 allude (see excursus). Hence, the Son of Man comes not to be served but to serve,[51] and to give his life as a ransom for many. Therefore, Jesus gives a powerful corrective to the disciples' delusions of grandeur. This story then serves as the climax to all the teaching Jesus is giving his disciples, in preparation for Jerusalem.

Excursus: The Suffering Servant of Isaiah 53 and Mark 10:45

We have argued consistently that in the Markan context the phrase "Son of Man" is to be understood primarily against the Danielic background, without denying the possibility of creative re-interpretation on the part of Jesus. However, the concepts of "service" and "giving one's life as a ransom" are best understood against the background of the Suffering Servant of Isaiah 53. This implies Jesus is appropriating scriptural traditions and stories, and understanding these to be an integral whole. So he can combine the Danielic image of the Son of Man with the Isaianic image of the Suffering Servant to clarify his vocation. Mark 10:45 may then be regarded as highly significant not just for understanding Jesus' sense of mission and vocation, but also his concept of Scripture.[52]

---

51. Cf. Gathercole, "Son of Man," where he argues that Jesus reversed the connotations associated with the Son of Man figure in Daniel 7:14.

52. The Jesus of the Gospels focuses more on the storyline of Scripture than on minute exegesis of passages, and often synthesizes passages to create meaning that is

Excursus: The Suffering Servant of Isaiah 53 and Mark 10:45

What evidence is there to support the claim that the Fourth Servant Song of Isaiah is being appropriated in Mark 10:45? This topic has been keenly discussed by scholars and we cannot hope to enter fully into this debate in this short commentary.[53] What we will do instead is identify the arguments for maintaining our case. The critical phrase to discuss is *dounai tēn psychēn autou lytron anti pollōn* (often translated as "to give his life as a ransom for many").

1. First it must be noted that "service" is connected with "the giving up of the life" in both Mark 10:45 and Isa 53:11. The term used in Mark 10:45 is *diakoneō*, while the related term in the LXX of Isa 53.11 is *douleuō*. But behind the LXX stands the Hebrew *'ābad*. It must be insisted that *diakoneō* is a legitimate translation of the Hebrew *'ābad*, and it is often used and understood as a synonym of *douleuō*, the LXX term. Hence, it is precarious to mount an objection based on the difference in Greek terminology, especially when the two terms are legitimate translation of the Hebrew. Moreover, in Mark 10:44 the term *doulos* (the noun) is found, and it is used as a synonym of *diakonos* in v. 43. Once the synonymous nature of the two terms is accepted, we may legitimately see a parallel between Mark 10:45 and Isaiah 53 LXX.

2. To be noted too is that "to give one's life" in Mark 10:45 approximates semantically the Hebrew phrase in 53:12, where the life is mentioned as being poured out.

3. The term *pollōn* (i.e., "many") recalls the *rabbîm* of Isa 53:11–12: the Servant dies for many who would be the beneficiaries of his self-offering.

4. The greatest objection to our case centers on the use of *lytron* (which may be translated as "ransom"). In the Hebrew text of Isa 53:10, the Servant is described as giving his life as an *'āšām*, which is the term for a guilt offering. The LXX never translates *'āšām* with *lytron*. Hence, if Mark is thinking of Isa 53:10, he is using a rather peculiar word to translate a key term in it. But if we think of Mark 10:45 as not meaning to be a translation of Isa 53:10, but a summary and a creative appropriation of the task of the Servant in that passage, the force of this objection will be ameliorated.[54]

---

untraditional, perhaps even shocking. See the essays in the forthcoming *Jesus and the Scriptures*, to be published as a volume of the LNTS and edited by T. Hägerland.

53. A good start may be made with the collection of essays in Bellinger 1998. See also Evans 2001: 120–22. The classic objections are found in Hooker 1959; and Barrett 1959: 1–18.

54. France 2002: 421.

5. Finally, apart from the Fourth Servant Song in Isaiah 53, there is no other biblical passage that comes close in terms of related themes and terminology. So what is being urged here is that if we think of all this cumulatively, the Fourth Servant Song stands as the best candidate for Mark 10:45, if ever there was a background to which the verse is alluding.

Restoring Bartimaeus' Sight (10:46–52)

This story, the last of the healing accounts in Mark, serves as a symbolic narrative, pointing to the possibility of the removal of spiritual blindness, an affliction that has plagued the Twelve. Mark narrates only two stories of restoring sight to the blind: the present story and the two-staged healing in Decapolis (8:22–26). That story began the major section of 8:22—10:52 that depicts Jesus on the road to Jerusalem. The present story concludes it. The two stories of healing serve, then, as a framing device for the entire major section, which has as its central concern the theme of discipleship and the need to eradicate misguided notions.

The travelling company now arrives in Jericho, only about fifteen miles from Jerusalem. Jericho has been regarded as the oldest continually inhabited city on earth. It was founded around 9,000 BC. Herod the Great built a new city not far from the ancient site, and erected his palace and a hippodrome there. He later died in this city.[55]

As they are about to leave the city[56] together with a large crowd, they pass by a blind beggar by the name of Bartimaeus. Mark's description of his location as *para tēn hodon* indicates he is not yet a disciple. He is "beside the way" but not on it yet. Later, he will be on it (*en tē hodō*, v. 52). Such phraseology strengthens our belief that this story serves as a parable of discipleship.

When Bartimaeus hears it is Jesus of Nazareth who is passing by, he shouts, "Jesus, Son of David, have mercy on me!" The term "Son of David" does not simply indicate genealogy, but speaks also of the hope of the coming scion of David who will rule over the nation (see excursus). Significantly, this title is used for the first time for Jesus in Mark's Gospel. Bartimaeus

---

55. Holland and Netzer 1992: 3:723-39.

56. In Luke Jesus meets a blind man (not named) as he is about to enter Jericho (Luke 18:35). In Mark, Jesus meets blind Bartimaeus when he is about to leave. Matthew follows Mark in the main, but he mentions two blind men (not named) instead (Matt 20:29-30)! These slight discrepancies should not distract us from the significance of the story in Mark.

connects this title with mercy. In Jewish thought the Son of David is usually regarded as a warlike figure who will deliver the nation from her enemies. Can it be that Bartimaeus is able to transcend the usual understanding of messianic function to grasp a neglected but important aspect of it? Note that the compassion of Jesus is the chief feature in the two feeding stories (6:34–44; 8:1–9).

Excursus: The Son of David

The Prophets never lost hope for the restoration of the Davidic rule, even in the face of destruction and deportation. The belief in a scion or branch of David, to be raised up by God at the end of days, is thus frequently found (Isa 11:1; Jer 23:5; 33:5; Zech 3:8; 6:12). This person is expected to rule as the vicegerent of God, in fulfillment of the covenant God made with David in 2 Sam 7:11–16. Later Jewish thought focuses on the militaristic aspect of this coming figure, who is also called the "Son of David" (*Pss Sol* 17–18).[57] Jesus' connection to David is not mentioned prior to this passage in Mark's Gospel. The title of "Messiah" may imply that he is from the line of David, but even this is not firm, as the term has also been used to depict a coming priest who would restore true worship in the Temple of Jerusalem. This as attested in the Qumran community (1QS 9:10–11).[58]

Although rebuked to be silent, Bartimaeus persists. The one on a resolute march to Jerusalem stops and asks for Bartimaeus to be brought to him. Mark provides the significant information that Bartimaeus throws away his cloak before jumping to his feet and coming to Jesus (v. 50). This is significant in a number of ways. First, according to the Torah a person's cloak cannot be taken away from him by any creditor, as it is deemed essential to his existence (Exod 22:26–27; Deut 24:12–13). For a blind beggar in the setting of first century Palestine, the cloak takes on an even greater significance, as it represents all his worldly goods and the one means of obtaining sustenance for himself (i.e., the cloak is used for begging).[59] Hence, Bartimaeus

57. Marcus 2009: 1119.
58. On the diversity of Jewish messianic speculations, see the collection of essays in Charlesworth 1992; and Neusner, Green and Frerichs 1987. However, the case for diversity has often been overstated. See Collins 1995; and Horbury 1998.
59. Taylor 1952: 449.

may be seen as renouncing all that he has to go to Jesus.[60] With this datum we may see a thematic line connecting us back to 1:14–20 and 2:13–14.

When Bartimaeus comes before Jesus, the latter asks him the same question he asked of James and John when they came to him (cf. v. 51 with v. 36). But instead of asking to sit either on the right or left of the Son of David, Bartimaeus asks that he may see! Such a request is indeed natural for a blind man to make, but in the setting of Mark's Gospel where perception is such an important motif, Bartimaeus's request takes on greater significance. This story may then be regarded as a counterpoint to the previous pericope.[61] It provides the right reply that those belonging to the inner circle of Jesus' disciples should make. Only by truly seeing could one be an authentic disciple of Jesus. So it is not surprising that Jesus replies with the significant: "Your faith has healed you!" (v. 52). It is faith that will restore sight, both physical and spiritual. Mark concludes this story with the information that not only is Bartimaeus' sight restored, but he also follows Jesus "on the way."

---

60. Cf. Ossandón 2012: 377–402, which argues that Bartimaeus is the only character who follows Jesus unconditionally.

61. Stein 2008: 497.

The Climax of the Gospel:
The Messiah and Jerusalem (11:1—16:8)

CHALLENGE IN JERUSALEM:
SYMBOLS OF FULFILLMENT AND JUDGMENT (11:1–26)

This section begins the final part of the book of Mark. All the action takes place in Jerusalem. Mark's Gospel only narrates one journey to this city. This stylized presentation serves to heighten the significance of the city for Jesus. In this city Jesus' prophecy of his own fate comes to pass.

We should also note that, alongside the change of location, there is also a change in profile. Everything important about Jesus' ministry comes into the open. So there is much confrontation between Jesus and the Jewish authorities. Furthermore, the actions performed by Jesus are provocative, challenging many accepted and hallowed notions and institutions. They are also mainly symbolic (the entry, the action in the Temple, the cursing of the fig tree, the last supper), and often made without explanatory remarks. Such challenging actions do not just speak of judgment, they also speak of fulfillment.

Why is there a change of profile with the change of locality? It may be argued that it is related to the mystique and significance of Jerusalem. These have been strengthened through years of traditioning, and they may be known as the Zion traditions. I have attempted to map out the significance of these traditions in a different book, especially their connection to eschatology, and demonstrate their appropriation by Jesus.[1]

All that said, what must still be pointed out is that if we accept that Jesus preaches the message of the kingdom in accordance with the background provided by Isa 52:7, God's reign in Zion is one theme that he cannot neglect. If God is to reign in Zion, Jesus' kingdom ministry must of necessity relate to the city of Jerusalem.

---

1. Tan 1997: 23–51.

The Entry to Jerusalem (11:1-11)

This story is in two parts: the finding of the animal (vv. 1-6), which is most probably a donkey,[2] and Jesus' riding it into Jerusalem (vv. 7-11) amidst jubilant chants, which are connected to the expectation of an eschatological Davidic king.

About two miles from Jerusalem, while still at Bethany and Bethphage,[3] Jesus instructs two of his disciples to look for a colt. The instructions indicate either that some prior arrangements have been made, or that Jesus is using the custom of impressment by which animals may be requisitioned for temporary service for a prominent rabbi or someone powerful, such as the king.[4] The term "Lord" (v. 3) is interesting, as nowhere else in Mark is Jesus given such a title. The term on its own can mean "Master," and the possibility that the Master here is the owner of the animal cannot be discounted. Alternatively, the Lord may refer to God here. If this is the case, the requisitioning is done in the name of God for his Messiah.[5]

What happens after this is significant. Cloaks are thrown on the colt for a makeshift saddle for Jesus to sit on; cloaks and leafy branches are also strewn on the road by many people; and an exclamation, utilizing the ancient traditions of Israel, is made. What do all these mean? The best place to start is the intentional action to ride on an animal to enter Jerusalem.

Stories of pilgrims and important visitors making their visits Jerusalem are frequently told. In all these stories it is assumed anyone visiting Jerusalem must walk on foot. Even the noble and royal have to comply. There is a story of Alexander the Great making his trip to Jerusalem, and this king of kings has to dismount from his horse and walk the whole way into the city (Josephus *Antiquities* 11:325-29). This is enforced because of the sacredness of the city. The practice is so important that anyone who cannot walk into Jerusalem because he or she is too sickly is exempted from making the pilgrimage, even for important festivals like Passover (*m. Hag.* 1:1). This reinforces the unspoken rule that a person must not ride into Jerusalem. In this regard, Jesus' action of riding into Jerusalem is extremely provocative.

---

2. Gundry 1993: 626, takes it as a young horse; but cf. France 2002: 431, who thinks it is a donkey. The latter is supported by the parallel accounts in Matthew and John.

3. Bethphage (meaning "house of figs") is mentioned with Bethany as though they form a unit. Presumably, this is because Bethphage was a small hamlet associated with Bethany. Scholars do not know exactly where Bethphage is, although according to Christian tradition, it is situated between Jerusalem and Bethany.

4. Derrett 1971: 241-58,

5. France 2002: 432.

If Jesus is consciously performing something provocative, we should expect him to explain what this is. But he does not, and this strange silence is found also in all the parallel accounts in the other three Gospels. Unless we think there is a total failure of communication, we must believe there is something in the traditions of Israel that can clarify Jesus' intention. Entries into Jerusalem on animals are mentioned twice in the OT: once for the coronation of Solomon (1 Kings 1:33), and the other in a prophecy of the eschatological Davidic king, who comes riding into Jerusalem to usher in what the city stands for: peace (Zech 9:9). This verse is not quoted in Mark, although we find it being used in the Matthean and the Johannine accounts (Matt 21:5; John 12:15). It is this royal background we propose is lurking behind Jesus' action. His riding into Jerusalem on an animal signifies that this long-expected prophecy is now coming to pass. Jerusalem is now confronted with the long-awaited king.

In this respect, the crowd strewing clothes on the road is meant to signify their acceptance of him as their ruler. This is certainly not done for the convenience of any traveler but is performed as a sign of honor and allegiance (cf. 2 Kings 9:13). The leafy branches that were cut from the fields and strewn on the road serve the same purpose: they provide a sort of carpeting for the one honored to tread on.[6]

What is most significant is the adulation of the crowd. The first important term in the adulation to note is "hosanna." This liturgical term comes from the Hebrew *hôšî'â-nā'* of Ps 118:25-26, one of the psalms chanted by pilgrims as they ascend Jerusalem during religious festivals.[7] Its basic meaning is "save us now," and was originally a cry for deliverance. The LXX translates the term as *sōson* (i.e., "save," thereby demonstrating that this basic sense is to be retained). That said, the strange use of hosanna in Mark 11:10 ("hosanna in the highest") may indicate that, in the course of its liturgical usage, the term may not always have strong connections to its original meaning. Hence, it may be used as a general term for praise.[8] In the OT such an acclamation is given either to God or the king (2 Sam 14:4; 2 Kings 6:26). Mark tells us that this hosanna is offered to Jesus, suggesting that he is to be identified with this Davidic tradition.

The phrase "Blessed is he who comes in the name of the Lord" is often used to greet pilgrims arriving in the Temple. This may be the case here, but the greeting to be extended to the Messiah when he finally comes to the Temple may also take this form (cf. Matt 23:39||Luke 13:15). The latter is

---

6. Evans 2001: 143-44.
7. Hooker 1991: 260.
8. Fitzmyer 1987: 110-18.

made clear by the next statement, which speaks of the blessed coming of the kingdom of David (v. 10).

The upshot of all this is that the crowd, according to Mark's narrative, certainly acclaims Jesus to be the long-awaited Davidic king. All the actions performed, and all the words uttered, take on this meaning. Significantly, Jesus does not silence them as he usually does in previous stories. In fact, his action of riding an animal into Jerusalem serves to encourage it!

The end of all Jewish religious pilgrimages in first century Palestine is the Temple, and so Jesus enters the Temple and takes a look at everything (v. 11). Since it is late, Jesus and the Twelve retire to Bethany, where Jesus' friends are. What may be of interest here is the description of Jesus looking around. It heightens suspense (i.e., is that all Jesus will do after the adulation of the crowd?) and also sounds an ominous note: is Jesus doing some sort of inspection visit? To unravel this, the Markan audience must listen to the sequel. Here, we see good story-telling technique at work.

The Cursing of the Fig Tree (11:12-14)

The sequel to the Entry story, which takes place the day after, comes in the form of a narrative sandwich. The framing story is the cursing of the fig tree (vv. 12-14; 20-21), and the story that is framed is the action in the Temple (vv. 15-19). The two stories are meant to be mutually illuminating and interpretative.

The story of the cursing of the fig tree has raised many questions for Christians. That there is a deeper layer of meaning, Mark indicates through two pieces of information. Mark begins the story by mentioning Jesus' hunger as he journeys from Bethany to Jerusalem (v. 12). This is peculiar since Bethany is only two miles from Jerusalem. Is it because his host failed to feed Jesus before the latter started the journey? This appears implausible. Or did Jesus set off deliberately without food in order to set the stage to convey some symbolic meaning? Mark does not tell us explicitly, but are there other clues that point in this direction?

Secondly, Mark states explicitly that it is not the season for figs, and that his disciples heard Jesus' curse clearly (vv. 13-14).[9] The datum either appears to make Jesus' action more reprehensible, or it points to a deeper meaning at work. The latter is to be preferred, as it is impossible to think Mark would want to make Jesus appear in a bad light. Mark does not yet tell us this deeper meaning, but the sandwich technique he uses hints at

---

9. This is the most cogent way of understanding the syntax. For discussion of the different scholarly proposals, see Telford 1980: 26.

what it may be. So we must take a closer look at the action performed in the Temple, before coming back to unravel the meaning of this strange episode.

Of course, one way of ameliorating Jesus' seemingly vindictive action is to appeal to botany. Some claim that the fig tree sprouts fruits first (the *paggîm*) before the leaves, and that these fruits would later ripen after the leaves have appeared. So the sight of a fig tree in bloom may indicate to Jesus that unripe fruits may at least be found. While not pleasant to the palate, they are still edible (*m. Sheni.* 4:7).[10] Mark's comment that it is not the season for fruits is correct as the full development of these early fruits will come later. So it is not unreasonable of Jesus to expect to find fruit on the fig tree after the leaves have sprouted. Such an explanation ameliorates a lot of the negative reactions to this story, and to some extent it is a good thing. However, it has not yet grappled with the symbolism Mark wants his audience to see. We must take a closer look at the Temple episode in order to grasp fully the message Mark intends for his audience.

The Action in the Temple (11:15-19)

The action of Jesus in the Temple has generated much controversy in recent scholarship, particularly over the symbolic meaning that he intended to convey.[11] Many competing theories have been propounded and to examine them all is too big a task for this commentary. What we shall do instead is look at the data Mark provides and from there, offer our line of interpretation. The data to be considered are the following:

(i) The significance of the Temple for Jewish self-understanding;
(ii) First-century realities pertaining to Jewish worship;
(iii) Elements of Jesus' *one* action: driving out those buying and selling; overturning tables of money-changers; overturning benches of the dove-sellers; not allowing anyone to carry a vessel through the temple courts;
(iv) OT quotations: Isa 56:7 and Jer 7:11;
(v) The reaction of the Temple authorities; and
(vi) The action's connection with the cursing of the fig tree.

The Jewish Temple is a national symbol for God's presence and Israel's election (i.e., her special identity over against other nations). As such, it is also used as a symbol of resistance to the inroads made by Hellenization and

---

10. Hunzinger 1997: 7:753; Bishop 1955: 217.
11. Sanders 1985 brought this to the fore of scholarship on the historical Jesus. Evans 2001 provides a good summary.

Roman imperialism.[12] Furthermore, it is a place around which much of the economy of Judea revolves, especially that of Jerusalem. Gifts flow into the Temple, and so do deposits, because it is believed this sacred place has been guaranteed by God to be the most secure on earth.[13] More than this, the Temple is linked to eschatological thought.[14] Many Jews believe that in the last days a new Temple, or at least the renewing of the present Temple, will come about. God's presence will then be experienced in an unprecedented way. This means nothing less than the vindication of Israel, and also her complete restoration to God, resulting in her glorification. Of course, such ideas entail the further notion of political freedom. In this regard, a demonstration in the Temple is not like an innocuous holding up of a placard. It is either a rejection of the Temple's significance or a direct challenge to the Temple authorities: not just on how the Temple is to be managed, but also on the kind of ideology and praxis connected with it.

Verse 15 tells us the target of Jesus' action is those who are buying and selling. Within this group, those who change money and sell doves are singled out: their tables and benches are overturned. All these data may easily suggest to a modern reader that Jesus is against the commercialization of a sacred place. But there is a deeper meaning when the background is taken into consideration, and the scriptural quotation of Jesus is scrutinized. Buying and selling are necessary in the Temple, because the offerings to be presented to God must receive priestly approval. Hence, it is unrealistic to expect the Israelites to bring their own animals, because they do not know whether the animals will meet with priestly approval. It makes sense therefore to provide such animals for the convenience of the worshippers. There is evidence that before AD 30, such services were found outside the Temple, but in its vicinity (Mount of Olives), and Caiaphas the high priest subsequently moved these services to the outer courts of the Temple.[15] It is hard to envisage that Jesus would be against such services.

Why are the money-changers and dove-sellers singled out in Mark's narrative? An annual tax on all males is collected for the running of the Temple, especially to fund the daily sacrifices (Exod 30:11–16), which are regarded as making atonement for the sins of Israel (*t. Seq.* 1.6). In the past, the financial cost of such an institution was defrayed by the kings, but after Israel lost its monarchy, the funds came from the common people.[16] Since

---

12. Hengel 1989: 206–24.
13. Hamilton 1974: 365–72.
14. See Brower 1999: 119–43.
15. Eppstein 1964: 42–58.
16. Schürer 1978: 2:271.

different types of coins were used throughout the Empire, some with a better quality of metal than others, it is hardly surprising the Temple authorities should insist on a particular coinage. In this instance, it is only the Tyrian silver statēr that is accepted.[17] If this is so, money-changing facilities should be provided, and so they were. The dove-sellers supplied sacrificial victims for the poor. The richer might bring bulls and lambs, but for the poor that was the one sacrificial victim they might use. Moreover, many other sacrifices to be made were related to doves, as commanded in the Torah (Lev 12:6; 15:14, 29; Num 6:10).

In the light of all these data, Jesus' action becomes transparent. Either he is attacking all these "services" as an extremist who does not think of practicalities, or he is attacking something fundamentally more important. Was he against the whole idea of sacrifice?[18] If this were so, it would be strange for him to take it out on the buyers and sellers. It would be better to stage the action where sacrifices were being made. So we need an alternative interpretation.

There is good and varied evidence to show there was corruption arising from the provision of such services.[19] This need not be surprising as any enterprise, however good its intention at the outset, may be easily corrupted by the love for money. If this evidence is considered seriously, Jesus may then be construed as staging a prophetic demonstration against the ongoing corruption. Such corruption harnesses the monopolistic power that the Temple authorities enjoy. They approve sacrificial victims, and they also provide them, albeit often through intermediaries. All this dovetails with the words of Jer 7:11, cited by Jesus. The Temple authorities have re-enacted the role of the generation before the exile, in that they do violence and rob with impunity and retreat, like bandits, to the safe haven of their robbers' cave, which in this context is the Temple. In so doing, the Temple becomes not a place for worship but a place for violent robbery. The money changers are singled out probably because Jesus does not believe in the mandatory collection of the Temple Tax (see Matt 17:24–27).[20] The dove sellers are also the special targets of his action because they supply sacrificial animals for the poor. There is an anecdote in the rabbinic literature (*m. Ker* 5:7) that has relevance for our understanding of the significance of this action of Jesus. The prices of doves were exorbitant, therefore making it difficult for the poor to offer sacrifices to God. Gamaliel I, a prominent rabbi, made a pro-

---

17. Abrahams 1917: 1:83–84.
18. Cf. Neusner 1989: 287–90.
19. Evans 1989: 522–39.
20. Bauckham 1986: 223.

nouncement that relaxed certain requirements, and this caused the prices to plunge. This incident demonstrates that the supply of such a "service" was not always offered with the convenience of the worshippers in mind; profiteering sometimes lurked.

What we are proposing, then, is that Jesus is demonstrating against the corrupt practices of the Temple authorities which have turned the Temple into a den of robbers. This crime is heightened because the hour of fulfillment has come, as demonstrated by Jesus' entry into Jerusalem. The failure of the current Temple establishment is a failure at the most crucial hour. This explains why Jesus tells a parable with these authorities as his target (12:1–12), and predicts the destruction of the Temple (13:1–2).

It must be emphasized that Jesus' action does not signify cleansing. If it did, why would Jesus proceed to predict its destruction, if it is *ex hypothesi* cleansed by him? Would this not mean the cleansing action had failed? So proponents of this theory cannot speak of the cleansing of the Temple, but of an attempted but failed cleansing.[21] Again, it is improbable Jesus' rationale is that such activities are conducted at a wrong place, namely the court of the Gentiles.[22] This court is not known as such in the first place. What we have is a boundary beyond which Gentiles cannot go (Josephus *Apion* 2:104). In other words, it is not *their* court although they are permitted to be there. If Jesus is really interested in clearing space for the Gentiles, the worst place to do it is where the merchants are, for this suggests the Gentiles are but second class worshippers, standing on that court while all of Israel may move close to the altar![23]

That said, Jesus does have in mind the Gentiles, not by clearing space for them but by demonstrating that the Temple should be ready to receive Gentiles at the fulfillment of the restoration of Jerusalem, signified by his entry. So Jesus quotes from Isa 56:7, a highly relevant verse. In its original context the prophecy speaks of the blessings to foreigners arising from the restoration of Israel. This also includes those who are excluded from worship in the Temple because of their failing to meet ritual requirements, such as the eunuchs. So the oracle speaks of an unprecedented gathering of those who were previously excluded. In this regard, the prophecy relates to the eschaton where the Temple will no longer be a boundary marker for the Jews, but embrace Gentiles from all walks of life in the worship of God.[24]

---

21. Sanders 1985: 61–68.
22. Stein 2008: 517.
23. Rightly noted by Borg 1984: 175.
24. Davies 1974: 350–51.

So we see how these data point in the direction of Jesus' staging a prophetic protest against the corrupt practices of a Temple that should be ready to welcome the long-expected king and fulfill its role as a house of prayer for all nations. What about the strange statement of v. 16: that Jesus does not allow anyone to carry a vessel across the Temple courts? This datum is unique to Mark. Since he does not explain why Jesus forbids anyone from carrying a vessel through the Temple, we are left guessing at Jesus' reason. The main scholarly proposals are the following: (i) Jesus was preventing people from taking a shortcut through the Temple (based on the evidence of *m. Ber.* 9:5);[25] (ii) Jesus was acting in fulfillment of Zechariah 14:20-21, where it is prophesied that every vessel in the Temple is holy; Jesus would then be forbidding people from carrying unclean vessels;[26] (iii) Jesus did not allow merchandise to be carried across the Temple courts, to prevent the corrupt sales from continuing.[27] Our interpretation favors (iii), which the NIV supports, but it must be admitted that the evidence as it stands does not permit firm conclusions.

In response to Jesus' action, the Temple establishment (the chief priests and the scribes) seek to have him killed because his action amounts to a shrill challenge to them. In their eyes, he has struck at the most important national and theological symbol. But no action is taken, only conniving. This is because the populace seem to be in favor of such an action (v. 18). The fact that he is not lynched to death by the people speaks volumes of the negative attitude the crowds may have towards the Temple establishment. It should also be pointed out that the crowd's allegiance can easily be swayed from one of astonishment to one of antagonism, if the Temple establishment plays its cards right by shifting the focus away from the elements of Jesus' action to the locus of the action (i.e., it was performed in and against the Temple, not the establishment). This explains why a few days later they shout, "Crucify him!"

To sum up our interpretation: there are two main considerations which inform Jesus' action in the Temple. The first is the perceived corruption of the Temple establishment, which is using its position for lucrative gain. Jesus' action may be regarded as a prophetic demonstration, performed in protest against this corruption. However, his statements which explain his actions, citing from Isaiah and Jeremiah, imply this is no ordinary prophet and no ordinary action. This leads us to the second reason. Jesus perceives that the hour of the fulfillment of the Zion promises has come. The Temple

25. Abrahams 1919: 1:84.
26. Chilton 1992: 135-36.
27. Bauckham 1988: 78.

has to be such that what it stands for harmonizes with the coming of the eschaton. But it fails abjectly at the most critical hour. Instead of being the house of prayer, drawing in the nations to worship God, it has become a den of robbers. What then would happen to it? The sequel which completes the Markan narrative sandwich explains.

The Withered Tree (11:20-26)

The next morning Jesus and the Twelve observe the fig tree has withered from the roots. The words of Peter serve as a reminder that it is so because of Jesus' curse (v. 21). In other words, Mark reiterates that this fig tree has been cursed by Jesus.

The response of Jesus to Peter's remark at first glance is puzzling but when it is connected to the Temple incident, the trend of thought becomes transparent. The first statement has to do with faith (v. 22),[28] and we have seen how important this is in Jesus' ministry. It is that which draws upon the gracious power of the in-breaking kingdom. But v. 23 connects this faith to the moving of a particular mountain,[29] and not just any other mountain. Bearing in mind Jesus' location, the mountain in question can either be the Mount of Olives, or the mountain on which the Temple is situated. Taking the cue from the Markan sandwich, it is best then to interpret "this mountain" as referring to the Temple mount. So Jesus is saying, if there is faith, the Temple mount may be cast into the sea.[30]

If the Temple becomes obsolete when there is faith, how does one approach God to make requests and offer sacrifice for atonement of sins? This implicit question is picked up in vv. 24-25. Verse 24 pronounces that the Temple is not needed for requests to be heard by God.[31] In fact when prayers are made in faith, even when that important national institution is removed, those prayers will still be heard and answered. Similarly in v. 25, forgiveness comes not through offering sacrifices at the Temple in Jerusalem, but may come through prayer and forgiveness exercised on others. So by faith,

---

28. The Greek actually says "have faith of God" (*echete pistin theou*). The genitive *theou* (i.e., "of God") can be construed in many ways. In this context the viable possibilities are "have faith in God" or "have the kind of faith that God gives." Whatever the case is, faith is now pitted against the Temple. In this context, it forms a new badge of identity for God's people. What marks them out is no longer their devotion to the Temple but the faith they have in God or from God (or both).

29. This is clear in the Greek text: *tō orei toutō*.

30. Marshall 1989: 168-69.

31. Recently Gray 2008: 53-55 draws upon Moloney 2002: 227-28 and argues that behind these sayings stand the notion of a new Temple.

prayers and forgiveness may come, especially when such faith is exercised in accordance with the character of the forgiving Father.[32]

In short, what Jesus utters are not general statements on effective prayer. Instead they relate particularly to his action in the Temple, and the self-understanding of his role in regard to the promises made to Zion: he has been acting out their fulfillment.[33] The Temple, its function and what it stands for as a sign of election, has been replaced by faith. In this light we can see that Jesus' response to Peter is not a *non sequitur*, like ships passing in the night. Jesus answers the disciples question in a profound way. The faith that can cast the Temple mount into the sea is connected with the withering of the fig tree.[34]

The Doomed Temple and the Withered Tree

We are now in a position to grasp more fully the meaning of this Markan sandwich. In the OT the fig tree is sometimes used to speak proverbially of peace and security, linked often with the eschaton (Mic 4:4; Zech 3:10). Moreover, its use in the eschatological speculation of Second Temple Judaism suggests it can be construed easily as a symbol for eschatological conditions.[35] In this regard, the cursing of the fig tree and the demonstration in the Temple may be seen as stemming from a unitary message of Jesus: the eschaton has come, but Israel as represented by her leaders and key institutions is found wanting. It is also instructive to note that in Jer 8:13, a passage close to Jer 7:11, the prophet speaks of God's judgment that results in barren vines and barren fig trees, offering us a further clue to the meaning intended by Mark. The barren fig tree presents a symbolic picture of the Temple: it is equally barren. Instead of being a house of prayer for all nations, it has become a den of robbers. Jesus' cursing of the fig tree and its subsequent withering symbolically expounds the fate awaiting this Temple. It is doomed; the king of Zion has entered the Temple, inspected it and rejected it. Just as the fig tree withers because it is cursed by Jesus, so will the Temple be removed to the sea (i.e., destroyed). So the story of the cursing of the fig tree is not about ethics but about theology.

---

32. Evans 2001: 188–89 comes to a similar conclusion. In fact, he argues that the metaphor of moving mountains is eschatological.

33. A similar conclusion is reached recently by Kirk 2012: 509–27.

34. Verse 26 is not found in early manuscripts and may be regarded as a scribal addition, made in the interest of clarity.

35. Telford 1980: 129–63.

Jesus' Authority Questioned (11:27–33)

This episode flows from the provocative actions Jesus performed in Jerusalem. It also serves as the head of a series of stories (11:27—12:44) that feature Jesus locking horns with the Jewish powers that be. This leads later to the explicit prediction of the destruction of the Temple in chapter 13. In some ways these stories mirror those of 2:1—3:6, where controversies are featured.

Mark locates the present episode in the Temple. Those arrayed against Jesus are identified as the ruling priests, the scribes and the elders (v. 27), an august grouping of sacerdotal, learned and traditional authorities. The two questions asked by them are closely related. The question of "what" asks Jesus for the nature of his authority. The question of "who" asks him for the source of that authority. Alternatively, they may be construed as unitary, with the second reiterating the first. This is because the Greek *poia* is often used synonymously with *tis*.[36]

Jesus' reply seems to indicate, on a superficial reading, that he is trying to dodge a difficult question, because he asks an equally (if not more) difficult one. Such a reading is inadequate because it fails to take into account that Jesus' identity and ministry are closely linked with John's baptism. In fact, it serves to prepare the nation for Jesus. All this means that if John's baptism is accepted as having come from heaven, the person of whom John is a herald should have the divine authority to challenge the Jewish powers that be. But if these Jewish authorities reject John's baptism as coming from heaven, no amount of explanation on the part of Jesus will suffice.

So it boils down to the reluctance to believe, not the inability to comprehend. As both are sent from heaven, to reject one is to reject the other. All the Jewish authorities can see is the political liability of Jesus' actions and teachings. This is precisely what Mark informs us in vv. 31–32. Since politics are uppermost in their minds, and not the truth, they have no choice but to claim ignorance. Confronted with such a group of people, Jesus would be wasting time explaining the source of his authority. Moreover, any answer Jesus gives could be twisted for political ends, including the premature termination of his ministry.

Further Controversies (12:1–44)

Together with 11:27–33, the stories in chapter 12 give the Markan audience a flavor of the issues surrounding Jesus' ministry in Jerusalem. Significantly,

---

36. BDAG s.v.

Mark does this by mentioning all the possible Jewish groupings as being in conflict with Jesus.

The Parable of the Tenants (12:1-12)[37]

The people referred to are not specified and are probably the same people who questioned Jesus about his authority (i.e., the chief priests), the scribes and the elders. Although Mark uses the plural "parables," only one is related (see 4:1-12 for a similar phenomenon). This shows that what Mark narrates here is just a sample, chosen because it sheds the most light on what is dividing Jesus and the Jewish authorities.

Mark tells us the audience of the parable understand it is spoken against them (v. 12), even though Jesus does not provide an interpretative key. The irony here is that the one parable that is understood by the "outsiders" is precisely the one that leads them to plot against Jesus. One reason why this parable is easily grasped, even by outsiders, must be that Jesus is using familiar images from the long story of Israel. The vine stands often for the nation (Ps 80:8-18; Isa 27:2-6; Jer 2:21; 12:10; Ezek 19:10-14; Hos 10:1). Coins minted by Jewish leaders would sometimes use this image too.[38] The parable may also allude to the song of the vineyard in Isaiah 5, where Israel is described as a failed vine.[39] That said, an important difference must be borne in mind: Jesus does not state that the vineyard will be abandoned, but the replacement of the tenants. Although Isaiah 5 may provide the background, it is not the determinant of the parable's meaning.

The different characters in the parable may now be identified. The vineyard is Israel, and the owner of the vineyard is therefore God. The tenants will be the leaders of the nation who have the responsibility of tending the vineyard. The servants who are repeatedly sent represent the prophets. The way the parable is told dovetails with many stories about them, featuring above all their violent fate,[40] which is indicative of the nation's obduracy (Jer 26:20-23; 2 Chron 24:20-22; cf. Matt 23:34, 37 and the first-century work, *Lives of the Prophets*). The Son must be understood as the Messiah,

---

37. The Gospel of Thomas also contains a parable about a vineyard, which scholars associated with the Jesus Seminar regard as being prior to the Markan version (see Funk and Hoover 1993: 100-101, 510-11). However, many scholars have serious objections to such a theory: Evans 2001: 217-19; France 2002: 457; Meier 1991: 1:134.

38. Hendin 1987: 94-95. The vine motif can be found on coins minted in the 2nd and 3rd year of the Jewish Revolt (AD 67-68). This is accompanied by an inscription in Hebrew which proclaims "the liberation of Zion."

39. Evans 2001: 224-28 provides a detailed analysis of the parallels.

40. Miller 1988: 225-40.

the heir of the vineyard. Instead of being received he is rejected, because the tenants are eyeing the vineyard for themselves. This theme parallels that of the preceding story: the authorities refused to face the "truth" of Jesus' question, because they were thinking only of their political position. It also dovetails with the Passion prediction: the heir of God will be ill-treated and killed by the Jewish authorities, the tenants of the vineyard.

Excursus: Problems of the Parable

Modern readers usually have two difficulties with the parable. The first pertains to the assumption of the vineyard owner (v. 6). As the story turns out, his assumption proves to be wrong. If this owner stands for God, is Jesus then teaching that God has miscalculated? Such a conclusion is unnecessary, as it is based on a misunderstanding of how parables function. Parables are not direct exposition—otherwise telling them would become superfluous. They are usually narratives, and these have their own local coloring and plot. The members of the audience are drawn into these narrative worlds to play certain roles or to see certain truths for themselves. The message is found not in the details but the whole narrative and the critical points that relate to the occasion for the giving of the parable.[41]

The second pertains to the assumption of the tenants (v. 7). There is certainly no Jewish law that says if the heir is killed, the vineyard will belong to the tenants. This lack of verisimilitude should not cause too much concern, since Jesus is aiming to show how absurd the assumption is, an absurdity that is comparable to the rejection of the Son by the Jewish aristocracy. That said, some scholars ameliorate the supposed difficulty by hypothesizing that the tenants may be thinking either that the son's appearance implies the owner is dead,[42] or that the owner is too old and frail to take action.

Some other pertinent points ought to be noted. The first is the assumption that the climax of Israel's story has come. This may be detected in the sequence of sendings, and the use of the phrase, "last of all" (v. 6). Since this is a tale about Israel's history, Jesus is depicting to his audience what obtains

41. Cf. Gerhardsson 1991: 321-35.
42. Jeremias 1954: 75-76.

at the climax of this tale: the leaders continue in the same evil spirit of their forbears; not only have they killed the servants sent, they have the temerity to kill the heir also. So judgment must fall. The owner of the vineyard will take action, personally seeing to it that these tenants are punished and the vineyard given to other tenants. So the judgment theme is followed by the replacement theme. The question then is, "Who are these replacement tenants?" Unfortunately, Mark does not make this clear. We could try guessing or regard the question of their identity to be a secondary concern. However, in view of how history panned out, Mark's audience would undoubtedly think of either the apostles or the church, comprising Jews and Gentiles, as the new tenants.[43]

The second theme is Jesus' identity, expressed through Ps 118:22–23. Once we take into account the Psalm's context (see excursus) and how it is interpreted, we can see Jesus' point. Just like the central character of the Psalm, he will be playing the role of a leader. Not only this, but he will also be the rejected stone. However, this rejected stone, in God's providence, will become the capping stone. This is the stone that either completes an arch or sits at the pinnacle of a building.[44] When this happens, those with eyes to see will understand how marvelous it is, and that God is behind it. So Jesus is pointing to the two stages in the unfolding of his identity: rejection and then vindication. If the stone image is to be construed as a synecdoche for the Temple, Jesus is pictured as the one who completes the eschatological Temple (cf. John 2:19). Hence, the Temple motif is still being maintained, if only in the background.

Excursus: The Appropriation of Psalm 118:22–23

The text used by Mark agrees with the LXX, which is also a close translation of the Masoretic Text. This passage contains the theme of reversal: the one rejected will be vindicated and glorified. In its original context, the entire Psalm is a thanksgiving liturgy, with the central character recounting his experience of troubles and subsequent deliverance by God, even though plural voices creep in at certain junctures (e.g., vv. 25–26). Verses 22–23, however, form part of the liturgy connected with the joyful entrance of the *central character*, whose role is annually re-enacted by a leader of the pilgrims. The Targums (*Tg. Ps* 118:19–27) understand this character

---

43. Evans 2001: 237; Stein 2008: 537.
44. France 2002: 463.

as David, who despite being despised by many became the most celebrated king of Israel. This may accord with the original setting of the Psalm, which is probably written for the celebration of military victory.[45]

Finally we should note that the scripture cited not only aptly expounds the fate of the Messiah, but also befits the occasion. Psalm 118 concludes the *Hallel* Psalms (Pss 113—18), which are sung as part of the Passover liturgy. It was also the psalm the crowd used to greet Jesus when he entered Jerusalem. Hence, Jesus is using what is in many people's minds.

Paying Taxes to Caesar (12:13-17)

Some Pharisees and Herodians are sent to trap Jesus with his own words. Although not specified, Mark probably intends his audience to think of the commissioners as the ruling priests, the scribes and the elders (11:27). We have here an interesting collusion of parties that are often opposed to each other in policies and beliefs (chief priests—mainly Sadducees—and Pharisees; Pharisees and Herodians; cf. 3:6).

The question asked is about whether a Jew should pay taxes to Caesar (v. 15). The tax in question is a form of poll tax of one denarius—the wage for a day's work.[46] In Jesus' day, only Jews in Judea paid this poll tax, because it became a Roman province in AD 6 when Archelaus, Antipas's brother, was forced to abdicate by Jewish protest and Roman greed. A Galilean Jew was not subjected to this Roman poll tax, as they had Herod Antipas as their ruler. When the legate Quirinius conducted a census to facilitate the proper collection of this tax, a revolutionary by the name of Judas the Galilean rose up and summoned many Jews to revolt against Roman rule. According to Josephus, the slogan used in this revolt was "only God is our king" (*Antiquities* 18:4-6, 23-25). Rome responded with great military might, and many lives were lost as a result. Hence, the question is meant to put Jesus between the rock and a hard place. If he answers "yes," the Zealots and many in Judea will turn against him, as paying the tax supports subjugation by a foreign power. If the answer is "no," Jesus may be hurled before a Roman magistrate and charged with sedition.

---

45. Allen 1983: 123–24.

46. Schürer 1973: 1:401–4. Rome imposes two forms of direct taxation: a *tributum soli* (tax on agriculture produce), and a *tributum capitis* (which is an amalgamated tax on both head count (poll tax) and property). Whatever the function or ends, the tax connotes subjugation to non-Romans.

Jesus asks for a denarius to be brought, which is the coin used to pay the poll tax. He also asks about the image imprinted on it. A typical coin would have the image of Tiberius, and the words "TI CAESAR DIVI AVG F AVGVSTVS."[47] On the reverse side there would be images connected with the Roman Empire, usually the goddess Pax.[48] Jesus' interlocutors acknowledge that the inscription and the image are all about Caesar. He now gives his pronouncement, which steers him away from the difficult dilemma the question was meant to create. "Pay back to Caesar what is Caesar's. And to God what is God's!" The Greek word *apodidōmi*, which is usually translated as "pay back," can suggest either pay the tax or reject Caesar by giving back to him what is his.[49] Hence, Jesus' answer does not give his opponents any cause to prosecute or denounce him, and yet at the same time it points in the direction of a full resolution. The emphasis is on loyalty to God,[50] as paying to God what is God's in the Jewish worldview means everything. Of course, different groups would interpret in different ways how this loyalty is shown (thus the adroitness in Jesus' answer). However, the main point stands, and Jesus is not simply trying to be evasive. What matters is loyalty to God. Seen in this way, it is no wonder Mark tells us the interlocutors marvel at his answer (v. 17).[51]

Marriage and the Resurrection (12:18-27)

In this story, those questioning Jesus are the Sadducees. Recent scholarship proposes that the term "Sadducees" is derived from the Hebrew *ṣādôq* (i.e., Zadok, the high priest appointed by David to oversee cultic activities; cf. 2 Sam 8:17), and refers not so much to a party that is tightly-knit as to some aristocratic and priestly families, loosely connected.[52] That said, the early sources (Josephus *Antiquities* 18:16; 20:199; *War* 2:165; cf. Acts 4:2; 23:6-8) imply that there must be sufficient distinctiveness in their beliefs and agenda for them to be spoken of as a group. One of these beliefs is mentioned in the present story: they do not believe in the resurrection (v. 18).[53]

---

47. Translated into English it means "Tiberius Caesar, Augustus, son of the divine Augustus."

48. Hart 1984: 241-48

49. Myers 1988: 312.

50. Tannenhill 1977: 175-76.

51. For a thorough examination of this pericope, see Förster 2012.

52. Wright 1992: 209-13; Porton 1992: 5:894.

53. On Jewish beliefs relating to the resurrection, see the treatment of Bauckham 1998; and Nickelsburg 1972.

There is one other tenet which Mark does not mention here, but knowing it will help us understand why Jesus answers them the way he does. It is that the Sadducees regard only the first five books of Moses (the Torah) to be authoritative. On this basis they claim that Scripture does not teach any resurrection of the dead, because the books of Job, Psalms, Isaiah, and Daniel, with their explicit (Isa 26:19; Dan 12:2) and implicit references (Pss 16:9-11; 49:15; 73:23-26; Job 19:25-26) to resurrection, are certainly not Scriptures to them. Perhaps one other reason why they do not believe in the resurrection may be that such a belief destabilizes society. Belief in resurrection can fan revolutions as it may embolden people to the point that they are prepared to give up their lives. In any revolution the reigning powers stand to lose most.

The Sadducees' hypothetical situation[54] is based on the law of levirate marriage (Deut 25:5-10; cf. Gen 38:8). A widow without issue is constrained by Torah to marry the brother of the deceased, so that any child born from this union may then carry on the deceased's name.[55] The point then is that resurrection creates messy situations, and what is worse, it undermines Torah. The woman in obedience to Torah ended up committing polyandry (marrying seven husbands altogether), which contradicts Torah.[56] In this light, the Sadducees are not just asking a mischievous question to trip Jesus up, for there are important issues at stake. Between holding to the integrity of Torah and following a teaching that is normally linked with the Pharisees, the Sadducees certainly know what they ought to choose.

The Sadducean perspective can only be corrected with good theology and an appeal to Torah. A quick glance at Jesus' answer will reveal that he is doing just that.[57] Matching the Sadducean concern for the upholding of Torah, Jesus answers with a passage from Torah. Matching their correct assumptions that ridiculous situations should not be contemplated, Jesus speaks of the power of God. The upshot is that it is the Sadducees' ignorance of the Torah and their poor appreciation of God's power that has landed them in such an erroneous position. We shall elaborate on these points below.

To answer the point about the resurrection's being messy and ridiculous, Jesus speaks of a transformation. The resurrection does not imply a

---

54. 2 Macc 7 and Tob 3:8, 15 may contain parallels: seven brothers who were martyred for their faith, and seven bridegrooms. In any case, what is important is not the putative background but the theological arguments that are being used.

55. Further on this topic see Burrows 1940: 22-33; Westbrook 1991: 68-89.

56. Commentators have not considered the importance of this point.

57. Although Jesus' view is similar to the Pharisees, there is a major difference in the way he establishes the foundations for such a belief.

repeat of conditions that are now obtaining in the world. Instead, it is about a new order, brought about by the power of God. People will be like the angels in heaven, and therefore will not marry.[58] So the question of whose wife that woman in the story will be does not arise at all.

Next, Jesus has to demonstrate that, far from contradicting Torah, resurrection is actually taught in the Mosaic corpus. The logic of Jesus' choice (Exod 3:6) is not clear, but it is certainly a passage that is fundamental for Israel's self-understanding. The revelation of God at the burning bush kick-started a series of events that finally resulted in the Exodus and this, in turn, led to the covenant-making at Sinai. In speculating on the underlying logic of Jesus' scriptural exposition, we bear in mind three points: the significance of the patriarchs, the concept of community embedded in the covenant, and the character of God.[59]

First, the point of the long string of titles that introduces the God of Israel is that he remains the God of those patriarchs still. This demonstrates the latter's significance in the birth of the nation and that God chooses and saves the nation because of them. A crass formula may be introduced here for clarity: no patriarchs, no Exodus, no covenant, and hence, no Israel! This being the case, it elicits an implicit question: "If there is a new order, will these significant founding fathers lose out on its blessings?"

Secondly, there is a profound corporate dimension to the covenant. In Jesus' view, this community stretches across time. So God's titling of himself in his speech to Moses mentions these patriarchs not only because they are foundational personages of the nation, but also because they are somehow part of the covenant community. The question that is thus engendered is: "When the climax of the covenant story comes, is it only for the fortunate few who live in the last days?"

Thirdly, God may be regarded by definition as the God of the living, because he does not want to be known as the God of the dead. If he is God only of the dead, he is no God at all, but simply an eternal being, existing all by himself. Since human existence must be embodied existence, their being alive with God must mean they will also be embodied one day. When God introduced himself to Moses the way he did, he was not reminiscing on a glorious past, but explaining the kind of God he is. This is also what we find in 4 Macc 7:18–19; 16:25, where it is affirmed that the patriarchs "do not die to God, but live to God."[60]

---

58. This can mean either resurrection humans will be celibates or that gender is no longer a characteristic. Whatever view is taken does not affect Jesus' point materially.

59. I am aware I am developing something novel here.

60. Cf. Culpepper 2007: 419.

The upshot of all this is that Torah and theology combine to give a resounding yes to resurrection. Covenant and community must mean that those who die in the Lord will not miss out when the denouement comes. The character of God guarantees this, for he does not wish to be known as the God of people who have long died. He is the God of the living.

The Greatest Commandment (12:28-34)

From the way Mark introduces this story, we may regard it as a sequel to the previous one. The scribe's question concerns the greatest commandment of Torah, just as the Sadducees' objection arose because of their intention to safeguard Torah. That said, the scribe's question is in itself significant, as similar questions have been asked before. Jews want to know what the heart of Torah is, as there are many commandments and regulations. So whenever there is a conflict of laws, the enquirer will know which has priority.[61] Furthermore, what really constitutes membership in the covenant will also be clarified. Indeed, the rabbi Hillel was asked a similar question: whether he could teach the whole of Torah while the learner was standing on one leg. His reply was: "Do not do to your neighbor what is hateful to you; this is the whole of Torah: the rest is commentary."[62]

Jesus cites what is known as the Shema. This comes from a Hebrew word that means "hear," and it serves as a peg for hanging the whole passage of Deut 6:4-5. The Shema may be regarded as the key confession of Israel, in which her covenantal status is summed up, and adherence to it marks her out as the special people of God (cf. Wisd 11-15; *SibOr* 3:8-45; Josephus *Antiquities* 5:1, 27, 112; Philo, *Decal.* 65). Deuteronomy 6:4-9 is also combined with 11:13-21 and Num 15:37-41 to form the whole creed. In *b. Suk.* 42a, we are told that once boys can speak, they will be taught the first line of the Shema (Deut 6:4).

In the Shema the fundamental belief and the primary praxis of Israel are given. The fundamental belief is that there is only one God, Yahweh (monotheism). The fundamental praxis for Israel to be truly monotheistic is to love this God with all her heart and all her soul and all her strength. Jesus includes "all your mind" (v. 30) for good measure, probably to connect with his interlocutor who is a scribe and is learned in the ways of Torah. As a scribe he has to think hard on what it means to love God truly. The

---

61. Which commandments were "heavy" (i.e., important), and which were "light" were discussed by rabbis. See *b. Ber.* 63a and *b. Mak.* 24a.

62. This is found in *b. Šab* 31a; cf. Rabbi Akiba's statement in *Sipre Lev.* §200 (on Lev 19:15-20).

scribe manages to pick up the cue of Jesus and indeed utilizes his mind well. Interestingly, the scribe uses three modifiers in his reply, as Deuteronomy 6:5 does. But he includes Jesus' unique modifier and omits "with all your soul" (v. 33)!

The fundamental relationality of the greatest commandment serves as the springboard for the giving of the second commandment. Love for God is actualized in love for neighbor. Although the love for neighbor is regarded as something of great importance to many Jews of Jesus' day, all the extant evidence points to Jesus as the only one who combines it with the Shema.[63] In its original OT context, the phrase "as yourself" in Lev 19:18 may be understood adjectivally or adverbially. The former produces the nuance of loving your neighbor because that neighbor is somehow also "you." This emphasizes the communal dimension. The latter produces the nuance of loving the neighbor in the same manner as you love yourself. Neither meaning excludes the other. That said, many OT scholars think that because of the occurrence of a similar phrase in Lev 19:34, the phrase "as yourself" should be interpreted adjectivally.[64] If this is the case, the immediate horizon the scribe may be thinking of would be the members of the covenant community. Of course there is an interesting twist to this concept of neighbor in Jesus' telling of the parable of the Good Samaritan (Luke 10:25–37), but that is another story.[65]

The scribe agrees with Jesus but also sees an important implication. Using language reminiscent of Hosea 6:6, he concludes that burnt offerings and sacrifices are secondary (v. 33). In other words, he understands that election (i.e., being the special people of God) is not bound up with the Temple and its sacrificial system (v. 34). So the scribe is in a position to see that although Jesus has demonstrated against the Temple and implicitly enacted its destruction, this does not mean he is against Torah.

This elicits from Jesus the observation that the scribe has answered wisely, and so is close to the kingdom (v. 34). Indeed, this is the only instance in Mark's Gospel, where Jesus commends a scribe. To put the Shema above the Temple, and love above the cult takes him to the heart of Torah. And if the kingdom means the fulfillment of Torah, grasping the essence of Torah places one in close proximity to God's kingdom.

---

63. Tan 2011: 2677–707.
64. See discussion in Milgrom 2001: 1646–56.
65. See my initial exploration in Tan 2005: 122–55.

The Messiah and David (12:35-37)

Mark depicts Jesus as the one now asking questions, breaking a pattern found in the earlier episodes. Jesus' question relates to his identity, using Ps 110:1 as the basis. This is significant, as the Psalm has been understood as a messianic psalm (cf. 11Q13), and plays an important role in helping the early Christians understand Jesus' identity (cf. 1 Cor 15:25-27; Eph 1:20-22; Heb 1:13—2:8).

The essence of Jesus' question seems to be: "How is David's son also David's lord?" Some background information is necessary to grasp the full significance of the question. Many Jews assume the Messiah will be from David's line. In this sense he is known as David's son (*Pss Sol* 17:21). It is also assumed by many Jews, and Jesus himself, that Psalm 110 is written by David. These two assumptions are brought together to frame a question that seeks to open up new vistas. David in that Psalm refers to his lord, who in v. 1 is being addressed by God himself. God invites this person to sit at his right hand, indicating he will have dominion over the world, and his enemies will be put under his feet. In Jewish theology the one to do this is identified as the Messiah, who will come from David's line (i.e., be David's son). If all this is true, how can David's son be called lord by David?

We can see what Jesus is driving at. This Messiah who will come to usher in God's rule cannot merely be known as the son of David, since David the great king addresses him as lord. Indeed, the Psalm that Jesus refers to speaks later of this lord as a priest of the order of Melchizedek, an order of eternal priesthood. What categories are then left for understanding the Messiah? Mark does not answer this in this passage but he has said enough in earlier passages for his audience to understand that Jesus bursts asunder the boundaries of messiahship traditionally established. He, the chosen Son of God, is also the One who shares some of God's special prerogatives.

Mark tells us that the characters in the story listen to this with delight (v. 37), but he will show later that they, too, have not grasped the actual answer that Jesus' question prompts.

The Widow's Mite (12:38-44)

Verses 12:38-40 and 12:41-44 are two scenes of one story. The first contains Jesus' warning about the scribes, for they desire to be seen and honored (vv. 38-39). In addition to this, they devour widows' houses. Widows were regarded as especially vulnerable in biblical times, as there was no social security system as we know it. Their houses were often their only means of security and shelter. Defrauding them of this was the most despicable thing a human being could do, and strongly condemned (Isa 10:2; Mal 3:5). Mark does not tell us how the scribes divested widows of their property, but many scholarly guesses have been given: mismanaging an estate of which they have become trustees;[66] taking their houses as pledges for unpaid debt;[67] promoting a kind of religion that actually ends up making the poor even poorer (usually widows);[68] or perhaps exploiting their hospitality and trust.[69]

The second scene brings us to the Court of Women[70] in the Temple, where chests for the collection of the Temple tax and offerings are set up (*m. Šeq.* 6:5). The contrast between the offering of the rich and the paltry sum of the widow provides a teaching point. The Greek word behind the NIV's "copper coin" is *lepton*, worth less than a hundredth of the denarius, a day's wage.[71] This is the smallest denomination in use. Mark also writes that the value of the two lepta is equal to a *kordrantē*, which is the Greek transliteration for the Latin *quadrans*, the least of the Roman coins. All this serves to show how small the amount is. However, the disciples are made to understand that despite the paltry amount, the widow has actually out-given the rich. The rich gave out of their wealth and remained rich; but the widow gave all that she had to live on (v. 44). According to the scale of values in the kingdom of God, that woman certainly gave more, as she had given herself.[72] Is this an echo of the discussion in Mark 10:41–45, which concluded by saying that the Son of Man gave his own life (i.e., gave up everything), in the name of serving the people of God?

Summary: the Controversies in Jerusalem

Is there a common thread suturing together the different conflict stories that are narrated in 11:27—12:44? In deriving this, the significance of some key data must be taken into consideration.

---

66. Derrett 1977: 118–27.
67. Evans 2001: 279.
68. Myers 1988: 321–22.
69. Jeremias 1969: 111–16.
70. France 2002: 492.
71. Schürer 1978: 2:62–66.
72. This is the traditional interpretation which posits that Jesus was praising the widow. It has become quite popular of late to regard Jesus as lamenting that the offertory led to deprivation of the poorest in the community (Evans 2001: 282–83; Myers 1988: 321). We remain unconvinced by this latest trend, as there appears precious little in the passage that supports this. See the discussion in Gundry 1993: 730–31.

The first is that Mark presents all the prominent groupings of first-century Judaism as being arrayed against Jesus. He does this nowhere else except in this collection of conflict stories. He introduces new groups in debate with Jesus, such as the chief priests, the elders and the Sadducees, groups hitherto unmentioned as interlocutors. But previously mentioned groups are also featured: the Pharisees and Herodians.

Secondly, the content of the debates shows Jesus is less reluctant to hide his messianic status. Jesus discusses with his interlocutors the special identity of the Son of David, and also implicitly refers to himself as the son of the owner of the vineyard of Israel. Furthermore, Mark informs us that the one parable Jesus tells in Jerusalem is no longer mystifying but is grasped by outsiders. All this contrasts with the secrecy orders of chapters 1–10. We get the impression that Mark's Jesus views his ministry in Jerusalem as the climax, in which issues are urgent and the need to conceal his identity is no longer appropriate.

All this takes place in the city of God, where promises of his return to reign as king are intimately bound. Jesus must therefore confront the city and her leaders with the gospel of God's return to Zion (cf. Isa 52:7). Not surprisingly, critical issues relating to Jesus' identity (the question about Jesus' authority, the parable of the talents, the question about David's son), covenantal identity (the question about the greatest commandment), Israel's relation to the powers that be (the question about paying taxes to Caesar), and the eschaton (the Sadducean question about the resurrection) are featured.

The Eschatological Discourse on the Mount of Olives (13:1–37)

This discourse of Jesus in Mark 13 has baffled many readers, leading to a great diversity of opinions and views being offered. Nevertheless, it is right to assume that the discourse is given in order to be understood. Perhaps what often prevents us from understanding it is the failure to consider the context or our making it answer questions it is not designed for. We cannot hope to interact with all the scholarly views available but we will simply explicate the view that is adopted and, at the same time, offer a sort of a map through the maze of the discourse.

The discourse is chiefly concerned with events connected with the destruction of the Temple because, after all, it is the context of the discourse. However, the destruction of the Temple is linked with the vindication of the

Son of Man, who will be shown in all his glory before Israel and the whole world at his Parousia. It is this linkage that needs some careful analysis.

To elaborate further: the prediction of the destruction of the Temple follows from Jesus' symbolic action in the Temple and his subsequent saying about casting the mountain into the sea (11:22–25). As readers will recall, this saying is interpreted by us as pointing to a new badge of election and a new mode of worship, without the need for a physical Temple. The destruction of the Temple is a clear signal to those who have eyes to see that it is *not the place but the person* to whom faithful Israelites and members of God's family are to look. What is only a signal at the destruction of the Temple will be glaringly obvious at the Parousia of the Son of Man. All this means that the disciples must remain committed to the message of the gospel that Jesus preaches. To put it in a nutshell, the following slogan may serve: at the end stands not the Temple but the Son of Man, and if this is so, loyalty is to be given only to him.

Regarding its themes, the first thing to note is that this discourse is not so much about the signs of the end as the discernment and attitudes Jesus' disciples must have, in order to face the ordeal awaiting them. In other words, the discourse is chiefly about *discipleship*: how they are to be discerning when the Jewish world is awash with speculation about the arrival of the end, and how they are to have fortitude and commitment to the gospel in spite of persecution. Commitment does not mean simply standing firm, it means also actively bearing witness (vv. 9–11). The twin concerns of discernment and commitment run through the entire discourse. The many repetitions of "watch" and "be on your guard" bear this out.

A second and related theme may be described as the *dampener* of overheated eschatological fervor.[73] Much of what Jesus says is calculated to cool such fervor. There are many warnings about being led astray and being caught in the maelstrom of revolutionary action, brought about by an overheated expectation of the coming of the Messiah. The disciples must remember that when wars and rumors of wars are prevalent, when many claim to be the Messiah, and when great earthly disturbances abound, the end is still not yet (v. 7). They need to know that the end is not ushered in by such events but by the glorious coming of the Son of Man, the One whom they are now following.

Although the dampener effect is pronounced, the message is also about the *denouement*. The destruction of the Temple is a signal of its being close. Indeed, if the disciples are alert, they will also realize that in Jesus' ministry, the eschaton is already present in seed form. This implies that the

---

73. Geddert 1989 emphasizes this.

person they will see at the denouement is not an unfamiliar figure, but one who has always been with them: incognito now but revealed in great glory at the end. That said, the destruction of the Temple remains a significant pointer to the denouement, because in this event God has demonstrated powerfully to speak of the end.

The above dovetails neatly with the final theme, which may be regarded as the most important theme of the discourse. Although it is often submerged, it emerges with clarity at vv. 24-27. This is about the *vindication of Jesus of Nazareth*.[74] He may be the despised and rejected of the nation, sacrificed in the name of maintaining the status quo, and cast away as expedient fodder to a voracious Empire. But he will be vindicated: both in the near future—with the destruction of the Temple—and at the end of the age. But before that day comes, the disciples have a message to bear to the nations, a message which he has preached and which is profoundly about him.

The themes elaborated above are relevant to the Twelve and also the Markan audience, who would be facing the prospect of persecutions. Hence, the eschatological discourse provides not esoteric knowledge about the end, but practical teaching for the long and arduous—but incomparably meaningful—road of discipleship. The disciples will need discernment and a cool head when fiery tempers control the agenda of society, and eschatological forecasting serves as news of the day. They will need strength for standing firm and remaining faithful to the end. What will help them do all this is the belief that Jesus of Nazareth is the Son of Man who will come again as the vindicated and the exalted, to consummate God's plan.

With the above themes serving as reference points, we are ready to enter the world of the discourse. But there is one more thing to take with us: the structure of the discourse. It may be argued that the progression of thought in the discourse has been carefully designed, in that an ABA'B' structure and two time-horizons, conceptually related, are being used.[75] Diagram 5 will make this clear.

---

74. Cf. Wright 1996: 342-43.

75. Witherington 2001: 340-41; Wenham 1982: 127-50; and recently Gray 2008: 103-106.

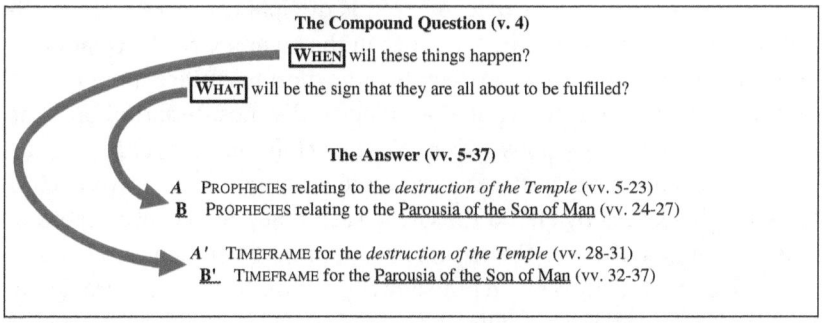

Diagram 5
Structure of the Olivet Discourse

The form the disciples' questions take (v. 2) may be collapsed into a compound question with two aspects: the first asks for the time, while the second, the sign. This may be further construed as presupposing two interrelated events, namely the destruction of the Temple and the coming of the Son of Man. One of the earliest interpreters of Mark, the evangelist Matthew, understood it in that way (Matt 24:3).[76] As to the structure, we note that v. 23 serves as a significant marker where it is stated *all* that needed to be foretold has been said. Hence, vv. 5–23 may be construed as forming one block, which may of course be broken down into smaller units. Furthermore, vv. 24–27 evince a different sort of language, concentrating on celestial phenomena. In this regard, they may be construed as forming another block. With v. 28, the material focuses on the time aspect, and may justifiably be broken down into two blocks of vv. 28–31 and vv. 32–37. All this produces an ABA'B' structure. The structure also shows that the two questions the disciples asked are answered in reverse order: the events (or signs leading to the key events) are first discussed (A and B material), followed by the teaching on the time (A' and B' material). We will now examine the passage closely.

The Setting (13:1–4)

This paragraph gives the audience the setting of the discourse. As such, it offers them and us an important hermeneutical reference point. It is important to note that what prompted the discourse is the disciples' awe over the Temple, and their subsequent question about its predicted destruction. In

---

76. We presuppose here the cogency of the Two Document Hypothesis.

this regard we should note that the discourse is first and foremost about the Temple's destruction, and the "end of the world" is not its main focus.

As Jesus leaves the Temple, one of his disciples remarks enthusiastically about the stones and the buildings in the complex. Such remarks are perfectly natural, as the Second Temple is the most magnificent building in Jerusalem. It even has the reputation of being the most beautiful building in the entire world (Josephus *War* 5:184–226; cf. *b. Suk.* 51b; *b. B. Bat.* 4a). Built as a small structure after the exiles returned, it was extensively refurbished and enlarged by Herod the Great, such that one may even speak of it as being a new Temple. The refurbishment project started around 20 BC. The bulk of it was completed in probably eight years, but the full completion came only a few years before its destruction in AD 70. Some of the stones used are still standing today in what is now known to many as the "Wailing Wall." Any visitor to Jerusalem today can appreciate what the Temple would have looked like, just by a glance at the massive stones still standing. Indeed, from Josephus we learn that some of these stones measured 67 feet long (*War* 5:224). One stone that was recently excavated by archaeologists actually measured 42 feet long, 11 feet high, and 14 feet deep.[77] It is estimated that the entire complex was about 1500 feet by 700 feet, and took up about one-sixth of the city's space.[78] When viewed from afar, with the sun shining on it, its gold and marble makes it resplendent in glorious colors (Josephus *War* 5:222–23). This magnificent building is indeed worthy of being the symbol of Israel's election. Indeed, a few decades after Jesus' crucifixion, it serves as the center of operations for the revolt against Rome, and is defended to the end.[79] All this explains the exuberance of the disciple's remark. However, Jesus gives an unexpected response. He predicts that not one stone will be left on another (v. 2).

Jesus' prediction is fascinating in that it does not mention any destruction by fire. According to Josephus, the Temple was first destroyed by fire in AD 70 by Titus and his troops, and only razed to the ground months later (cf. *War* 6:250; 7:1–4). The omission of this datum may indicate that Mark writes before AD 70, since he is not averse to giving editorial comments or explanations. The reason for Jesus' mentioning only stones may be that he is using a biblical idiom (2 Sam 17:13; cf. LXX Hag 2:15), a sort of stock phrase, or adapting his answer to the disciples' description, as they were impressed by the massive stones.

---

77. Bahat 1995: 39.
78. Finegan 1969: 118; Parrot 1957: 76–100; Sanders 1992: 57.
79. Hengel 1989: 221.

From the Mount of Olives, which offers a magnificent view of the Temple and has eschatological significance itself (Zech 14:1–4), Jesus' disciples ask questions about his prophecy. Their questions may be understood as referring to one event, although two aspects of it are being asked. The first is about the time, and the second, the sign. Interestingly, the event is spoken of in the plural ("these things"), even though Jesus has spoken only of the destruction of the Temple. The reason for this is that the Temple is not simply a building of bricks and mortars. It also represents Jewish national identity and God's election.[80] Consequently, the destruction of the Temple cannot be a solo event without consequences. In this light, "these things" may be appropriate, as they refer to all the tragic circumstances surrounding the destruction of the Temple. One can understand why in the Matthean version (Matt 24:3) the question is linked with the end of the age. Many in Israel believe the period preceding the denouement will be full of woes and tribulation.[81] One event that qualifies as the climax of such woes is the destruction of the Temple. All this explains why the disciples ask for the sign that will kick off "these things." However, we will see that Jesus separates the destruction of the Temple chronologically from the end of the age.

Rumors of the End (13:5–8)

The first word in Jesus' answer is "Watch" (v. 5). The Greek *blepō*, as used here, means both discernment (seeing beyond appearances) and alertness (being ready to take proper action). This word sets the tone for the whole discourse, as we see from its repetition in vv. 9, 23 and 33. "To watch" is related to something tangible. Hence, Jesus proceeds to speak about false signs.

Speculations about the end will become rife as wars and rumors of wars spread, and natural disasters such as earthquakes and famines occur. These events are often associated with eschatological expectations in Jewish thought (Isa 19:2; 4 *Ezra* 13:31; Mic 1:3–4; Hab 3:6–10; Zech 14:5; 2 *Bar* 27:2, 6; *b. Ber.* 55a). There will even be people coming in Jesus' name, or claiming to be the person himself. Many will be deceived because distress and ominous events make them vulnerable to the persuasions of messianic claimants. Against such runaway speculation, Jesus warns the end has not yet come. It is hard to take the word "end" in v. 7 as referring merely to the destruction of the Temple (i.e., to translate "end" as "completing the

---

80. Cf. Wardle 2010: 14–30.
81. Allison 1987.

process").⁸² Quite clearly, more is at stake. Furthermore, the events mentioned are often connected with the end of the world in much Jewish and pagan thought. In Jesus' view, however, the events of v. 7 represent only the beginning of birth pangs. The true "birth" is yet to come.

Persecution and Betrayal (13:9-13)

Such rumors of the end are harmless if they remain as such. But rumors can whip up fervor, and fervor can bring about drastic actions. The disciples must expect to find themselves at the receiving end of an acrimonious attitude, especially if they do not conform to the national agenda inspired by the Temple.⁸³ Since their message contradicts the expectation of the populace, or the propaganda of the religious or political authorities, they will be persecuted. Astonishingly, the disciples are counselled to use such painful circumstances for bearing witness (vv. 9-10). When arraigned before the authorities, the disciples should not be afraid of being tongue-tied; neither do they need to prepare an eloquent speech for their own justification. Instead, the Holy Spirit, the agent who inspired Jesus to preach the kingdom message, will be with them to do the same.

Verse 10 has often been misunderstood. Far from serving as a sign for the end, it speaks actually of the indomitable progress of the gospel.⁸⁴ Interestingly, the one means of achieving this comes from the most unlikely source. Persecution, far from hampering the growth of the gospel, results in its spread instead. This means for the disciples that their one duty, when under duress, is to bear witness to Jesus' kingdom message.

Poignantly, the disciples will be opposed not just by official bodies but also by family members. Verse 12 speaks of betrayal in a domestic setting, alluding to Micah 7:6.⁸⁵ Such depraved actions can only mean the rise of iniquity, or a fanatical loyalty to the national agenda of preserving Jerusalem, especially the Temple, to the detriment of everything else. Verse 13 sums up the section by mentioning that the disciples will be hated by all because of Jesus. In such a climate they are not to give up being disciples, but remain

---

82. *Pace* France 2002: 511.

83. The harsh punishments against Gentile trespassers (Philo, *Embassy to Gaius*, 212) and Jews who spoke/acted against the Temple (Josephus *War* 6:301; *m. Sanh.* 9:6) provide evidence for us to believe that the lack of conformity to the Temple's ideology can bring about great reprisals. This would have been intensified when an external threat to its safety loomed. On the topic of the temple as a national symbol of loyalty and resistance see Borg 1984.

84. Boring 2006: 364-65.

85. Intra-familial conflict has become a feature in Jewish speculations of the eschaton. See *Jub* 23:19; *1 En* 100:1-2; *3 Bar* 4:17.

firm, as only those who endure to the end[86] will be saved. The word "saved" here probably refers to eschatological salvation.[87]

The Abomination of Desolation (13:14–20)

Jesus has been focusing on dampening eschatological speculation. Now he speaks of the sign the disciples need to watch, which is the "abomination of desolation." Our thesis needs some defense.

Jesus counsels those in Judea to flee to the mountains when they see the abomination of desolation, implying the need for urgent response. Moreover, the editorial remark,[88] "let the reader understand" (v. 14) implies that the event, although significant, is not transparent to all. Furthermore, the fact that urgent action has to be taken when the abomination happens supports the thesis that it is indeed the sign. If Jesus intends to say there can be no sign at all for the Temple's destruction, as it has been argued recently,[89] all the foregoing data become incomprehensible.

Having established that the abomination of desolation is the sign the disciples are to watch for, what remains to be done is to identify this event. Some interesting clues are already given, especially in v. 14. We note first that Jesus counsels those in Judea—and not all Israel—to flee to the mountains. This signals that the catastrophic event is going to happen in Judea, and will affect mainly Judeans. The topographically limited scope is to be borne firmly in mind. Secondly, the abomination of desolation is a phrase taken from Daniel (Dan 11:31; 12:11; cf. 8:13; 9:27), which refers to the desecration of the Temple by Antiochus Epiphanes IV. He set up a pagan altar in the Temple to sacrifice a sow to Zeus Olympius in 167 BC (1 Macc 1:54–59; 2 Macc 6:2). With this as a cue, we may regard the phrase as meaning "the abomination that makes the Temple desolate" (i.e., devoid of the divine presence). A similar event should be envisaged, unless otherwise indicated. Hence, Jesus is telling his disciples to look out for a great sacrilege of the Temple. Just as it was momentous in the Maccabean period, so also will this event be to the generation of Jesus' disciples. Thirdly, Mark's editorial words also imply that although the event is significant, it will not be

---

86. The Greek *eis telos* can be construed as an idiomatic phrase to mean "completely" or as referring to something concrete such as the eschaton.

87. Evans 2001: 313.

88. This is surely Mark's editorial remark, since if they were Jesus' words we should expect "Let the hearer understand." Till now Mark has not addressed any hortatory word of his own to his audience, although he has explained things once in a while. This implies that what is given is a very important sign.

89. Geddert 1989: 29–58, 203–6, 257.

transparent to all. The coded language may be unraveled only by insiders who understand Scriptures and Jesus' ministry.[90] We may summarize the clues given: the abomination of desolation speaks of a great sacrilege of the Temple, but this is not apparent to all; special insight is needed to see that it is so; when it happens Judeans—and not all Israel—are to flee.

The above prepares us to decode the sign given in v. 14. The strange Greek syntax needs closer scrutiny. The word *bdelygma* ("abomination") is neuter in gender, but it is later modified by a participle in the masculine (the Greek is *hestēkota*). So we may ask, "Is Jesus referring to a thing[91] or a person?"[92] In other words, is he referring to something that is set up as an abomination, or to someone who is the abomination? Our view is it refers to an event, but brought about by human agency.[93] Someone will set himself up, out of pure caprice or pressured by others, and brings about an abomination that leads to desecration.

The exact event that Jesus is referring to has teased many scholarly minds. The chief proposals are: (i) Caligula's attempt to place his image in the Temple;[94] (ii) the Zealot party's appointing their own high priest during the Jewish Revolt, which also featured much internecine strife (*War* 4:147-57);[95] (iii) the desecration by Titus's troops when they sacrificed to their standards after quelling the Jewish revolt;[96] and (iv) the awaited Antichrist.[97] Option (ii) is what we support, and the justification for this will be made below. But we start with the options we reject.

Caligula certainly wanted his image to be set up in the Temple and be regarded as divine. The trouble with this proposal is that this intention was never realized, as he was persuaded to rescind the edict (Josephus *Antiquities* 18:261, 271). Option (iii) is certainly related to the desecration of the Jerusalem Temple. After storming it and defeating the Jewish resistance, Titus' troops sacrificed to their standards in the Temple (Josephus *War* 6:316; cf. also 6:260, where it is recorded that Titus and his generals went into the inner sanctum of the Temple). However, all this was done *after* the Temple had been destroyed. It could not therefore serve as a sign of its destruction, as signs are always chronologically prior to the events. Option

---

90. Boring 2006: 266-67.
91. Evans 2001: 319-20.
92. Marcus 2009: 890.
93. Stein 2008: 603.
94. Gnilka 1979: 2:194; Manson 1937: 329-30.
95. Lane 1974: 469; Marcus 2009: 890-91.
96. Pesch 1980: 2:291.
97. Evans 2001: 320; Taylor 1952: 511.

(iv) is popular amongst Christians brought up on a dispensationalist diet, but the trouble with this is that it sucks away any relevance the discourse may have for the disciples. Instead, it makes the discourse relevant only for the last generation before Christ comes. This makes us wonder whether it is relevant for us now, as we have no way of knowing whether we are the last generation. Sadly, this plays into the hands of many exploitative preachers.

Option (ii) fits the prediction of v. 14 best. In the winter of AD 67/8, the Zealot party occupied the Temple and appointed by lot the reluctant Phanias as the high priest. Josephus informs us Phanias did not have the slightest clue what such an office entailed. He was forcefully dragged from his abode, draped in priestly vestments and taught how to sacrifice! This mockery of the high priestly office aroused popular indignation, which in turn led to internecine bloodshed in the Temple (Josephus *War* 4:147–57, 201). All this shows that what the Temple was meant to symbolize in God's intention was no longer respected. Instead, it had become the place for the shedding of blood, defiling the sacred place. Moreover, it had also become the symbol not of God's presence but of great iniquity in Israel. However, this great affront to God was not apparent to many Jews. They probably thought that if Zealots were sinners, the Romans were even greater sinners. So many Jews remained convinced that God would still protect the Temple, even if their own people were not getting their act right. Tragically they failed to see that the woes of the nation were not brought about by external forces, but by their own iniquity.

Once the sign is seen, the disciples are to "flee to the mountains." This means abandoning the cause of Jerusalem, and fleeing to places of refuge. Instead of doggedly believing in the inviolability of the city, the disciples are to move out and move on in their task of witnessing. Indeed, the actions described in vv. 15–16 are drastic. They are not to return to the house, even to grab a cloak (an important garment for self-preservation), but to flee. This is because when the Romans come, they cannot count on God's protection of the Temple or the city. Indeed, the Romans may well be the agents God uses to punish the nation for the abomination of desolation. As events panned out, we can see the wisdom of this saying.[98]

All this goes against the grain of popular Jewish expectation. Since the archetypal abomination of desolation caused the Maccabean revolt, which resulted in victory for the Jewish cause, if a similar incident occurred Jews would most likely take up arms and defend the holy place. The successful

---

98. Eusebius preserves a tradition that speaks of Christians fleeing to the city of Pella, before the war started, because of an oracle (*H.E.* 3:5:3). We are not sure whether Eusebius has preserved an authentic tradition, and even if he has, the oracle might have been something other than Mark 13:14. This is so because Pella is below sea level.

Maccabean revolt remained an inspiration for many Jews. In this light, Jesus' exhortation is jarring to Jewish ears. Indeed, the implication is that loyalty to the covenant will not be shown by an ardent defense of the Temple. Instead, it is shown by persevering in the gospel.

In such hazardous times, pregnant women, or those who are nursing children, will suffer dreadfully. The words of v. 19 recall Daniel 12:1. They must not be interpreted without bearing in mind the context and the implied geographical limitation. This will preempt the temptation of comparing this event with, say, the Holocaust. In the case of the Judeans, no other event can be equal to this in terms of distress and suffering. Stories of Roman atrocities and great bloodshed abound in many ancient sources.[99] So dreadful is all this that if God does not shorten it, no one will be left alive. However, for the sake of the elect—and this must mean those in Israel who follow Jesus—those days will be shortened (v. 20). From history we know that the siege of Jerusalem lasted only a few months.[100]

Reiteration of Exhortation (13:21-23)

The trend of thought in this section may be summarized thus. In view of the fact that calamitous events can be exploited by people to push their own theological agenda or their own brand of eschatological speculation, Jesus reiterates his exhortation to his disciples to be alert and discerning. Charlatans will perform signs and miracles to claim they are the prophets of God, or his messiahs. Verse 23 is important for it serves as a sort of *inclusio* with v. 5, which opened the discourse. Through this *inclusio*, the Markan audience will discern that Jesus' focus is on discernment.

The significance of v. 21 must not be missed. The words of Jesus assume that false reports of the arrival of the Messiah will be given in those days. The disciples are warned against believing such reports, and this must imply that Jesus envisages a situation where he is no longer with them physically. We then have here the implicit idea of the returning Messiah, and that his return is ardently expected. Otherwise there is no need for such a warning. Indeed, the warning against listening to the reports and claims of false prophets and messiahs invariably raises the question about when the true Messiah will come. All this implies that the Mark 13 cannot just be about the Temple's destruction.

---

99. Josephus provides a terrifying account of what the Romans did to their captives in *War* 5: 449-51. See also Schürer, 1973: 1:507.

100. From *Nisan* to *Ab* of AD 70 (i.e., March/April to Jul/August). See Schürer 1973: 1:502-506.

The disciples are to stand firm on the teaching that the Messiah's "arrival" (for the disciples, this is the "return") will not take place during those events. When he comes in the clouds with great power he will be seen by all, so there will be no need to depend on reports. Read in this way, the controversial vv. 24–27 can then be seen as answering the need of the disciples to know when the Parousia will take place.

Verse 23 indicates the intent of Jesus in the discourse up to this stage. This is to inform his disciples of the things to come that are connected to the Temple, ahead of time. This will, in turn, help the disciples to be on their guard so that they will not be led astray.

The Parousia of the Son of Man (13:24–27)

This section bristles with difficulties. It is laden with scriptural language, and should be seen as metaphorical in many ways. But what it is a metaphor of is precisely the question. To unravel this, we start with the time indicators of v. 24.

The strong adversative "but" (the Greek is *alla*) is eminently appropriate for referring to a new phase in the eschatological drama. Furthermore, the phrase "in those days" echoes the temporal formula found in many OT prophecies that speak of the eschaton (Jer 3:16; 33:15–16; Joel 3:2; Zech 8:23).[101] To be sure, the phrase also has an exact parallel in verses 17 and 19, which refer to the days of tribulation. This may suggest that what is being described in vv. 24–27 may be construed as belonging to those events. However, the phrase that follows on its heels is "after the distress," indicating that a new phase to the eschatological drama is being envisaged.[102] Hence, the destruction of the Temple is not to be confused with the coming of the Son of Man.

The metaphorical language is taken from Isa 13:10 and 34:4. In their original contexts the oracles speak of the destruction of Babylon and Edom respectively. This has led some scholars to associate such images only with the destruction of cities.[103] It may then be argued that the phrases should refer to the destruction of Jerusalem. However, a closer inspection shows that such phrases are not invariably connected with the destruction of cities, but with theophanies in which God suddenly appears in great power either to judge or to save (see especially Isa 13:9, 11 and 34:2, 8).[104] Such pow-

---

101. Evans 2001: 327.
102. Boring 2006: 372.
103. France 2002: 532–33; Wright 1996: 354–65.
104. Beasley-Murray 1993: 424–25.

erful intervention is either preceded or is accompanied by such heavenly phenomena. One confirmation of this view comes from Jewish writings, especially the apocalyptic type (*TMos* 10:1-5; *SibOr* 3:796-803), and also other OT passages such as Ezek 32:7 and Joel 2:10, where clearly such celestial phenomena are linked with God's taking powerful action, rather than the destruction of cities per se. Hence, we may conclude that these phrases are better understood as stock imagery accompanying or preceding a theophany. Of course, the astonishing thing here is that these passages refer to a Christophany.

This paves the way for us to construe the event as the Parousia of the Son of Man. Nevertheless, the Parousia and the destruction of the Temple are conceptually connected in that both express the idea of the vindication of Jesus of Nazareth as God's Messiah and the Son of Man. Incidentally, if vv. 24-27 contain coded language for the destruction of the Temple, it will give the discourse a substantial element of incongruence, because it means the Temple is destroyed *after* the tribulation (v. 24). Most Jews would regard its destruction as preceding or a part of that tribulation. Indeed, the end of tribulation should logically mean salvation.

There is one more issue to tackle, and this concerns the "movement" of the Son of Man (v. 26). The Greek word *erchomai* can mean coming or going. So some scholars argue it should be translated as "going to," in line with the original context of Dan 7:13, from which such words are taken. Accordingly, the discourse speaks of the Son of Man's going to the Ancient of Days to receive power and authority, which signifies the vindication of the Son of Man, seen concretely in the destruction of the Temple.[105] This is an attractive explanation and might be adopted if not for the difficulties pointed out earlier. It may be better to regard such language as speaking of a "coming to," since early Jewish interpretation of this Danielic text interprets it in the way that speaks of the Son of Man coming to earth to judge (4 *Ezra* 13.3; cf. *b. Sanh.* 98a).[106] In other words, the Jewish logic in such writings may be that even if the Son of Man did go to the Ancient of Days to receive authority and power, it is done so that he could come to earth to deliver his beleaguered people. And his coming will be with the clouds of heaven, full of power and glory. Furthermore, the next verse (v. 27) which speaks of the Son of Man sending his angels to gather his elect may support our contention in that the only other occurrence in Mark that associates the Son of Man with angels is Mark 8:38, which refers to the Parousia. Hence, the event envisaged in 13:27 should be identical, and that "angels" in this pas-

---

105. France 2002: 534-35.
106. Collins 1992: 448-66.

sage should not refer to the preachers of the gospel.[107] To be noted further is that all the other occurrences of *angelos* in Mark—and there are not many (1:13; 8:38; 12:25; 13:32)—refer to heavenly agents.[108]

The gathering of the elect from the four winds connotes also the notion of the re-gathering of Israel's exiles (Zech 2:6). This means the salvation of the elect, and is most suitable as language of the denouement. In the previous section the elect were described as being beleaguered. In this section, what answers to that beleaguered condition must be the denouement.

After a long trek through the previous difficult paragraphs, we need to recapitulate the key message given thus far: there will be no divine deliverance for the Temple. The Son of Man comes after its destruction and not before. There is indeed divine rescue, but it is not for the Temple. Instead, it is for God's elect, defined by their links with the Son of Man. This being the case, loyalty to the Temple is seen as wrong-headed. Furthermore, Jesus' disciples must not be caught in the vortex of extreme eschatological speculations which often lead to violent revolutions. Instead, they are to continue preaching the gospel of the kingdom.

Lesson from the Fig Tree (13:28–31)

Just as the discourse in the earlier paragraphs presupposes a two-phase drama (the destruction of the Temple and the coming of the Son of Man), the answer on the question of time also splits into two parts (vv. 28–31 and vv. 32–37). The first concerns the time for the Temple's destruction and the second, the Parousia.[109]

The fig tree is to be understood in its normal sense and not as a symbol for Israel, even though it was used as such in chapter 11.[110] Since there are many fig trees in Palestine, it can be used as a good illustration (the Greek is actually "a parable.") The lesson is that there is a short time between its budding and the arrival of summer. Similarly, there will be a short time between the sign (v. 14), and the destruction of the Temple. To make the

---

107. France 2002: 536 is aware of the potency of this argument, but he insists that these angels are given the missionary task. This appears dubious as the discourse specifically links the missionary task with the work of the disciples (vv. 10–11). It appears inescapable that verse 27 speaks not of a worldwide mission but a worldwide gathering for the coming of the Son of Man (which is also the language of the parallel in Matt 24:30–31).

108. High Christology is contained here, for in the OT only God may send his angels to perform tasks. See Evans 2001: 329.

109. Cf. also Stein 2008: 610, 617.

110. See our treatment of the relevant passage.

sense of imminence doubly clear, Jesus pronounces that "this generation will not pass away until all these things happen" (v. 30). The solemnity of this pronouncement is indicated by the formula "Amen I say to you," and the declaration of the utter reliability of Jesus' words, the permanence of which exceeds that of creation (Isa 40:7-8; 51:6; 54:9-10; Jer 33:20-21).[111]

The statement of v. 30 therefore impresses on Jesus' disciples that he is not making one last bid for respectability by predicting events what would come to pass only after hundreds of years, where no one present would be able to check on the authenticity. Rather, the generation hearing these words from Jesus would be present when they happened. This being the case, interpretations which speak of the last generation before the Second Coming of Christ[112] or that the Jewish race would never perish actually miss the whole point.[113] Our proposal enables us to see that Jesus is not playing mind games with his disciples, but he is actually answering their questions in a very relevant way.

The Unknowable Hour (13:32-37)

The present section speaks of the coming of the Son of Man. Otherwise, the section sits uncomfortably with the previous one because that section clearly gave a time-frame, while the present passage is agnostic about it. One possible harmonization is to construe Jesus as knowing roughly when (i.e., in a generation's time), but not exactly when. However, this seems a ponderous way of stating it. We prefer to regard the time horizon as having been switched to the Parousia, and will now seek to justify it.

As we pointed out earlier, the destruction of the Temple and the Parousia, although separate events, are conceptually related. Furthermore, we note many grammatical indicators that point in the direction of a change in time-horizon. The opening two words in Greek (*peri de*) are often used as a section marker or a break in a discourse (cf. 12:26 and especially 1

---

111. We take the "words" to refer to the entire discourse (*pace* Cranfield 1959). Again, high Christology is implied here, as in the OT only God's word has this quality, and not that of mortal man. Some have construed that Jesus is equating his words with Torah. Even so, it must be borne in mind that Torah is eternal only (Bar. 4:1; Wisd 18:4) because it is regarded as given by God.

112. As France observes, if this is what Jesus intended, shouldn't he have said "*that* generation," rather than "*this* generation"? Moreover, it makes the expression trite, since by definition there would always be a last generation to welcome Jesus' Second Coming (see France 2002: 539). Cf. the remark of Gundry: "Of course this generation would not pass away if by definition it could extend out indefinitely!" (Gundry 1993: 791).

113. Construing *genea* as "race," an interpretation which may be traced back to Jerome (see France 2002: 539).

Corinthians.) Moreover, Jesus now speaks of a particular day (singular) when throughout the discourse he has spoken of days in the plural. Biblical literature is notorious for the ambiguous use of the singular and the plural. Hence, we must not set too much store by it. Nevertheless, we may also note the parallel found in Matthew, which understands Mark as pointing to a different event, especially when he uses the Greek word *parousia* to describe it (Matt 24:37–39).

The upshot of all this is that Jesus speaks of the "unknowability" of the time of his second coming. Such knowledge belongs only to the Father, as he is the one who determines when it is to take place. What all this means for the disciples is that they will know the time frame for the Temple's destruction. They will know that Jesus' Parousia cannot take place until after that; but they won't know the length of the interval between the Temple's destruction and the Parousia. Notwithstanding, they are still to be vigilant at all times. The key word in the discourse, *blepō* ("see") is now accompanied by *agrypneō* ("do not sleep" or "keep watch"), heightening the call for vigilance (v. 33). This heightening points to the profound significance of the subject matter, which is the Parousia.

Just as a comparison was made in the earlier paragraph, a comparison is also made now to teach about the time of the Parousia. In this comparison the absentee landlord is used. This man assigns responsibilities to his servants while he is away, even assigning someone to keep watch at the door. There is no indication when he is coming back, and so his servants must always be on the alert. The comparison is apt, as it alludes to Jesus' going away and his assigning of duties to his servants. His absence must not be taken as an opportunity for sloth or complacency, but for faithful discharging of responsibilities assigned. So the servants must be "alert" (v. 35).

The discourse ends by universalizing the exhortation to watch (v. 37). When it comes to portents of the destruction of the Temple and rumors of the end, the disciples must be discerning. But when it comes to the Parousia, they are to keep vigil, and discharge faithfully the responsibilities given to them. So at the end of the discourse the discipleship thrust becomes clear again.

Introduction to the Passion Narrative (14:1—15:47)

From this point on, Mark's Gospel slows down dramatically as the key moment approaches. Indeed, one scholar has even provocatively called Mark's Gospel a passion narrative with a long introduction.[114]

---

114. Kahler 1964: 80.

The audience of Mark has been prepared for this key event in the earlier chapters, especially 11–13 which feature Jesus in conflict with the Jewish leaders and the Temple establishment. Now Mark narrates the plot and the subsequent actions the Jewish authorities take, and what proactive response Jesus makes to prepare his disciples for his passion.

All this takes place against the backdrop of the Passover, a festival which marks Israel's special elect status because it recalls the founding of the nation.[115] So it is poignant that during this festival an unjust action, taken for political expediency against someone sent by God, was contrived and carried out. In the midst of this poignancy, however, the good news that Mark offers should not be lost sight of. For what Jesus does in the final chapters relates in a profound way to the way of the Lord, the good news of the kingdom, and the fulfillment of what the Passover truly stands for.

The Anointing at Bethany (14:1–11)

Complicated as the historical question may be,[116] the story as set in Mark's Gospel presents teaching that is clear, cleverly formulated, and easily assimilated. The opening verse of chapter 14 sets the story against the backdrop of the feasts of the Passover and Unleavened Bread. Originally separate, the two festivals in the course of time became identified with each other as the "Feast of the Passover." Passover recalls the slaying of the firstborns of Egypt, but the preservation of those of Israel (Exod 12:6–20). This formed the prelude to the deliverance from enslavement, with the intention of making Israel the special people of God. So this festival relates profoundly to Israel's self-understanding and identity (cf. Num 9:2–14; Deut 16:1). The Feast of Unleavened Bread lasts for a week (Num 28:15–16) and has its origins in the great deliverance from Egypt, with the emphasis on being pure before God (the concept of being unleavened).[117]

During this fused festival Jewish pilgrims from all over the world would return to Palestine to celebrate it in Jerusalem. Thus the festival is often regarded as being congenial for revolutions in the name of freedom and being God's special people to occur.[118] So Roman troops are on the alert

---

115. Segal 1963.

116. Matthew comes closest to Mark's version, followed by John. Luke seems to have narrated a different story, even though the key elements are identical (Simon as the host; anointing by a woman, which led to misgivings). The focus here is on understanding Mark's presentation. For a succinct summary of the issues and proposals, see France 2002: 550.

117. De Vaux 1965: 2:484–93.

118. Evans 2001: 355, provides copious evidence.

and Jewish authorities are on their toes. Moreover, since any action taken against a popular person when the city is thronged is politically risky, the chief priests and the scribes judge it is better to have Jesus arrested after the festival (v. 2).

Against this plot is set the story of the anointing of Jesus by an unnamed woman in the home of Simon the leper at Bethany. Mark tells his audience that the ointment used is expensive (v. 3), as it is worth a year's wages (v. 5). So this draws the comment from those present that what is done is sheer wastage (v. 4). The statement "It could have been sold ... and the money given to the poor" (v. 5) is intended to heighten the wrongness of the action because during Passover the poor are to be specially remembered. The ointment in question is pure[119] spikenard, often used for anointing specially-honored guests or the dead, especially when they are held in high regard.[120] The woman's action of breaking the container speaks of a deliberate intent to use it all, without holding back.[121]

The deeper significance of her action is lost to those around Jesus. So they focus on what is most tangible: the exhausting of a year's wages in one profligate act. Mark describes her being rebuked harshly with the same word used for Jesus' rebuke of demons.[122] In her defense Jesus extols her act, and makes essentially three points. First, she has performed a good or beautiful work for him. Throughout Mark's Gospel it is Jesus who performs good work on people. Not once do people perform work on Jesus. This act of the woman breaks the pattern. At the narrative level, Mark's audience can see that her work stands in stark contrast to that of the authorities and Judas, which frame her action.

Secondly, her act recognizes that Jesus is to be held in higher regard than the poor. Certainly giving to the poor is emphasized in Mark's Gospel (10:21), but this must be done out of a commitment to Jesus. The poor will always be with them, but not Jesus. There will always be opportunity to give to the poor, but the significant moment must be grasped: Jesus will be going to the cross soon.[123]

---

119. Reading *pistikēs* to mean "pure."

120. Hooker 1991: 329.

121. It has often been misunderstood that the container is made in such a way that it must be broken in order to use the spikenard, but there is absolutely no evidence for this. Instead, the following assumption is more cogent: as the spikenard is expensive, it would have been stored in containers that are stoppered, so that the unused contents would not be wasted. See Marcus 2009: 934; Gundry 1993: 802, 813.

122. The Greek is *embrimaomai*.

123. France 2002: 554.

Thirdly, the woman's action points to Jesus' burial. She recognizes that Jesus' messianic ministry must end in death, as it is part and parcel of the way of the Lord.[124] This death is not a tragic accident or something Jesus must avoid at all costs. Instead it forms the warp and woof of his vocation, and in this regard is the key ingredient of the gospel. Just as he was anointed for the messianic task at the beginning of his ministry, so he is now anointed for the same task at the close of it.

These points bring us to the climactic statement of this story found in v. 9. So solemn is this declaration that it is prefaced with "Amen I say to you." Wherever the gospel is preached, what she has done must be told in memory of her. Why should her action earn such a remembrance, and what is its connection with the gospel? Perhaps the reason is the profligacy of the woman's action,[125] which Mark also emphasizes. It mirrors the gospel which is equally profligate because it speaks of the giving up of the Son of Man for the ransom of the undeserving many. In the work of the gospel Jesus gives himself unreservedly; the alabaster box of his life is broken, without any intention of resealing it. Furthermore, the woman's action points to Jesus' death and burial, even during the lull of a friendly dinner at Simon's home. It seems to say that no matter how peaceful the situation may be, Jesus' vocation involves his going to the vortex of a "storm" to offer his life. Jesus' death on the cross is connected profoundly to the gospel.

The peculiar thing about this episode is that the woman is not named, even though her action is deeply significant! The parallel in John provides a name, which is Mary, the sister of Lazarus; John 12:3. The silence in Mark is probably due to his desire to put the spotlight on the action and not the person. She is famous only in so far as her action is significant for the gospel.[126]

Judas's departure is a reaction to Jesus' remark (v. 10). We may speculate that it seals for him the belief that Jesus' messianic program is wrongheaded and dangerous. It is wrongheaded because it involves death; it is dangerous because it speaks of God's profligate love. In this regard, one may further surmise that behind Judas's treachery stands a fanatical intent to do what he thinks is right for the nation.[127] Certainly, Judas's offering of himself provides the chief priests with just what they need: someone who can give

---

124. Hooker 1991: 327–29.

125. Evans 2001: 361–62.

126. Recently, Bauckham 2008: 194–97 has suggested that the silence over the name was meant for the woman's protection from the attention of the authorities in the early years of the church's existence. This was not needed when the Gospel of John was written, and consequently her name might be divulged as Mary of Bethany.

127. Some attempts at rehabilitating the "tainted" character of Judas, but at the expense of the Early Church, may be found in Klassen 2005.

them inside information on Jesus' activities and claims, and guide them to solitary places that Jesus frequents in order to arrest him without causing any commotion.

The Last Supper (14:12-31)

During a meal Jesus performs an action that speaks of the emptying of himself for the new people of God. This answers the action performed by the unnamed woman who profligately emptied a jar of expensive perfume to anoint Jesus.

Much has been discussed regarding the apparently differing chronologies provided by the Synoptic writers and John.[128] Arising from this discussion, the question of what really is the type of meal envisaged by Mark is also asked.[129] The position taken by this commentary is that Jesus intended to hold the Passover meal one day in advance of the official celebration (see excursus).

Excursus: The Chronology of the Last Supper in the Four Gospels

Four main proposals, with variations, have been made in scholarship:

1. There was a calendrical dispute amongst the Jews and the different Gospel writers use different calendars to narrate Jesus' last meal;[130]

2. John's chronology is historically inaccurate because of his theological interest to depict Jesus as the sacrificed Passover lamb;[131]

3. John's chronology is correct and the Synoptic Gospels got it wrong, as the meal was not intended to be a Passover meal. It was thought to be so only in retrospect;[132] and

4. The Synoptic Gospels can be harmonized with John's Gospel, by postulating either that, despite appearances, the former did not intend us to understand the meal to be a Passover meal, or that their accounts leave open the possibility that a Passover meal was celebrated in advance of the official one.[133]

---

128. Brown 1994: 1361–73, Keener 2009: 372–74
129. For a succinct presentation of the issues, see Evans 2001: 370–72.
130. Made famous by Jaubert 1965.
131. Jeremias 1966a: 41–62.
132. Evans 2001: 372; Hooker 1991: 333; Taylor 1952: 664–67.
133. France 2002: 559–64; Lane 1974: 498; Schweizer 1971: 297.

Option (1) makes recourse to the Qumran community that peculiarly followed the solar calendar instead of a lunar one, giving rise to the possibility that they might have celebrated the Passover on a different day. However, it is dubious to regard the majority of the Jews as taking cognizance of the issue, or even considering it as important.[134] Option (2) sacrifices John to save the Synoptic Gospels, and militates against the early evidence that Jesus was understood as the Passover Lamb even in the Pauline churches (1 Cor 5:7). Indeed, the rabbinic tradition has it that Jesus died on the eve of Passover (*b. Sanh.* 43a; cf. 67a). Similarly, option (3) requires a hypothesis that assumes a blunder in the Early Church, and it is not necessary if option (4) or (2) can be sustained. Much may be said for option (4), especially the theory that Jesus intended to celebrate the Passover in advance. The following are the considerations.

1. The term "Passover" looms large in the first half of Mark 14. Verses 12, 14, and 16 clearly indicate that the meal to be eaten is the Passover meal.

2. The meal is eaten in Jerusalem and not at Bethany, where Jesus is hosted. Having the meal in Jerusalem runs the risk of being spotted and arrested. There is no need for this unless the location for the meal is important. Passover meals are customarily eaten in Jerusalem (Deut 16:2; *m. Pesaḥ.* 7:9).

3. Jesus acts as the presider of the meal and speaks words of interpretation over the different elements of the meal. This dovetails with the liturgy performed at Passover meals.

4. The singing of the Hallel Psalms forms part of the Passover liturgy. The singing of a hymn to conclude the meal at v. 26 fits reasonably with such a liturgy.

5. The failure to mention the Passover lamb may speak against this theory, but there is a good explanation for this omission.

The Markan evidence does not tell us clearly *whether the meal is held on the official day* itself or a day before it. It has been plausibly suggested by France that the question about the Passover preparation could have been asked on the beginning of 14th of Nisan (i.e., in the evening), which is followed by the meal immediately (i.e., during the night, but still part of the 14th of Nisan).[135] This means no lamb is mentioned because it cannot be obtained, as (i.e., on the afternoon of the next solar day but it is still

---

134. But note Saulnier 2012 for a recent attempt to defend Jaubert's thesis.

135. France 2002: 559–63. Jews began the day with the evening.

the 14th of Nisan). The sacrificing of lambs took place on the afternoon of the 14th of Nisan, so that in the evening (i.e., 15th of Nisan), the Passover meal may be held. This allows us to fit Mark's chronology with John's, which clearly states that Jesus dies on the day the lambs are sacrificed (i.e., afternoon of 14th of Nisan). All this means that Jesus held the meal a day in advance of the official one. There are good reasons for this: to throw his enemies off his trail, and to fulfill his vocation of being sacrificed like the Passover lamb for the new covenant.

The Preparation for the Meal (14:12-16)

Verse 12 gives us a time note again—the first day of the Festival of Unleavened Bread—and even specifies this to be the day the Passover lambs are to be sacrificed, indicating that Mark is stressing the backdrop against which his readers are to understand the Last Supper. We have previously commented on the link between the Unleavened Bread festival and Passover. Suffice it here to reiterate that. Quite plausibly, it is in the evening of the 14th of Nisan, and not the afternoon of the next solar day (still 14th of Nisan) that the question of the disciples was asked.

The instructions of Jesus in vv. 13-15 suggest some prior arrangements have been made, and with pre-arranged signals agreed upon for security and secrecy. Mark also tells his audience this meal is held in a big upper room (v. 15).[136]

The Meal and the Interpretative Words (14:17-26)

Two key moments in the meal may be identified: first, the prediction that a member of the Twelve will betray Jesus (vv. 18-21), and secondly, the giving of interpretative words over the key elements in the meal, transforming a time-hallowed meal into something new (vv. 22-25).

During the meal Jesus takes the initiative to inform the Twelve of his impending betrayal. The words "one who is eating with me" (v. 18) are shocking in the ancient context because they indicate great betrayal. Partaking of a meal together is often symbolic of intimacy or reconciliation. Indeed, such words also echo the Psalmist's complaint in Ps 41:9 of being

---

136. Swete 1898: 330 argues that the room would have been carpeted and the couches upholstered.

betrayed by a close associate.¹³⁷ This understandably leads to sadness in the company, and questions about the identity of this person.

Jesus' reply deepens the discomfort. He repeats the point that it will be one of the Twelve who will betray him, with a heightening of the intimacy involved (v. 18). Not only does this person eat with Jesus, but he will also be dipping bread into the same bowl with him. If a dastardly deed such as this can happen to Jesus, does it mean the movement he started is falling apart, and his ministry heading for irretrievable loss? So the statement of v. 21 plays an important function by preempting such thoughts, as it speaks of the fulfillment of Scripture. The dastardly deed is inscrutably connected with God's plan. What this Scripture is, Mark does not tell us.¹³⁸

In other words, as horrifying as the news may be, underlying it is a note of hope. Scripture is being fulfilled and God's will is being done. The wrath of man is still under the control of God and may thus be directed towards ends that are faithful to his covenantal promises. Note that the use of the title "Son of Man" in this connection is important (v. 21). It harmonizes with the Markan depiction of the Son of Man as someone who is not only the kingdom inaugurator, but also one who suffers for human redemption. Furthermore, it reminds the audience that the person whom Judas is betraying is no ordinary mortal.

The theme of betrayal prepares for the narration of the meal proper. As the presider of the meal, Jesus leads the Passover liturgy. This liturgy ingrains in the minds of the Jewish nation the story of the Exodus, and the divine election through which a covenant is established. In this way the founding story of the nation—the story which gives the people their unique identity—is constantly retold (see excursus). But this is no ordinary Passover meal, as Jesus transforms it by juxtaposing his story with the story of the Exodus. The broken and distributed bread is interpreted as Jesus' body. The words uttered over the bread in the traditional Passover liturgy probably went something like this: "This is the bread of affliction which our fathers ate in the land of Egypt. Let everyone who hungers come and eat; let everyone who is needy come and eat the Passover meal."¹³⁹ But Jesus transforms its meaning, and defines it according to his own identity and vocation. The Greek word *sōma* probably translates an underlying Aramaic *gěšēm*, which is used to signify not just the physical body (flesh), but also physical life. In effect Jesus is saying that just as the bread is offered to the disciples, so also

---

137. Cranfield 1959: 423.
138. See Evans 2001: 377 for speculations.
139. Marcus 2009: 964.

is his whole life given for them. The reason for this is answered by the next interpretative word, spoken over the cup.

Excursus: The Passover Meal

The traditional Passover meal, as this is gathered from the extant evidence available to us (*m. Pes.* 10:1–7), follows the structure below:

The Preliminary Course
- Words of dedication spoken by the presider over the first cup.
- Preliminary dish consisting, among other things, of green herbs, bitter herbs and a sauce of fruit purée.
- The meal proper is served but not yet eaten; the second cup is mixed and put in its place but not yet drunk.

The Passover Liturgy
- Passover haggadah led by the presider.
- First part of the Passover *hallel* (Pss 113–14).
- Drinking the second cup (*haggadah* cup).

The Main Meal
- Grace spoken by the presider over the unleavened bread.
- Meal, consisting of Passover lamb, unleavened bread, bitter herbs (Exod 12:8), with fruit purée and wine.
- Grace over the third cup (cup of blessing).

The Conclusion
- Second part of the Passover *hallel* (Pss 115—18).
- Praise over the fourth cup (*hallel* cup).

So one may conjecture that the cup over which the saying is given is the third cup or the cup of blessing. And the hymn Jesus and his disciples sing at the conclusion of the meal might plausibly be the Hallel Psalms, specifically Psalms 115—18.

The cup saying[140] completes the meaning of the bread saying. It speaks of Jesus' blood as the blood of the covenant. To understand the full impor-

---

140. The phrase recalls Exodus 24:8, which speaks about the establishment of the Sinaitic covenant through the shedding of blood. Matthew follows Mark here, but Luke and Paul speak of the new covenant. Scholars have therefore identified two strands of tradition relating to the cup-saying: a Markan one and a Lukan-Pauline one. In an

tance of this, we must think of two parallel stories which are intertwined: the story of the Exodus and the story of Jesus. The Passover meal reminds the Jews of the deliverance from Egypt and the covenant at Mt Sinai that ensued. In the establishment of this covenant, the blood of an animal was shed. Hence, when Jesus identifies the cup as his blood of the covenant, he seeks to communicate two propositions. The first is that his ministry and death are connected intimately with Israel's covenant with God. Far from being a religious deviant, Jesus is actually a faithful Israelite. However, if the blood of the Sinaitic covenant has already been shed, why does blood need to be shed again? This brings us to the second proposition. What Moses originally ratified is no longer tenable, otherwise there would be no need for further blood to be shed. In other words, what Jesus is offering is either a renewal of the covenant, or a new covenant altogether.[141] Prophets such as Jeremiah and Isaiah looked forward to a time when the intransigence of Israel would be eradicated, leading to the fulfillment of the true intent of the Sinaitic covenant (e.g., Isa 59:15–21; Jer 31:31–34). Jesus is then conveying that what the Prophets looked for is now being fulfilled. The new people to be brought about once this new or eternal covenant is established are represented by those partaking of the meal with Jesus. The upshot of all this is that the open-ended covenantal story of Israel and God is completed by Jesus' offering of his life. The new locus of covenant identity is no longer to be found in Moses but in Jesus. This does not mean what Moses ratified was an evil to be done away with. Rather it means that covenant had an in-built obsolescence. It awaited a completion from outside of itself.

The phrase "poured out for many" probably recalls Isa 53:12, which speaks of the Servant pouring out his life for many.[142] The "many" here is not intended to limit the scope of Jesus' death, to make it short of being universal. Instead, it appropriates a biblical idiom to speak about Jesus' redemptive death for *others*, without defining its scope.

Verse 25 speaks of Jesus' expectation of drinking wine again with the disciples in a new setting: when the kingdom of God is consummated. Drinking wine is often a metaphor associated with the in-breaking of God's

---

earlier work I argue that this difference in terminology is insignificant, since Jewish theology did not strive for terminological precision (Tan 1997: 215–16). What is significant is the juxtaposing of Jesus' story with the covenant story, a story that many Jews believe awaits completion.

141. On the consistent overlap of the two concepts in Jewish thought, see Nicholson 1986: 3–117; Tan 1997: 205–16.

142. Note the candid observation of Jeremias 1971–72: 203: "Without Isa 53 the eucharistic words would remain incomprehensible."

kingdom (cf. Isa 25:6),[143] which also ushers in unprecedented blessings. Interestingly, this statement has been interpreted as referring either to Jesus' abstinence from banqueting (i.e., during the interval framed by his death and the consummation of the kingdom),[144] or to his expectation of post-mortem survival and confidence in the certain consummation of the kingdom of God, in which he would play the central role.[145] Both ideas are not mutually exclusive. That said, there is a more profound dimension that needs explication. First, the saying communicates to the disciples that Jesus' fellowship with them will be renewed. Jesus has spoken about his passion many times. With this verse, he is saying that his death ends not in tragedy. A greater fellowship awaits them instead: they will drink wine together *again* in the kingdom of God. Secondly, this fellowship will be of a different order, as it is indicated by the Greek word *kainon*. This points to the consummation of the kingdom. Thirdly, all this is meant to show the vindication of Jesus' message and vocation. Reunion in a new mode at the consummation of the kingdom certainly entails it. The kingdom's program will not be derailed by his death, but comes, in an inscrutable way, to fruition.

The Prediction of Peter's Denial (14:27-31)

En route to the Mount of Olives, Jesus predicts abandonment by the Twelve and Peter's denial. This indicates that the theme of discipleship, so much a part of the eschatological discourse of chapter 13 and the middle segment of Mark, has not been forgotten.

Again, the initiative is with Jesus. The prediction is offered, without the disciples' asking for it. Coming after the explanation of what Jesus' impending death stands for, the prediction amounts to being a major disappointment for the disciples. Like the prediction of betrayal in 14:18, it is backed up by Scripture (Zech 13:7). The book of Zechariah prophesies not just the coming of a peaceable king, riding on a donkey, but also the mysterious rejection of a shepherd close to God.[146] Jesus may have connected these themes together to speak of the fate of God's chosen king. In this sense the disciples' defection is also foretold in Scripture, but that is not the end of the story. Jesus moves on to predict his rising again (v. 28), which means

---

143. The so-called messianic banquet; see Boring 2006: 391; Evans 2001: 395.
144. Jeremias 1966a: 207-9.
145. Cf. de Jonge 1996: 265-86.
146. Zech 13:7 is also used in CD 19:7-13 in a similar way (sheep = adherents; shepherd = Teacher of Righteousness).

nothing less than his leading them once more.¹⁴⁷ In other words, the scattering of the flock that comes from Jesus being struck down ends in a regathering. Just as 10:32 speaks of his leading his flock to Jerusalem, so this prediction answers it by speaking of his leading them back to Galilee, away from the city of danger.

The prediction draws from Peter the boast that he would be different (v. 29). Hence, Jesus' revelation to Peter is shocking. It is also prefaced with the solemn words, "Amen I say to you." Peter would not simply abandon Jesus, but he would also disown him verbally: not just once but three times! Far from being a cut above the rest, he would do what the others would not contemplate doing: to disown Jesus verbally thrice. Cock crowing signals the approach of dawn, and is often used symbolically for the coming of hope.¹⁴⁸ In this instance the point made is different. Instead of offering hope, it seals for Peter what he dreads most: his abject failure. To add to his culpability, Jesus informs him all this will happen before the cock crows twice (i.e., Peter will not take heed even after hearing the first cock-crow). All this leaves Peter no ground whatsoever to excuse his falling away.

Upon hearing this, Peter reaffirms his loyalty and speaks of unswerving attachment even to the point of death (v. 31). So do the other disciples. Vows made with ease are often recanted in the face of terror.

GETHSEMANE AND THE ARREST OF JESUS (14:32–52)

The route Jesus takes from Jerusalem to his intended destination winds through an orchard (cf. John 18:1), by the name of Gethsemane. It is here that the company stops and Jesus prays in great ordeal. It is also here that the disciples fail miserably to stay loyal to their Master. Succumbing to the natural inclination to preserve the self, the disciples flee when Jesus is arrested.

The Ordeal (14:32–42)

The name of the orchard is most probably derived from the Aramaic *gat šĕmānê*, which means "olive press" and is therefore eminently suitable for the place of Jesus' great ordeal.¹⁴⁹ According to tradition, it is located on the western slope of the Mount of Olives, just across the Kidron valley. The

---

147. This is the significance of the Greek *proagō*, which is better translated as "leading before," and is often used to speak of leadership, especially in a military context (2 Macc 10:1; Thucydides *Peloponnesian War* 7:6).

148. Brown 1994: 137.

149. Evans 2001: 407.

opening words of Jesus' speech to his disciples echo the refrain found in Psalms 42–43 (42:5, 11; 43:5), which are psalms of lament. Mark also provides his audience with the content of Jesus' prayer for the first time, even though he has earlier referred to his habit (1:35; 6:46).

Jesus addresses God as "Abba," and this word is found only once in Mark's Gospel (14:36). There is good evidence to show that this Aramaic word represents an intimate form of address,[150] notwithstanding the strictures of James Barr,[151] although it must be pointed out that its use is not limited only to children. The combination of an Aramaic term with the translation "Father" appears also in Paul's writings, which were addressed to people who spoke Greek (Rom 8:15-16; Gal 4:6). This implies that the term "Abba" has become theologically loaded, and used for describing the Christian's relationship with God. This further implies there must be something quite distinctive with the way it was used by Jesus in order for it to gain such significance. All this explains why when a translation is provided the original term is not expunged.

Addressing God as "Abba" sets Jesus' request on a familial tone of trust. The specific request is for the cup to be removed, predicated upon the understanding that all things are possible with the Father. However, the request is also qualified by submission to the Father's will. All this indicates clearly the struggle that Jesus is going through. What is the cup he seeks to avoid?

We suggested the metaphor of cup in 10:38-39 stood for the destiny to which one had been divinely appointed, whether it meant blessing or judgment. Drawing upon this insight, we may then conclude that for Jesus to struggle with this cup must mean it speaks of his suffering, perhaps even his suffering of wrath—certainly not for his wrongdoing but for the sins of many (cf. 10:45). If this is correct, we can then understand what sort of ordeal Jesus is going through. He is expecting not just any kind of suffering to come to him but that which is somehow linked with the wrath of God. Holiness that reaches out to cleanse and heal can only make a person recoil at the prospect of divine wrath. But how could this be if God is Jesus' Abba? The riddle is solved when we remember the Son of Man comes to give his life as a ransom for many (10:45).

Upon returning to his disciples, Jesus finds them sleeping (v. 37). Jesus' rebuke is stinging: the disciples are not able to keep watch even for an hour. Peter is specially singled out, and for good reason. He has already been warned about his frailty, and should therefore be even more watchful. The

---

150. Jeremias 1966b; Evans 2001: 412-13.
151. Barr 1988: 28-47.

injunction to watch and pray stems from the antithesis of spirit and flesh (v. 38). This antithesis is also mentioned in the OT (Isa 31:3) and the Pauline writings (Rom 7–8). It is not to be understood as a form of Platonic or proto-Cartesian thought (i.e., a sort of "ghost in the machine" metaphysics). Rather, the spirit denotes the so-called orientation towards God, something belonging to the order of the life-giving Spirit, or even the higher faculties of a human being.[152] In this light, Jesus is not speaking of a split between the material and immaterial parts of a man, but the dilemma a man encounters when temptations come his way.[153] Should he follow the directions of the divine or should he succumb to his basal instincts? The weakness of the flesh can only be overcome by watching and praying. Mark informs his audience that this injunction of Jesus is repeated twice (vv. 40–41). In all the cases, the same results are obtained. The disciples are too sleepy to keep watch and pray.

The incident at Gethsemane thus showcases the unswerving loyalty of one person to the will of God, and the abject failure that humanity could sink into at crunch time. Yet this failure must not be understood as something that would inevitably happen. An antidote has been given by the One who stayed loyal to God's will: watch and pray.

The Arrest (14:43–52)

Judas comes with people armed with swords and clubs. They are to be identified as the Temple police and not the Roman soldiers.[154] This was quite a substantial force and well organized in Jesus' day. The fact they are sent by the chief priests, the teachers of the law and the elders demonstrates not only that this is officially sanctioned, but also what sort of people are against Jesus: they belong to the powerful establishment in Jerusalem. Temple, Torah (as interpreted by the best teachers), and tradition stand ready to condemn him.

The pre-arranged signal for Jesus' arrest is heavily ironic (v. 44), as the kiss is commonly used for showing affection, or as a form of greeting, often given by a student to his rabbi.[155] Interestingly, in the midst of such commotion someone (John 18:10 tells us it is Peter) takes a sword and cuts off

---

152. Wolff 1974: 32–39.

153. Marcus 2009: 979–80.

154. Boring 2006: 401; Collins 2007: 684. Regarding them as "a hired rabble" (Taylor 1952: 558) is unnecessary and anachronistic.

155. See Marcus 2009: 991, for discussion on the possible nuances, concluding that the kiss is merely a conventional form of greeting. We think there is no need to limit the possibilities.

the ear of the servant of the high priest (v. 47). The definite article in Greek (*ton doulon tou archiereōs*) indicates he is someone significant enough to be singled out. So he is possibly the leader of this group of armed men, or someone who has been specially commissioned by the high priest to ensure the arrest is performed.[156]

In response to such a show of force, Jesus asks some rhetorical questions (v. 48). Their function is to convey the point that all this is unnecessary, since he is not a bandit (the meaning of the Greek *epi lēstēn*). Banditry was quite a problem in first-century Palestine; these bandits usually targeted Roman trains and supplies, and often enjoyed local protection and support.[157] In this sense they may be regarded as revolutionaries acting against Rome. The point Jesus wishes to make is that bandits do not engage in teaching or discussions in the Temple (v. 49). Do note, however, that although Jesus distances himself from being identified as a bandit, he will later be crucified between two bandits (15:27). It is plausible that the irony is intended. Be that as it may, Jesus' words certainly point out what the official delegates should grasp: his kingdom is of a different order, and so there will be no resistance to this unjust arrest.

Now that things have come to such a head, the instinct to flee for safety takes over the disciples' resolve. Mark inserts here an intriguing story of the flight of an unnamed young man, the details of which are somewhat comical (vv. 51–52). This apparently inconsequential element of the story of Jesus' arrest has led many scholars to suspect some symbolism must be at work.[158] Frankly, it is difficult to see any symbolic quality in this rather strange incident. Perhaps it is best to regard it as historical reminiscence, especially memorable to a member of Mark's intended audience.[159] This need not mean Mark is writing himself into the story, as many commentators in the nineteenth and twentieth centuries have thought.[160]

---

156. Cf. Viviano 1989: 71–80. The act amounted to mutilation which would disqualify the victim from Temple duties. In other words, the act was intended to destroy the victim's career.

157. Horsley and Hanson, *Bandits* 1985: 190–243.

158. Gundry 1993: 862–63: the young man in white prefigures the resurrection of Jesus; Myers 1988: 368–69: symbolizing the restoration of the disciples that is to come; Evans 2001: 428: suggesting a Joseph typology but only to reject it; Kermode 1979: 55–64: a type of all Christians who desert the faith, since being divested of clothes by captors is a sign of shame.

159. Hooker 1991: 352.

160. Marcus 2009: 1124. A good summary of the history of interpretation is found in Collins 2007: 688–93.

The Hearing by the Sanhedrin (14:53–72)

Studies on the trial narrative are often bedeviled by historical problems. Two questions that recur concern the charge made against Jesus and the legality of the trial.[161] Does what Mark narrates appear credible when set against what we know of Jewish religion and Roman administration of the first century? The question about the charge will be addressed in the course of the commentary; the question about the legality of the trial may be treated at the outset.

According to the Mishnah, it is stipulated that trials relating to capital punishment must be conducted in the day, and certainly not held on the eve of a festival. Moreover, it must be held in the specified courtrooms, and any verdict to be given must not be made on the same day. This is to prevent any miscarriage of justice due to haste. The trial in Mark breaks these rules, and therefore raises doubts over whether his account is credible. Two things need to be said in reply. First, the regulations in the Mishnah were codified at the end of the second century. How many of these were being practiced in the first century remains uncertain.[162] Secondly, there is no indication in Mark that this was a formal trial. In fact, it has all the appearances of an out-of-court hearing to decide whether the matter should be handed over to the Roman authorities.[163] On both counts it may legitimately be concluded that the Mishnaic regulations may not be as relevant as they are often thought.

In fact, Mark's account is historically plausible. We have already been informed the Temple establishment has a great interest in seeing Jesus' condemned. As the administration of capital punishment has been taken away from the Jewish authorities by the Romans (Josephus *Antiquities* 18:63–64),[164] it becomes expedient that a preliminary hearing be conducted so as to bring a credible charge before the Romans.

The Jewish Hearing (14:53–65)

With the opening two verses of this passage, Mark introduces us to two settings in which significant action will take place. The first is the high priest's house,[165] where charges against Jesus will be heard before the chief priests,

---

161. The classic study is Winter 1961; cf. the later Catchpole 1971, who interacts copiously with it. A good summary of the issues is provided in Marcus 2009: 1126–30.
162. Stein 2008: 677.
163. Marcus 2009: 1127–28.
164. See the discussion in Keener 2009: 377–78; *contra* Winter 1961: 10–15.
165. Donahue and Harrington 2002: 420.

the elders and the scribes. The second is the courtyard where Peter, after following the party from a distance, settles down to warm himself at the fire with the guards. In other words, two stories are running on parallel tracks. While Jesus is being tried, Peter also faces a sort of "trial."

Verses 55–56 inform us that initially the eyewitnesses' testimonies cannot agree. The accusation that Jesus claimed to destroy the Temple is then made. For the Jewish context, this may be regarded as a heinous crime (Josephus *War* 6:300–309; cf. Acts 21:27–36). To be sure, there is evidence for the belief among Jews that the Messiah would be the one to build a new Temple, but this does not envisage his destroying it in order to build it again (Zech 6:12; *Tg. Zech.* 6:12; 4QFlor 1:6–7).[166] The scenario is usually this: the Temple is already destroyed or defiled before the Messiah comes to the rescue of Israel and reinstates her sacrificial system.[167] This being the case, the idea that Jesus' opponents were trying to elicit from Jesus a messianic confession appears weak. There is strong evidence, however, to show that any talk or prediction of the Temple's destruction was construed as a threat to it. This would make the person liable to punishment or even execution. In AD 62 a person by the name of Jesus ben Ananias repeatedly predicted the Temple's destruction. This caused consternation amongst the leading men of Jerusalem. Some of them were so incensed that they wanted him dead, but he was brought before the Romans and was flogged to the bone before being released (Josephus *War* 6:300–309). Such a harsh reaction may be explainable as the attempt to safeguard the one symbol that speaks of the unique Jewish identity, and the non-negotiable belief that God's presence is found among the Jews precisely because he has chosen to dwell in the Temple.

There is, however, no unanimous agreement even for this charge (v. 59). However, the fact that Mark highlights this shows how important the charge is, for there is a grain of truth to it. Jesus did predict the Temple's destruction, and he did perform a provocative action to signify its rejection (13:2; 11:15–17, 22–25). Of course, the way it has been interpreted by the so-called eyewitnesses is far from Jesus' original intent.

---

166. There is a remote possibility that *Lam. Rab.* 1:5 may testify to this. In that passage, Rabban Yohanan ben Zakai proleptically hailed Vespasian as the king, since only a king can destroy the Temple and he would be the very person to do so. He proceeded to cite Isa 10:34 about the fall of Lebanon (= Temple) by a mighty one (= king). But it takes a conceptual leap to think that this provides evidence that there was a belief of the Messiah's destroying the Temple. A more straightforward way of reading it is that only an enemy with the status of king can destroy the Temple. All this may mean that Mark 14:58 is unprecedented, and that it could very well have been concocted out of sheer malice.

167. Gaston 1970: 150–54.

With eyewitness testimonies becoming more like an embarrassing cacophony of contradictions, the high priest (see excursus for discussion on his identity) has two important cards left to play. The first is to get the accused to incriminate himself by making him answer unadvisedly to leading questions (v. 60). Jesus wisely remains silent. The second card—the final and desperate one—has now to be played. The high priest asks whether Jesus is the Messiah, the Son of the Blessed One.[168] The title "the Son of the Blessed One" is usually regarded as being synonymous with the royal Messiah (2 Sam 7:12, 14; Ps 2:2, 7; 4QFlor 3:11–12; 4Q246), even if the early Church would later treat it as containing a meaning greater than that. We may detect in the high priest's question the cunning that is honed by years of serving in the highest Jewish office, surviving countless politicking from competitors, and handling many sensitive diplomatic issues with an imperialistic overlord. The question puts Jesus between the rock and a hard place. An answer in the affirmative could easily land Jesus in trouble with the Romans, for he could then be charged with sedition. If it were answered in the negative, much of what Jesus came to teach and do would be discredited. Imagine what would happen if an official statement was issued that Jesus had denied all messianic claims? The nation would then regard him as a hot head, who had acted thoughtlessly and impulsively.

Excursus: Caiaphas the High Priest

Mark does not tell us who the high priest is although we learn from other sources (cf. Luke 3:2; John 18:13; Josephus *Antiquities* 18:95) that he is Caiaphas. He has an extraordinarily long tenure (AD 18–37). Most high priests in that period had an average tenure of about four years.[169] According to the Babylonian Talmud, this was because the high priestly office could be bought with money. As a result, the Romans were pleased to replace the incumbent with a new candidate frequently (*b. Yoma* 8b), as this would generate income for them. For Caiaphas to have remained for such a long period he must have had powerful backers or great political acumen himself.[170]

---

168. Evans 2001: 448–49 rightly argues that the question is not double, but contains one compound reference.
169. For a descriptive of the high priests, see Vanderkam 2004.
170. Bond 2004: 42–44. Striking a very cautious note is Reinhartz 2013: 11–23.

Locked between these two horns of the dilemma, what would Jesus do? Things have come to a head, and any attempt at being reticent at this point would only lead to greater misunderstanding. But a simple answer of "This is correct" plays too much into the hands of the priest. So Jesus answers "I am," but together with a qualification of what being Messiah means. Just as Jesus has responded to Peter's confession by couching his messianic claim in terms of the Son of Man designation (8.29–31), so also does he qualify his affirmation here with the Son of Man's role. In other words, the Messiah or the Son of the Blessed One is also the Son of Man who sits at the right hand of the Almighty and comes in the clouds of heaven. Properly speaking, the reply of Jesus in Greek spoke of "the right hand of the Power" (the Greek used is *dynamis*). "Power" is a well-known circumlocution for God (cf. *Mekilta of Rabbi Simon* 14:21; *Sifre on Numbers* 15.31). Here two OT passages are being combined: Psalm 110 and Daniel 7. The effect is that not only does this speak of vindication, but also the Son of Man's sharing sovereign authority with the Almighty. The claim is made more potent by Jesus' stating that those who are now charging him will see this event. Jesus does not specify when this is to happen, except that it is to happen in the lifetime of these people. Many scholars suggest it refers either to (i) the world-wide spread of the Jesus movement,[171] the originator whom they are now trying, (ii) the destruction of the Temple,[172] or (iii) the Parousia, during which they would be judged by the one who is now judged by them.[173]

Upon hearing this claim, the high priest tears his clothes (v. 63). Tearing clothes is an expression of grief in oriental culture (Gen 37:34; Josh 7:6; 2 Sam 1:11). That said, according to the Mishnah, when it becomes clear that a blasphemy has been committed, the judges are "to stand up on their feet and rend their garments, and they may not mend them again." (*m. Sanh.* 7:5). The charge of blasphemy is entirely tenable, as it may be understood either in the strict sense of speaking against the Almighty (Lev 24:15–16; 1 Kings 21:13), or loosely for lesser offences such as threatening his representative (1QpHab 10:12–13; CD 12:8) or the high priest (cf. Exod 22:28).[174] Of course, non-verbal actions can also fall into this category. Such actions make a person liable for capital punishment.[175]

---

171. Hooke 1991: 362; cf. Taylor 1952: 568.
172. France 2002: 612–13.
173. Evans 2001: 451–52.
174. Detailed evidence is provided by Evans 2001: 453–55.
175. Bock 1998: 30–112.

In Mark's narrative the strict sense of blasphemy is probably intended.[176] Jesus makes a claim that may be regarded as an affront to Jewish religious sensibilities. The whole Sanhedrin (see excursus) agrees that Jesus should be sentenced to death (v. 64). Animosity which has been seething is now expressed. Jesus is spat upon, insulted, and beaten in the manner worthy of a despised criminal.[177]

Excursus: Sanhedrin

The term is actually borrowed from the Greek *synedrion*, which mean basically "council." The term as used in the Jewish context has either a generic or technical sense (i.e., it may loosely refer to any local council or speak specifically of a supreme council that was located in Jerusalem [cf. the evidence from Josephus *Life of Josephus* 386; *Antiquities* 20:216–17]). With respect to the latter, there are keen scholarly debates on whether there were in fact two great Sanhedrins: one led by the high priests and his aristocratic colleagues that was political in nature, and the other that was dominated by the Pharisees that was religious or halakhic in nature. Although it is to be borne in mind that what we know about this institution comes from post-70 sources (e.g., the Mishnah)—and we therefore cannot be certain about its exact composition, structure, and function—we none the less side with those scholars who posit that there was only one such Sanhedrin. The chief reason being that what we know of first-century realities dictates that politics and religion, or the spiritual and the mundane, cannot be separated into neat compartments. They were all intertwined.

In the present Markan context, the term is used restrictively and not generically (i.e., it refers to the Great Sanhedrin [or Jerusalem Sanhedrin] and not any local council [cf. 13:9]). This comprises around seventy to seventy-two members, who met in the Chamber of Hewn Stone on the Temple Mount.[178] After the two wars with Rome, the Great Sanhedrin was superseded by the Beth Din (judicial court), which had charge over religious or moral matters only.[179]

---

176. Collins 2004: 398–400.
177. Collins 2007: 707 argues that such actions were performed by the judges.
178. Schürer 1978: 2:210–11.
179. Saldarini 1992: 5:975–80.

Peter's Denial (14:66–72)

Mark adroitly shifts the scene to Peter, depicting another "trial," that of Peter's loyalty. The Greek word for "servant girl" here (v. 67) is *paidiskē*, which is the feminine diminutive of *pais*. This can mean either the girl is very young or, more probably, her social status is insignificant (i.e., the lowliest servant). A person who usually poses no threat by virtue of her social position now sends shivers down the spine of this Galilean with just a simple statement: "You also were with that Nazarene, Jesus" (v. 67). This statement threatens Peter's much desired anonymity, and so he denies it. Sensing that his cover could be blown if this conversation were allowed to be prolonged, he leaves the fireside for the entrance of the courtyard (v. 68). The servant girl now gets others involved by telling them who she thinks Peter is (v. 69). Peter issues another denial. Finally, these people become convinced Peter was with Jesus because his Galilean accent gives him away (v. 70). The only way for Peter to escape suspicion is to issue an even stronger denial, one which is backed up by curses and swearing (v. 71).

On whom precisely are the curses called? Mark does not indicate. It could be Peter or, more plausibly, Jesus. The Greek verb *anathematizō* is actually transitive (i.e., it needs a grammatical object to complete its meaning). But it appears to be used reflexively in Acts 23:12, 14, 21. However, the reflexive force is clear in Acts only because it is accompanied by the Greek reflexive *heautous*. This is absent in Mark 14:71. If we accept therefore that there is no grammatical support for understanding Mark's *anathematizō* as having reflexively force, the conclusion is that Peter is calling down curses on someone other than himself. The inescapable entailment of this conclusion will be that the one being cursed is Jesus.[180] This actually serves to give Peter's denial greater veracity but poignantly, it also heightens his guilt.

Mark has thus shown us how Peter's denial became progressively severe, and how he moved further and further away from the ideals of discipleship. However, the story has not ended yet, as Mark moves on to narrate that just when Peter has finished denying and swearing, a cock crows the second time (v. 72). Mark does not narrate the first crowing, and the intention may be that he is once again heightening Peter's failure.[181] The point is that warning has already been served by the first crowing, but Peter did not take heed, as he was absorbed in self-preservation. He woke up from this "spiritual slumber" only with the second crowing. With this, Peter's guilt

---

180. *Pace* Cranfield 1959: 447–48; but cf. Evans 2001: 466.

181. Some manuscripts add *kai alektōr ephōnēsen* (i.e., "and a cock crowed") to v. 68 in order to make Jesus' prediction and its fulfillment seamless but it is certainly a scribal gloss. All this means Mark does not inform us of the first crowing of the cock.

now comes home to him with full force, as he remembers what Jesus has predicted (14:30). Greatly disappointed with the failure, Peter breaks down and weeps.

Mark has sketched vividly contrasting stories to his audience. On the one hand, Jesus has stood firm when all the slings and arrows of human cunning have been thrown at him. On the other hand, the key member of the Twelve has wilted: not under trial but by a simple observation made by a servant girl and those around her: that Peter had been with Jesus (v. 67). But wasn't this precisely what Peter was called to do when he became an apostle (3:14)?

THE ROMAN TRIAL (15:1–20)

Two key themes emerge in the Roman trial. The first is that Jesus is charged as claiming to be the king of the Jews. The second is the rejection of Jesus in favor of an insurrectionist by the name of Barabbas. All this strikes a poignant note: he who has been sent as God's final envoy, and he who has offered God's kingdom to the nation is now rejected in favor of him whose type would later on lead the nation into a catastrophic confrontation with Rome in AD 66–70.

The Rejection of Jesus by the Jewish Crowd (15:1–15)

The arrival of dawn often signifies hope, but in this instance it means further suffering for Jesus. Having decided that Jesus is worthy of death, the Jewish leadership has now the task of formally charging him before the Roman prefect, since the right to administer the death penalty has been taken away from them (Josephus *Antiquities* 18:63–64). The question asked by Pilate (v. 2) implies it is the charge of claiming to be king that the Jewish leadership brings before him. This charge has teeth because Rome is always on the lookout for revolutionaries who may lead the people to rise up against her. Jesus does not deny the charge.

Excursus: Pontius Pilate

Pontius Pilate was prefect[182] of Judea in AD 26–37, and as such he was directly answerable to the Senate in Rome. His official residence was in

---

182. Not "procurator", as in some versions, basing on Tacitus *Annals*, 15:44. The inscription discovered at Caesarea testifies otherwise. A prefect is commissioned by the

Caesarea Maritima but during the Passover and other important festivals, he would reside in Jerusalem for assizes, and to ensure peace and security during such heady times. He was a protégé of Sejanus, the commander of the Praetorian Guard (the Emperor's special troops), who was influential on the Emperor Tiberius. Unfortunately, Sejanus was anti-Semitic, and such an attitude would certainly have influenced his protégé. From two extant Jewish sources (Josephus *Antiquities* 18:55–62; Philo's *Embassy to Gaius* 299–305), Pilate appears to be a rather insensitive ruler who despised the Jews. Apart from the incident alluded in Luke 13:1, two other incidents bear mentioning for they typify the kind of attitude Pilate had towards the Jews.

The first may be known as the "standards incident." Roman standards bearing the Emperor's image were brought into Jerusalem, rousing the ire of the Jewish populace because they regarded them as idolatrous and therefore defiling to a holy city such as Jerusalem. Military force was used to quell the Jewish protest, but to no avail as the Jews willingly bared their necks before the soldiers' swords. They would rather die than to have the city defiled. Sensing that a massacre could easily ignite a revolution, Pilate backed down and withdrew the standards (Josephus *War* 2:169–74; *Antiquities* 18:55–59).

In the second incident, Pilate took Corban funds from the Temple treasury to build an aqueduct to carry water into Jerusalem. Although the project would bring practical benefits to the Jews, the use of such sacred funds was deemed highly offensive for they were dedicated to God. There was a massacre this time round (Josephus *War* 2:175; *Antiquities* 18:60–62). The two incidents probably took place before Jesus was arraigned before him.[183]

As it is expedient for overlords to win over the goodwill of the subjects, certain forms of amnesty are sometimes given, especially in the context of national or religious festivals.[184] So Mark informs us it is a Roman practice to release a prisoner requested by the Jewish people during the Feast of the Unleavened Bread (cf. *m. Pes.* 8.6). The Jewish crowd duly ask for a prisoner to be released (v. 8; but do note that Mark's narrative is compressed here; he

---

Emperor to take charge mainly of civil or criminal matters, while a procurator's sphere of responsibility was mainly fiscal in nature.

183. Brown 1994: 693–705. Cf. Bond 1998 for a thorough sifting of the evidence.
184. Brown 1994: 817.

is focusing only on the key actions without dwelling on details). Sensing an opportunity to thwart the chief priests' plan, Pilate turns to the Jewish crowd and asks them whether they want Jesus released. The rejection of the crowd is poignant. What was offered to them was the king of the Jews and but they wanted Barabbas,[185] a murderer, instead (vv. 9–11). Mark informs us that behind the crowd's rejection of Jesus lay the influence and maneuvering of the chief priests (v. 11). More seriously, the crowd wants Jesus crucified— punished with the most painful sort of sentence reserved only for slaves and seditious people (v. 13). When asked to reconsider, the crowd only hardens its resolve (v. 14). Indeed, in the Markan narrative this crowd speaks only two words and nothing else: "Crucify him" (the Greek is *staurōson auton*). And this is all there is to their eloquence. Up until now the verb "crucify" has not been used in Mark's tale (but cf. 8:34 where the noun is used) and it must be intentional that the first use of the word in Mark's narrative belongs to the Jewish crowd. Crucifixion may be described as one of the cruelest form of punishment, as the victim is not only slowly tortured to death but also shamed and made a public example.[186] It is a punishment greatly feared by Jews, as crucified victims are regarded as cursed (cf. Gal 3:13).

The die is now cast. Both leaders and people want Jesus dead. And why should a Roman prefect, who has no respect for the Jewish people, stand up for an accused Jew? So even if Pilate knows that trumped-up charges have been made against Jesus (cf. v. 10), he acquiesces. Barabbas is duly released, and Jesus sentenced to be crucified. In keeping with Roman practise, Jesus is flogged, as a preliminary to crucifixion (Josephus *War* 2:306-308; 5:449; 7:200-202). The word "flog" and its Greek counterpart (*phragelloō*) are borrowed from the Latin *flagello*. The term denotes a lashing with whips that are normally made of leather, and may sometimes have metal or bone pieces at their tips. This ensures the whips cut deeply into a person's flesh so as to inflict maximum pain. True to Jesus' prediction, the Gentiles have now taken over the process of executing him (see 10:33-34).

Jesus Mocked by Roman Soldiers (15:16-20)

Jesus is now in the hands of the Roman soldiers for torture and execution. Led into the Praetorium (i.e., the official residence of the Roman prefect),[187] he is now subjected to sadistic insults and torture. The operative principle

---

185. Barabbas means "son of Abba," and "Abba" here can refer either to God or Abraham. See Abrahams 1924: 2:202.

186. Marcus 2009: 1131-33; Hengel 1977: 33-63.

187. Collins 2007: 725.

here is that a condemned man has no more rights left, and soldiers may do as they please. Often bored with their vocation or tired of being under subjection to commanders, soldiers relish the opportunity for comic relief and venting their pent-up feelings. Commanders allow for this to happen to keep the troops happy.[188] A mock enthronement ceremony is staged, with biting sarcasm and buffeting blows. Having satisfied their cruel inclinations, they dress Jesus now in his own clothes and lead him out to be crucified (v. 20). The chief priests might have been pleased that Jesus was so treated, but little did they realize it was the entire nation that had been insulted.

Jesus' Crucifixion and Death (15:21–41)

The climax to which earlier stories looked forward has now arrived. And with this the distinctive symbol of Christianity is born. Mark therefore slows his tale down to speak of Jesus' crucifixion and the events surrounding it, including the different people who are involved or impacted by it. The listeners of Mark's tale, if they are steeped in the OT, will certainly be able to detect many echoes of Psalm 22.

The Crucifixion of Jesus (15:21–32)

Just as it was with 14:51–52, so we have here a detail not found in any other Gospel. It is probably included because the characters are well-known to the first Markan audience. Simon of Cyrene[189] is compelled to carry the *patibulum* (i.e., the crossbeam) for Jesus, presumably because the latter was too wounded to do so.[190]

The whole band of soldiers and criminals come to the place of execution, which is called Golgotha. This Aramaic word means "the place of the skull," as Mark himself informs us (v. 22). Wine mixed with myrrh is offered to Jesus, for the purpose of numbing the senses to the excruciating pain of crucifixion. In the Babylonian Talmud it is recorded that women, guided by the teaching of Prov 31:6 would offer wine mixed with frankincense to help dull the pain of tortured people (*b. Sanh.* 43a). Perhaps a similar practice is being performed here. The only difference is that instead of frankincense

---

188. As an indication of this see the account in Josephus *War* 5:450–51, where Titus allowed his soldiers to do as they pleased to the victims, even though he was supposedly moved by pity to give them a more humane treatment.

189. The name is Jewish. Cyrene was the capital of Cyrenaica, in which a sizeable Jewish community was present since the time of Ptolemy I (fourth cent. BC).

190. Marcus 2009: 1041. This datum is missing in John 19:17, which states that Jesus carried the cross.

we have myrrh. Although Pliny informs us that wine mixed with myrrh is a luxury drink (*Natural History* 14:15, 92–93), the army physician Dioscorides Pedanius of the first century attests to myrrh's having narcotic properties (*Materia Medica* 1:64:3). It is this property which induces the unnamed people to offer Jesus the drink. However, Jesus refuses to accept it, probably because he must drink to the full the cup the Father has reserved for him.

After furnishing his audience with the setting of the crucifixion, Mark now focuses on the cross, offering many details. Some of them bear great significance. The first is that the crucifixion takes place at the third hour (v. 25). According to the Jewish reckoning of time, the third hour is roughly our nine o'clock in the morning. Innocuous as this may seem, the detail has actually generated scholarly discussion because the parallel in John speaks of the sixth hour instead (John 19:14). Since this is a commentary on Mark and not a work on Gospel harmony, it shall stay focused on Mark's tale (but see the excursus for some proposed solutions).

Excursus: Mark and John on the Hour of Crucifixion

Mark's time note occasions difficulty only when it is compared with the parallel provided by John, as the latter puts it at "about the sixth hour" (John 19:14). The major proposals for solving this discrepancy are: (i) to regard Mark 15:25 as an insertion by scribes during the earliest phase of the transmission of Mark's Gospel. This explains why although it is not part of the original text, there is currently no textual variants that indicate otherwise;[191] (ii) to regard Mark 15:25 as being theologically motivated in that Mark wants to align the time of Jesus' death with the daily sacrifice (the Tamid);[192] (iii) to regard John's account as theologically motivated in that he wants to align the time of Jesus' death with the sacrifice of the Passover lambs;[193] and (iv) to treat both time notes as approximations arising from observing the position of the sun.[194] The jury is still out on this issue. That said, it must be emphasized that Mark's chronology is coherent: the trial before Pilate takes place "very early in the morning" (the Greek here is *prōi*),

---

191. Cf. Lane 1974: 567.
192. Pobee 1970: 95.
193. Cranfield 1959: 455–56; Gundry 1993: 957.
194. Carson 1991: 605.

and the crucifixion can plausibly be fixed at the third hour (i.e., about 9:00 AM).

The second detail has to do with the *titulus* (v. 26). In Latin, this is probably IESUS NAZARENUS REX IUDAEORUM (translated into English it means "Jesus of Nazareth, King of the Jews"), which accounts for the use of INRI in much of Christian art on the crucifixion. When a criminal is crucified under Roman administration, his crime is written down on a placard and often hung on the neck of the condemned.[195] Where this is placed in Jesus' case Mark does not inform us, although from other Gospels we may gather it is above his head, on the vertical beam (Matt 27:37; John 19:19). The charge against Jesus could well be written as a title with, of course, a sarcastic tone. The point is to humiliate Jesus and the Jews. But the Markan audience would have seen beyond this sarcasm to detect a paradoxical reality here. All along Jesus has commanded silence about his kingly status, but now it is made known to all in a paradoxical setting. In other words, it is when he is crucified that the whole crowd gets to read his kingly claims. It may be a joke to the Romans, and a sick joke to the Jewish leaders (see John 19:19–22), but Mark's audience knows it is truer than these people dare to believe. The king is now finally enthroned, not on a throne of velvet but on a Roman gibbet.

The third detail concerns those who are crucified on both sides of Jesus (v. 27). The Greek term used to describe these two criminals is *lēstai*, and it refers not so much to robbers as to violent rebels or bandits.[196] These are probably patriots who are set on overthrowing Roman rule. Their positions relative to Jesus are significant, as the Greek replicates almost verbatim that used by James and John when they requested to sit on the right and left of Jesus (10:37). If there is an intended irony here, it is that when the moment comes to drink the cup of Jesus and be on his right and left, James and John are nowhere to be found.

Verses 29–30 record the fourth detail: the reaction of those who are witnessing the crucifixion. It is one of scorn and mockery. That which is connected with the Temple is vented: Jesus is challenged to come down from the cross to save himself if he wants to back his claim to be able to destroy the Temple and rebuild it in three days. In other words, in the minds of these people a form of poetic justice is now being played out: the would-be Temple destroyer is himself destroyed, while the Temple stands. The Jewish

---

195. Bammel 1984: 353.
196. Lane 1974: 568.

leaders also taunt Jesus to save himself, but express the irony that the one who could save others cannot even save himself. There may also be an intended pun, as the name "Jesus" means "Yahweh saves." Whatever the case, it is highly plausible that Mark intends a profound irony: Jesus cannot save himself not because of impotence, but because of a greater salvific work he is accomplishing.

Sadly, those who are crucified with him also insult him. All this can only mean that the chosen one of God is totally rejected: by common people, by leaders and even by those condemned to suffer the same fate. Jesus is a lonely figure: everywhere he turns he sees only taunting faces. In this sense Jesus has truly become the stone that the builders reject (12:10). Moreover, what he asked of his disciples he himself has accomplished: taking up the cross, denying himself, and suffering betrayal and rejection for the gospel's sake (8:34–35).

The Death of Jesus (15:33–37)

Up to this stage in the procession and the crucifixion, the Markan Jesus has not uttered a word. In fact, attention has been focused on those around him: the soldiers, the crowd, the Jewish leaders, and even those who are crucified alongside him. However, in this passage poignant and significant words will issue from his lips. And what theological reflection and debates these words have generated!

However, Mark first informs us of a supernatural event—an unnatural darkness—from the sixth to the ninth hour (i.e., during the brightest part of the day). Its significance is probably to be gathered from the OT, where darkness over the land during the day is a sign of divine displeasure or judgment (Deut 28:29; Amos 8:9; Jer 15:9). To our loss, Mark does not clarify whether the divine wrath is directed against Jesus or the conspirators.

At the ninth hour, probably towards the end of the darkness, Jesus cries out in Aramaic, which Mark translates as "My God, my God, why have you forsaken me?" The cry of dereliction and god-forsakenness has engendered much theological reflection in later Christian tradition.[197] Not surprisingly, there is a textual variant in the manuscript tradition which reads instead: "My God, my God, why have you heaped insults (the Greek here is *ōneudisas*) upon me?" (D, fifth century). This is probably because some Christian scribes found it hard to envisage Jesus as being forsaken by God. Later on, when the doctrine of the divinity of Christ was firmly established in the Christian Church, theological questions were posed such as "Could

---

197. Augustine *Letter* 140 speaks of Christ's identification with vulnerable humanity.

God be forsaken by God?" or "If Jesus is forsaken by God, does it mean he had died spiritually, and thus God has suffered hell?" As important as such questions may be, they actually take us away from the original intention of Mark.

The words are derived from the first verse of Psalm 22. We have pointed out earlier that this Psalm has had a great influence on the composition of the Passion Narrative, and should therefore be used as a template for interpretation.[198] In its original context, the Psalm features the complaint of the righteous person, who, because of the treatment he has received from friends and foes, feels he is as good as forsaken by God. However, it ends on a note of hope that God would hear him and come to his aid. The complaint may then be regarded as being made in faith and hope. Using this as a cue, what we may legitimately claim is that at this moment Jesus is the suffering righteous one par excellence. Just as the Son of Man sums up Israel's history in himself, so does the suffering Jesus sum up the unjust suffering of the righteous. Since Jesus is steeped in Scripture, we may expect him to think of the vindication that comes after all this suffering, which is indicated in the Psalm. Hence we may conclude that as painful as the complaint may be, it is voiced in the hope of restoration and vindication,[199] without belittling the suffering Jesus experiences.

The use of the verb *boaō* ("cry out") here reinforces the above observations. First of all, Jesus does not die like other crucified victims in that he cries out loudly before death comes. Crucifixion kills by exhaustion and asphyxiation, and most victims die with a whimper (Seneca *Epistula* 101).[200] In this regard there is a rather distinctive quality to his death. Secondly, the fact that the word is used only twice in Mark invites us to think of their relation. The cry in 1:3 sounds out the way of the Lord at the beginning of the gospel. The derelict cry concludes this way. In this regard, the cry signifies not a loss of hope because it is related to God's way. This means as agonizing as the experience may be, there is an implicit trust in divine vindication. All this has great mileage for Mark's audience, as their being persecuted would raise all sorts of questions about God's administration of justice.[201]

---

198. Cf. Boring 2006: 428. On how the Psalms of Lament, of which Psalm 22 is a member, shaped the Passion Narrative, see Athearne-Kroll 2007.

199. Pesch 1980: 2:494. But note the cautionary remarks of Marcus 2009: 1063–64, so as not to lessen the shock effect of the cry.

200. Donahue and Harrington 2002: 454; Hartman 2010: 603–604; Hengel 1977: 30–31.

201. Cf. the recent work of Rindge 2012: 755–74, who argues for this Markan intention based on reading the cry of dereliction from the perspective of a reconfigured Akedah.

Upon hearing those words, the crowd thinks mistakenly that Jesus is calling for Elijah. Popular Jewish piety regards Elijah as not only the agent to restore all things, but also the person who can deliver Jews out of duress and calamities. The Babylonian Talmud tells the story of Rabbi Eleazar who is rescued from a Roman trial by Elijah, who is disguised as a Roman official (b. 'Avod. Zar. 17b). Such expectation has its roots in the belief that Elijah was taken up to heaven without dying (cf. 2 Kings 2:11), and therefore could come back to earth to offer help. The offering of vinegar to Jesus is peculiar. Perhaps it is meant to awaken him so that he too can wait a little longer, in case Elijah does come.[202] Or possibly, the words of v. 36 may be sarcastic and derisory.[203] Of course, to Jesus Elijah has already come, and humans have done to him what they wished. So with another cry, Jesus breathes his last.

Two Responses to Jesus' Death (15:38-39)

Two significant things happen at the death of Jesus. The first is a portent, located in the Temple. We cannot be certain exactly which curtain Mark is referring to, although construing it as that which separates the Holy of Holies from the Holy Place makes good theological sense (i.e., the inner veil and not the outer curtain).[204] This must have been a dramatic sign, as this curtain is probably 90 feet in length.[205] Being the curtain for shielding the Holy of Holies from prying eyes, its rending must have been greatly significant to all who witnessed it. However, the exact significance Mark hopes to convey with this account is not entirely clear. It may mean there is now free access to the presence of God, as the writer of Hebrews construes it (Heb 10:19-20; cf. 6:19-20),[206] or that the Temple is desecrated, as the Holy of Holies is now profaned.[207] What should not be missed, however, is that the tearing of the curtain is intended to be a divine response to the death of Jesus.

The other significant happening concerns a Roman centurion. As the first human being in Mark's Gospel to confess Jesus as the authentic Son of God, there are at least two theological points being made. The first is that it is only when Jesus is crucified that human beings may see clearly and

202. Boring 2006: 431.
203. Marcus 2009: 1067.
204. Brown 1994: 1111.
205. This is conjectured from the datum that the height of the hall just before the Holy of Holies was 60 cubits high (Josephus *War* 5:215-19). Cf. France 2002: 656.
206. Marcus 2009: 1066-67.
207. France 2002: 657.

confess he is the Son of God.²⁰⁸ The "secrecy theme" that has been developing over many chapters is now at its terminal point. Without the crucifixion, the meaning of true messiahship is liable to be misunderstood.

The second point concerns ethnicity. This profound confession is made by a Gentile centurion of all people! Might Mark be saying three further things in this connection? One, Gentiles may recognize in the crucified Jesus the Messiah of God. Two, the possibility is open even for those working for the Empire to come to faith. There is no disbarment for them even when the Empire appears to be attacking Christianity. Three, the Empire's concept of the son of god is subverted.²⁰⁹ The usual notion is that of a charismatic and victorious Emperor, worthy of the reverence and worship of his subjects. His glory is best seen in a Roman triumph. This means that what Mark presents here is surely one of the most profound paradoxes known to Roman citizens and subjects. He who was crucified on a Roman gibbet is confessed as authentically (the Greek used is *alēthōs*) the Son of God! A Roman soldier who is so used to aligning the title "Son of God" with Caesar and all his pomp realizes there is an alternative—displayed in the crucifixion and death of Jesus.

The Female Witnesses (15:40–41)

Interestingly, Mark singles out a group of people that writers of the ancient world would usually ignore. These are the women followers of Jesus. Mark's explicit comment in v. 41 implies that there is a deeper layer of meaning here: they were Jesus followers' when he was active in Galilee. Perhaps the quiet ways of these women in their following of Jesus stand up to the test better than the bravado of Jesus' male disciples, since these male followers are conspicuously absent.

In this group of women followers, three are singled out for special mention: Mary Magdalene, Mary the mother of James the younger and of Joses, and Salome. These women will play a key role in the resurrection narrative, as the first witnesses of Jesus' resurrection.

---

208. Even if the comment was meant to be ironic or sarcastic (Burchard 1983: 1–11), in Mark's hand it serves the purpose of furthering the theme of saturoformic revelation (so Marcus 2009: 1059).

209. Collins 2007: 768.

THE BURIAL OF JESUS (15:42–47)

Since crucifixion is designed to show the masses the terrible fate awaiting anyone going against the Roman Empire, the burial of crucified victims is not guaranteed. Indeed, they are often left on the crosses to decompose, producing a horrifying sight.[210] Special permission must be sought from magistrates or governors for such burials. If this is granted, the corpses are often buried in mass graves unless someone influential comes forward to claim the body and bury it in an individually assigned grave (Horace *Epistulae* 1:16, 18; cf. Tacitus *Annals* 6:29).[211] So this story in Mark is by no means an anti-climax to the death of Jesus, because it relates that Jesus is properly buried. Furthermore, it also introduces a character hitherto unmentioned. This is Joseph of Arimathea, a member of the Sanhedrin.

Mark informs us in v. 42 that it is Preparation Day, and he explains this as the day before the Sabbath. If corpses cannot be left unburied at nightfall because of an OT injunction (Deut 21:22–23), this is even more so if that nightfall begins the Sabbath day. And if we were right that Jesus died on the 14th of Nisan, nightfall would begin the celebration of the Passover meal. All this means Joseph of Arimathea has to take quick action to give Jesus an honorable burial.

Who is this Joseph of Arimathea? The toponym is probably to be identified as Ramathaim-zophim (cf. 1 Sam 1:1), a town situated about twenty miles northeast of Jerusalem.[212] More importantly, Mark informs us he is a prominent member of the Sanhedrin who is also yearning for the kingdom of God to come (v. 43). This implies he is a disciple of Jesus, since his message concerns the kingdom. Confirmation of this is found in the description that he goes to Pilate for permission to bury Jesus. A request from a prominent member of the Sanhedrin is not a small matter. If that august body has condemned Jesus to death, they will also have no wish for him to be given an honorable burial. So Joseph's request testifies to his disagreement with the Sanhedrin's decision. Although Mark does not mention explicitly that Joseph will use his own tomb for burying Jesus (cf. Matt 27:60), this may be legitimately inferred.

Pilate expresses surprise that Jesus has died so quickly—most victims would have lasted longer. After receiving confirmation from the centurion who has supervised the crucifixion, Pilate gives permission for Jesus' body to be given to Joseph. Verse 46 informs us that the necessary procedures

---

210. See the evidence assembled in Hengel 1977: 22–32.
211. Schneider 1966: 3:411–12.
212. Marcus 2009: 1070.

linked with burial have been carried out, before the stone is rolled to seal the tomb which is cut out of rock. Witnessing this are two women: Mary Magdalene and Mary the mother of Joses. Mark mentions explicitly that these women know where Jesus is buried, preparing the audience for the next important story.

Fusing the Horizons: Mark's Achievement

At the end of the Passion narrative Mark may be seen as having achieved the following. He has told his audience in some detail how Jesus' prediction of his suffering has actually come to pass. There is but one more element left, and this is the resurrection, which is related in the next story. He has also shown in lurid detail the kind of treatment the Son of Man was subjected to. One could not but recoil at all this and wonder whether it had to be the case. However, such suffering is part and parcel of the message of the Christian gospel. The gospel is not about an esoteric experience where adherents may be taken away from their troubles. It is about confronting problems head-on, without flinching.

The disciple's failure has now come to a nadir. It seems that what Jesus has attempted to do by gathering a group of people and teaching them has come to naught. However, there is a small glimmer of hope. Against this depressing picture, Mark tells us there were faithful women disciples who were at the crucifixion and bore witness to all that was done. Indeed, a member of the Sanhedrin by the name of Joseph of Arimathea came forward to ask what may be regarded as a request that could jeopardize his political career. Even if many have seemingly abandoned the call to discipleship, the Lord has left for himself some who stand firm.

Furthermore, Mark has mentioned frequently in this narrative that what was happening to Jesus was already anticipated in Scripture, principally in Psalm 22. Just as Jesus was the last envoy to sum up all the prophetic overtures made to Israel, so he also summed up all the sufferings of the righteous. What Scripture relates, even when it is about the most unjust suffering, is truly about the Son of Man. In this regard, Mark recounts a detail that has puzzled so many: the cry of dereliction taken from Ps 22:1. This is not to be understood merely as a desperate or hopeless cry. Even if we give the cry its full excruciating weight, the note of hope cannot be expunged still. This is so because the cry in context testifies that beyond the terrible injustice lies divine vindication, and beyond the suffering stands glory. What is most crucial for the understanding of the Christian religion, however, is that this was taken up by none other than he who would be the vicegerent of God, the Son of Man himself! Hence righteous sufferers will never feel lonely anymore.

There is still one more point to note that is highly relevant to the times we live in and it concerns the foundational narratives of religions and some current tendencies. The foundational narrative of a religion inevitably shapes its outlook and praxis. If this narrative is about how a leader led his followers to fight for freedom and won against all odds, this will become a key theme in this religion, and later followers will have no qualms unsheathing swords against anything that appears to threaten it. If their hero did it, why shouldn't they? Indeed, if their hero won against all odds, small numbers or poor equipment will be of no hindrance to them. However, if this narrative is about the acceptance of an excruciating death because of love for humanity and obedience to God's will, a powerful check is put on the human tendency to take up the sword to propagate religion. Of course, it does not always work out that way, but followers of this religion will know that if they resort to violence, they are liable to be criticized by other followers and stand condemned before the Almighty. He who lives by the sword will die by the sword, and cause misery for many because the effects of violence do last a long time.

Jesus' death on the cross will therefore have powerful ethical implications for Christians. The vicegerent of God believed his vocation was to drink the cup assigned by the Father. This involved his sacrificial death for the sins of the world. In other words, violence was not met with violence, but in an inscrutable way absorbed and conquered. And rightly the one symbol that identifies Christianity before the world is the cross, a symbol of torture, cruelty and death. Yet, the one who died on it was not weak but strong and courageous, because he accepted it as God's will and as the necessary means for the reconciliation of the world. Indeed, he who died on it did not stay dead but was raised again to life. The cross then speaks of courageous and obedient love, and the indomitable spirit that entrusts things to God and believes that beyond death lies the resurrection. Death does not have the last word but life, which is offered to all.

The Resurrection of Jesus (16:1–8)

Because of who Jesus is and what he has predicted, the story of Mark cannot simply end with Jesus' Passion. Many other themes point in that direction: the messianic secret which could only be fully revealed when the resurrection takes place; the promise of renewal for the distraught, discouraged, and disappearing disciples; and the vindication of Jesus' claims, made in the face of much skepticism and opposition. This is what an ancient reader would have expected of Mark's conclusion. However, as the Markan text now stands, there is a problem.

The Problem of Mark's Ending

The first thing to note in this connection is that it is almost the unanimous opinion of all textual critics that Mark 16:9-20 is not an original part of Mark's text.[213] The earliest Greek manuscripts do not have them (ℵ and B, fourth cent.) nor do some early versions. Prominent Church Fathers either do not know them (e.g., Clement and Origen) or testify to the fact that they are not found in the majority of manuscripts available to them (e.g., Eusebius and Jerome). Furthermore, even if the majority of the manuscripts emanating from the later period of Church history do have these verses as the ending, other manuscripts from roughly the same period (083, sixth to seventh cent.) have a shorter ending,[214] and some even conflate the endings (L Ψ 099, earliest seventh cent.), or attest to unique materials (W, fifth cent.).[215] Indeed, of the manuscripts which attest to the Longer Ending (vv. 9–20), some of them (f1.22) mark this off with signs or comments to indicate its doubtful status. The above phenomenon is best explained by positing that the original text as we have it now ends at v. 8. This explains why a multiplicity of endings arose. Moreover, the last twelve verses read like a pastiche of traditions deriving from Luke, John and Acts.[216] Furthermore, there is a high concentration of unique words found in these verses (i.e., vocabulary not found elsewhere in Mark).[217] Manuscript evidence,

---

213. See the fine study of Elliott 1971: 254–62

214. The translation of Marcus 2009: 1089 is: "And all the things that they had been commanded they promptly announced to those around Peter. And after these things Jesus himself also sent out through them, from east to west, the sacred and imperishable announcement of eternal salvation."

215. Known as the Freer Logion. The classic study is Gregory 1908.

216. Evans 2001: 546–47; France 2002: 686–87.

217. Elliott 1971: 254–62.

transcriptional probability and intrinsic probability combine together to point to the secondary status of these last twelve verses.

Accepting v. 8 as the end of the Markan text as we now have it may solve the textual problem but it creates another. Endings are composed to wrap things up: defusing potential contradictions and providing closure. However, v. 8 ends with the description of the women's fears, with no narration of their seeing Jesus raised or his restoring the disciples, which were predictions he himself made. Could Mark end with loose ends untied?

Recently, scholars have used modern literary theories to argue that this is indeed the intention: not to end with a damaging conclusion, but rather to goad the readers to better discipleship by providing an open ending. There are many variations to such a proposal, but the common thread uniting them may be summarized thus: Mark's ending is meant to be ironical, and even downright discouraging, in order to convey the message that the story goes on in the lives of the readers. They are really the people who are in the position to fulfill Jesus' predictions and provide closure to Mark's text.[218]

The one problem with such theories is that it appears highly improbable ancient readers would detect this surreptitious message. Most ancient tales are told with rather explicit conclusions so that their message gets through without misunderstanding.[219] Furthermore, since it is mentioned explicitly, and in a significant way, that Jesus would restore his disciples after his resurrection (14:28; 16:7), the failure to give an account of this fulfillment, and the reporting instead that the women were afraid and told no one appears to destroy Mark's plot.[220] In other words, this is a case of having *contradictory* developments introduced into the plot without resolution, and not a simple one of leaving loose ends untied. To reiterate, such theories are to be rejected because they are anachronistic and damaging to the plot.[221]

---

218. See Wedderburn 1999: 135-44 for a helpful survey of the scholarly proposals available.

219. Magness 1986 has tried to defuse this strong objection. In our view, he has not reckoned with the fact that Mark intends to tell a revolutionary tale that he hopes will change the world. Such a message would not be easily accepted; the majority would even ridicule it. This being the case, to leave an ending such as 16:8 amounts to committing something close to literary suicide, making the gospel even more laughable. In other words, such creatively ambiguous stuff, while laudable, is usually tried only when a religion is institutionalized, but not during its nascent stages, or when it is fighting for survival. Early Church history has more in common with the latter than the former. Moreover, Mark shows fondness for adding editorial remarks at important junctures. This is done for the very reason of preventing misunderstandings. See France 2002: 670-73 for similar objections.

220. Croy 2003: 33-71.

221. Much discussion has revolved around whether a book can end with the Greek conjunction *gar*, the final word of Mark 16:8. In our view this is a red herring. We think

If what we have argued above is correct, we are driven to only one conclusion: either Mark could not complete his Gospel because of extenuating circumstances, or that the original ending was lost at an early stage.[222] Is there any way whereby we can reconstruct this ending? Some scholars think this can be done.[223] If it is true that Matthew and Luke have used Mark, it can then be conjectured that the similar elements between Matthew's and Luke's resurrection accounts would most probably be from Mark, especially since Q (or the common material that Matthew and Luke have that is not found in Mark) probably did not contain the Passion narrative and Resurrection narrative.

Furthermore, much of Matthew's resurrection account in the first seven verses follows Mark's closely. It may then be conjectured, based on Matthew's penchant for following Mark and diverging only when certain Matthean motifs are being fleshed out, that Mark's resurrection account would most probably contain the story of the women's report to the disciples, Jesus' meeting up with the disciples again, and probably a sort of commissioning, where the disciples' role is once again reaffirmed.

The Empty Tomb (16:1–5)

The resurrection story of Mark, as we have it, focuses on two motifs: the discovery of the empty tomb by three women, and the report of the young man, which explains what has happened and commissions them to do what is necessary.

Mark has cleverly set the stage for the resurrection story by informing his audience in 15:40 of the presence of three special women: Mary Magdalene, Mary the mother of James, and Salome. Since Jesus was buried hurriedly and without proper embalming, these three women wanted to make up for this lack at the earliest opportunity, on the first sunrise of the week, straight after the Sabbath (i.e., early Sunday morning [vv. 1–2]). The question occupying the thoughts of these women concerns the stone that seals the entrance of the tomb. There may be a touch of humor here: shouldn't the women have thought of this before they set off?[224] Or could it be that there was no male disciple they could turn to because they had all gone into

---

more in terms of contents and plot.

222. This was the dominant theory up till the middle of the twentieth century, before the rise of post-modernism.

223. France 2002: 674; Trompf 1971–72: 308–30.

224. France 2002: 678.

hiding?²²⁵ Whatever the case may be, when they "look up," they see that the large stone has already been rolled away. The Greek for the phrase "looked up" (*anablepō*) plays an interesting role in Mark's Gospel. It can mean "looking upwards" (6:41; 7:34) or a restoration of sight (8:24; 10:51–52). The latter may be alluded here.²²⁶ When they could see properly, they would see that the obstacle was gone.

Upon entering the tomb they see a young man, dressed in white and sitting on the right side. The description of this young man is done to indicate his significance. White robes are associated with festivities such as weddings. The dress of those participating in heavenly worship in Jewish apocalyptic literature is also white (cf. Rev 7:9, 13). More importantly, white is also often the color of the clothing of heavenly beings (cf. Dan 7:9; 1 *En.* 62:15–16; 87:2). In addition, being seated on the right side conveys the notion of pre-eminence and authority (Ps 110:1). The combined effect is that this person has the authority to break the news to the women. He cannot be any ordinary man, and certainly not the young man of 14:51–52.²²⁷ He should be regarded as an angel sent from God (cf. Matt 28:2, 5; Luke 24:4–5).²²⁸

Mark also tells us that the women are alarmed. This is the expected behavior of human beings when they are confronted with the supernatural or things beyond their comprehension. Many times in the Gospel the disciples have evinced such behavior, but the injunction of Jesus to them is that they should not be afraid but have faith in him. A similar message, as we shall see, is also given to the women.

The Commissioning Explanation (16:6–8)

The words of the young man both explain what is happening and commission the women to do the necessary. In fact, they summarize concisely the key themes of the resurrection story: (i) the encouragement to be unafraid; (ii) the loving rebuke that the women's assumptions are wrong because they expected to see a dead Jesus; (iii) Jesus is risen; (iv) the evidence for this is present; (v) resurrection speaks of Jesus' vindication, indicating also the trustworthiness of Jesus' words; and (vi) Jesus will restore and lead his disciples. We will expand on some of these points below.

---

225. This means the women's question amounts to being a lament. See Marcus 2009: 1079–80.
226. Mann 1986: 664–65.
227. Collins 2007: 795, provides a good refutation of the idea.
228. Marcus 2009: 1080.

Jesus wants to re-gather his distraught and discouraged disciples, so the women must not keep the story to themselves, but proclaim it to the disciples and Peter. The singling out of Peter implies there is restoration even for Peter, the disciple who has failed so miserably. In addition, the women are commissioned to inform the disciples that Jesus would be going ahead of them into Galilee, repeating the promise of 14:28. It should also be noted that "going ahead" here (the Greek used is *proagō*) has the same nuance as that of 10:32 (i.e., it refers to Jesus' leading them especially in critical times). The word "there" is interesting. It may refer to a specific place such as Galilee, or to the position of Jesus in relation to the disciples (i.e., he will be leading them). Perhaps a double meaning is present, as the alternatives are not mutually exclusive. The restoration of Jesus as the disciples' shepherd is thus emphasized and the Galilean setting indicates that the precious lessons of discipleship will be taught once more.

The concluding phrase of v. 7 "just as he told you" is important, as it speaks of the vindication of Jesus. All this has happened not as an accident of history but has been foreseen by Jesus. This implies, of course, his controversial teaching about his messianic role has proven to be correct. His word may then be trusted.

Verse 8 informs us that the women are bewildered and flee from the tomb with fear, qualities unbecoming of Jesus' disciples. While outshining the male disciples, they are not immaculate. We have argued earlier that the putative ending would have described the women's overcoming their fear probably because Jesus appears to them, and with renewed courage they inform the other disciples of the good news of Jesus' resurrection. The historical datum that women were the first messengers of Jesus' resurrection[229] would not be something that Mark would want to contradict.

---

229. Allison 2005: 328; Wright 2003: 607–8.

A Sketch of Mark's Theology

Mark announces his primary subject matter at the very start. Two items are mentioned: the Messiah Jesus, (also known as the Son of God, if the longer text is followed), and the gospel. What is not mentioned in this announcement, but is implied and would be given prominence in the tale, is that the Messiah's proclamation of the gospel through word and deed produces a people. The following nexus of ideas is then obtained: Messiah—Gospel—People. However, this gospel is the gospel of the kingdom (1:15). So the nexus may be modified thus: Messiah—Gospel/Kingdom—People. What follows is a brief sketch of the themes of this nexus; supporting arguments for the elements of this nexus may be found in the comments of the relevant passages.

CHRISTOLOGY

Since Jesus is the central character of Mark's narrative, any discussion of the thought of Mark must start with Christology (i.e., how Jesus is presented). Indeed, as Boring observes, Christology is the book's generative and driving force.[1]

The character of Jesus is fleshed out with recourse mainly to the OT.[2] All other traditions, notions or cultural mores, even when they are promoted by a mighty Empire, pale before this. The OT is treated as an authoritative tradition, which contains in itself an open-ended narrative that needs completion (1:2–3; 1:11; 10:45; 12:10–11; 14:27; 14:49). It also reveals the pattern of God's action in the world, and speaks of promises that need to be fulfilled. If there is a *sensus plenior* to this tradition, Jesus is regarded as the *sensus plenus*. That said, the OT's central character is Yahweh, and we therefore should expect the portrayal of Jesus to be related to him. And indeed, this is what we find.

---

1. Boring 2006: 248.
2. The key scriptural books are the Pentateuch, Isaiah, Daniel, Psalms and Zechariah. Scriptures are mined, juxtaposed and utilized creatively to flesh out Jesus' identity (see comments in 1:14–15; 10:45; 11:1–11; 12:1–37; 14:27). See the informative summary of Boring 2006: 404–8.

Jesus is certainly presented as the Messiah, the one who fulfills God's promises in the OT and brings to climax the story of God and his people (1:1; 8:29; 9:14).³ However, Mark sometimes goes beyond Jesus' messianic identity and puts him on an equal footing with God: not in the use of the title of Son of God (as this means primarily God's chosen king, and may therefore be regarded as challenging the claim of the Roman Emperor)⁴ but in stories and allusions to Yahweh's role in Scripture (2:1–11, 23–28; 6:45–52).⁵ In this regard the messianic category, while important, is deemed insufficient. Of course, Jesus is never once addressed as God. The constraint of Jewish monotheism prevents this. However, Jesus is presented as more than a man, with concepts and actions that are unique to God.⁶ Here many scholars see it fit to invoke functional categories to speak of Jesus' divinity (i.e., Jesus is not ontologically divine but functionally so). However, this is anachronistic and confuses the issue. For Jews, what makes God *God* is that he can do certain things that no other being can.⁷ Perhaps all this means Mark has not yet found the language for the phenomenon he is attesting to. That said, Mark is not alone in this, as other NT writers evince such an approach (see especially Paul's writings).⁸

In Mark, Jesus' favorite self-designation is the Son of Man. This is used for the first time in the first controversy story in which Jesus is accused of blasphemy (2:1–11), and at his trial where he is also charged with blasphemy (14:61–64). All this indicates how important this self-designation is. While it introduces a sense of mystery, as it could mean man in general, it could also refer to the figure of Dan 7:13.⁹ In this commentary, we take

3. See especially 1:1; 8:29; 9:41; 11:1–11; 12:1–12. For recent discussions on the Messiah, see Charlesworth 1992.

4. To be sure, the Son of God title and its associate appellations are significant, and rightly scholars have deemed them to be so despite their paucity of occurrences (e.g., Evans 2001: lxxiii). However, it must be insisted that this family of appellations is used in what may be called disclosure events (except for 1:1, but there is textual uncertainty here), and must therefore be understood in relation to such. What these are will be covered in the later paragraphs. Furthermore, the backdrop against which these appellations are understood must serve as hermeneutical control, and in this light messianic or imperial-cult categories are key (see Collins 1999: 393–408 and 2000: 85–100). All this implies that the title of Son of God should not be understood as the key christological theme. Instead, it belongs to a constellation of equally important themes, and the gravitational center may very well be Jesus' favorite self-designation: the Son of Man.

5. See especially 1:2–3; 2:1–11, 23–28; 6:45–52; 13:27; 14:61–64.

6. Cf. Marcus 2000: 222, 340: "a Messiah who bears the marks of divinity."

7. See Bauckham 2008: 31.

8. Kreitzer 1987; Capes 1992; and Richardson 1994.

9. The secondary literature on this is legion. For recent discussion see Burkett 1999; Casey 2007; Müller 2008; and Hurtado and Owen 2011.

Jesus as meaning primarily the latter. Hence, the self-designation dovetails with the very important kingdom theme, since the Son of Man in Daniel is a figure used to depict the irruption of God's kingdom. That said, Jesus redefines this role by juxtaposing it with the Suffering Servant of Isaiah. This means the Son of Man who is expected to bring in God's kingdom must also suffer in the process. It must be stressed that this suffering is to be linked to service and redemption (10:45).

The above provides a framework for understanding the secrecy theme, which is prominent in Mark. Jesus is often portrayed as adjuring silence about his true identity, when this is precisely what he hopes to demonstrate through spectacular deeds. To cite just an example: why should Jesus command silence over the raising of Jairus's daughter from death (5:43), when he has been teasing the crowd into active thought about his identity (5:35–36)? Since the seminal work of Wilhelm Wrede, this phenomenon is given the name of "messianic secret."[10]

The scope of this commentary does not allow for protracted discussion of the different scholarly explications of this theme,[11] but we will simply explain our position. At one level it may be possible to explain Jesus' command of silence as stemming from prudence, as he wanted to avoid being identified with bellicose ideas of messiahship.[12] Much speculation on the role of the Messiah at that time focused on his liberation of the nation from political foes (*Pss Sol* 17; 1QSb 5:20–29). Without a proper theological framework for understanding this, the claim to be the Messiah might incite an armed revolution.

At another level, this secrecy theme dovetails with Jesus' teaching of the time of the kingdom's coming. It comes secretly now and in a hidden form; only the eyes of faith can perceive it. However, it will be manifested gloriously one day, at the consummation of history. The same is true of Jesus. His true status remained hidden but would be revealed one day. The theme also captures much of what Jesus taught about the nature of the kingdom. Profoundly covenantal in nature (14:24–25), it involved the death of the Messiah. Indeed, the confession of the Roman centurion serves to highlight this in Mark's plot (15:39). It is when Jesus is crucified that the authentic

---

10. Wrede 1971. Although the moniker "messianic secret" has been criticized in some scholarly circles, it is still useful for describing Mark's Christology. See recently G. Steele 2012: 169–85.

11. For starters, see the collection of essays in Tuckett 1983. Cf. the recent attempts to resolve this by resurrecting the concept of Messiah-designate, to be enthroned in the future in Marcus 2001: 381–401; Allison 2010: 290. Cf. Dalman 1902: 315–16.

12. Collins 2007: 53–58.

Son of God is seen. In other words, Christology is profoundly linked to the cross.

Hence, the secrecy theme arises not just from Jesus' clear grasp of the currents of his day, but also from his vision of what the kingdom is, his understanding of his role in it, and his unique identity. Although these are profoundly connected with Israel's scriptures and covenant, they come to full expression only in the event of the cross and resurrection (9:9). The theme serves then as a foil to a deeper understanding of Christology and Jesus' kingdom theology, which we will explore in the next section.

Since this series is entitled *New Covenant Commentary Series*, something about Jesus and the covenant has to be said. The theme is not explicit, but it may be cogently argued that it functions as the invisible glue that holds things together. Indeed, as Sanders has reminded us, the theme of covenant holds the worldview of the Jews together even if it is seldom expressed.[13] So it is a worthwhile venture to examine this theme in Mark.

The term covenant (the Greek for this is *diathēkē*) occurs only once in Mark, but it is found at a highly significant passage (14:24). There Jesus explains what the meaning of his death is, which is also the meaning of his vocation. The inescapable conclusion is that Jesus' death must be understood in covenantal terms. If Jesus establishes a covenant by his blood, it implies that what Moses has ratified before is no longer efficacious. Such a trend of thought is not unprecedented, as the OT story is one in which covenant-breaking on the part of Israel is highlighted. This was what the exile meant. However, prophets looked to a time when God would establish an everlasting or new covenant with Israel that would be immune from further breaches. The OT does not clarify whether this would be an entirely new covenant or a renewal of a broken one. Happily, how this question is resolved does not affect what we are here explicating. What obtains from all this is that the OT attests to an ongoing story of God and his people, defined by the covenant, which has yet to receive closure. Using this lens to look at Jesus' ministry, one can then say that Jesus conceived of his vocation, especially his death, as the climax of this covenantal story, in which an eschatological covenant is established that would create the new people of God.

Covenantal ideas are found not only in the Last Supper passage, but may be regarded as profoundly undergirding Jesus' preaching of the kingdom. In Jesus' explanation of why his disciples do not need to fast, he uses the metaphor of the bridegroom at his wedding (2:18–20). As we have argued in our exegesis, the primary background for understanding this metaphor

13. Sanders 1977.

is the covenantal story of God and his people. The prophets looked to a time when Yahweh the bridegroom would return and marry Israel once again. If this is indeed the background for Jesus' answer, what he is then saying is that his ministry brings about this marriage.

As a spin-off from the concept of Jesus' ministry as the climax of the covenant, we can more properly understand what it means to describe Jesus' ministry as eschatological. It is not eschatological in the sense that it brings about the end of the world or human history. Instead, it is eschatological in the sense that what has been predicted and longed-for in the ongoing story of God and his people has reached its climactic point in Jesus. At this climactic point, God cuts a new or eternal covenant with his people, a covenant that brings about all the attendant blessings and ramifications for them, and for his creation. The relational aspect of God's program receives the dominant beat.

The Kingdom of God

The kingdom of God is the primary theme of Jesus' message (1:14–15).[14] As it is true for Jesus' identity, this theme is also fleshed out with recourse to Scriptures. Hence, the arrival of God's kingdom means the fulfillment of his promises found in Scriptures. In this regard, the Book of Isaiah plays a key role.[15] This kingdom is eschatological in nature, signaling God's return to his people and their restoration to their true elect status, with ramifications for the created order, including both flora and fauna. It is another way of saying that Yahweh has returned to Zion.[16]

What is fascinating is that the kingdom is presented as coming in the future, and in some sense as having already arrived in Jesus' ministry, albeit in hidden form.[17] Such a notion supports the importance of faith, as only the eyes of faith may perceive its presence in Jesus' ministry.[18] This is made clear in chapter 4, which contains mainly seed parables. Seed is the appropriate image because its planting in the ground speaks of hiddenness, and its smallness speaks of how the kingdom begins. If we are to stay with Jesus' botanical imagery, we may say that for many Jews the kingdom should come as a full-grown tree, transplanted from heaven to earth,[19] and not as a

---

14. See the seminal work of Weiss 1900.
15. Schneck 1994; Watts 1997.
16. Wright 1996 exploits this theme.
17. Ambrozic 1972.
18. Marshall 1989.
19. See our discussion on 4:26–32.

seed that is planted in the ground. All this must not be taken to mean that for Jesus the kingdom remains as seed. No, it will grow. And the smallest of seeds will become the largest of plants. The glory of the consummation far outstrips the glory of the inauguration. The hiddenness of the kingdom dovetails with the hiddenness of Jesus' identity.

Kingdom proclamation and activity is intimately linked to exorcism, a prominent theme in Mark which is unfortunately seldom examined.[20] The importance of this motif is seen in that the first miraculous and awe-inspiring deed Jesus performs after his announcement of the kingdom's imminence is an exorcism. Furthermore, this exorcism is intentionally labelled as a piece of new teaching with authority (1:27). The calling of the Twelve and the sending of them for mission are explicitly linked with such a theme. The first mentioned role of the apostles is that of preaching and having authority over demons (3:15; cf. 6:7). Their kingdom proclamation involves exorcistic activity. The important passage of Mark 3:20–30 further supports the significance of exorcism. Jesus defends his exorcism by using images that speak of the kingdom. Indeed, misunderstanding Jesus' exorcisms may make one liable for committing the eternal sin.

It must also be pointed out that Jesus is depicted not just as the proclaimer of the kingdom, but he also embodies it.[21] To reject one is to reject the other (8:38). This theme is deeply embedded in the Passion narrative. The "vow of abstinence" (14:25) may be understood as speaking of Jesus' central role in the realization and consummation of the kingdom. His death does not mean the kingdom's project is derailed. In a paradoxical way, it is essential to its completion. This dovetails with the Markan motif of the necessity of Jesus' going to Jerusalem to be crucified (8:31; 9:31–32; 10:33–34).

Finally, something must be said about this kingdom theme and the situation of Mark's first readers, where imperial power and propaganda were prominent. Mark encourages them to think along this line: the kingdom message of Jesus subverts the imperial propaganda of Rome.[22] This is seen to be at work already in the very first verse, and climaxing at 15:39, where a centurion, who is under Rome's employ proclaims the crucified Jesus as the

---

20. But see recently, Evans 2009: 151–79; and Iwe 1999. Cf. Käsemann 1969: 58, where he argues for the importance of exorcism for understanding eschatology and Christology.

21. Allison 2010: 245–47 observes that God is seldom explicitly called king in the Synoptic Tradition, despite the fact that sayings relating to the Kingdom are plentiful. This phenomenon stands in stark contrast with the OT. What may explain this is that Jesus is intentionally portrayed as the king of the eschatological kingdom.

22. See the provocative treatment on the clash between Jesus' message and the imperial propaganda in Horsley 2002.

authentic Son of God, a claim made by Roman Emperors. The subversion theme is also found in the story of the Gerasene demoniac (5:1–20). This is written to allude to the Roman annexation of lands through its military might. Like the legion of demons that has possessed the man, Roman legions have taken over lands and oppressed people. Jesus' exorcism of the demoniac is told in such a way as to hint at Jesus' power to cast out Roman subjection. This is done not by violent means, however, but by the exorcistic word. If there is any destruction in the encounter between Jesus and the demoniac, it is not one that is performed by Jesus. The possessed pigs run into the lake and drown themselves, probably suggesting Rome will destroy itself. So there is a clash of kingdoms, but this is not done in a bellicose way, as was the case with the Jewish Zealots. Instead, it is done through non-violent means. Being non-violent does not mean being impotent, for Jesus' word has the power to drive out legions.

All this speaks powerfully to the reality confronting Mark's first readers, a situation in which Rome has started to rear its demonic head. These readers would not be encountering many who are demon-possessed, but they would certainly come across many who are Empire-possessed. The continuing work of the Church in relation to the Empire must be that of removing Rome from peoples' hearts, whether this refers to its nefarious influence or its dehumanizing presence. This could only be done through the preaching of the gospel. The binding of this strong man will be a continuous task for the Church, even as she waits for the consummation of the kingdom.

Discipleship (The Way of the Lord)

The theme of discipleship in Mark has been much discussed in scholarly circles.[23] This is not surprising, as Jesus is seldom alone in Mark's tale. He exercises his ministry in public, appeals to the crowd to follow him, and has a band of followers. The theme of discipleship is developed through the use of a few motifs.

The first motif concerns the authoritative call of Jesus.[24] People do not choose to follow Jesus, but it is he who calls, and they obey (1:17–18, 20; 2:14). The call is to be with him, follow him, learn from him, and model their lives after him. So special is this call that Mark does not shy away from using the word "creation" (3:14, 16). The disciples may therefore be regarded as the reconstituted people of God, made possible only by divine action.

---

23. Best 1986; Black 1989; and the recent Henderson 2006.
24. Hengel 1981.

The second concerns "the way."²⁵ The Greek word *hodos* occurs sixteen times in Mark's Gospel. This is impressive but what needs to be discerned beyond mere statistics is that it appears in important contexts. At the start of the Gospel, Mark cites a composite text to set the tone: the "way" of the Lord is being prepared by John the Baptist (1:2–3). The way of the Lord turns out to be the way of Jesus Christ. When fleshed out later, this way leads to the cross, and beyond it, the resurrection. Furthermore, Jesus is described by his opponents as "teaching the way of God in accordance with the truth" (12:14). Jesus is thus identified with the way of the Lord in different forms. But what is more important in this connection is that discipleship may then be justifiably described as "following in the way." Many passages that contain the phrase "in the way" (the Greek is *en tē hodō*) bear this out. To cite a couple of examples: in 8:27 Jesus asks his disciples who they think he is while "in the way"; and in 9:33–34 the disciples argue about who among them is the greatest while "in the way." The juxtaposing of discipleship concerns with the phrase "in the way" serves to show how the latter is a rubric for what discipleship means. Jesus is in the way of the Lord; to be his disciple means following in this way.

The book of Acts demonstrates how apt and powerful this language is for describing discipleship, where the early Christians are frequently described as "people of the way" (Acts 9:2; 19:9, 23; 22:4; 24:14, 22). If there is any historical reliability to Luke's account, it may be said that they were so called because they were followers of Jesus' way, which is also the way of the Lord.²⁶ Followers of Jesus were known in this manner before they were called "Christians."

The missionary role of the disciples is the third motif.²⁷ Jesus' disciples are called not only to learn from Jesus but also to further his work (3:13–19). In 6:7–13 we see how this is accomplished. Jesus sends them out in pairs all over Israel for the purpose of preaching, exorcising and healing. The eschatological discourse in chapter 13 adds a significant datum to the concept of mission. When many people are carried away by apocalyptic ferment and re-establishing group loyalty through sanctions and persecutions, the disciples are to be on a mission to bear witness to the gospel (13:5–11).

We come finally to the motif of failure and restoration. The way of Jesus is a paradoxical way, containing many revolutionary values. Hence, being a disciple of Jesus is not easy, and Mark pulls no punches when it

---

25. Marcus 1992; Watts 1997.

26. Fitzmyer 1998: 424. Seminal work on this topic is done by Repo 1964.

27. Not much has been done here but note the assessment of Pesch 1980: 1:60: "The entire book of Mark is a missionary book!"

comes to portraying the disciples' failure. The disciples are portrayed as lacking faith and understanding (4:13, 40; 6:37, 52; 7:18; 8:4, 14–21, 32–33; 9:5–6, 10, 14–29, 32–41; 10:10, 24–26, 32, 35–41). When the crunch comes, they abandon Jesus. However, the failure of the disciples is only part of the story. The finale of the Gospel speaks of restoration: the risen Christ will once again shepherd them, including Peter, the one who denied him (16:7). So the failure of the disciples must be related to the theme of restoration. A pastoral message is therefore sounded out, which will be relevant and encouraging to all listeners of Mark's tale.[28] Such people will be able to identify with the disciples' frailty and find solace in the restorative Shepherd.

---

28. Hartman 2010: 664.

Bibliography

Books and articles on Mark are legion. So I present here only a small sampling of this great abundance. Three criteria govern the choice of items listed here. First, they are chosen because they have been mentioned in the commentary. Secondly, those that are deemed to be of special significance for the further study of Mark's Gospel are included. And finally, literature that provides quick and convenient handles to bring the student up to speed on Markan scholarship is also included.

COMMENTARIES ON MARK

Boring, E. 2006. *Mark: A Commentary*. NTL. Louisville: Westminster John Knox.
Collins, A. Y. 2007. *Mark: A Commentary*. Hermeneia. Minneapolis: Fortress.
Cranfield, C. E. B. 1959. *The Gospel According to Saint Mark*. Cambridge Greek Testament Commentary. Cambridge: Cambridge University Press.
Culpepper, R. A. 2007. *Mark*. SHBC. Macon: Smyth & Helwys.
Donahue J. R. and Harrington D. J. 2002. *The Gospel of Mark*. Sacred Pagina 2. Collegeville: Liturgical.
Edwards, J. R. 2002. *The Gospel According to Mark*. PNTC. Grand Rapids: Eerdmans.
Evans, C. A. 2001. *Mark 8:27–16:20*. WBC 34B. Nashville: Thomas Nelson.
France, R. T. 2002. *The Gospel of Mark: A Commentary on the Greek Text*. NIGTC. Grand Rapids: Eerdmans.
Gnilka, M. 1978–79. *Das Evangelium nach Markus*. 2 vols. Evangelisch-katholischer Kommentar zum Neuen Testament 2. Zürich: Benzinger; Neukirchen: Neukirchener Verlag.
Guelich, R. A. 1989. *Mark 1:1—8:26*. WBC 34A. Dallas: Word.
Gundry, R. H. 1993. *Mark: A Commentary on His Apology for the Cross*. Grand Rapids: Eerdmans.
Hartman, L. 2010. *Mark for the Nations: A Text – and Reader-Oriented Commentary*. Eugene: Pickwick.
Hooker, M. D. 1991. *The Gospel According to St. Mark*. BNTC. London: A&C Black.
Hurtado, L. W. 1983. *Mark*. NIBC. Peabody: Hendrickson.
Klostermann, E. 1950. *Das Markusevangelium erklärt*. Handbuch zum Neuen Testament 3. 4th ed. Tübingen: Mohr Siebeck.
Lagrange, M. J. 1911. *Évangile selon Saint Marc*. Études bibliques. Paris: Gabalda.
Lane W. L. 1974. *The Gospel According to Mark*. NICNT. Grand Rapids: Eerdmans.
Lührmann, D. 1987. *Markusevangelium*. HNT 3. Tübingen: Mohr Siebeck.

Mann, C. S. 1986. *Mark: A New Translation with Introduction and Commentary*. AB 27. New York: Doubleday.

Marcus, J. 2000. *Mark 1–8: A New Translation with Introduction and Commentary*. AB 27. New York: Doubleday.

———. 2009. *Mark 8–16: A New Translation with Introduction and Commentary*. AB 27A. New Haven and London: Yale University Press.

Moloney, F. J. 2002. *The Gospel of Mark: A Commentary*. Peabody: Hendrickson.

Myers, C. 1988. *Binding the Strong Man: A Political Reading of Mark's Story of Jesus*. Maryknoll, NY: Orbis.

Pesch, R. 1980. *Das Markus-Evangelium*. 2 vols. Herders Theologischer Kommentar zum Neuen Testament 2. 3rd ed. Freiburg: Herder.

Schweizer, E. 1971. *The Good News According to Mark*. ET. London: SPCK.

Stein, R. H. 2008. *Mark*. BECNT. Grand Rapids: Baker Academic.

Swete, H. 1898. *The Gospel According to St Mark*. London: Macmillan.

Taylor, V. 1952. *The Gospel According to St. Mark*. London: Macmillan.

Van Iersel, B. M. F. 1989. *Reading Mark*. ET. Edinburgh: T. & T. Clark.

Wellhausen, J. 1909. *Das Evangelium Marci Ubersetzt und Erklärt*. 2nd ed. Berlin: G. Reimer.

Witherington, B. 2001. *The Gospel of Mark: A Socio-Rhetorical Commentary*. Grand Rapids: Eerdmans.

Other Scholarly Literature

Abrahams, I. 1917, 1924. *Studies in Pharisaism and the Gospels*. 2 vols. Cambridge: Cambridge University Press.

Allen, L. C. 1983. *Psalms 101—150*. WBC 21. Waco: Word.

Allison, D. C. 1987. *The End of the Ages Has Come: Early Interpretation of the Passion and Resurrection of Jesus*. Edinburgh: T. & T. Clark.

———. 1993. *The New Moses: A Matthean Typology*. Minneapolis: Fortress.

———. 1998. *Jesus of Nazareth: Millenarian Prophet*. Philadelphia: Fortress.

———. 2005. *Resurrecting Jesus: The Earliest Christian Tradition and Its Interpreters*. New York: T. & T. Clark.

———. 2010. *Constructing Jesus: Memory, Imagination and History*. Grand Rapids: Baker Academic.

Alonso, P. 2011. *The Woman Who Changed Jesus: Crossing Boundaries in Mk 7:24–30*. BTS 11. Leuven: Peeters.

Ambrozic, A. M. 1972. *The Hidden Kingdom: A Redaction-critical Study of the References to the Kingdom of God in Mark's Gospel*. CBQMS 2. Washington: Catholic Biblical Association.

Athearne-Kroll, S. P. 2007. *The Psalms of Lament in Mark's Passion: Jesus' Davidic Suffering*. SNTSMS 142. Cambridge: Cambridge University Press.

Aus, R. D. 2000. *The Stilling of the Storm: Studies in Early Palestinian Judaic Traditions*. International Studies in Formative Christianity and Judaism. Binghamton: Global.

Bahat, D. 1995. "Jerusalem Down Under: Tunneling along Herod's Temple Mount Wall." *BAR* 21/6:30–47.

Bammel, E. 1984. "The *Titulus*." In *Jesus and the Politics of His Day*, edited by E. Bammel and C. F. D. Moule, 353–64. Cambridge: Cambridge University Press.

Bammel, E., editor. 1970. *The Trial of Jesus: Cambridge Studies in Honour of C. F. D. Moule*. Studies in Biblical Theology 13. London: SCM.

Barr, J. 1988. "Abba Isn't Daddy." *JTS* 39:28–47.

Barrett, C. K. 1959. "The Background of Mark 10:45." In *New Testament Essays: Studies in Memory of Thomas Walter Manson, 1893–1958*, edited by A. J. B. Higgins, 1–18. Manchester: Manchester University Press.

Batto. B. F. 1987. "The Sleeping God: An Ancient Near Eastern Motif of Divine Sovereignty," *Bib* 68:153–77.

Bauckham, R. J. 1986. "The Coin in the Fish's Mouth." In *Gospel Perspectives 6: The Miracles of Jesus*, edited by D. Wenham and C. L. Blomberg, 219–52. Sheffield: JSOT Press.

———. 1988. "Jesus' Demonstration in the Temple." In *Law and Religion*, edited by B. Lindars, 72–89. Cambridge: Clarke.

———. 1998. *The Fate of the Dead: Studies on the Jewish and Christian Apocalypses*. NovTSup 93. Leiden: Brill.

———. 2002. "Paul and Other Jews with Latin Names in the New Testament." In *Paul, Luke and the Graeco-Roman World: Essays in Honour of Alexander J. M. Wedderburn*, edited by A. Christophersen, C. Claussen, J. Frey, and B. Longenecker, 202–20. JSNTSup 21. Sheffield: Sheffield Academic.

———. 2008a. *Jesus and the Eyewitnesses: The Gospels as Eyewitness Testimonies*. Grand Rapids: Eerdmans.

———. 2008b. *Jesus and the God of Israel: God Crucified and Other Studies on the New Testament's Christology of Divine Identity*. Grand Rapids: Eerdmans.

Bauckham, R. J., editor. 1998. *The Gospel for All Christians: Rethinking the Gospel Audiences*. Grand Rapids: Eerdmans.

Baumgarten, A. I. 1984. "*Korban* and the Pharisaic *Paradosis*." *JANES* 16:5–17.

———. 1987. "The Pharisaic *Paradosis*." *HTR* 80:5–17.

———. 1997. *The Flourishing of Jewish Sects in the Maccabean Era: An Interpretation*. JSJSup 55. Leiden: Brill.

Beale, G. K. 1999. *John's Use of the Old Testament in Revelation*. JSNTSup 166. Sheffield: Sheffield Academic.

Beasley-Murray, G. R. 1986. *Jesus and the Kingdom of God*. Exeter: Paternoster.

———. 1993. *Jesus and the Last Days: The Interpretation of the Olivet Discourse*. Peabody: Hendrickson.

Beavis, M. A. 1989. *Mark's Audience: The Literary and Social Setting of Mark 4:11–12*. JSNTSup 33. Sheffield: Sheffield Academic.

Becker, Eve-Marie. *Das Markus-Evangelium im Rahmen antiker Historiographie*. WUNT 1/194. Tübiingen: Mohr Siebeck, 2006.

Bellinger, W. H., editor. 1998. *Jesus and the Suffering Servant*. Harrisburg, PA: Trinity.

Best, E. 1986. *Disciples and Discipleship: Studies in the Gospel According to Mark*. Edinburgh: T. & T. Clark.

Bird, M. 2003. "The Crucifixion of Jesus as the Fulfillment of Mark 9:1." *Trinity Journal* 24:23–36.

Bishop, E. F. F. 1955. *Jesus of Palestine: The Local Background to the Gospel Documents*. London: Lutterworth.

Black, C. C. 1989. *The Disciples According to Mark: Markan Redaction in Current Debate*. JSNTSup 27. Sheffield: Sheffield Academic.

Black, M. 1967. *An Aramaic Approach to the Gospels and Acts.* 3rd edition. Oxford: Clarendon.
Boccaccini, G., editor. *Enoch and the Messiah Son of Man: Revisiting the Book of Parables.* Grand Rapids and Cambridge: Eerdmans, 2007.
Bock, D. L. 1998. *Blasphemy and Exaltation in Judaism and the Final Examination of Jesus: A Philological-Historical Study of the Key Jewish Themes Impacting Mark 14:61–64.* WUNT 2/106. Tübingen: Mohr Siebeck.
Bond, H. K. 1998. *Pontius Pilate in History and Interpretation.* SNTSMS 100. Cambridge: Cambridge University Press.
———. 2004. *Caiaphas: Friend of Rome and Judge of Jesus?* Louisville: Westminster John Knox.
Borg, M. 1984. *Conflict, Holiness and Politics in the Teaching of Jesus.* SBEC 5. Lewiston: Edwin Mellen.
Borgen, P. 1965. *Bread from Heaven: An Exegetical Study of the Concept of Manna in the Gospel of John and the Writings of Philo.* NovTSup 10. Leiden: Brill.
Braund, D. C. 1992. "Herod Antipas." *ABD* 3:160.
Brower, K. E. 1999. "Temple and Eschatology in Mark." In *Eschatology in the Bible and Theology,* edited by K. E. Brower and M. Elliott, 119–43. Downers Grove: IVP.
Brown, M. L. 1995. *Israel's Divine Healer.* SOTBT. Grand Rapids: Zondervan.
Brown, R. E. 1994. *The Death of the Messiah: From Gethsemane to the Grave.* 2 vols. ABRL. New York: Doubleday.
Bryan, C. 1993. *A Preface to Mark: Notes on the Gospel in Its Literary and Cultural Settings.* New York: Oxford University Press.
Buckner, R. 1993. *The Joy of Jesus: Humour in the Gospels.* Norwich: Canterbury Press.
Bultmann, R. 1963. *The History of the Synoptic Tradition.* ET. Oxford: Blackwell.
Burchard, C. 1983. "Markus 15, 34." *ZNW* 74:1–11.
Burkett, D. 1999. *The Son of Man Debate: A History and Evaluation.* SNTSMS 107. Cambridge: Cambridge University Press.
Burridge, R. A. 1992. *What are the Gospels? A Comparison with Graeco-Roman Biography.* SNTSM 70. Cambridge: Cambridge University Press.
Burrows, M. 1940. "Levirate Marriage in Israel." *JBL* 59:23–33.
Camery-Hoggart, J. 1992. *Irony in Mark's Gospel: Text and Subtext.* SNTSMS 72. Cambridge: Cambridge University Press.
Capes, D. B. 1992. *Old Testament Yahweh Texts in Paul's Christology.* WUNT 2/47. Tübingen: Mohr Siebeck.
Carson, D. A. 1984. "Matthew." Vol. 8. *The Expositor's Bible Commentary,* edited by F. E. Gaebelein. Grand Rapids: Zondervan.
———. 1991. *The Gospel According to John.* PNTC. Leicester: IVP.
Casey, P. M. 1988. "Culture and Historicity: The Plucking of the Grain (Mark 2:23–28)." *NTS* 34:1–23.
———. 2007. *The Solution to the "Son of Man" Problem.* LNTS 343. London: T. & T. Clark.
Catchpole, D. R. 1971. *The Trial of Jesus: A Study in the Gospels and Jewish Historiography from 1770 to the Present Day.* Studia Post-Biblical duodevicesimum. Leiden: Brill.
Charlesworth, J. H., editor. 1992. *The Messiah: Developments in Earliest Judaism and Christianity; the First Princeton Symposium on Judaism and Christian Origins.* Minneapolis: Fortress.

Chilton, B. D. 1980-81. "The Transfiguration: Dominical Assurance and Apostolic Vision." *NTS* 27:115-24.

———. 1987. *God in Strength: Jesus' Announcement of the Kingdom*. Sheffield: JSOT.

———. 1992. *The Temple of Jesus: His Sacrificial Program within a Cultural History of Sacrifice*. University Park, PA: Pennsylvania State University Press.

Collins, A. Y. 1999. "Mark and His Readers: The Son of God among Jews." *HTR* 92:393-408.

———. 2000. "Mark and His Readers: The Son of God among Greeks and Romans." *HTR* 93:85-100.

———. 2004. "The Charge of Blasphemy in Mark 14.64." *JSNT* 26:379-401.

Collins, J. J. 1992. "The Son of Man in First-century Judaism." *NTS* 38:448-66.

———. 1993a. *Daniel: A Commentary on the Book of Daniel*. Hermeneia 27. Minneapolis: Fortress.

———. 1993b. "The *Son of God* Text from Qumran." In *From Jesus to John: Essays on Jesus and New Testament Christology in Honour of Marinus de Jonge*, edited by M. C. De Boer, 65-82. JSTNSup 84. Sheffield: JSOT Press.

———. 1995. *The Scepter and the Star. The Messiahs of the Dead Sea Scrolls and Other Ancient Literature*. New York: Doubleday.

Cope, O. L. 1976. *Matthew: A Scribe Trained for the Kingdom of Heaven*. CBQMS 5. Washington, DC: Catholic Biblical Association of America.

Crossan, J. D. 1991. *The Historical Jesus: The Life of a Mediterranean Jewish Peasant*. San Francisco: HarperCollins.

Croy, N. C. 2003. *The Mutilation of Mark's Gospel*. Nashville: Abingdon.

Dalman, G. 1902. *The Words of Jesus Considered in the Light of Post-biblical Jewish Writings and the Aramaic Language*. Edinburgh: T. & T. Clark.

Danker, F. W. 1982. *Benefactor: Epigraphic Study of a Graeco-Roman and New Testament Semantic Field*. St Louis: Clayton.

Davies, W. D. 1974. *The Gospel and the Land: Early Christianity and Jewish Territorial Doctrine*. Berkeley: University of California Press.

De Jonge, M. 1996. "Jesus Role in the Final Breakthrough of God's Kingdom." In *Geschichte—Tradition—Reflexion. Festschrift für Martin Hengel zum 70. Geburtstag, Band III. Frühes Christentum*, edited by H. Lichtenberger, 265-86. Tübingen: Mohr Siebeck.

De Vaux, R. 1965. *Ancient Israel*. New York: McGraw Hill.

Deines, R. 1997. *Die Pharisäer: Ihr Verständnis im Spiegel der christlichen und jüdischer Forschung seit Wellhausen und Graetz*. WUNT 1/101. Tübingen: Mohr Siebeck.

Derrett, J. D. M. 1971. "Law in the NT: The Palm Sunday Colt." *NovT* 13:241-58.

———. 1975. "Judaica in Saint Mark." *Journal of the Royal Asiatic Society of Great Britain & Ireland* (new series) 107:2-15.

———. 1977. *Studies in the New Testament*. Vol. 1. Leiden: Brill.

———. 1981. "Why and How Jesus Walked on the Sea." *NovT* 23:330-48.

Dewey, J. 1980. *Markan Public Debate: Literary Technique, Concentric Structure, and Theology in Mark 2:1—3:6*. Chico, CA: Scholars Press.

Dittenberg, W. 1960. *Orientis Graeci Inscriptions Selestae*. Vol. 2. Hildesheim: Olms.

Dodd, C. H. 1941. *The Parables of the Kingdom*. London: Nisbet.

Dowd, S. E. 1988. *Prayer, Power and the Problem of Suffering: Mark 11:22-25 in the Context of Markan Theology*. SBLDS 105. Atlanta: Scholars Press.

Donahue, J. R. 1992. "Tax Collector." *ABD* 6:337-38.

Dunn, J. D. G. 2003. *Jesus Remembered. Christianity in the Making*. Vol. 1. Grand Rapids: Eerdmans.
Edwards, D. 1992. "Gennesaret." *ABD* 2:963.
Elliott, J. K. 1971. "The Text and Language of the Endings of Mark." *TZ* 27:254–62.
Eppstein, V. 1964. "The Historicity of the Gospel Account of the Cleansing of the Temple." *ZNW* 55:42–58.
Evans, C. A. 1989a. "Jesus' Action in the Temple and Evidence of Corruption in the First-Century Temple." In *SBL 1989 Seminar Papers*, edited by D. J. Lull, 522–39. SBLSP 28. Atlanta: Scholars Press.
———. 1989b *To See and Not Perceive: Isaiah 6:9–10 in Early Jewish and Christian Interpretation*. JSOTSup 64. Sheffield: JSOT.
———. 2009. "Exorcisms and the Kingdom: Inaugurating the Kingdom of God and Defeating the Kingdom of Satan." In *Key Events in the Life of the Historical Jesus: A Collaborative Exploration of Context and Coherence*, edited by D. L. Bock and R. L. Webb, 151–79. Grand Rapids: Eerdmans.
Filson, F. V. 1960. *A Commentary on the Gospel According to St. Matthew*. New York: Harper & Row.
Finegan, J. 1969. *Archaeology of the New Testament: The City of Jesus and the Beginning of the Early Church*. Princeton: Princeton University Press.
Fishbane, M. 1985. *Biblical Interpretation in Ancient Israel*. Oxford: Clarendon.
Fitzmyer, J. A. 1959 "The Aramaic Qorban Inscription from Jebel Hallet Et-turi and Mk 7:11/Mt 15:5." *JBL* 78:60–65.
———. 1987. "Aramaic Evidence Affecting the Interpretation of *Hosanna* in the New Testament." In *Tradition and Interpretation in the New Testament*, edited by G. F. Hawthorne and O. Betz, 110–18. Tübingen: Mohr Siebeck; Grand Rapids: Eerdmans.
———. 1993. "4Q246: The Son of God Document from Qumran." *Bib* 74:153–74.
———. 1998. *The Acts of the Apostles: A New Translation with Introduction and Commentary*. AB 31. New York: Doubleday.
Förster, N. 2012. *Jesus und die Steuerfrage. Die Zinsgroschenperikope auf dem religiösen und politischen Hintergrund ihrer Zeit mit einer Edition von Pseudo-Hieronymus*. WUNT 1/294. Tübingen: Mohr Siebeck.
Fowler, R. M. 1981. *Loaves and Fishes: The Function of the Feeding Stories in the Gospel of Mark*. Chico: Scholars Press.
Funk, R. and Hoover, R. 1993. *The Five Gospels: The Search for the Authentic Words of Jesus*. New York: Scribner.
Gaston, L. 1962. "Beelzebul." *TZ* 18:247–55.
———. 1970. *Not One Stone on Another: Studies in the Significance of the Fall of Jerusalem in the Synoptic Gospels*. NovTSup 23. Leiden: Brill.
Gathercole, S. 2004. "The Son of Man in Mark." *ExpT* 115:366–72.
Geddert, T. J. 1989. *Watchwords: Mark 13 in Markan Eschatology*. JSNTSup 26. Sheffield: Sheffield Academic.
Gerhardsson, B. 1967/86. "The Parable of the Sower and Its Interpretation." *NTS* 14:165–93.
———. 1991. "If We Do Not Cut the Parables Out of Their Frames" *NTS* 37:321–35.
Gibson, J. B. 1986. "The Rebuke of the Disciples in Mark 8:14–21." *JSNT* 27:31–47.
———. 1990. "Jesus' Refusal to Produce a Sign (Mk 8.11–13)." *JSNT* 38:37–66.
Glöckner, R. 1979. *Biblischer Glaube ohne Wunder?* Einsiedeln: Johannes.

Gray, R. 1993. *Prophetic Figures in Late Second Temple Palestine: The Evidence from Josephus*. New York: Oxford University Press.
Gray, T. C. 2008. *The Temple in the Gospel of Mark: A Study in Its Narrative Role*. WUNT 2/242. Tübingen: Mohr Siebeck.
Gregory, C. R. 1908. *Das Freer Logion*. Leipzig: Hinrichs.
Hägerland, T. 2011. *Jesus and the Forgiveness of Sins: An Aspect of His Prophetic Mission*. SNTSMS 150. Cambridge: Cambridge University Press.
Hamilton, N. Q. 1964. "Temple Cleansing and Temple Bank." *JBL* 83:365–72.
Harrington, D. J. 2004. *What Are They Saying about Mark?* New York: Paulist.
Harris, W. V. 1991. *Ancient Literacy*. Cambridge, MA: Harvard University Press.
Hart, H. St J. 1984. "The Coin of 'Render Unto Caesar' ... (A Note on Some Aspects of Mark 12:13–17; Matt. 22:15–22; Luke 20:26)." In *Jesus and the Politics of His Day*, edited by E. Bammel and C. F. D. Moule, 241–48. Cambridge: Cambridge University Press.
Hartvigsen, K. M. 2012. *Prepare the Way of the Lord: Towards a Cognitive Poetic Analysis of Audience Involvement with Characters and Events in the Markan World*. BZNW 180. Berlin: de Gruyter.
Hawthorne, G. F. 1992. "Amen." In *Dictionary of Jesus and the Gospels*, edited by J. B. Green and S. McKnight, 7–8. Downers Grove: IVP.
Head, P. M. 1991. "A Text-Critical Study of Mark 1.1: 'The Beginning of the Gospel of Jesus Christ.'" *NTS* 37:621–29.
Heil, J. P. 2000. *The Transfiguration of Jesus: Narrative Meaning and Function of Mark 9:2–8, Matt 17:1–8 and Luke 9:28–36*. Analecta Biblica 144. Rome: Editrice Pontificio Instituto Biblico.
Henderson, S. W. 2006. *Christology and Discipleship in the Gospel of Mark*. SNTSMS 135. Cambridge: Cambridge University Press.
Hendin, D. 1987. *Guide to Biblical Coins*. New York: Amphora.
Hengel, M. 1977. *Crucifixion in the Ancient World and the Folly of the Message of the Cross*. ET. Philadelphia: Fortress.
———. 1981. *The Charismatic Leader and His Followers*. ET. Edinburgh: T. & T. Clark.
———. 1985. *Studies in the Gospel of Mark*. ET. London: SCM.
———. 1989. *The Zealots: Investigations into the Jewish Freedom Movement in the Period from Herod I until 70 A.D.* ET. Edinburgh: T. & T. Clark.
———. 2000. *The Four Gospels and the One Gospel of Jesus Christ*. London: SCM.
Hezser, C. 2001. *Jewish Literacy in Jewish Palestine*. Tübingen: Mohr Siebeck.
Hock, R. F. 1992. "Cynics." *ABD* 1:1221–26
Hoehner, H. W. 1972. *Herod Antipas*. SNTSMS 17. Cambridge: Cambridge University Press.
Hofius, O. 1994. "Jesu Zuspruch der Sündenvergebung: Exegetische Erwägungen zu Mk 2,5b." In *Sünde und Gericht*, edited by I. Baldermann et al., 125–43. JBT 9. Neukirchen-Vluyn: Neukirchener.
Hogan, L. P. 1992. *Healing in the Second Temple Period*. NTOA 21. Freiburg: Universitätsverlag Freiburg; Göttingen: Vandenhoeck & Ruprecht.
Holland, T. A., and Netzer, E. 1992. "Jericho." *ABD* 3:723–39.
Hooker, M. D. 1959. *Jesus and the Servant: The Influence of the Servant Concept in Deutero-Isaiah in the NT*. London: SPCK.
———. 1983. *The Message of Mark*. London: Epworth.
Horbury, W. 1998. *Jewish Messianism and the Cult of Christ*. London: SCM.

———. 2003. *Messianism among Jews and Christians: Twelve Biblical and Historical Studies.* London: T. & T. Clark.
Horsley, R. A. 2002. *Jesus and Empire: The Kingdom of God and the New World Disorder.* Philadelphia: Fortress.
Horsley, R. A. and Hanson, J. S. 1985. *Bandits, Prophets and Messiahs: Popular Movements in the Time of Jesus.* San Francisco: Harper and Row.
Hull, J. M. 1974. *Hellenistic Magic and the Synoptic Tradition.* SBT 28. London: SCM.
Hunzinger, C. H. 1979. "Sykē." *TDNT* 7:753.
Hurtado, L. and Owen, P., editors. 2011. *Who is This Son of Man? The Latest Scholarship on a Puzzling Expression of the Historical Jesus.* LNTS 390. London: Bloomsbury T. & T. Clark.
Incigneri, B. J. 2003. *The Gospel to the Romans: The Setting and Rhetoric of Mark's Gospel.* Biblical Interpretation 65. Leiden: Brill.
Iverson, K. R. 2013. "Incongruity, Humor, and Mark: Performance and the Use of Laughter in the Second Gospel (Mark 8:14–21)." *NTS* 59:2–19.
Iwe, J. C. 1999. *Jesus in the Synagogue of Capernaum: The Pericope and Its Programmatic Character for the Gospel of Mark. An Exegetico-Theological Study of Mark 1:21–28.* TGST 57. Rome: Gregorian University Press.
James, E. O. 1966. *The Tree of Life: An Archaeological Study.* NumenSup. Leiden: Brill.
Jaubert, A. 1965. *The Date of the Last Supper.* Staten Island, NY: Alba House.
Jeremias, J. 1954. *The Parables of Jesus.* ET. London: SCM.
———. 1966a. *The Eucharistic Words of Jesus.* ET. London: SCM.
———. 1966b. *Abba. Studien zur neutestamentlichen Theologie und Zeitsgeschichte.* Göttingen: Vandenhoeck & Ruprecht.
———. 1969. *Jerusalem in the Time of Jesus: An Investigation into the Economic and Social Conditions during the NT Period.* ET. London: SCM.
———. 1971. *New Testament Theology: The Proclamation of Jesus.* ET. London: SCM.
———. 1971–72. "This is My Body ..." *ExpT* 83:196–203.
Johnson, E. S. 1979. "Mark 8.22–26: The Blind Man from Bethsaida." *NTS* 25:370–83.
Kahler, M. 1964. *The So-called Historical Jesus and the Historic Biblical Christ.* ET. Philadelphia: Fortress.
Käsemann, E. 1969. *Jesus Means Freedom.* ET. Philadelphia: Fortress.
Keck, L. 1970–71. "The Spirit and the Dove." *NTS* 17:41–67.
Kee, H. C. 1977. *Community of the New Age: Studies in Mark's Gospel.* London: SCM.
Keener, C. S. 2009. *The Historical Jesus of the Gospels.* Grand Rapids: Eerdmans.
Kermode, F. 1979. *The Genesis of Secrecy: On the Interpretation of Narrative.* Cambridge, MA: Harvard University Press.
Kiilunen, J. 1985. *Die Vollmacht im Widerstreit: Untersuchungen zum Werdegang von Mk 2,1–3,6.* Annales Academiae Scientiarum Fennicae Dissertationes Humanarum Litterarum 40. Helsinki: Suomalainen Tiedeakatemia.
Kingsbury, J. D. 1983. *The Christology of Mark's Gospel.* Philadelphia: Fortress.
Kirk, J. R. D. 2012. "Time for Figs, Temple Destruction, and Houses of Prayer in Mark 11:12–25." *CBQ* 74:509–27.
Klassen, W. 2005. *Judas: Betrayer or Friend of Jesus.* Minneapolis: Fortress.
Kreitzer, L. J. 1987. *Jesus and God in Paul's Eschatology.* JSNTSup 19. Sheffield: Sheffield Academic.
Kümmel, W. G. 1957. *Promise and Fulfilment: The Eschatological Message of Jesus.* SBT 1/23. London: SCM.

Lee, S. S. 2009. *Jesus' Transfiguration and the Believer's Transformation: A Study of the Transfiguration and Its Development in Early Christian Writings*. WUNT 2/265. Tübingen: Mohr Siebeck.
Leifeld, W. L. 1974. "Theological Motifs in the Transfiguration Narrative." In *New Dimensions in New Testament Studies*, edited by R. N. Longenecker and M. C. Tenney, 162–79. Grand Rapids: Zondervan.
Lindars, B. 1983. *Jesus Son of Man: A Fresh Examination of the Son of Man Sayings in the Gospels*. London: SPCK.
Lövestam, E. 1968. *Spiritus blasphemia. Eine Studie zu Mk 3,28f par Mt 12,31f, Lk 12,10*. Lund: Gleerup.
Magness, J. L. 1986. *Sense and Suspense: Structure and Suspension in the Ending of Mark's Gospel*. SBLSS. Atlanta: Scholars Press.
Manson, T. W. 1935. *The Teaching of Jesus*. 2nd ed. Cambridge: Cambridge University Press.
———. 1937. *The Sayings of Jesus as Recorded in the Gospels According to St. Matthew and St. Luke: Arranged with Introduction and Commentary*. London: SCM.
Marcus, J. 1992. *The Way of the Lord: Christological Exegesis of the Old Testament in the Gospel of Mark*. Edinburgh: T & T Clark.
———. 2001. "The Once and Future Messiah in Early Christianity and Chabad." *NTS* 47:381–401.
Marshall, C. D. 1989. *Faith as a Theme in Mark's Narrative*. SNTSM 64. Cambridge: Cambridge University Press.
Marxsen, W. 1969. *Mark the Evangelist: Studies on the Redaction History of the Gospel*. ET. Nashville: Abingdon.
McArthur, H. K. 1973. "Son of Mary." *NovT* 15:38–58.
McKnight, S. 1999. *A New Vision for Israel: The Teachings of Jesus in National Context*. Grand Rapids: Eerdmans.
Meier, J. P. 1991–2009. *A Marginal Jew: Rethinking the Historical Jesus*. ABRL. 4 vols. New York: Doubleday.
———. 2000. "The Historical Jesus and the Historical Herodians." *JBL* 119:740–46.
Metzger, B. M. 1994. *A Textual Commentary on the Greek New Testament*. 2nd ed. Stuttgart: Deutsche Bibelgesellschaft.
Metzger B. M., and Ehrman, B. 2005. *The Text of the New Testament: Its Transmission, Corruption and Restoration*. 4th ed. Oxford: Oxford University Press.
Milgrom, J. 1991–2001. *Leviticus: A New Translation with Introduction and Commentary*. 3 vols. AB 3, 3A, 3B. New York: Doubleday.
Millard, A. R. 2000. *Reading and Writing in the Time of Jesus*. Sheffield: Sheffield Academic.
Miller, R. J. 1988. "The Rejection of the Prophets in Q." *JBL* 107:225–40.
Mitchell, M. M. 2005. "Patristic Counter-Evidence to the Claim that 'The Gospels were Written for ALL Christians.'" *NTS* 51:36–79.
Moltmann-Wendel, E. and Moltmann, J. 1983. *Humanity in God*. Boston: Pilgrim.
Moore, M. S. 1987. "Yahweh's Day." *Restoration Quarterly* 29:193–205.
Moule, C. F. D. 1959. *An Idiom Book of New Testament Greek*. 2nd ed. Cambridge: Cambridge University Press.
Müller, M. 2008. *The Expression "Son of Man" and the Development of Christology: A History of Interpretation*. London: Equinox.

Neusner, J. 1973. *From Politics to Piety: the Emergence of Pharisaic Judaism*. Englewood Cliffs, NJ: Prentice-Hall.

———. 1989. "Money-Changers in the Temple: The Mishnah's Explanation." *NTS* 35:287–90.

Neusner, J., Green, W. S. and Frerichs, E. S. 1987. *Judaisms and Their Messiahs at the Turn of the Christian Era*. Cambridge: Cambridge University Press.

Nickelsburg, G. W. E. 1972. *Resurrection, Immortality and Eternal Life in Intertestamental Judaism*. HTS 26. Cambridge, MA: Harvard University Press.

Nicholson, E. W. 1986. *God and His People: Covenant and Theology in the Old Testament*. Oxford: Clarendon.

Ossandón, J. C. 2012. "Bartimaeus' Faith: Plot and Point of View in Mark 10.46–52." *Biblica* 93:377–402.

Parrot, A. 1957. *The Temple in Jerusalem*. London: SCM.

Payne, P. B. 1978. "The Order of Sowing and Ploughing in the Parable of the Sower." *NTS* 25:123–29.

———. 1980. "The Authenticity of the Parable of the Sower and Its Interpretation." In *Gospel Perspectives: Studies of History and Tradition in the Four Gospels*. Volume 1, edited by R. T. France and D. Wenham, 163–207. Sheffield: JSOT Press.

Peppard, M. 2010. "The Eagle and the Dove: Roman Imperial Sonship and the Baptism of Jesus (Mark 1.9–11)." *NTS* 56:431–51.

Pesch, R. 1994. "'He Will be Called a Nazorean:' Messianic Exegesis in Matthew 1–2." In *The Gospels and the Scriptures of Israel*, edited by C. A. Evans and W. R. Stegner, 129–78. Sheffield: Sheffield Academic.

Pobee, J. 1970. "The Cry of the Centurion—A Cry of Defeat." In *The Trial of Jesus: Cambridge Studies in Honour of C. F. D. Moule*, edited by E. Bammel, 91–102. London: SCM.

Pokorný, P. 1995. "From a Puppy to a Child: Some Problems of Contemporary Biblical Exegesis Demonstrated from Mark 7.24–30/Matt 15.21–8." *NTS* 41:321–37.

Porton, G. G. 1992. "Sadducess." *ABD* 5:894.

Quesnell, Q. 1969. *The Mind of Mark: Interpretation and Method through the Exegesis of Mark 6.52*. Analecta Biblica 38. Rome: Biblical Institute Press.

Reinhartz, A. 2013. *Caiaphas the High Priest*. SPNT. Minneapolis: Fortress.

Repo, E. 1964. *Der "Weg" als Selbstbezeichnung des Urchristentums*. AASF B131/2. Helsinki: SuomalainenTiedeakatemia.

Richardson, N. 1994. *Paul's Language about God*. JSNTSup 99. Sheffield: Sheffield Academic.

Rindge, M. S. 2012. "Reconfiguring the Akedah and Recasting God: Lament and Divine Abandonment in Mark." *JBL* 131:755–74.

Riesenfeld, H. 1947. *Jésus transfigure*. ASNU 17. Copenhagen: Munksgaard.

Roubos, K. 1986. "Biblical Institutions." In *The World of the Bible*, edited by A. S. van der Woude, 350–92. Grand Rapids: Eerdmans.

Rubenstein, J. L. 1994. "The Symbolism of the Sukkah." *Judaism* 43:371–87.

Saldarini, A. J. 1988. *Pharisees, Scribes and Sadducees in Palestinian Society: A Sociological Approach*. Wilmington: Glazier.

———. 1992. "Sanhedrin." *ABD* 5:975–80.

Sanders, E. P. 1977. *Paul and Palestinian Judaism*. London: SCM.

———. 1985. *Jesus and Judaism*. London: SCM.

———. 1992. *Judaism: Practice and Belief, 63 BCE–66 CE*. London: SCM.

Saulnier, S. 2012. *Calendrical Variations in Second Temple Judaism: New Perspectives on the "Date of the Last Supper" Debate.* JSJSup 159. Leiden: Brill.

Schmidt, T. E. 1987. *Hostility to Wealth in the Synoptic Gospels.* JSNTSup 15. Sheffield: JSOT Press.

Schneck, R. 1994. *Isaiah in the Gospel of Mark I-VIII.* Bibal Dissertation Series 1. Vallejo, CA: Bibal.

Schneider, J. 1966. "*Kathaireō.*" *TDNT* 3:411–12.

Schürer, E. 1973–87. *The History of the Jewish People in the Age of Jesus Christ (175 B.C.– A.D. 135).* 3 vols. Rev. and ed. G. Vermes, F, Millar and M. Goodman. Edinburgh: T. & T. Clark.

Segal, J. B. 1963. *The Hebrew Passover from Earliest Times to AD 70.* London: Oxford University Press.

Snodgrass, K. 1983. *The Parable of the Wicked Tenants: An Inquiry into Parable Interpretation.* WUNT 27. Tübingen: Mohr Siebeck.

———. 2008. *Stories with Intent: A Comprehensive Guide to the Parables of Jesus.* Grand Rapids: Eerdmans.

Stanton, G. N. 1974. *Jesus of Nazareth in New Testament Preaching.* SNTSMS 27. Cambridge: Cambridge University Press.

———. 1985. "Aspects of Early Christian-Jewish Polemic and Apologetic." *NTS* 31:377–92.

———. 2002. *The Gospels and Jesus.* Oxford Bible Series. 2nd ed. Oxford: Oxford University Press.

———. 2004. *Jesus and Gospel.* Cambridge: Cambridge University Press.

Steele, G. 2012. "The Theology of Hiddenness in the Gospel of Mark: An Exploration of the Messianic Secret and Corollaries." *Restoration Quarterly* 54:169–85.

Stein, R. H. 1979. "Is It Lawful for a Man to Divorce His Wife?" *JETS* 22:115–21.

———. 2008. "The Ending of Mark." *Bulletin for Biblical Research* 18:79–98.

Strange, J. F. "Bethsaida." 1992. *ABD* 1:692–93.

Stuhlmacher, P. 1968. *Das paulinische Evangelium. Vorgeschichte.* Forschungen zur Religion und Literatur des Alten und Neuen Testaments 95. Göttingen: Vandenhoeck & Ruprecht.

Tan, K. H. 1997. *The Zion Traditions and the Aims of Jesus.* SNTSMS 91. Cambridge: Cambridge University Press.

———. 2005. "Community, Kingdom and Cross: Jesus' View of Covenant." In *The God of Covenant: Biblical, Theological and Contemporary Perspectives*, edited by J. A. Grant and A. I. Wilson, 122–55. Leicester: Apollos.

———. 2008. "The Shema in Early Christianity." *Tyndale Bulletin* 58:181–206.

———. 2011. "Jesus and the Shema." In *Handbook for the Study of the Historical Jesus.* Vol. 3, edited by T. Holmen and S. E. Porter, 2677–707. Leiden: Brill.

Tannenhill, R. C. 1977. "The Disciples in Mark: The Function of a Narrative Role." *Journal of Religion* 57:486–505.

Taylor, J. E. 1997. *The Immerser: John the Baptist within Second Temple Judaism.* Grand Rapids: Eerdmans.

Telford, W. R. 1980. *The Barren Temple and the Withered Tree: A Redaction-Critical Analysis of the Cursing of the Fig-Tree Pericope in Mark's Gospel and Its Relation to the Cleansing of the Temple Tradition.* JSNTSup 1. Sheffield: JSOT Press.

———. 1999. *The Theology of the Gospel of Mark.* Cambridge: Cambridge University Press.

Theissen, G. 1983. *The Miracle Stories of the Early Christian Tradition.* SNTW. Edinburgh: T. & T. Clark.

———. 1991. *The Gospels in Context: Social and Political History in the Synoptic Tradition.* ET. Minneapolis: Fortress.

Trompf, G. W. 1971–72. "The First Resurrection Appearance and the Ending of Mark's Gospel." *NTS* 18:308–30.

Tuckett, C. M., editor. 1983. *The Messianic Secret.* Issues in Religion and Theology 1. London: SPCK.

Van Oyen, G. 1992. "Intercalation and Irony in the Gospel of Mark." In *The Four Gospels 1992: Festschrift Franz Neirynck.* BETL 100, edited by van Sogbroeck et al., 949–74. Leuven: Peeters.

Vanderkam, J. C. 2004. *From Joshua to Caiaphas: High Priests after the Exile.* Minneapolis: Fortress.

Viviano, B. T. 1989. "The High Priest's Servant Ear: Mark 14:47." *RB* 96:71–80.

Von Rad, G. 1959. "The Origin of the Day of Yahweh." *JSS* 4:97–108.

Wardle, T. 2010. *The Jerusalem Temple and Early Christian Identity.* WUNT 2/291. Tübingen: Mohr Siebeck.

Wasserman, T. 2011. "The 'Son of God' Was in the Beginning (Mark 1:1)." *JTS* 62:20–50.

Watts, R. E. 1997. *Isaiah's New Exodus and Mark.* WUNT 2/88. Tübingen: Mohr Siebeck.

Webb, R. L. 1991. *John the Baptizer and Prophet: A Socio-Historical Study.* JSNTSup 62. Sheffield: Sheffield Academic.

Wedderburn, A. J. M. 1999. *Beyond Resurrection.* London: SCM.

Weeden, T. J. 1968. "The Heresy that Necessitated Mark's Gospel." *ZNW* 59:145–58.

Weiss, J. 1971. *Die Predigt Jesu vom Reiche Gottes.* Göttingen: Vandenhoeck & Ruprecht.

Wenham, D. 1982. "'This Generation will not Pass . . . ' A Study of Jesus' Future Expectation in Mark 13." In *Christ the Lord: Studies in Christology Presented to Donald Guthrie*, edited by H. H. Rowdon, 127–50. Leicester: IVP.

Wenham, J. W. 1950. "Mark 2:26." *JTS* 1:156.

Westbrook, R. 1991. "The Law of the Biblical Levirate." In *Property and the Family in Biblical Law,* 68–89. JSOTSup 113. Sheffield: Sheffield University Press, 1991.

White, K. D. 1964. "The Parable of the Sower." *JTS* 15:301–03.

Widengren, G. 1951. *The King and the Tree of Life in Ancient Near Eastern Religion.* King and Saviour IV. Uppsala Universitets Arsskrift 1951:4. Uppsala: A.-B. Lundequistska Bokhandeln.

Williams, C. H. 2000. *I am He: The Interpretation of 'ănî hû' in Jewish and Early Christian Literature.* WUNT 2/113. Tübingen: Mohr Siebeck.

Wilson, S. G. 1995. *Related Strangers: Jews and Christians 70–170 CE.* Minneapolis: Fortress.

Winn, A. 2008. *The Purpose of Mark's Gospel: An Early Christian Response to Roman Imperial Propaganda.* WUNT 2/245. Tübingen: Mohr Siebeck.

Winter, P. 1961. *On the Trial of Jesus.* SJFWJ 1. Berlin: de Gruyter.

Witmer, A. 2012. *Jesus, the Galilean Exorcist: His Exorcisms in Social and Political Context.* LNTS 459. London: T. & T. Clark International.

Wolff, H. W. 1974. *Anthropology of the Old Testament.* London: SCM.

Wong, E. K. C. 2002. "The Deradicalization of Jesus' Ethical Sayings in 1 Corinthians." *NTS* 48:181–94.

Wrede, W. 1971. *The Messianic Secret.* ET. Cambridge: James Clarke.

Wright, N. T. 1992. *The New Testament and the People of God*. Christian Origins and the Question of God. Vol. 1. London: SPCK.
———. 1996. *Jesus and the Victory of God*. Christian Origins and the Question of God. Vol. 2. Minneapolis: Fortress.
———. 2003. *The Resurrection of the Son of God*. Christian Origins and the Question of God. Vol. 3. Minneapolis: Fortress.
Wyatt, N. 2001. *Space and Time in the Religious Life of the Near East*. Biblical Seminar 85. Sheffield: Sheffield Academic.

Scripture Index

OLD TESTAMENT

Genesis

1:2	20
1:27	133
2:2–3	41
2:24	133
12:1–3	139
14:18–20	66
15:9	20
22:2	20
37:34	205
38:8	166
40:17	55
40:19	55

Exodus

3:6	167
3:14	88
4:21	43
7:3	43
8:32	43
12:6–20	188
12:8	195
14:4	43
14:24	87
17:1–7	105
18:21	83
19:19	121
20:10	41
20:12	50
22:26–27	147
22:28	205
23:30	17
24:1	121
24:8	195n140
24:9	121
24:16	121
25:30	42
30:11–16	154
30:18–21	91
30:35	131
33:9	120
33:17ff.	88
34:6–7	34
34:21	41
34:29–35	124
34:30	121
40:30–32	91
40:35	121

Leviticus

1:14	20
2:13	131
11:7–8	66n110
12:6	20, 155
13–14	30
13:2–6	29
13:45–46	29
15:14	20, 155
15:19–33	69
15:29	20, 155
16:29–31	39
18:16	80
19:9–10	41
19:18	169
19:34	169
20:10–12	134
20:21	80
23:22	41
23:26–29	39
23:33–43	120

Leviticus (continued)

24:5–9	42
24:8	41
24:10–16	34
24:15–16	205

Numbers

6:10	155
9:2–14	188
9:18–23	121
12:9–15	29
15:37–41	168
24:16	66
27:17	82, 85
28:15–16	188
29:12–38	120

Deuteronomy

6:4	168
6:4–5	34, 54, 168
6:4–9	168
6:5	168
6:16	105
9:22	105
10:16	133
14:8	66n110
16:1	188
16:2	192
17:6	75
21:22–23	218
21:23	115
23:24–25	41
24:1–4	79, 132, 133
24:12–13	147
25:5–10	166
27:15–26	49
28:1–14	138
28:26	55
28:27	33
28:29	214
28:49	101
29:18	43
32:39	88
33:8	101

Joshua

7:6	205
15:25	47

Judges

6:36–40	106

1 Samuel

1:1	218
12:6	46n61
17:43	97

2 Samuel

1:11	205
7:11–16	147
7:12	204
7:14	204
8:17	165
14:4	151
16:9	97
17:13	176

1 Kings

1:33	151
8:41	101
12:31	46n61
13:33	46n61
14:11	55
16:4	55
17:8–16	84
18:24	106
18:36–38	106
19:11–13	88
19:19–21	25
21:13	205
22:17	82, 85

2 Kings

1:8	18
2:11	216
4:9	27
4:42–44	84
5:7	29
6:26	151

6:31	105
9:13	151

1 Chronicles

16:36	49

2 Chronicles

24:20–22	161
26:16–21	29

Ezra

6:9	131
7:22	131

Nehemiah

8:14–17	120

Esther

5:3	80
5:6	80
7:2	80
9:31	39

Job

1:10	138
9:8	88
19:25–26	166
26:11–12	64
31:1	130
31:5	130
31:7	130
38:1	121

Psalms

2:2	204
2:7	20, 204
3:5	63
4:8	63
11:6	143
16:5	143
16:9–11	166
19	60
22	211, 215, 221
22:1	221
22:16	97
23	83
33:6	60
41:3–4	33
41:9	193
42:5	199
42:11	199
43:5	199
46:5	87
49:15	166
73:23–26	166
75:8	143
77:19	88
79:2	55
80:8–18	161
81:15	43
95:7–11	105
106:16	27
107:4	64
107:17–18	33
110	170, 205
110:1	170, 224
113–14	195
113–18	164
115–18	195
116:13	143
118:22–23	163
118:25–26	151
119:105	60
128:1–2	138
145:10–13	23

Proverbs

3:24	63
6:16–19	130
31:6	211

Ecclesiastes

3:11	100
4:9–12	75

Isaiah

2:2	119
2:2–4	98
6:9–10	59
7:13–14	106

Isaiah (continued)

10:2	171
10:34	203n166
11.1	147
11:2	18, 73
13:9	183
13:10	183
13:11	183
13:14	82
18:6	55
19:2	177
25:6	98, 197
26:19	166
27:2–6	161
28:2	18
29:13	92
31:3	200
32:14–20	51
32:15	18
34:2	183
34:4	183
34:8	183
35:5–6	100
35:6	100
38:17	33
40:2	51
40:3	17
40:7–8	186
40:9	14
41:4	88
41:10	88
41:13	88
42:1	20
43:1	89
43:1–25	89
43:5	89
43:10–11	88
43:25	34, 51
44:3	18
44:22	24, 34, 51
49:6	46, 98
49:26	18
51:6	186
51:9–10	64
51:10–12	89
51:17–23	143
52:7	14, 23, 122, 149, 172
53	122, 144, 145, 146, 196n142
53:4–6	33
53:10	145
53:11	145
53:11–12	145
53:12	145, 196
54:5	39
54:9–10	186
55:10–11	54, 60
56:7	153, 156
56:10–11	97
59:15–21	51, 196
59:20–21	24
60:4	101
61:1	14
61:1–8	24
62:5	39
64:1	19
65:16	49n74
65:17	17
66:24	130

Jeremiah

2:2	39
2:21	161
3:10–14	24
3:16	183
3:17	43
4:3	56
4:4	133
7:11	153, 155, 159
7:24	43
7:33	55
8:13	159
9:14	43
11:8	43
12:10	161
13:10	43
15:9	214
16:12	43
16:16	25
23:5	147
25:15–29	143
26:20–23	161
31:12	56
31:27–28	54

31:31–34	24, 196	3:26	66
31:32	110n5	4:2	66
31:34	51	4:20–22	63
33:5	147	7	35n37, 43, 112, 113n7, 122, 123, 205
33:6–9	35		
33:8	51		
33:15–16	183	7:9	119, 224
33:20–21	186	7:13	35, 36, 184, 227
34:20	55	7:13–14	36, 144
41:24	47	7:14	144n51
46:27	101	7:18	112
		7:21–22	112

Lamentations

4:21	143

7:25	112
8:13	179
9:27	179
11:31	179
12:1	182
12:2	71, 166
12:11	179

Ezekiel

1:4	121
11:19	18
16	39
17:1–10	63
17:23	62
19:10–14	161
23:31–34	143
29:4–6	25
29:5	55
31:6	63
32:4	55
32:7	184
34:5	82
34:5–16	85
34:23	82
36:24–36	51
36:26–27	18
36:33	51
37:1–14	51
37:14	18
37:21–28	24
37:24	82
39:21–29	51
43:24	131
45:8	46

Hosea

1:2	12
2	39
2:16–23	35
2:18–23	24
2:21–22	56
2:21–23	54
6:2	113
6:6	95, 169
10:1	161
14:1–9	24

Joel

2:10	184
2:22	56
2:28–29	18
3:2	183
3:13	62

Amos

4:2	25
5:21–27	95
8:9	214
9:13	56
9:13–15	54

Daniel

2:18–19	57
2:27–30	57
2:40	57

Micah

1:3–4	177
4:4	159
5:4	82
7:6	178

Habakkuk

1:14–17	25
2:16	143
3:6–10	177
3:15	88

Haggai

2:15	176

Zechariah

2:6	185
3:8	147
3:10	159
6:12	147, 203
8:12	54, 56
8:19	39
8:23	183
9:9	151
10:2	82
13:4	18
13:7	85, 197
14:1–4	177
14:5	177
14:20–21	157

Malachi

3:1	17
3:5	171
4:4–5	120
4:5–6	77, 123

∽

APOCRYPHA

Tobit

3:8	166n54
3:15	166n54

Judith

16:17	130

Wisdom of Solomon

4:3	56
18:4	186n111

Sirach

7:17	130
23:25	56
24:5–6	88
40:15	56
48:10	124

Baruch

4:1	186n111

1 Maccabees

1:54–59	179
3:47	39
4:46	77
14:41	77

2 Maccabees

3:31	66
6:2	179
7	166n54
10:1	198n147

∽

NEW TESTAMENT

Matthew

3:11	19
3:16	19
5:15	61n99
7:6	66n110
8:5–13	26
8:5–17	26

8:28	65	11:33	61n99
9:9	37, 46	12:50	143
10:3	37	13:1	209
10:10	76	13:15	151
11:4–6	100	18:12	39
11:14	123	18:35	146n56
11:20	110	22:30	46
12:38–41	104	24:4–5	224
14:1	76		
15:28	99	**John**	
15:31	102		
16:18	46	1:45	74
17:24–27	155	2:19	163
19:10–12	134	6:4	74, 83n143, 85
19:28	46	6:4–15	85
20:29–30	147n56	6:9	84n152
21:5	151	6:15	28
23:34	161	6:42	74
23:37	161	9:2–3	33
23:39	151	10:20	48
24:3	175, 177	10:41	77
24:30–31	185n107	12:3	190
24:37–39	187	12:15	151
27:37	213	14:22	47
27:60	218	18:1	198
28:2	224	18:10	200
28:5	224	18:13	204
		19:14	212
Luke		19:17	211n190
		19:19	213
1:32	66	19:19–22	213
3:1	79		
3:2	204	**Acts**	
3:16	19		
3:21	19	1:13	47
4:22	74	2:1–4	19
5:29	37	2:42	8
6:15	47	4:2	165
7:1–10	26	5:42	8
7:22–23	100	9:2	233
8:16	61n99	12:12	3
9:3	76	12:25	3
9:10	86	13:5	3
9:31	119	13:13	3
9:54	46	13:51	75
10:4	76	15:37	3
10:25–37	169	16:17	66
11:29–32	104	18:6	75

18:27–28	127
19:9	233
19:13	66n109
19:23	233
21:27–36	203
22:4	233
23:6–8	165
23:12	207
23:14	207
23:21	207
24:14	233
24:22	233

Romans

1:4	117
1:16	96
7–8	200
8:15–16	199

1 Corinthians

1:22–24	97
5:7	192
13:11	95
15:25–27	170

Galatians

3:13	115, 210
4:6	199
4:14	127

Ephesians

1:20–22	170
2:13	101

Colossians

4:10	3
4:15	8

2 Timothy

4:11	3

Philemon

24	3

Hebrews

1:13 – 2:8	170
6:19–20	216
10:19–20	216

James

5:14	76n128

1 Peter

5:13	3

2 Peter

2:22	66n110

Revelation

2:7	85
4:4	119
7:9	119, 224
7:13	224
19:7–8	39
21:1–3	39
21:9–10	39

Ancient Sources Index

JEWISH SOURCES

Dead Sea Scrolls

CD
4:20—5:2	132
11:9–10	43
11:13–17	41
12:8	205
19:7–13	197n146
19:10–11	111

1Q30 27

1QH
4:7–15	92

1QM
4:13	111
14:4–8	111

1QpHab
10:12–13	205

1QS
4:18–23	27
4:20–22	18
8:14	17
9:10–11	147
9:19–21	17

1QSb
5:20–29	228

4Q242 34

4Q246 15, 66, 204

4Q252 111

4Q521
1:6	20

4Q558 124

4QFlor
1:6–7	203
1:10–13	14
1:18–19	14
3:11–12	204

11Q13 170

11QT
57:17–19	132

Josephus

Against Apion
1:70	96
1:197	110n4
2:104	156

Antiquities of the Jews
4:253	134
5:1	168
5:27	168

Antiquities of the Jews (continued)

5:112	168
7:280–81	113
8:45–48	26n8
11:325–29	150
13:171–73	38
13:297	91
14:9	80
14:313–21	96
15:363–64	110
17:41	92
17:41–47	44
18:4	38
18:4–6	164
18:11–25	38
18:16	165
18:23–25	164
18:28	110
18:55–59	209
18:55–62	209
18:60–62	209
18:63–64	202, 208
18:95	204
18:109	78
18:112	78
18:116–19	77
18:117–19	18
18:118	78
18:119	78
18:136	79, 80
18:261	180
18:271	180
18:356	87
20:199	165
20:216–17	206

Jewish War

1:123	80
1:319	44
1:404–6	110
1:571	44
2:162–66	38
2:165	165
2:169–74	209
2:175	209
2:306–8	210
2:478	96
3:506–8	25
3:516–21	26
4:147–57	180, 181
4:201	181
5:184–226	176
5:215–19	216n205
5:222–23	176
5:224	176
5:449	210
5:449–51	182n99
5:450–51	211n188
6:250	176
6:260	180
6:300–309	203
6:301	178n83
6:316	180
7:1–4	176
7:200–202	210

Life of Josephus

290	39
341	68n115
386	206
410	68n115
426	134

Philo

Decalogue

65	168

Embassy to Gaius

212	178n83
299–305	209

Life of Moses

2:22	41

Pseudepigrapha

2 Baruch

14:18	42
27:2	177
27:6	177
29:8	85
59:10	130

70:2	54
85:13	130

3 Baruch

4:17	178n85

1 Enoch

27:1–2	130
37–71	35
54:1ff	130
56:3–4	130
62:15	119
62:15–16	224
87:2	224
89:42	97
89:46–47	97
89:48	97
90:26	130
90:30	62
100:1–2	178n85

Epistle of Aristeas

305	92

4 Ezra

7:36	130
8:41	54
9:31	54
13:3	184
13:31	177

Joseph and Aseneth

14:1–2	87

Jubilees

2:17	42
11:11	55
23:19	178n85

3 Maccabees

7:9	66

Psalms of Solomon

17	111, 228

17–18	147
17:21	170
17:21–32	14
17:23	73

Sibylline Oracles

2:187–88	124
3:8–45	168
3:796–803	184

Testament of Moses

10:1–5	184

Rabbinic Literature

Mishnah

Abot

1:1	91

Berakot

5:5	46
9:5	157

'Eduyyot

8:7	124

Gittin

9:10	132

Hagigah

1:1	150

Keritot

5:7	155

Nazir

1:5	62

Nedarim

3:4	37
5:6	93

Niddah

5:2	62

'Oholot

2:3	75

Parah

11:5	92

Pesahim

7:9	192
8:6	209
10:1–7	195

Sabbat

7:2	41
14:3–4	43

Sanhedrin

7:5	26, 161
9:6	178n83

Sheni

4:7	153

Sheqalim

6:5	171

Sotah

9:15	124

Ta'anit

14:5	39

Toharot

4:5	75
7:6	37

Yadaim

1:1	91
2:3	91

Yoma

8:6	43

Tosephta

Sabbat

7:2	55

Sanhedrin

12:10	100

Babylonian Talmud

'Avodah Zarah

17b	216

Baba Batra

4a	176
126b	100

Berakot

53b	20
55a	177
55b	139
63a	168n61

'Erubin

30a	25

Hagigah

15a	20

Ketubbot

66a	25
11b–12a	56

Makkot

24a	168n61

Nedarim

41a	33

Pesahim

12b	26n8

Sabbat

31a	168n62
49a	20
73b	55

Sanhedrin

26a	75
43a	75, 192, 211
67a	192
97b-98a	39
98a	184

Sukkah

42a	168
51b	176

Ta'anit

10a	39
24b	136
24b-25a	84n148

Yoma

8b	204
38b	74
85b	42, 43

Midrashic Literature

Mekilta on Exodus

16:5	85

Mekilta of R. Simon

14:21	205

Leviticus Rabbah

32:3	41n48

Numbers Rabbah

19:8	27

Lamentations Rabbah

1:5	203n166

Hekhalot Rabbati

18	69

Pesiqta Rabbati

36:1	27
37:2	40

Pirqe Rabbi Eleazar

29	97

Sipre on Leviticus

§200	168n62

Sipre on Numbers

15:31	205

Targums

Psalms

118:19–27	163

Canticles

2:12	20

Zechariah

6:12	203

∾

EARLY CHRISTIAN LITERATURE

Didache

11.1–2	127
12.1	127
81	39

Epiphanius

Heresies

6:10	6n19

Eusebius

Church History

2:16:1	6n18
3:5:3	181n98
3:9:15	2n11

Irenaeus

Against Heresies

3:2:2	3n12

Origen

Commentary on Matthew

12:38	120n23

∾

GRECO-ROMAN SOURCES

Diodorus Siculus

Bibliotheca Historica

19:26:1	87

Dioscorides Pedanius

Materia Medica

1:64:3	212

Galen

Natural Faculties

3:7	100

Herodotus

Histories

9:109	81

Horace

Epistles

1:16	218
1:18	218

Juvenal

Satires

3:14	84n149
6:54	84n149

Philostratus

Epistles

44	73

Life of Apollonius

1:3–5	26n8
1:19	26n8

Pindar

Nemean Odes

1:60	66
11:20	66

Pliny the Elder

Natural History

5:15	25
6:18	68n115
6:74	68n115
14:15	212
14:92–93	212

Plutarch

Apophthegm Laconica

230F	38n42

Seneca

Epistles
101   215

Strabo

Geography
16:2   25

Tacitus

Annals
6:29   218
15:44   208n182

Thucydides

Peloponnesian War
7:6   198n147

Modern Authors Index

Abrahams, I. 96n170, 155n17, 157n25, 210n185
Allen, L. C. 164n45
Allison, D. C. 23n1, 73n123, 104n188, 177n81, 225n229, 228n11, 231n21
Alonso, P. 99n175
Ambrozic, A. M. 230n17
Athearne-Kroll, S. P. 215n198
Aus, R. D. 63n104
Bahat, D. 176n77
Bammel, E. 213n195
Barr, J. 199
Barrett, C. K. 145n53
Batto, B. F. 64n104
Bauckham, R. J. 80n137, 155n20, 157n27, 165n53, 190n126, 227n7
Baumgarten, A. I. 38n41, 90n126, 93n166
Beale, G. K. 17n13
Beasley-Murray, G. R. 183n104
Beavis, M. A. 106n190
Becker, Eve-Marie 12n3
Bellinger, W. H. 145n53
Best, E. 232n23
Bird, M. 117n17
Bishop, E. F. F. 153n10
Black, C. C. 232n23
Black, M. 58n91
Boccaccini, G. 35n36
Bock, D. L. 34n30, 205n175
Bond, H. K. 204n170, 209n183
Borg, M. 156n23, 178n83
Borgen, P. 84n150
Boring, E. 6n20, 12n2, 17n14, 19n17, 23n2, 28n10, 40n45, 46n62, 47n68, 50n76, 55n83,
 61n101, 67n113, 76n129, 178n84, 180n90, 183n102, 197n143, 200n154, 215n198, 216n202, 226
Braund, D. C. 76n131
Brower, K. E. 154n14
Brown, M. I. 33n25
Brown, R. E. 47n68, 191n128, 198n148, 209n183, 209n104, 216n204
Bryan, C. 8n28
Buckner, R. 94n167
Bultmann, R. 73n121
Burchard, C. 217n208
Burkett, D. 35n34, 227n9
Burridge, R. A. 7n26
Burrows, M. 166n55
Camery-Hoggart, J. 98n173
Capes, D. B. 227n8
Carson, D. A. 76n130, 212n194
Casey, P. M. 42n55, 227n9
Catchpole, D. R. 202n161
Charlesworth, J. H. 14n9, 147n58
Chilton, B. D. 116n12, 157n26
Collins, A. Y. 1n2, 4n13, 7n24, 12n1, 29n11, 31n19, 33n22, 34n29, 38n42, 40n45, 40n47, 42n52, 47n66, 47n67, 48n70, 63n104, 64n105, 67n112, 72n120, 77n132, 84n146, 84n151, 107n194, 200n154, 201n160, 206n176, 206n177, 210n187, 217n209, 224n227, 227n4, 228n12
Collins, J. J. 63n103, 66n108, 113n7, 147n58, 184n100
Cranfield, C. E. B. 117n15, 186n111, 194n137, 207n180, 212n193

Croy, N. C. 222n220
Culpepper, R. A. 71n118, 104n187, 167n60
Dalman, G. 228n11
Danker, F. W. 13
Davies, W. D. 156n24
De Jonge, M. 197n145
De Vaux, R. 188n117
Deines, R. 38n41
Derrett, J. M. D. 42n51, 87n156, 150n4, 171n66
Dewey, J. 31n20, 32n21, 42n54
Dodd, C. H. 23n3
Donahue, J. R. 37n38, 49n73, 62n102, 94n168, 98n169, 127n33, 130n37, 202n165, 215n200
Dowd, S. E. 138n47
Dunn, J. D. G. 35n35
Edwards, D. 89n161
Edwards, J. R. 117n16
Ehrman, B. 30n13
Elliott, J. K. 221n213
Eppstein, V. 154n15
Evans, C. A. 4n13, 57n89, 124n29, 131n39, 145n53, 151n6, 153n11, 155n19, 159n32, 161n37, 161n39, 163n43, 171n67, 171n72, 179n87, 180n91, 180n97, 183n101, 185n108, 188n118, 190n125, 191n129, 191n132, 194n138, 197n143, 198n149, 199n150, 201n158, 204n168, 205n173, 205n174, 204n180, 221n216, 227n4, 231n20
Filson, F. V. 98n173
Finegan, J. 176n78
Fishbane, M. 17n13
Fitzmyer, J. A. 66n108, 93n166, 151n8, 233n26
Förster, N. 165n51
Fowler, R. M. 83n141
France, R. T. 5n14, 7n24, 12n1, 13n4, 14n10, 19n21, 23n2, 29n11, 31n17, 33n23, 34n27, 41n49, 42n54, 46n63, 46n65, 48n70, 49n74, 66n109, 68n114, 76n130, 82n138, 88n158, 97n172, 102n183, 104n184, 108n194, 110n4, 124n31, 131n38, 142n50, 145n54, 150n2, 150n5, 161n37, 163n44, 171n70, 178n82, 183n103, 184n105, 185n107, 186n112, 186n113, 188n116, 189n123, 191n133, 192, 205n172, 216n205, 216n207, 221n216, 222n219, 223n223, 223n224
Funk, R. 161n37
Gaston, L. 5, 203n167
Gathercole, S. 144n51
Geddert, T. J. 173n73, 179n89
Gerhardsson, B. 54n80, 161n41
Gibson, J. B. 104n186, 107
Glöckner, R. 74
Gnilka, M. 30n16, 180n94
Gray, R. 104n188, 174n75
Gray, T. C. 159n31, 174n75
Green, W. S. 147n58
Gregory, C. R. 221n215
Guelich, R. A. 4n13, 7n23, 14n8, 19n19, 29n11, 31n17, 83n144, 102n181, 104n185
Gundry, R. H. 2n10, 5n16, 7n25, 29n11, 34n29, 102n182, 124n29, 150n2, 171n72, 186n112, 189n121, 201n158, 212n193
Hägerland, T. 34n31, 145n52
Hamilton, N. Q. 154n13
Hanson, J. S. 201n157
Harrington, D. J. 49n73, 62n102, 94n168, 98n169, 127n33, 130n37, 202n165, 215n200
Harris, W. V. 8n27
Hart, H. St. J. 165n48
Hartman, L. 116n10, 128n34, 215n200, 234n28
Hartvigsen, K. M. 8n28
Hawthorne, G. F. 49n72
Head, P. M. 14n10
Heil, J. P. 120
Henderson, S. W. 232n23
Hendin, D. 161n38

Hengel, M. 2n9, 25, 99n76, 115n8, 154n12, 176n79, 210n186, 215n200, 218n210, 232n24
Hezser, C. 8n27
Hoehner, H. W. 80n137
Hofius, O. 34n27
Hogan, L. P. 34n31
Holland, T. A. 146n55
Hooker, M. D. 30n15, 55n82, 106n191, 113n7, 117n13, 124n30, 130n36, 145n53, 151n7, 189n120, 190n124, 191n132, 201n159, 205n171
Hoover, R. A. 161n37
Horbury, W. 14n9, 147n58
Horsley, R. A. 16n12, 201n157, 231n22
Hull, J. M. 26n9
Hunzinger, C.-H. 153n10
Hurtado, L. W. 35n34, 35n37, 61n100, 61n101, 227n9
Incigneri, B. J. 5n17
Iverson, K. R. 94n167
Iwe, J. C. 231n20
James, E. O. 63n103
Jaubert, A. 191n130
Jeremias, J. 37n40, 49n73, 49n74, 56n87, 60n96, 83n140, 84n147, 162n42, 171n69, 191n131, 196n142, 197n144, 199n150
Johnson, E. S. 100n6
Kahler, M. 187n114
Käsemann, E. 231n20
Keck, L. 19n20
Kee, H. C. 6n20
Keener, C. S. 73n123, 191n128, 202n164
Kermode, F. 201n158
Kiilunen, J. 32n21
Kingsbury, J. D. 15n11
Kirk, J. R. D. 159n33
Klassen, W. 190n127
Klostermann, E. 34n28
Kreitzer, L. J. 227n8
Kümmel, W. G. 23n4, 117n13

Lane, W. L. 37n39, 39n44, 43n57, 180n95, 191n133, 212n191, 213n196
Lee, S. S. 119n21
Leifeld, W. L. 119n20
Lövestam, E. 51n77
Lührmann, D. 99n176
McArthur, H. K. 74n126
McKnight, S. 117n18
Magness, J. L. 222n219
Mann, C. S. 224n226
Manson, T. W. 58n91, 180n94
Marcus, J. 1n6, 6n20, 23n2, 29n11, 30n16, 33n23, 35n33, 39n44, 40n46, 40n47, 41n49, 43n58, 44n60, 46n62, 46n64, 49n75, 55n85, 59n94, 61n102, 64n104, 64n106, 65n107, 67n111, 71n120, 74n125, 74n126, 79, 82n138, 83n142, 84n146, 84n150, 88n159, 90n164, 100n178, 104n184, 105n189, 106n192, 109n1, 110n5, 110n6, 113n7, 116n11, 117n15, 120n24, 121n28, 135n41, 137n46, 142n50, 147n57, 180n92, 180n95, 189n121, 194n139, 200n153, 200n155, 201n160, 202n161, 202n163, 210n186, 211n190, 215n199, 216n203, 216n206, 217n208, 218n212, 221n214, 224n225, 224n228, 227n6, 228n11, 233n25
Marshall, C. D. 68n116, 158n30, 230n18
Meier, J. P. 44n59, 161n37
Metzger, B. M. 30n13, 29n11
Milgrom, J. 169n64
Millard, A. R. 8n27
Miller, R. J. 161n40
Mitchell, M. M. 6n22
Moloney, F. J. 159n31
Moore, M. S. 117n14
Moule, C. F. D. 58n90
Müller, M. 227n9
Myers, C. 67n111, 84n152, 165n49, 171n68, 171n72, 201n158

Netzer, E. 146n55
Neusner, J. 38n41, 90n163, 91n165, 147n58, 155n18
Nicholson, E. W. 196n141
Nickelsburg, G. W. E. 165n53
Ossandón, J. C. 148n60
Owen, P. 35n34, 35n37, 227n9
Parrot, A. 176n78
Payne, P. B. 55n84, 56n88
Peppard, M. 20n22
Pesch, R. 1n6, 4n13, 104n185, 180n96, 215n199, 233n27
Pobee, J. 212n192
Pokorný, P. 99n174
Porton, G. G. 165n52
Quesnell, Q. 106n192
Reinhartz, A. 204n170
Repo, E. 233n26
Richardson, N. 227n8
Riesenfeld, H. 120n26
Rindge, M. S. 215n201
Roubos, K. 33n24
Rubenstein, J. L. 120n26
Saldarini, A. J. 34n26, 38n41, 206n179
Sanders, E. P. 24n5, 90n163, 153n11, 156n21, 176n78, 229
Saulnier, S. 192n134
Schmidt, T. E. 139n48
Schneck, R. 59n93, 230n15
Schneider, J. 218n211
Schürer, E. 68n117, 154n16, 164n46, 171n71, 182n99, 182n100, 206n178
Schweizer, E. 126n32, 191n131
Segal, J. B. 188n115
Snodgrass, K. 60n97
Stanton, G. N. 7n26, 13n5, 24n6, 55n86
Steele G. 228n10
Stein, R. H. 35n33, 39n43, 43n55, 47n66, 119n19, 120n22, 125n42, 148n61, 156n22, 163n43, 180n93, 185n109, 202n162

Strange, J. F. 87n154
Stuhlmacher, P. 14n8
Swete, H. 193n136
Tan, K. H. 34n32, 137n45, 149n1, 169n63, 196n140
Tannenhill, R. C. 165n50
Taylor, J. E. 18n15
Taylor, V. 87n156, 147n59, 180n97, 191n132, 200n154, 205n171
Telford, W. R. 152n9, 159n35
Theissen, G. 6n20, 96n171, 100n177
Trompf, G. W. 223n223
Tuckett, C. M. 228n11
Van Iersel, B. M. F. 8n29
Van Oyen, G. 48n69
Vanderkam, J. C. 204n169
Viviano, B. T. 201n156
Von Rad, G. 114n14
Wardle, T. 177n80
Watts, R. E. 58n92, 142n50, 230n15, 233n25
Webb, R. L. 18n15
Wedderburn, A. J. M. 222n218
Weeden, T. J. 7n25
Weiss, J. 230n14
Wenham, D. 174n75
Wenham, J. W. 41n50
Westbrook, R. 166n55
White, K. D. 56n88
Widengren, G. 63n103
Williams, C. H. 89n160
Wilson, S. G. 74n125
Winn, A. 7n23
Winter, P. 202n161
Witherington, B. 34n28, 174n75
Wolff, H. W. 200n153
Wong, E. K. C. 135n43
Wrede, W. 228
Wright, N. T. 14n9, 23n1, 55n81, 165n52, 174n74, 183n103, 225n229, 230n16
Wyatt, N. 63n103

www.ingramcontent.com/pod-product-compliance
Lightning Source LLC
Chambersburg PA
CBHW022002220426
43663CB00007B/918